THE RECIPE
SCRAPBOOK

Published in 2010 by Bay Books, an imprint of Murdoch Books Pty Limited

Murdoch Books Australia
Pier 8/9, 23 Hickson Road
Millers Point NSW 2000
Phone: +61 (0)2 8220 2000
Fax: +61 (0)2 8220 2558
www.murdochbooks.com.au

Murdoch Books UK Limited
Erico House, 6th Floor
93–99 Upper Richmond Road
Putney, London SW15 2TG
Phone: +44 (0)20 8785 5995
Fax: +44 (0)20 8785 5985
www.murdochbooks.co.uk

Chief Executive: Juliet Rogers
Publishing Director: Chris Rennie

Publisher: Lynn Lewis
Senior Designer: Heather Menzies
Designer: Margaret McCutcheon
Project Manager: Paul McNally
Production: Alexandra Gonzalez
Index: Jo Rudd

ISBN: 978-0-68135-877-5

Printed by Hang Tai Printing Company Limited, China

IMPORTANT: Those who might be at risk from the effects of salmonella poisoning
(the elderly, pregnant women, young children and those suffering from immune
eficiency diseases) should consult their doctor with any concerns about eating raw eggs.

OVEN GUIDE: You may find cooking times vary depending on the oven you are using.
For fan-forced ovens, as a general rule, set the oven temperature to 20°C (35°F) lower than indicated in the recipe.

THE RECIPE SCRAPBOOK

MORE THAN 650 RECIPES
FOR MORNING, NOON AND NIGHT

bay books

CONTENTS

WHO WANTS TO SPEND HOURS SEARCHING THROUGH COUNTLESS RECIPE BOOKS AND MAGAZINES — THEN EVEN MORE TIME PREPARING THE MEAL — WHEN COOKING SHOULD BE A FUSS-FREE AFFAIR? **THE RECIPE SCRAPBOOK** TAKES THE STRESS OUT OF CHOOSING AND CREATING MEALS — IT'S THE GO-TO RECIPE BOOK FOR BUSY PEOPLE. FOR IMPRESSIVE, RELIABLE AND EASY-TO-MAKE MEALS — FROM BREAKFASTS AND MORNING TEAS, TO SOUPS AND SALADS, AND HEARTIER EVENING FARE —**THE RECIPE SCRAPBOOK** HAS THE DAY COVERED. WITH MORE THAN 650 TRIPLE-TESTED RECIPES TO CHOOSE FROM, YOU CAN BE SURE YOU'LL FIND THE RIGHT RECIPE FOR ANY TIME OF DAY OR OCCASION — AND THE RESULTS WILL BE PERFECT EVERY TIME. AND, AS A HANDY EXTRA, EACH OF THE RECIPES HAS BEEN NUMBERED — SO, ONCE YOU HIT UPON A FAVOURITE DISH, YOU CAN QUICKLY FLICK STRAIGHT TO IT.

MORNING

1   SAVOURY BREAKFAST TARTS

220 g (7¾ oz/1¾ cups) plain (all-purpose) flour
140 g (5 oz) butter, diced
9 eggs
4 slices ham
2 tablespoons chopped flat-leaf (Italian) parsley
2 tomatoes, finely chopped
125 ml (4 fl oz/½ cup) cream
4 tablespoons grated parmesan cheese

Preheat the oven to 200°C (400°F/Gas 6). Sift the flour and ½ teaspoon of salt into a food processor, add the butter and process for a few seconds until the mixture resembles breadcrumbs. Bring the dough together using your hands and shape into a ball. Wrap the ball in plastic wrap, flatten slightly, and put in the fridge for 10 minutes.

Roll the pastry out on a floured work surface until it is very thin. Cut out four 16 cm (6½ inch) circles and use them to line four 10 cm (4 inch) tartlet tins. Press the pastry gently into the flutes of the tins. Line each tin with a piece of crumpled baking paper and some uncooked rice. Bake the pastry for 5 minutes, then take out the paper and rice and bake for another minute.

Line each pastry base with the ham (you may need to cut it into pieces to make it fit neatly). Sprinkle with the parsley and add the tomato. Gently break two eggs into each tin, then pour a quarter of the cream over the top of each, sprinkle with parmesan and dust with salt and pepper. Put the tarts in the oven and bake for 10–12 minutes, or until the egg whites are set. Serve hot or cold. Serves 4

2   SCRAMBLED EGGS & SALMON ON BRIOCHE

4 fresh eggs
4 tablespoons cream
40 g (1½ oz) unsalted butter
125 g (4½ oz) smoked salmon, sliced
2 teaspoons finely chopped dill
2 individual brioche buns or 2 croissants

Crack the eggs into a bowl, add the cream and beat well together. Season with some salt and freshly ground black pepper.

Melt the butter in a non-stick frying pan. When it starts to sizzle, add the eggs and turn the heat down to low. Using a flat-ended wooden spoon, push the mixture around until it starts to set, then add the salmon and dill. Continue to cook, gently folding the salmon and dill through the mixture until the eggs are mostly cooked, and just a little liquid left in the pan.

Cut the top off the brioche or croissants, scoop out some of the filling, then pile the scrambled eggs on top and serve. Serves 2

3   PIPERADE

2 tablespoons olive oil
1 large onion, thinly sliced
2 red capsicums (peppers), seeded and cut into batons
2 garlic cloves, crushed
750 g (1 lb 10 oz) tomatoes
pinch of cayenne pepper
8 eggs, lightly beaten
20 g (¾ oz) butter
4 thin slices of ham, such as Bayonne

Heat the oil in a large, heavy-based frying pan over medium heat, then add the onion. Cook for about 3 minutes, or until soft. Add the capsicum and garlic, cover and cook for 8 minutes, stirring frequently to ensure the mixture doesn't brown.

Score a cross in the base of each tomato. Put in a large bowl of boiling water for 20 seconds, then drain and plunge into a bowl of cold water. Remove the tomatoes and peel the skin away from the cross. Chop the flesh and discard the cores. Add the chopped tomato and cayenne to the capsicum mixture, cover the pan and cook for a further 5 minutes.

Uncover the pan and increase the heat. Cook for 3 minutes, or until the juices have evaporated, shaking the pan often. Season well with salt and freshly ground black pepper. Add the eggs and scramble into the mixture until fully cooked. Heat the butter in a small frying pan over medium heat and fry the ham. Arrange the piperade on four plates, top with the cooked ham and serve with buttered toast. Serves 4

4   CLASSIC OMELETTE

12 eggs
40 g (1½ oz) butter

Break the eggs into a bowl. Add 8 tablespoons water, season with salt and freshly ground black pepper, and beat together well. Heat 10 g (¼ oz) of the butter in a small frying pan or omelette pan over high heat. When the butter is foaming, reduce the heat to medium and add one-quarter of the egg mixture. Tilt the pan to cover the base with the egg and leave for a few seconds. Using a spatula or egg flip, draw the sides of the omelette into the centre and let any extra liquid egg run to the edges.

If you are adding a filling to the omelette, sprinkle it over the egg. As soon as the egg is almost set, use an egg slide to fold the omelette in half in the pan. It should still be soft inside. Slide it onto a warm serving plate and repeat to make 3 more omelettes. Serves 4

5

6

7

8

5 FRENCH TOAST WITH CRISPY PROSCIUTTO

3 tablespoons thickened cream or milk
3 eggs
3 tablespoons caster (superfine) sugar
pinch of cinnamon
about 80 g (2³/₄ oz) butter
8 thick slices bread, cut in half diagonally
1 tablespoon olive oil
12 slices prosciutto

Put the cream, eggs, sugar and cinnamon in a wide, shallow bowl and mix together. Soak the bread in the egg mixture, one slice at a time, shaking off any excess.

Melt half the butter in a frying pan. When it is sizzling, add 3–4 slices of bread in a single layer and cook until golden brown on both sides. Cook the remaining bread in batches, adding more butter as needed, and keeping the cooked slices warm in the oven until all are done.

Next, in a separate frying pan, heat the olive oil. When hot, add the prosciutto and fry until crisp. Remove and drain on paper towels. Place the prosciutto on top of the French toast and serve. Serves 4

6 CHEESE & ONION WAFFLES

4 roma (plum) tomatoes, halved
1 tablespoon each olive oil and balsamic vinegar
1 teaspoon sugar
1 tablespoon chopped oregano
310 g (11 oz/1¹/₄ cups) low-fat ricotta cheese
4 tablespoons chopped herbs (oregano, sage, rosemary, parsley)
185 g (6¹/₂ oz/1¹/₂ cups) self-raising flour
3 tablespoons each grated parmesan and cheddar cheese
3 large spring onions (scallions), finely chopped
1 egg and 2 egg whites
250 ml (9 fl oz/1 cup) low-fat milk
oregano sprigs, to garnish

Preheat the oven to 160°C (315°F/Gas 2–3). Lightly grease an oven tray. Place the tomato halves on the tray and drizzle the cut surface with olive oil and balsamic vinegar. Sprinkle with the sugar, oregano and salt. Bake for 1 hour, or until very soft. Meanwhile, put the ricotta in a bowl and fold in the chopped herbs. Season to taste. Divide the mixture into 4 even portions. Refrigerate until needed.

Meanwhile, place the flour, parmesan, cheddar, spring onion, whole egg and milk in a bowl. Season then mix well. Whisk the egg whites until soft peaks form and gently fold into the cheese and egg mixture. Preheat a waffle iron and brush lightly with olive oil. Pour in 80 ml (2¹/₂ fl oz/¹/₃ cup) batter and cook until golden on both sides. Keep warm in the oven while you cook the remaining waffles. To serve, arrange the waffle halves on each plate with two tomato halves and some herbed ricotta mixture on the side. Garnish with oregano. Serves 4

7 EGGS BENEDICT

12 eggs, straight from the fridge
8 slices prosciutto
4 English muffins, split
200 g (7 oz) butter
2 tablespoons lemon juice

Turn on the grill (broiler). Put a large frying pan full of water over high heat. When the water is bubbling, turn the heat down to a simmer. Crack an egg into a cup and slip the egg into the water. The egg should start to turn opaque as it hits the water. Do the same with 7 more eggs, keeping them separated. Turn the heat down and leave the eggs for 3 minutes.

Put the prosciutto on a baking tray, place it under the grill for 2 minutes, then turn it over and cook the other side. Put the muffins in a toaster or under the grill to toast. Crack the remaining 4 eggs into a blender, put the lid on and leave the top hole open. Heat the butter in a small pan, until it has melted.

Start the blender and pour in the butter in a steady stream through the top hole. The eggs should thicken straight away to make a thick sauce. Add the lemon juice and season the hollandaise with salt and black pepper. Put the muffins on plates and put a slice of prosciutto on each. Lift each egg out of the water, drain and put them on top of the prosciutto. Spoon some hollandaise over each egg. Serves 4

8 BAGELS WITH SMOKED SALMON & CAPER SALSA

4 plain or rye bagels
100 g (3¹/₂ oz) neufchatel cream cheese
200 g (7 oz) smoked salmon, sliced
2 spring onions (scallions), chopped
2 roma (plum) tomatoes, finely chopped
2 tablespoons baby capers
2 tablespoons finely chopped dill
2 tablespoons lemon juice
1 tablespoon extra virgin olive oil

Cut the bagels in half and spread the base generously with cream cheese, then top with the salmon.

Combine the spring onion, tomato, capers, dill, lemon juice and olive oil in a bowl. Pile this mixture onto the salmon and serve. Serves 4

9

10

11

12

9 GRILLED SARDINES WITH BASIL & LEMON

1 lemon, cut into thin slices
8 whole sardines, gutted, scaled and cleaned
coarse sea salt
80 ml (2½ fl oz/⅓ cup) olive oil
3 tablespoons torn basil or whole small leaves

Preheat a grill (broiler) or chargrill pan to very hot. Insert a couple of slices of lemon inside each sardine and season on both sides with the sea salt and some freshly ground black pepper. Drizzle them with half of the olive oil.

Put the sardines on a baking tray and grill (broil) for 3 minutes on each side or place the fish directly onto the chargrill pan. Check to see if the fish are cooked by lifting the top side and checking the inside of the fish. The flesh should look opaque. Remove and place in a shallow serving dish. Scatter the basil over the sardines and drizzle with the remaining olive oil. Serve warm or at room temperature. Serves 4

10 GRILLED FIELD MUSHROOMS WITH GARLIC & CHILLI

4 large or 8 medium field mushrooms
40 g (1½ oz) butter, softened
1 garlic clove, crushed
1–2 small red chillies, finely chopped
4 tablespoons finely chopped flat-leaf (Italian) parsley
4 thick slices ciabatta
tomato chutney or relish, to serve
crème fraîche, to serve

Put the grill (broiler) on and cover the grill rack with a piece of foil so any juices stay with the mushrooms as they cook. Gently pull the stalks out of the mushrooms and peel off the skins.

Mix together the butter, garlic, chilli and parsley and spread some over the inside of each mushroom. Make sure the butter is quite soft so it spreads easily. Season well. Grill the mushrooms under a medium heat for about 8 minutes — they need to be cooked right through. Test the centres with the point of a knife if you are not sure.

Toast the bread, spread some tomato chutney or relish on each slice, then top with a mushroom (or two) and serve straight away. Serve with a dollop of crème fraîche. Serves 4

11 TOMATO & PESTO BRUSCHETTA

8 thick slices ciabatta
80 ml (2½ fl oz/⅓ cup) olive oil
125 ml (4 fl oz/½ cup) pesto
8 ripe roma (plum) tomatoes
75 g (2¾ oz/⅓ cup) mascarpone cheese

Turn the grill (broiler) to its highest setting. To make the bruschetta, brush both sides of each piece of bread with olive oil and put the bread on a baking tray. Grill for 3 minutes on each side, or until crisp and golden brown.

Spread a teaspoon of pesto over each piece of bruschetta and take them off the tray. Slice the tomatoes into four pieces lengthways and drain them for a minute on a piece of paper towel — this will stop the juice from the tomatoes making the bruschetta soggy. Put the tomato slices on the baking tray.

Grill the tomato for about 5 minutes, by which time it will start to cook and brown at the edges. When the tomato is cooked, layer four slices onto each piece of bruschetta. Put the bruschetta back on the tray and grill it for another minute to heat it through. Add a dollop of mascarpone and a little more pesto to each bruschetta and serve hot. Serves 4

12 BRUNCH BURGER WITH THE WORKS

750 g (1 lb 10 oz) minced (ground) beef
1 onion, finely chopped
1 egg
40 g (1½ oz/½ cup) fresh breadcrumbs
2 tablespoons tomato paste (concentrated purée)
1 tablespoon worcestershire sauce
2 tablespoons chopped flat-leaf (Italian) parsley
30 g (1 oz) butter
3 large onions, cut into thin rings
6 slices cheddar cheese
butter, extra, for cooking
6 eggs, extra
6 bacon slices
6 large hamburger buns, lightly toasted

TO SERVE
lettuce, tomato, beetroot, pineapple, tomato ketchup

Mix together the beef, onion, egg, breadcrumbs, tomato paste, worcestershire sauce and parsley with your hands. Season well. Divide into six portions and shape into patties. Cover and set aside.

Heat the butter on a barbecue flat plate. Cook the onion until well browned. Brush the barbecue with oil. Cook the patties for 3–4 minutes each side or until cooked through. Place a slice of cheese on each burger. Heat some butter in a large frying pan and fry the eggs and bacon until golden. Fill the buns evenly with the burger ingredients and serve. Serves 6

13

14

15

16

13 CROQUE MADAME

3 eggs
1 tablespoon milk
30 g (1 oz) butter, softened
4 slices good-quality white bread
1 teaspoon dijon mustard
4 slices gruyère cheese
2 slices leg ham
2 teaspoons vegetable oil

Crack 1 egg into a wide, shallow bowl, add the milk and lightly beat. Season with salt and freshly ground black pepper. Butter the bread using one-third of the butter and spread half the slices with dijon mustard. Place a slice of cheese on top, then the ham and then another slice of cheese. Top with the remaining bread.

Heat the remaining butter and vegetable oil in a large non-stick frying pan over medium heat. While the butter is melting, dip one sandwich into the egg and milk mixture, coating the bread on both sides. When the butter is sizzling but not brown, add the sandwich and cook for 1½ minutes on one side, pressing down firmly with a spatula. Turn over and cook the other side, then move it to the side of the pan. Gently break an egg into the pan and fry until it is done to your liking.

Transfer the sandwich to a plate and top with the fried egg. Keep warm while you repeat with the remaining sandwich and egg, adding more butter and oil to the pan if necessary. Serve immediately. Makes 2 sandwiches

14 HUEVOS RANCHEROS

1½ tablespoons olive oil
1 white onion, finely chopped
1 green capsicum (pepper), finely chopped
2 red chillies, finely chopped
1 garlic clove, crushed
½ teaspoon dried oregano
2 tomatoes, chopped
2 x 400 g (14 oz) tins chopped tomatoes
8 eggs
4 flour tortillas
100 g (3½ oz/⅔ cup) crumbled feta cheese

Put the olive oil in a large frying pan (one with a lid) over a medium heat. Add the onion and capsicum and fry them gently together for 3 minutes, or until they are soft.

Add the chilli and garlic and stir briefly, then add the oregano, fresh and tinned tomatoes, and 185 ml (6 fl oz/¾ cup) water. Bring to the boil, then turn down the heat, cover with a lid and simmer gently for 8–10 minutes, or until the sauce thickens. Season with salt and pepper.

Smooth the surface of the mixture, then make eight hollows with the back of a spoon. Break an egg into each hollow and put the lid on the pan. Cook the eggs for 5 minutes, or until they are set.

While the eggs are cooking, heat the tortillas according to the instructions on the packet and cut each into quarters. Serve the eggs with some feta crumbled over them and the tortillas on the side. Serves 4

15 MUSHROOM OMELETTE WITH CHORIZO

50 g (1¾ oz) butter
1 medium chorizo sausage, sliced
100 g (3½ oz) mushrooms, finely sliced
6 eggs
2 tablespoons chives, finely chopped

Heat 30 g (1 oz) of the butter in a small omelette pan or frying pan over medium heat. Add the chorizo and fry for about 5 minutes, or until golden. Remove from the pan using a slotted spoon. Add the mushrooms to the pan and cook, stirring frequently, for about 4 minutes, or until soft. Add to the chorizo.

Break the eggs into a bowl and season with salt and freshly ground black pepper. Add the chives and beat lightly with a fork. Put half the remaining butter in the pan and melt over medium heat until foaming. Add half the eggs and cook for 20 seconds, in which time they will start to set on the bottom, then quickly stir the mixture with a fork. Work quickly, drawing away some of the cooked egg from the bottom of the pan and allowing some of the uncooked egg to set, tilting the pan a little as you go.

Once the eggs are mostly set, arrange half the mushrooms and chorizo on top. Cook for 1 minute more, if necessary. Tip the omelette out onto a plate and keep warm while the second omelette is cooking. Repeat with the remaining ingredients. Serve as soon as both omelettes are cooked. Serves 2

16 SPRING ONION POTATO CAKES

300 g (10½ oz) potatoes, peeled and roughly chopped
1 egg yolk
50 g (¾ oz) cheddar cheese, grated
3 spring onions (scallions), trimmed and finely chopped
2 tablespoons finely chopped flat-leaf (Italian) parsley
1 tablespoon plain (all-purpose) flour
2 tablespoons olive oil

Boil the potatoes in a saucepan of salted water until tender. Drain, then return the potatoes to the pan over low heat to evaporate off any moisture. Remove the pan from the heat and mash the potatoes.

Stir in the egg yolk, cheese, spring onion and parsley and season. Form into 4 patty shapes. Tip the flour onto a plate and lightly coat the patties with it. Cover and chill for 30 minutes.

Heat the olive oil in a large frying pan over medium heat. Fry the patties for 4–5 minutes on both sides until golden brown. Serve the spring onion potato cakes with fried eggs and tomatoes. Serves 2

17

18

19

20

17 CREAMED RICE WITH MINTED CITRUS COMPOTE

150 g (5½ oz/¾ cup) basmati rice
500 ml (17 fl oz/2 cups) milk
4 cardamom pods, bruised
½ cinnamon stick
1 clove
3 tablespoons honey
1 teaspoon natural vanilla extract

MINTED CITRUS COMPOTE
2 ruby grapefruit, peeled and segmented
2 oranges, peeled and segmented
3 tablespoons orange juice
1 teaspoon grated lime zest
3 tablespoons honey
8 mint leaves, finely chopped

Cook the rice in a large saucepan of boiling water for 12 minutes, stirring occasionally. Drain and cool.

Place the rice, milk, cardamom pods, cinnamon stick and clove in a saucepan and bring to the boil. Reduce the heat to low and simmer for 15 minutes, stirring occasionally, until the milk is absorbed and the rice is creamy. Remove the spices, then stir in the honey and vanilla.

To make the compote, combine the ruby grapefruit, orange segments, orange juice, lime zest, honey and mint and mix until the honey has dissolved. Serve with the rice. Serves 4

18 CINNAMON PORRIDGE WITH CARAMEL FIGS & CREAM

200 g (7 oz/2 cups) rolled (porridge) oats
¼ teaspoon ground cinnamon
50 g (1¾ oz) butter
115 g (4 oz/½ cup) soft brown sugar
300 ml (10½ fl oz) cream
6 fresh figs, halved
milk, to serve
thick (double/heavy) cream, to serve

Place the oats, 1 litre (35 fl oz/4 cups) water and cinnamon in a saucepan and stir over a medium heat for 5 minutes, or until the porridge becomes thick and smooth. Set the porridge aside.

Melt the butter in a large frying pan, add all but 2 tablespoons of the brown sugar and stir until it dissolves. Stir in the cream and bring to the boil, then simmer for 5 minutes, or until the sauce starts to thicken slightly.

Place the figs onto a baking tray, sprinkle with the remaining sugar and grill (broil) until the sugar is melted. Spoon the porridge into individual bowls, top with a little milk, then divide the figs and the caramel sauce among the bowls. Top each serving with a large dollop of thick cream. Serves 4

19 HEALTHY NUT & SEED MUESLI

100 g (3½ oz) puffed corn
150 g (5½ oz/1½ cups) rolled (porridge) oats
100 g (3½ oz/1 cup) pecans
135 g (4¾ oz/1 cup) macadamia nuts, roughly chopped
100 g (3½ oz) flaked coconut
200 g (7 oz) LSA (linseed, sunflower and almond mix)
100 g (3½ oz) dried apples, chopped
200 g (7 oz) dried apricots, chopped
125 g (4½ oz) dried pears, chopped
125 ml (4 fl oz/½ cup) maple syrup
1 teaspoon natural vanilla extract

Preheat the oven to 180°C (350°F/Gas 4). Place the puffed corn, oats, pecans, macadamia nuts, coconut, LSA, apples, apricots and pears in a bowl and mix to combine.

Place the maple syrup and vanilla in a small saucepan and cook over a low heat for 3 minutes, or until the maple syrup becomes easy to pour. Pour the maple syrup over the mixture and toss lightly to coat.

Divide the muesli mixture between two non-stick baking dishes. Bake for about 20 minutes, turning frequently, until the muesli is lightly toasted. Allow the mixture to cool before transferring it to an airtight container. Makes 1 kg (2 lb 4 oz)

20 STUFFED MUSHROOMS WITH SPICED COUSCOUS

8 field mushrooms
95 g (3½ oz/½ cup) couscous
1 tablespoon extra virgin olive oil
1 teaspoon ground cumin
¼ teaspoon cayenne pepper
2 teaspoons finely grated lemon zest
125 ml (4 fl oz/½ cup) chicken stock
1 tomato, finely chopped
1 tablespoon lemon juice
2 tablespoons chopped flat-leaf (Italian) parsley
2 tablespoons chopped mint

Peel the mushrooms and remove the stalks, then grill (broil) them, top side up. Place the couscous, olive oil, cumin, cayenne pepper and lemon zest in a bowl. Season, then stir the flavourings through the couscous.

Bring the chicken stock to the boil and stir it into the couscous. Cover and leave for 5 minutes, then fluff the grains with a fork. Stir in the tomato, lemon juice, parsley and mint. Fill each mushroom with some of the couscous mixture and pack down firmly. Grill until the couscous is golden. Serve hot or cold. Makes 8

21

22

23

24

21 BLUEBERRY PANCAKES

250 ml (9 fl oz/1 cup) buttermilk
1 egg, lightly beaten
20 g (^{3}/$_4$ oz) melted butter
1 teaspoon natural vanilla extract
115 g (4 oz/^{3}/$_4$ cup) plain (all-purpose) flour
1 teaspoon baking powder
^{1}/$_2$ teaspoon salt
2 ripe bananas, mashed
100 g (3^1/$_2$ oz/^{2}/$_3$ cup) blueberries
1 teaspoon vegetable oil
maple syrup, to serve

Put the buttermilk, egg, butter and vanilla extract in a bowl and whisk together. Sift in the flour, baking powder and salt, then stir, making sure not to over blend as the batter should be lumpy. Add the fruit.

Heat the oil in a frying pan over medium heat. Add 3 tablespoons of batter to the pan for each pancake. Cook for 3 minutes, or until the pancakes are golden brown on the bottom. Turn over and cook for 1 minute more. Repeat with the rest of the batter, keeping the cooked pancakes warm. Serve immediately, drizzled with maple syrup. Makes about 12 pancakes

22 GRILLED STONE FRUITS WITH CINNAMON TOAST

2 tablespoons low-fat margarine
1^1/$_2$ teaspoons ground cinnamon
4 thick slices good-quality brioche
4 ripe plums, halved and stones removed
4 ripe nectarines, halved and stones removed
2 tablespoons warmed blossom honey

Place the margarine and 1 teaspoon of the ground cinnamon in a bowl and mix until well combined. Grill (broil) the brioche on one side until golden. Spread the other side with half the cinnamon spread, then grill until golden. Keep warm in the oven.

Brush the plums and nectarines with the remaining spread and cook under a grill (broiler) or on a ridged grill plate, until the spread is bubbling and the fruit is tinged at the edges.

To serve, place 2 plum halves and 2 nectarine halves on each toasted slice of brioche. Dust with the remaining cinnamon and drizzle with the warmed honey. Serves 4

Note: Tinned plums or apricots may be used in place of fresh stone fruits.

23 RASPBERRY BREAKFAST CREPES

250 g (9 oz/2 cups) plain (all-purpose) flour
pinch of salt
1 teaspoon sugar
2 eggs, lightly beaten
500 ml (17 fl oz/2 cups) milk
20 g (^{3}/$_4$ oz) melted butter
400 g (14 oz/3^1/$_3$ cups) raspberries
icing (confectioners') sugar, for dusting
maple syrup or honey, to serve

Sift the flour, salt and sugar into a bowl and make a well in the centre. In a bowl, mix the eggs and milk together with 100 ml (3^1/$_2$ fl oz) water. Slowly pour the mixture into the well, whisking all the time to incorporate the flour and ensure a smooth batter. Stir in the melted butter. Cover and refrigerate for 20 minutes.

Heat a crepe pan or a small non-stick frying pan over medium heat and lightly grease. Pour in enough batter to coat the base of the pan in a thin, even layer. Tip out any excess. Cook for 1 minute, or until the crepe starts to come away from the side of the pan. Turn over and cook on the other side for 1 minute more until just golden. Repeat the process until all the batter is used up.

To serve, put one crepe on a serving plate. Arrange some raspberries on a quarter of the crepe. Fold the crepe in half, then in half again, so that the raspberries are wrapped in a little triangular pocket. Repeat with the remaining crepes and raspberries. Dust with icing sugar, drizzle with maple syrup or honey, and serve. Makes 8 large crepes

24 MIXED BERRY COUSCOUS

185 g (6^1/$_2$ oz/1 cup) couscous
500 ml (17 fl oz/2 cups) apple and cranberry juice
1 cinnamon stick
150 g (5^1/$_2$ oz) raspberries
150 g (5^1/$_2$ oz) blueberries
150 g (5^1/$_2$ oz) blackberries
150 g (5^1/$_2$ oz) strawberries, halved
zest of 1 lime
zest of 1 orange
200 g (7 oz) Greek-style yoghurt
2 tablespoons golden syrup
mint leaves, to garnish

Place the couscous in a bowl. Place the apple and cranberry juice in a saucepan with the cinnamon stick. Bring to the boil, then remove from the heat and pour over the couscous. Cover with plastic wrap and allow to stand for 5 minutes, or until all the liquid has been absorbed. Remove and discard the cinnamon stick.

Separate the grains of the couscous with a fork, add the raspberries, blueberries, blackberries, strawberries, lime zest and orange zest and fold through gently. Spoon the mixture into four bowls and serve with a generous dollop of yoghurt and a drizzle of golden syrup. Garnish with mint leaves. Serves 4

25

26

27

28

25 GINGER & RICOTTA FLATCAKES WITH FRESH HONEYCOMB

150 g (5$\frac{1}{2}$ oz/1 cup) wholemeal (whole-wheat) flour
2 teaspoons baking powder
2 teaspoons ground ginger
2 tablespoons caster (superfine) sugar
55 g (2 oz/1 cup) flaked coconut, toasted
4 eggs, separated
500 g (1 lb 2 oz/2 cups) ricotta cheese
310 ml (10$\frac{3}{4}$ fl oz/1$\frac{1}{4}$ cups) milk
4 bananas, sliced
200 g (7 oz) fresh honeycomb, broken into large pieces

Sift the flour, baking powder, ginger and sugar into a bowl. Stir in the coconut and make a well in the centre. Add the combined egg yolks, 350 g (12 oz) of the ricotta and all of the milk. Mix until smooth. Beat the egg whites until soft peaks form, then fold into the pancake mixture.

Heat a frying pan over a low heat and brush lightly with a little melted butter or oil. Pour 3 tablespoons of the batter into the pan and swirl gently to create an even pancake. Cook until bubbles form on the surface. Flip and cook the other side for 1 minute, or until golden. Repeat until all the batter is used up.

Stack three pancakes onto each plate and top with a generous dollop of ricotta, banana and a large piece of fresh honeycomb. Serves 4

26 CORNBREAD WITH SCRAMBLED EGGS

6 eggs
125 ml (4 fl oz/$\frac{1}{2}$ cup) cream
small basil leaves, to garnish

CORNBREAD
155 g (5$\frac{1}{2}$ oz/1$\frac{1}{4}$ cups) self-raising flour
1 tablespoon caster (superfine) sugar
2 teaspoons baking powder
1 teaspoon salt
110 g (3$\frac{3}{4}$ oz/$\frac{3}{4}$ cup) fine polenta
60 g (2$\frac{1}{4}$ oz/$\frac{1}{2}$ cup) grated cheddar cheese
1 handful chopped mixed herbs (chives, dill, parsley)
2 eggs
250 ml (9 fl oz/1 cup) buttermilk
80 ml (2$\frac{1}{2}$ fl oz/$\frac{1}{3}$ cup) macadamia or olive oil

Preheat the oven to 180°C (350°F/Gas 4). Grease a 20 x 10 cm (8 x 4 inch) loaf (bar) tin. Sift the flour, sugar, baking powder and salt into a bowl. Add the polenta, cheddar, herbs, eggs, buttermilk and oil and mix to combine. Spoon the mixture into the tin and bake for 45 minutes, or until a skewer inserted into the centre comes out clean. Remove from the tin.

To make the scrambled eggs, whisk together the eggs and cream and season with salt and pepper. Pour the mixture into a non-stick frying pan and cook over a low heat, stirring occasionally until the egg is just set. (The more you stir the eggs, the more scrambled they become.) Serve the scrambled eggs with slices of buttered cornbread. Sprinkle with basil leaves. Serves 4

27 MOROCCAN STUFFED SARDINES

75 g (2$\frac{1}{2}$ oz) couscous
2 tablespoons olive oil
2 tablespoons chopped dried apricots
3 tablespoons raisins
1 tablespoon flaked almonds, toasted
1 tablespoon each chopped flat-leaf (Italian) parsley and mint
grated zest of 1 orange
2 tablespoons freshly squeezed orange juice
1 teaspoon finely chopped preserved lemon
1 teaspoon ground cinnamon
$\frac{1}{2}$ teaspoon harissa
16 whole large sardines, butterflied
16 large fresh vine leaves or preserved vine leaves
400 g (14 oz) Greek-style yoghurt

Put the couscous in a bowl, add half the oil and 2$\frac{1}{2}$ tablespoons boiling water. Stir and leave for 10 minutes. Fluff the couscous with a fork and add the apricots, raisins, almonds, herbs, orange zest and juice, preserved lemon, cinnamon, harissa and the remaining oil. Season with salt and pepper and mix.

Divide the stuffing between the sardines, folding the two fillets of each fish together to enclose. Blanch the vine leaves, in batches, in boiling water for 30 seconds. Pat dry on paper towels. If using preserved vine leaves, rinse and dry them. Wrap a leaf around each sardine and secure it with a toothpick. Preheat a chargrill pan or barbecue flatplate. Cook the sardines for 6 minutes, turning them over halfway through. Serve each one with a dollop of yoghurt and any extra couscous. Serves 4

28 CORN PANCAKES

6 corn cobs or 325 g (11$\frac{1}{2}$ oz) tin corn kernels, drained
4 spring onions (scallions), finely chopped
1 garlic clove, crushed
1 teaspoon curry powder
2 tablespoons self-raising flour
1 teaspoon soy sauce
1 egg
oil, for shallow-frying

If using fresh corn, remove the kernels with a sharp knife. Combine the corn, spring onion, garlic, curry powder, flour, soy sauce and egg, mashing lightly with a potato masher. Cover with plastic wrap and chill for 1 hour.

Heat 4 tablespoons of oil in a frying pan. Drop tablespoons of the corn mixture into the pan — avoid overcrowding. Cook over medium heat for 2–3 minutes, on each side, or until golden brown — turn carefully to prevent the pancakes breaking. Remove from the pan and drain on paper towels. Repeat with the remaining mixture. Delicious served with sweet chilli sauce, if desired. Makes 12

29

30

31

32

29 ROASTED FIELD MUSHROOMS WITH TARRAGON & LEMON CRÈME FRAÎCHE

80 ml (2 1/2 fl oz/1/3 cup) olive oil
2 tablespoons lemon juice
4 garlic cloves, crushed
12 large flat field mushrooms, brushed and stems trimmed
2 tablespoons finely chopped flat-leaf (Italian) parsley
toasted bread, to serve

LEMON CRÈME FRAÎCHE

3 tablespoons crème fraîche
2 teaspoons lemon juice
1 garlic clove, crushed
2 teaspoons chopped tarragon

Preheat the oven to 200°C (400°F/Gas 6). In a large roasting tin, combine the oil, lemon juice and garlic. Add the mushrooms, and gently toss until coated. Season well with salt and pepper and arrange in a single layer. Roast for 30 minutes, turning to cook evenly.

Meanwhile, in a small bowl, combine the crème fraîche, lemon juice, garlic and tarragon. Sprinkle the mushrooms and their cooking juices with parsley, and serve with the lemon crème fraîche and toasted bread. Serves 4

30 ASPARAGUS & PROSCIUTTO BUNDLES WITH HOLLANDAISE

24 asparagus spears, trimmed
8 prosciutto slices, cut into thirds lengthways

HOLLANDAISE

175 g (6 oz) butter
4 egg yolks
1 tablespoon lemon juice
ground white pepper

Blanch the asparagus in boiling salted water for 2 minutes, then drain and refresh in cold water. Pat dry, then cut the spears in half. Lay the bottom half of each spear next to its tip, then secure together by wrapping a piece of prosciutto around them.

To make the hollandaise, melt the butter in a small saucepan. Skim any froth off the top. Cool the butter a little. Combine the egg yolks and 2 tablespoons of water in a small heatproof bowl placed over a saucepan of simmering water, making sure the base of the bowl does not touch the water. Using a wire whisk, beat for about 3–4 minutes, or until the mixture is thick and foamy. Make sure the bowl does not get too hot or you will end up with scrambled eggs. Add the butter slowly, a little at a time at first, whisking well between each addition. Keep adding the butter in a thin stream, whisking continuously, until all the butter has been used.

Try to avoid using the milky whey in the bottom of the pan, but don't worry if a little gets in. Stir in the lemon juice and season with salt and white pepper. Place in a bowl and serve warm with the asparagus. Makes 24 bundles

31 ASPARAGUS GREMOLATA

50 g (1 3/4 oz) butter
80 g (2 3/4 oz/1 cup) coarse fresh white breadcrumbs
3 tablespoons chopped flat-leaf (Italian) parsley
2 garlic cloves, very finely chopped
3 teaspoons very finely chopped lemon zest
400 g (14 oz) green asparagus, trimmed
1 1/2 tablespoons virgin olive oil

Melt the butter in a heavy-based frying pan over high heat. Add the breadcrumbs and, using a wooden spoon, stir until the crumbs are golden and crisp. Remove to a plate to cool slightly. Combine the parsley, garlic and lemon zest in a bowl, add the breadcrumbs, and season to taste with freshly ground black pepper.

Bring a large, wide saucepan of water to the boil, add the asparagus and cook for 2–3 minutes, or until just tender when pierced with a fine skewer. Drain well and arrange on a warmed serving plate. Drizzle with the olive oil and sprinkle gremolata over the top. Serve immediately. Serves 4

32 ROSEMARY SKEWERS WITH TOMATO CONCASSÉ

12 long rosemary sprigs, leaves removed, leaving a 5 cm (2 inch) tip
18 Swiss brown mushrooms, cut in half, stems intact
1 small eggplant (aubergine), cut into 2 cm (3/4 inch) cubes
3 tablespoons olive oil
2 tablespoons balsamic vinegar
2 garlic cloves, crushed
1 teaspoon sugar
sea salt, to sprinkle (optional)
olive oil, for brushing

TOMATO CONCASSÉ

1 tablespoon olive oil
1 small onion, finely chopped
1 garlic clove, crushed
5 tomatoes, peeled, seeds discarded, diced
1 tablespoon tomato paste (concentrated purée)
2 teaspoons each sugar and balsamic vinegar
1 tablespoon chopped flat-leaf (Italian) parsley

Marinate the mushrooms and eggplant in the oil, vinegar, garlic, sugar and salt in a bowl for 15 minutes. Thread alternating mushroom and eggplant pieces onto the rosemary sprigs. Oil a chargrill pan or barbecue hotplate and cook the skewers for 7–8 minutes.

Meanwhile, for the concassé, heat the oil in a saucepan over medium heat. Cook the onion and garlic for 2–3 minutes, or until soft. Reduce the heat, add the remaining ingredients and simmer for 10 minutes. Serve the skewers with the concassé, rosemary leaves and salt. Serves 4

33

34

35

36

33 SPINACH & ZUCCHINI FRITTATA

1 tablespoon olive oil
1 red onion, thinly sliced
2 zucchini (courgettes), sliced
1 garlic clove, crushed
300 g (10½ oz) baby English spinach leaves, stalks removed
6 eggs
2 tablespoons cream
80 g (3 oz) emmenthal cheese, grated

Heat the oil in a non-stick frying pan and fry the onion and zucchini over medium heat until they are a pale golden brown. Add the garlic and cook it for a minute. Add the spinach and cook until the spinach has wilted and any excess moisture has evaporated off — if you don't do this, your frittata will end up soggy in the middle, as the liquid will continue to come out as it cooks. Shake the pan so you get an even layer of mixture. Turn the heat down to low.

Beat the eggs and cream together and season with salt and pepper. Stir in half of the cheese and pour the mixture over the spinach. Cook the bottom of the frittata for about 4 minutes, or until the egg is just set. While you are doing this, turn on the grill (broiler). When the bottom of the frittata is set, scatter on the rest of the cheese and put the frying pan under the grill to cook the top. Turn the frittata out of the pan after leaving it to set for a minute. Cut it into wedges to serve. Serves 4

35 ZUCCHINI OMELETTE

80 g (2¾ oz) butter
400 g (14 oz) zucchini (courgettes), sliced
1 tablespoon finely chopped basil
pinch ground nutmeg
8 eggs, lightly beaten

Melt half the butter in a non-stick 23 cm (9 inch) frying pan. Add the zucchini and cook over medium heat for 8 minutes, or until lightly golden. Stir in the basil and nutmeg, season with salt and pepper and cook for 30 seconds. Transfer to a bowl and keep warm.

Wipe out the pan, return it to the heat and melt the remaining butter. Lightly season the eggs and pour into the pan. Stir gently over high heat. Stop stirring when the mixture begins to set in uniform, fluffy small clumps. Reduce the heat and lift the edges with a fork to prevent it catching. Shake the pan from side to side to prevent the omelette sticking. When it is almost set but still runny on the surface, spread the zucchini down the centre. Using a spatula, fold the omelette over and slide onto a plate. Serve immediately. Serves 4

34 SPANISH OMELETTE WITH SMOKED SALMON

1 tablespoon olive oil
400 g (14 oz) potatoes, peeled and cubed
1 onion, finely chopped
8 eggs
2 tablespoons chopped dill
8 slices smoked salmon
80 g (2¾ oz/⅓ cup) mascarpone cheese
4 handfuls salad leaves

Heat the oil in a non-stick frying pan and add the potato cubes. Fry them gently, stirring them so they brown on all sides and cook through to the middle. This should take about 10 minutes. Cut a cube open to see if they are cooked through completely.

When the potato is cooked, add the onion and cook it gently for a few minutes until it is translucent and soft. Switch on the grill (broiler). When the onion is almost ready, break the eggs into a bowl and whisk them together with some salt and freshly ground pepper and the dill.

Tear the smoked salmon into pieces and add it to the frying pan. Add the mascarpone in blobs. Using a spatula, pull the mixture into the centre of the pan and level it off. Pour the eggs over the top and cook for 5–10 minutes, or until the omelette is just set.

Put the frying pan under the grill for a minute or two to lightly brown the top of the omelette. Slide the omelette out of the frying pan and cut it into eight wedges. Arrange a handful of salad leaves on each plate and top with two wedges of omelette. Serves 4

36 CHARGRILLED ASPARAGUS WITH SALSA

3 eggs
2 tablespoons milk
1 tablespoon olive oil
2 cobs corn
1 small red onion, diced
1 red capsicum (pepper), finely chopped
2 tablespoons chopped thyme
2 tablespoons olive oil, extra
2 tablespoons balsamic vinegar
24 asparagus spears
1 tablespoon macadamia oil
toasted wholegrain bread, to serve

Beat the eggs and milk to combine. Heat the oil in a non-stick frying pan, add the egg and cook over a medium heat until just set. Flip and cook the other side. Remove and allow to cool, then roll up and cut into thick slices.

Cook the corn on a chargrill pan or in boiling water until tender. Set aside to cool slightly, then slice off the corn kernels. Make the salsa by gently combining the corn, onion, capsicum, thyme, olive oil and balsamic vinegar.

Trim off any woody ends from the asparagus, lightly brush with macadamia oil and cook on the chargrill until tender. Serve the asparagus topped with a little salsa and the finely shredded egg, accompanied by fingers of buttered, toasted bread. Serves 4–6

37

38

39

40

37 POTATO TORTILLA

500 g (1 lb 2 oz) potatoes, cut into 1 cm (1/2 inch) slices
3 tablespoons olive oil
1 brown onion, thinly sliced
4 garlic cloves, thinly sliced
2 tablespoons finely chopped flat-leaf (Italian) parsley
6 eggs

Place the potato slices in a large saucepan, cover with cold water and bring to the boil over high heat. Boil for 5 minutes, then drain and set aside.

Heat the oil in a deep-sided non-stick frying pan over medium heat. Add the onion and garlic and cook for 5 minutes, or until the onion softens. Add the potato and parsley to the pan and stir to combine. Cook over medium heat for 5 minutes, gently pressing down into the pan.

Whisk the eggs with 1 teaspoon each of salt and freshly ground pepper and pour evenly over the potato. Cover and cook over low–medium heat for about 20 minutes, or until the egg is just set. Slide onto a serving plate or serve directly from the pan. Serves 6–8

38 MUSHROOMS WITH MARINATED FETA

2 large oxheart tomatoes
20 asparagus spears
300 g (10½ oz) marinated feta cheese
3 tablespoons extra virgin olive oil
zest of 1 lemon
2 garlic cloves, crushed
2 tablespoons lemon juice
4 large field mushrooms, brushed clean and stems removed
4 eggs
oregano leaves, to garnish

Cut the tomatoes into thick slices. Trim the ends from the asparagus. Drain the oil from the feta and place into a non-metallic bowl. Stir in the olive oil, lemon zest, garlic and lemon juice. Season with freshly ground black pepper.

Place the mushrooms and tomatoes in a shallow dish and pour the oil mixture over them. Toss gently to coat, and marinate for 15 minutes. Drain the mushrooms, reserving the marinade, and cook them, together with the tomatoes, on a lightly oiled barbecue grill plate until tender.

Add the asparagus towards the end of cooking, and lastly the eggs. Place the mushrooms on a plate, top each one with some asparagus spears, a slice of tomato, an egg and some sliced feta. Drizzle with the oil marinade and garnish with oregano. Serves 4

39 CRISPY LAVASH TILES WITH BUTTER MUSHROOMS

3 pieces lavash or pitta bread
2 tablespoons olive oil
3 tablespoons finely grated parmesan cheese
100 g (3½ oz) butter
4 spring onions (scallions), sliced
750 g (1 lb 10 oz) mixed mushrooms (field, button, Swiss brown, pine, enoki), sliced
1 tablespoon chervil leaves

Preheat the oven to 180°C (350°F/Gas 4). Cut the lavash bread into 3 cm (1¼ inch) wide strips and brush lightly with 1 tablespoon of the oil. Sprinkle with the grated parmesan cheese and bake for 10 minutes, or until crispy.

Heat the butter and the remaining oil in a large frying pan until it is sizzling. Add the spring onion and the field mushrooms and cook over a medium heat until the mushrooms are tender. Add the button, swiss brown and pine mushrooms and cook until the liquid has evaporated. Remove from the heat and stir through the enoki mushrooms.

Arrange the toasted strips of lavash bread into an interlocking square. Pile the mushrooms in the centre, garnish with chervil and serve immediately. Serves 4

40 CHEESY BUBBLE & SQUEAK CAKES WITH BACON

4 large or 8 small floury potatoes
2 tablespoons milk
40 g (1½ oz) butter
480 g (1 lb 1 oz) savoy cabbage, shredded
125 g (4½ oz/1 cup) grated cheddar cheese
1 tablespoon oil
8 bacon slices, rinds cut off

Cut the potatoes into pieces and cook them in simmering water for 15 minutes, or until they are soft. Drain well, put them back in the pan with the milk and mash until they are smooth. Season with salt and pepper.

Melt the butter in a non-stick frying pan and cook the cabbage until it is soft. Add this to the potato along with the cheese. The mixture should be stiff enough to form the potato into cakes — it is up to you whether you make large ones or small ones.

Heat the oil in the same frying pan over a medium heat and cook the bacon on both sides until it is crisp. Remove the bacon from the pan, keep warm. Add the potato cakes to the pan and fry them on both sides until they are well browned and slightly crisp. Shake the pan occasionally to move the cakes around so they don't stick. Serve with the bacon. Serves 4

41

42

43

44

41 CHARGRILLED ASPARAGUS

500 g (1 lb 2 oz) asparagus
2 garlic cloves, crushed
2 tablespoons balsamic vinegar
2 tablespoons olive oil
50 g (1^3/$_4$ oz) parmesan cheese shavings

Break off the woody ends from the asparagus by gently bending the stems until the tough end snaps away. Cook the asparagus on a hot, lightly oiled barbecue grill or flat plate for 3 minutes, or until bright green and just tender.

To make the dressing, whisk the garlic, vinegar and olive oil. Pour the dressing over the warm asparagus and top with the parmesan shavings and lots of black pepper. Serves 4

42 HERBED GARLIC MUSHROOMS WITH GOAT'S CHEESE BRUSCHETTA

80 g (2^3/$_4$ oz) butter
4 garlic cloves, crushed
1 large handful flat-leaf (Italian) parsley, chopped
4 large field mushrooms (100 g/3^1/$_2$ oz each), stalks removed
4 large slices crusty Italian bread, sliced on the diagonal
2 tablespoons olive oil
150 g (5^1/$_2$ oz) goat's cheese, at room temperature
40 g (1^1/$_2$ oz) baby rocket (arugula) leaves

Preheat the oven to 180°C (350°F/Gas 4). Melt the butter in a small saucepan, add the garlic and parsley, and cook, stirring, for 1 minute, or until well combined. Spoon the mixture evenly over the underside of the mushrooms. Line a baking tray with baking paper. Place the mushrooms on the tray, filling side up, and cover with foil. Bake for 20 minutes, or until softened and cooked through.

Towards the end of the cooking time, brush both sides of the bread with the olive oil and grill or chargrill until crisp and golden on both sides. Spread the bruschetta with the soft goat's cheese and top with the rocket. Cut the hot garlic mushrooms in half and place two halves on each bruschetta, then drizzle with the cooking juices and season with ground black pepper. Serve immediately to prevent the bread from going soggy. Serves 4

43 POLENTA WITH MUSHROOMS, SPINACH & TOMATOES

4 roma (plum) tomatoes, halved lengthways
4 large field mushrooms
80 ml (2^1/$_2$ fl oz/^{1}/$_3$ cup) garlic-flavoured oil
900 ml (32 fl oz) vegetable stock
175 g (6 oz) instant polenta
150 g (5^1/$_2$ oz) goat's cheese, chopped
50 g (1^3/$_4$ oz/^{1}/$_2$ cup) grated parmesan cheese
300 g (10^1/$_2$ oz) baby English spinach leaves

Place the tomato and mushrooms in a non-metallic dish, brush with half the garlic oil, and leave to marinate for 30 minutes. Preheat the oven to 200°C (400°F/Gas 6).

Place the tomato in a baking dish and bake for 20 minutes. Meanwhile, place the stock in a large saucepan and bring to the boil, add the polenta in a slow steady stream and cook, stirring, for 10 minutes, or until creamy. Stir in the goat's cheese and half the parmesan. Remove from the heat and keep warm.

Heat 1 tablespoon garlic oil in a frying pan, add the mushrooms and cook, turning once, for 3–4 minutes, or until cooked, but not starting to release too much juice. Remove from the pan. Add the remaining oil to the pan, add the spinach and cook for 3–4 minutes, or until just wilted. Spoon the polenta onto four warm serving plates, arrange the spinach on top, then a mushroom and top with two tomato halves. Sprinkle with the remaining parmesan and serve. Serves 4

44 ZUCCHINI & HALOUMI FRITTERS

300 g (10^1/$_2$ oz) zucchini (courgette)
4 spring onions (scallions), thinly sliced
200 g (7 oz) haloumi cheese, coarsely grated
3 tablespoons plain (all-purpose) flour
2 eggs
1 tablespoon chopped dill, plus sprigs, to garnish
3 tablespoons oil
1 lemon, cut into very thin slices, seeds removed
90 g (3^1/$_4$ oz/^{1}/$_3$ cup) Greek-style yoghurt

Coarsely grate the zucchini and squeeze out as much liquid as possible in your hands or in a clean cloth. Combine the zucchini with the spring onion, haloumi, flour, eggs and dill. Season well with salt and freshly ground black pepper.

Heat the oil in a large heavy-based frying pan. Form fritters (using heaped teaspoons of the mixture) and cook in batches for 2 minutes each side, or until golden and firm. Drain on crumpled paper towels.

Cut each slice of lemon into quarters or eighths, depending on the size, to make small triangles. Top each fritter with ^{1}/$_2$ teaspoon yoghurt, a piece of lemon and a small sprig of dill. Makes 45

45

46

47

48

45 DAMPER

375 g (13 oz/3 cups) self-raising flour
1–2 teaspoons salt
90 g (3¼ oz) butter, melted
125 ml (4 fl oz/½ cup) milk
milk, extra, to glaze
flour, extra, to dust

Preheat the oven to 210°C (415°F/Gas 6–7). Grease a baking tray. Sift the flour and salt into a bowl and make a well. Combine the butter, milk and 125 ml (4 fl oz/½ cup) water and pour into the well. Stir with a knife until just combined. Turn the dough onto a lightly floured surface and knead for 20 seconds, or until smooth. Place the dough on the baking tray and press out to a 15 cm (6 inch) circle.

Using a sharp pointed knife, score the dough into 6 sections about 1 cm (½ inch) deep. Brush with milk, then dust with flour. Bake for 10 minutes. Reduce the oven temperature to 180°C (350°F/Gas 4) and bake the damper for another 15 minutes, or until the damper is golden and sounds hollow when the surface is tapped. Serve with butter. Makes 1 damper

46 FRIED EGG & RED ONION WRAP

1½ tablespoons olive oil
3 red onions, thickly sliced
1 large red capsicum (pepper), sliced
3 tablespoons balsamic vinegar
4 eggs
4 lavash breads
4 tablespoons sour cream
sweet chilli sauce

Heat the olive oil in a non-stick frying pan and add the onion. Cook it slowly, stirring occasionally until it softens and turns translucent. Add the capsicum and continue cooking until both the onion and capsicum are soft. Turn the heat up and stir for a minute or two, or until they start to brown, then stir in the balsamic vinegar. Remove the mixture from the pan and keep warm.

Carefully break the eggs into the frying pan, keeping them separate if you can. Cook over a gentle heat until the eggs are just set.

Heat the lavash breads in a microwave or under a grill (broiler) for a few seconds (you want them to be soft and warm). Lay the breads out on a board, spread a tablespoon of sour cream onto the centre of each, then drizzle with a little chilli sauce. Put a heap of the onion and capsicum mixture on each and top with an egg. Season with salt and pepper. Fold in one short end of each piece of lavash bread and then roll each one up lengthways. Serves 4

47 CORN BREAD

125 g (4½ oz/1 cup) self-raising flour
150 g (5½ oz/1 cup) fine cornmeal
1 teaspoon salt
1 egg
250 ml (9 fl oz/1 cup) buttermilk
3 tablespoons oil

Preheat the oven to 220°C (425°F/ Gas 7). Generously grease a 20 cm (8 inch) cast-iron frying pan with an ovenproof or screw off handle, or round cake tin, with oil. Place in the oven to heat while making the batter.

Sift the flour into a bowl, add the cornmeal and salt and make a well in the centre. Whisk together the egg, buttermilk and oil, add to the dry ingredients and stir until just combined. Take care not to overbeat. Spoon into the hot cast iron pan or cake tin and bake for 25 minutes, or until firm to the touch and golden brown. Cut into wedges and serve. Makes 1 loaf

48 MEDITERRANEAN BLT

4 small vine-ripened tomatoes, halved
1 head garlic, halved
1 tablespoon extra virgin olive oil
3 tablespoons sliced basil
1 loaf Italian woodfired bread
8 slices provolone cheese
8 slices mortadella
1 large handful rocket (arugula) leaves
extra virgin olive oil, to drizzle
balsamic vinegar, to drizzle

Preheat the oven to 200ºC (400ºF/Gas 6). Place the tomato and garlic in a roasting pan and drizzle with the oil. Sprinkle with sea salt and freshly ground black pepper and roast for 40 minutes, or until the garlic is soft and the tomatoes are slightly dried. Add the basil leaves and continue cooking for 5 minutes, or until the leaves are crisp. Remove from the oven.

Cut four thick slices from the loaf of woodfired bread and lightly toast on both sides. Peel the roasted garlic cloves and spread half onto the toast. Top with the provolone, mortadella, rocket, basil and roasted tomatoes. Sprinkle with the remaining roasted garlic, drizzle with extra olive oil and the balsamic vinegar and serve immediately. Serves 4

49

50

51

52

49 SPICED PARSNIP & BACON CAKE

8 parsnips, cut into pieces
80 g (2³/₄ oz) butter
8 bacon slices, rinds cut off, chopped
2 red chillies, finely chopped
4 French shallots, finely chopped
1¹/₂ teaspoons garam masala
2 tablespoons wholegrain mustard
1 tablespoon honey
125 ml (4 fl oz/¹/₂ cup) cream
green salad leaves, to serve

Bring a saucepan of water to the boil and cook the parsnips at a simmer for 15 minutes. Drain them well.

Melt half the butter in a large non-stick frying pan, add the bacon and cook until browned. Add the chilli and shallot and cook for 2 minutes. Stir in the garam masala and remove from the heat. Mash the parsnips and mix them into the bacon mixture. Put the frying pan back over the heat with the remaining butter, pile the parsnip mixture into the pan and flatten it out with a spatula. Cook it for a few minutes — it should hold together in a cake. Loosen the cake, slide it out onto a plate, then invert the plate back over the frying pan and flip the cake back in so you can cook the other side.

While the cake is cooking, mix the mustard, honey and cream together in a small saucepan over low heat until the mixture bubbles. When both sides of the cake are brown, turn the cake out onto a board. Cut the cake into wedges and serve with the honey and mustard sauce and some green salad leaves. Serves 4

50 SPINACH & LEEK FRITTERS

40 g (1¹/₂ oz) butter
3 tablespoons pine nuts
1 leek, white part only, thinly sliced
100 g (3¹/₂ oz) baby English spinach, chopped
3 eggs
1 egg yolk
1 tablespoon cream
75 g (2³/₄ oz/³/₄ cup) grated parmesan cheese
1 tablespoon chopped flat-leaf (Italian) parsley
1 tablespoon olive oil

Melt half the butter in a heavy-based frying pan over low–medium heat and cook the pine nuts and leek for 3 minutes, or until the pine nuts are golden. Add the spinach and cook for 1 minute. Remove the mixture from the pan and allow to cool slightly. Wipe out the pan with paper towels.

Whisk the eggs, yolk and cream together in a large bowl. Add the cheese and parsley and season with salt and freshly ground black pepper. Stir in the spinach mixture.

Melt half of the remaining butter and half of the oil in the frying pan. Place four 5–7 cm (2–2³/₄ inch) egg rings in the pan, and pour 3 tablespoons of the spinach mixture into each. Cook over low heat for 2–3 minutes, or until the base is set. Gently flip and cook the other side for 2–3 minutes, or until firm. Transfer to a plate and slide out of the egg rings. Repeat with the remaining butter, oil and spinach mixture. Serve immediately. Makes 8

51 MINI FRITTATAS

1 kg (2 lb 4 oz) orange sweet potato
1 tablespoon oil
30 g (1 oz) butter
4 leeks, white part only, finely sliced
2 garlic cloves, crushed
250 g (9 oz) feta cheese, crumbled
8 eggs
125 ml (4 fl oz/¹/₂ cup) cream

Preheat the oven to 180°C (350°F/Gas 4). Grease or brush a tray of twelve 250 ml (9 fl oz/1 cup) muffin holes with oil or melted butter. Cut small rounds of baking paper and place into the base of each hole. Cut the sweet potato into small cubes and boil, steam or microwave until tender. Drain well and set aside.

Heat the oil and butter in a frying pan and cook the leek for 10 minutes, stirring occasionally, or until very soft and lightly golden. Add the garlic and cook for a further 1 minute. Cool, then stir in the feta and sweet potato. Divide the mixture evenly among the muffin holes.

Whisk the eggs and cream together and season with salt and freshly ground black pepper. Pour the egg mixture into each hole until three-quarters filled, then press the vegetables down gently. Bake for 25–30 minutes, or until golden and set. Leave in the tins for 5 minutes, then ease out with a knife and cool on a wire rack. Makes 12

52 POTATO RÖSTI

750 g (1 lb 10 oz) waxy potatoes, peeled
1 small onion, finely sliced
2 tablespoons chopped flat-leaf (Italian) parsley
30 g (1 oz) butter
2 teaspoons olive oil

Boil the potatoes for 10–15 minutes, or until they just begin to soften. Drain, and allow to cool. Grate the potatoes and place in a large bowl with the onion and parsley, and season well with salt and pepper.

Heat the butter and oil in a non-stick frying pan over medium–low heat. When the butter has melted, add the potato mixture to the pan, spreading the mixture out, but not pressing too firmly. Cover the pan and cook for 8–10 minutes, or until golden and crispy. Halfway through the cooking time, check to ensure the rösti is not burning. Carefully turn by flipping the whole rösti onto a plate then sliding it, uncooked side down, back into the pan. Cover and cook for 5 minutes, or until golden brown. Cut into four pieces and serve. Serves 4

53

54

55

56

53 APPLE & BERRY CRUMBLE MUFFINS

150 g (5^1/$_2$ oz/1 cup) self-raising flour
150 g (5^1/$_2$ oz/1 cup) wholemeal (whole-wheat) self-raising flour
^{1}/$_4$ teaspoon ground cinnamon
pinch ground cloves
115 g (4 oz/^{1}/$_2$ cup) soft brown sugar
185 ml (6 fl oz/^{3}/$_4$ cup) milk
2 eggs
125 g (4^1/$_2$ oz) unsalted butter, melted and cooled
2 granny smith apples, peeled, cored and grated
155 g (5^1/$_2$ oz/1 cup) blueberries

CRUMBLE

5 tablespoons plain (all-purpose) flour
3 tablespoons raw (demerara) sugar
35 g (1^1/$_4$ oz/^{1}/$_3$ cup) rolled (porridge) oats
40 g (1^1/$_2$ oz) unsalted butter, chopped

Preheat the oven to 190°C (375°F/Gas 5). Line 12 regular muffin holes with muffin papers. Sift the flours, cinnamon and cloves into a large bowl, add the husks and stir in the sugar. Make a well in the centre. Put the milk, eggs and butter in a jug, whisk and pour into the well. Fold gently until just combined — the batter should be lumpy. Fold in the fruit. Divide among the muffin holes.

For the crumble, put the flour, sugar and oats in a bowl. Rub the butter in with your fingertips until most of the lumps are gone. Sprinkle 2 teaspoons of the crumble over each muffin. Bake for 25 minutes, or until golden. Cool for 5 minutes, then transfer to a wire rack. Makes 12

54 BLUEBERRY MUFFINS

375 g (13 oz/3 cups) plain (all-purpose) flour
1 tablespoon baking powder
165 g (5^3/$_4$ oz/^{3}/$_4$ cup) soft brown sugar
125 g (4^1/$_2$ oz) unsalted butter, melted
2 eggs, lightly beaten
250 ml (9 fl oz/1 cup) milk
185 g (6^1/$_2$ oz/1^1/$_4$ cups) fresh or thawed frozen blueberries

Preheat the oven to 210°C (415°F/Gas 6–7). Grease or brush two trays of six 125 ml (4 fl oz/^{1}/$_2$ cup) muffin holes with melted butter or oil. Sift the flour and baking powder into a large bowl. Stir in the sugar and make a well in the centre.

Add the combined melted butter, eggs and milk all at once, and fold until just combined. Do not overmix — the batter should look quite lumpy. Fold in the blueberries. Spoon the batter into the prepared tin. Bake for 20 minutes, or until golden brown. Cool on a wire rack. Makes 12

55 CORN MUFFINS

310 g (11 oz/2^1/$_2$ cups) self-raising flour
75 g (2^3/$_4$ oz/^{1}/$_2$ cup) cornmeal
250 ml (9 fl oz/1 cup) milk
125 g (4^1/$_2$ oz) butter, melted
2 eggs, lightly beaten
130 g (4^1/$_2$ oz) tin corn kernels, drained
2 spring onions (scallions), finely chopped
60 g (2^1/$_4$ oz/^{1}/$_2$ cup) grated cheddar cheese

Preheat the oven to 210°C (415°F/Gas 6–7). Grease two trays of six 125 ml (4 fl oz/^{1}/$_2$ cup) muffin holes with butter. Sift the flour and cornmeal into a large bowl and make a well in the centre.

Whisk together the milk, butter, eggs, corn, spring onion, cheddar and salt and pepper in a separate bowl and pour into the well. Fold gently with a metal spoon until all the ingredients are just combined. Do not overmix — the mixture should still be very lumpy.

Spoon the mixture into the tin and bake for 20–25 minutes, or until lightly golden. Leave for 5 minutes before removing from the tin. Serve split in half spread with butter or cream cheese. Delicious warm or at room temperature. Makes 12

56 CHEESE, OLIVE & SUN-DRIED TOMATO TOASTS

250 g (9 oz/2 cups) self-raising flour
125 g (4^1/$_2$ oz/1 cup) grated cheddar cheese
3 tablespoons freshly grated parmesan cheese
50 g (1^3/$_4$ oz/^{1}/$_3$ cup) pine nuts
250 ml (9 fl oz/1 cup) milk
1 egg, lightly beaten
30 g (1 oz) butter, melted
60 g (2^1/$_4$ oz/^{1}/$_2$ cup) pitted black olives, chopped
3 tablespoons sun-dried tomatoes, finely chopped
40 g (1^1/$_2$ oz/^{1}/$_3$ cup) grated cheddar cheese, extra

Preheat the oven to 200°C (400°F/Gas 6). Lightly grease two 8 x 26 cm (3^1/$_4$ x 10^1/$_2$ inch) loaf (bar) tins and cover the bases with non-stick baking paper. Combine the flour, cheeses and pine nuts in a bowl. Make a well in the centre of the mixture.

Pour in the combined milk, egg, butter, olives and sun-dried tomato, and stir to form a slightly sticky dough. Divide the mixture between the tins. Smooth the surface and sprinkle with the extra cheese. Bake for 45 minutes, or until cooked through when tested with a skewer. Leave in the tins for 5 minutes, then turn onto wire racks to cool.

Cut into 5 mm (^{1}/$_4$ inch) slices and place on baking trays lined with baking paper. Bake for 15–20 minutes, or until the toasts are golden and crisp. Makes about 50

57

58

59

60

57 APRICOT & RAISIN BRAN LOAF

150 g (5¹/₂ oz/³/₄ cup) dried apricots, chopped
160 g (5³/₄ oz/1 cup) raisins
70 g (2¹/₂ oz/1 cup) processed bran cereal
95 g (3¹/₂ oz/¹/₂ cup) soft brown sugar
375 ml (13 fl oz/1¹/₂ cups) warm milk
125 g (4¹/₂ oz/1 cup) self-raising flour, sifted
75 g (2³/₄ oz/¹/₂ cup) wholemeal (whole-wheat)
   self-raising flour, sifted
1 teaspoon mixed spice

Preheat the oven to 180°C (350°F/Gas 4). Grease a deep 18.5 x 11 cm (7¹/₄ x 4¹/₄ inch) loaf (bar) tin and line the base and sides with baking paper. Soak the apricots, raisins, bran cereal and brown sugar in the milk in a large bowl for 30 minutes, or until the milk is almost completely absorbed. Stir in the flours and mixed spice to form a stiff moist batter. Spoon the mixture into the tin and smooth the surface.

Bake for 50 minutes, or until a skewer comes out clean when inserted into the centre of the cake — cover with foil during cooking if it browns too much. Leave in the tin for 10 minutes, then turn out onto a wire rack to cool. Cut into thick slices. If desired, serve with butter and dust with icing (confectioners') sugar. Serves 6–8

58 BANANA & HONEY LOAF

125 g (4¹/₂ oz) unsalted butter, softened
140 g (5 oz/³/₄ cup) soft brown sugar
2 eggs, lightly beaten
2 tablespoons honey
1 large (175 g/6 oz) ripe banana, cut into chunks
225 g (8 oz/1¹/₂ cups) wholemeal (whole-wheat) self-raising flour
2 teaspoons ground cinnamon

Preheat the oven to 180°C (350°F/Gas 4). Grease a 22 x 12 cm (8¹/₂ x 4¹/₂ inch) loaf (bar) tin. Combine the butter and sugar in a food processor for 1 minute, or until lighter in colour. Add the egg and process until combined.

Put 1 tablespoon of the honey in a saucepan over low heat and warm for 1 minute, or until runny. Add to the food processor with the banana and blend until smooth. Add the flour and cinnamon and process until well combined.

Spoon evenly into the tin and bake for 35–40 minutes, or until a skewer comes out clean when inserted into the centre of the cake. Leave in the tin for 5 minutes before turning out onto a wire rack. Warm the remaining honey in a saucepan over low heat for 1 minute, or until runny. Brush the warm cake with the warm honey. Serve warm or cool. Serves 8

59 BANANA BREAD

3 ripe bananas, well mashed
2 eggs, well beaten
2 teaspoons grated orange zest
250 g (9 oz/2 cups) plain (all-purpose) flour
1 teaspoon ground cinnamon
1 teaspoon salt
1 teaspoon bicarbonate of soda (baking soda)
180 g (6¹/₄ oz/³/₄ cup) caster (superfine) sugar
75 g (2¹/₂ oz) walnuts, coarsely chopped

Preheat the oven to 180°C (350°F/Gas 4). Grease a 17 x 8 cm (6¹/₂ x 3¹/₄ inch) loaf (bar) tin.

Combine the bananas, eggs and orange zest in a large bowl. Sift in the flour, cinnamon, salt and bicarbonate of soda, mix, then add the sugar and walnuts. Mix thoroughly, then tip into the prepared tin. Bake for 1 hour and 10 minutes, or until a skewer inserted into the centre comes out clean. To serve, eat warm or allow to cool, then toast and serve buttered. Makes 1 loaf

60 ZUCCHINI & WALNUT LOAF

245 g (8³/₄ oz/2¹/₂ cups) walnuts
500 g (1 lb 2 oz) zucchini (courgettes)
250 ml (9 fl oz/1 cup) canola oil
330 g (11³/₄ oz/1¹/₂ cups) raw (demerara) sugar
3 eggs
310 g (11 oz/2¹/₂ cups) self-raising flour, sifted
1¹/₂ teaspoons ground cinnamon
1 teaspoon ground nutmeg

Preheat the oven to 170°C (325°F/Gas 3). Grease a 22 x 12 cm (8¹/₂ x 4¹/₂ inch) loaf (bar) tin and line the base and two long sides with a sheet of baking paper.

Roughly chop 185 g (6¹/₂ oz/1³/₄ cups) of the walnuts. Grate the zucchini, then put the zucchini in a large bowl with the oil, sugar, eggs and chopped walnuts and mix well. Stir in the flour, cinnamon and nutmeg.

Spoon the mixture into the tin and arrange the remaining walnuts on top. Bake for 1 hour 10 minutes, or until a skewer comes out clean when inserted into the centre of the cake. Leave in the tin for 20 minutes before turning out onto a wire rack to cool. Cut into slices and serve. Serves 6–8

61

62

63

64

61 CHOCOLATE BANANA CAKE

3 ripe bananas, mashed
185 g (6^1/$_2$ oz/^{3}/$_4$ cup) caster (superfine) sugar
185 g (6^1/$_2$ oz/1^1/$_2$ cups) self-raising flour
2 eggs, lightly beaten
3 tablespoons light olive oil
3 tablespoons milk
100 g (3^1/$_2$ oz) dark chocolate, grated
90 g (3^1/$_4$ oz/^{3}/$_4$ cup) walnuts, chopped

Preheat the oven to 180°C (350°F/Gas 4). Grease a 20 x 10 cm (8 x 4 inch) loaf (bar) tin and line the base with baking paper.

Mix the mashed banana and sugar in a large bowl until just combined. Add the sifted flour, eggs, oil and milk. Stir the mixture gently for 30 seconds with a wooden spoon. Fold in the chocolate and walnuts.

Pour the mixture into the tin and bake for 55 minutes, or until a skewer comes out clean when inserted into the centre of the cake. Leave to cool in the tin for 5 minutes before turning onto a wire rack. If desired, serve warm with cream. Serves 6–8

62 PINEAPPLE PECAN CAKE

80 g (2^3/$_4$ oz) unsalted butter, softened
250 g (9 oz/1 cup) sugar
2 eggs, lightly beaten
185 g (6^1/$_2$ oz/1^1/$_2$ cups) plain (all-purpose) flour
1^3/$_4$ teaspoons baking powder
40 g (1^1/$_2$ oz/^{1}/$_3$ cup) finely chopped pecan nuts, toasted
180 g (6^1/$_4$ oz/^{3}/$_4$ cup) finely chopped glacé pineapple
170 ml (5^1/$_2$ fl oz/^{2}/$_3$ cup) milk

Preheat the oven to 180°C (350°F/Gas 4). Grease a 23 cm (9 inch) round cake tin and line the base with baking paper. Beat the butter and sugar with electric beaters until combined. Add the egg and beat until pale and creamy.

Sift together the flour, baking powder and ^{1}/$_4$ teaspoon salt. Add to the butter mixture with the pecans, pineapple and milk, then beat on low for 1 minute, or until almost smooth.

Spoon the mixture evenly into the prepared tin and smooth the surface. Bake for 1 hour, or until a skewer comes out clean when inserted into the centre of the cake. Leave in the tin for 10 minutes before turning onto a wire rack to cool. If desired, dust with icing (confectioners') sugar just before serving. Serves 8–10

63 HONEY PICNIC CAKE

300 g (10^1/$_2$ oz/1^1/$_4$ cups) sour cream
165 g (5^3/$_4$ oz/^{3}/$_4$ cup) soft brown sugar
1 egg
300 g (10^1/$_2$ oz/2 cups) wholemeal (whole-wheat) plain
    (all-purpose) flour
1 teaspoon baking powder
3 tablespoons honey, warmed
50 g (1^3/$_4$ oz/^{1}/$_2$ cup) pecan nuts, chopped

Preheat the oven to 150°C (300°F/Gas 2). Grease a 22 x 12 cm (8^1/$_2$ x 4^1/$_2$ inch) loaf (bar) tin and line the base and the two long sides with baking paper.

Blend the sour cream, sugar and egg in a food processor until combined. Add the flour and baking powder and process until well blended. Add the honey and process until mixed. Add the nuts and process just long enough for them to mix through.

Spoon into the prepared tin and bake for 1 hour, or until a skewer comes out clean when inserted into the centre of the cake. Leave in the tin for 15 minutes before turning out onto a wire rack to cool. Serves 8–10

64 PECAN & ORANGE LOAF CAKE

185 g (6^1/$_2$ oz/^{3}/$_4$ cup) caster (superfine) sugar
140 g (5 oz) unsalted butter, softened
2 eggs, lightly beaten
100 g (3^1/$_2$ oz/^{3}/$_4$ cup) ground pecan nuts
1 tablespoon grated orange zest
185 g (6^1/$_2$ oz/1^1/$_2$ cups) self-raising flour
125 ml (4 fl oz/^{1}/$_2$ cup) milk
125 g (4^1/$_2$ oz/1 cup) icing (confectioners') sugar

Preheat the oven to 180°C (350°F/Gas 4). Grease a 22 x 12 cm (8^1/$_2$ x 4^1/$_2$ inch) loaf (bar) tin and line the base and the two long sides of the tin with baking paper.

Beat the sugar and 125 g (4^1/$_2$ oz) of the butter with electric beaters until pale and creamy. Gradually add the eggs, beating well after each addition. Add the pecans and 3 teaspoons of the orange zest, then gently fold in the sifted flour with a metal spoon alternately with the milk. Spoon the mixture into the prepared tin and smooth the surface.

Bake for 50–60 minutes, or until a skewer comes out clean when inserted into the centre of the cake. Leave in the tin for 10 minutes before turning onto a wire rack to cool.

To make the icing (frosting), place the icing sugar, the remaining orange zest and 1–2 tablespoons hot water in a bowl and mix until smooth and combined. Spread the icing over the cooled cake with a flat-bladed knife. Serves 8–10

65

66

67

65 APPLE TEACAKE

150 g (5½ oz) unsalted butter, chopped
200 g (7 oz/1 cup) caster (superfine) sugar
2 eggs, lightly beaten
1 teaspoon natural vanilla extract
185 g (6½ oz/1½ cups) self-raising flour, sifted
185 g (6½ oz/¾ cup) vanilla yoghurt
1 granny smith apple, peeled, cored and thinly sliced
1 teaspoon ground cinnamon

Preheat the oven to 180°C (350°F/Gas 4). Grease a deep 20 cm (8 inch) round cake tin and line the base with baking paper. Beat 130 g (4½ oz) of the butter and 185 g (6½ oz/¾ cup) of the sugar with electric beaters until light and creamy.

Gradually add the egg, beating well after each addition until combined. Add the vanilla. Fold in the flour, then the yoghurt and stir until smooth. Spoon the mixture into the prepared tin and smooth the surface.

Arrange the apple slices evenly over the mixture in a circular pattern starting in the centre. Sprinkle with the cinnamon and the remaining sugar. Melt the remaining butter, then drizzle over the top.

Bake for 1 hour, or until a skewer comes out clean when inserted into the centre of the cake. Leave in the tin for 30 minutes before turning out onto a wire rack to cool. If desired, combine a little extra cinnamon and sugar and sprinkle over the apple. Serves 8

67 PUMPKIN FRUITCAKE

250 g (9 oz) pumpkin (winter squash), peeled
and cut into small pieces
125 g (4½ oz) unsalted butter, softened
140 g (5 oz/¾ cup) soft brown sugar
2 tablespoons golden syrup or treacle
2 eggs, lightly beaten
250 g (9 oz/2 cups) self-raising flour, sifted
200 g (7 oz/1 cup) mixed dried fruit
2 tablespoons chopped glacé ginger

Preheat the oven to 150°C (300°F/Gas 2). Grease a deep 20 cm (8 inch) round cake tin and line the base and side with baking paper.

Steam the pumpkin for 10 minutes, or until cooked through. Mash with a potato masher or a fork until smooth. Measure 200 g (7 oz/¾ cup) and set aside until ready to use.

Beat the butter and sugar together with electric beaters until pale and creamy. Add the golden syrup or treacle and beat well. Gradually add the egg, beating well after each addition. Fold in the pumpkin until combined. Combine the flour, dried fruit and ginger, then fold into the butter mixture with a metal spoon until combined. Spoon the mixture into the prepared tin and smooth the surface. Bake for 1 hour 40 minutes, or until a skewer comes out clean when inserted into the centre of the cake. Cool in the tin for 20 minutes before turning out onto a wire rack. Serves 8–10

66 RAISIN BUTTER CAKE

160 g (5¾ oz/1 cup) raisins
3 tablespoons rum
1 tablespoon soft brown sugar
250 g (9 oz) unsalted butter, softened
230 g (8¼ oz/1 cup) soft brown sugar, extra
3 eggs, lightly beaten
310 g (11 oz/2½ cups) self-raising flour, sifted
185 ml (6 fl oz/¾ cup) buttermilk

COFFEE BUTTERCREAM
3 teaspoons instant coffee powder
125 g (4½ oz) unsalted butter, softened
185 g (6½ oz/1½ cups) icing (confectioners') sugar, sifted
½ teaspoon natural vanilla extract
2 teaspoons milk

Preheat the oven to 180°C (350°F/Gas 4). Lightly grease a 23 cm (9 inch) round cake tin and line the base with baking paper. Combine the raisins, rum and brown sugar in a small saucepan. Bring to the boil, reduce the heat and simmer for 30 seconds, or until the rum is absorbed. Set aside to cool.

Beat the butter and extra brown sugar with electric beaters until pale and creamy. Add the egg gradually, beating well after each addition — the mixture may look curdled but once you add the flour, it will bring it back together. Using a metal spoon, fold in the flour and buttermilk in two batches, then fold in the raisin and rum mixture.

Spoon the mixture into the tin and bake for 1 hour 30 minutes, or until a skewer comes out clean when inserted into the centre of the cake. Leave in the tin for 10 minutes before turning it out onto a wire rack to cool.

To make the buttercream, dissolve the coffee in 2 tablespoons boiling water. Beat the butter and icing sugar with electric beaters until pale and creamy. Add the vanilla, coffee mixture and milk and beat for 2 minutes, or until smooth and fluffy. Spread over the cool cake. Serves 10

68

69

70

68 APPLE SHORTCAKE

250 g (9 oz/2 cups) plain (all-purpose) flour
1 teaspoon baking powder
125 g (4½ oz) unsalted butter, chilled and chopped
3 tablespoons caster (superfine) sugar, plus 2 tablespoons, extra
1 egg, lightly beaten
1 tablespoon cold milk, plus 1 tablespoon, extra
4 small red apples, peeled, quartered and cored
1 teaspoon ground cinnamon
raw (demerara) sugar, to sprinkle

Preheat the oven to 180°C (350°F/Gas 4). Lightly grease a baking tray and line with baking paper, leaving it hanging over the two long sides. Sift the flour and baking powder into a large bowl, add the butter and rub with your fingers until the mixture resembles fine breadcrumbs. Stir in the sugar. Make a well in the centre and add the combined egg and milk. Mix with a flat-bladed knife using a cutting action until the mixture comes together in beads. Gently gather together and lift out onto a lightly floured work surface. Press together into a ball, flatten slightly, cover in plastic wrap and chill for 20–30 minutes.

Halve the dough — keep one half in the refrigerator and roll the other half into an even 20 cm (8 inch) square. Put on the baking tray. Cut the apple quarters into thin slices and arrange in rows, to form a double layer of apples over the pastry. Sprinkle with the cinnamon and extra caster sugar. Roll the remaining pastry into a 20 cm (8 inch) square and put over the apple. Brush with milk and sprinkle with raw sugar. Bake for 40–45 minutes, or until crisp and golden. Makes 9 pieces

70 DATE CARAMEL SHORTCAKE

125 g (4½ oz) unsalted butter, softened, plus 10 g (¼ oz), extra
125 g (4½ oz/½ cup) caster (superfine) sugar
1 teaspoon natural vanilla extract
1 egg
250 g (9 oz/2 cups) plain (all-purpose) flour
1 teaspoon baking powder
175 g (6 oz/1 cup) roughly chopped seedless dates
1 tablespoon soft brown sugar
2 teaspoons unsweetened cocoa powder
icing (confectioners') sugar, to sprinkle

Preheat the oven to 180°C (350°F/Gas 4). Lightly grease an 18 x 27 cm (7 x 10¾ inch) shallow baking tin. Line with baking paper, leaving it hanging over the two long sides. Beat the butter, sugar and vanilla with electric beaters until light and fluffy. Beat in the egg, then transfer to a bowl. Fold in the combined sifted flour and baking powder in batches with a metal spoon. Press half the dough into the tin. Form the other half into a ball, cover and refrigerate for 30 minutes.

Place the dates, brown sugar, cocoa, extra butter and 250 ml (9 fl oz/1 cup) water in a saucepan. Bring to the boil, stirring, then reduce the heat and simmer, stirring, for 12–15 minutes, or until the dates are soft and the water absorbed. Spread onto a plate and refrigerate to cool quickly.

Spread the filling over the pastry base with a metal spatula, then grate the remaining dough over the top. Bake for 35 minutes, or until light brown and crisp. Cool in the tin for 15 minutes, then lift onto a wire rack. Sprinkle with icing sugar and cut into squares. Makes 12 pieces

69 VANILLA SLICE

500 g (1 lb 2 oz) ready-made puff pastry
250 g (9 oz/1 cup) caster (superfine) sugar
90 g (3¼ oz/¾ cup) cornflour (cornstarch)
60 g (2¼ oz/½ cup) custard powder (see Note)
1 litre (35 fl oz/4 cups) cream
60 g (2¼ oz) unsalted butter, cubed
2 teaspoons natural vanilla extract
3 egg yolks

ICING
185 g (6½ oz/1½ cups) icing (confectioners') sugar
3 tablespoons passionfruit pulp
15 g (½ oz) unsalted butter, melted

Preheat the oven to 210°C (415°F/Gas 6–7). Lightly grease two baking trays with oil. Line the base and sides of a shallow 23 cm (9 inch) square cake tin with foil, leaving the foil hanging over two opposite sides.

Divide the pastry in half, roll each piece to a 25 cm (10 inch) square 3 mm (⅛ inch) thick and put on a baking tray. Prick all over with a fork and bake for 8 minutes, or until golden. Trim each pastry sheet to a 23 cm (9 inch) square. Put one sheet, top side down, in the cake tin.

Combine the sugar, cornflour and custard powder in a saucepan. Add the cream, stirring constantly over medium heat for 2 minutes, or until it boils and thickens. Add the butter and vanilla and stir until smooth. Remove from the heat and whisk in the egg yolks until combined. Spread the custard over the pastry in the tin, then cover with the other pastry sheet, top side down. Cool completely.

To make the icing (frosting), combine the icing sugar, passionfruit pulp and butter in a bowl, and stir until smooth. Lift the slice out of the tin using the foil as handles. Ice (frost) the top and leave to set before cutting with a serrated knife. Makes 9 pieces

Note: Instant vanilla pudding mix can be used as a replacement to the custard powder in this recipe.

71

72

73

74

71 MADEIRA CAKE

180 g (6¼ oz) unsalted butter, softened
185 g (6½ oz/¾ cup) caster (superfine) sugar
3 eggs, beaten
165 g (5¾ oz/1⅓ cups) self-raising flour, sifted
2 teaspoons finely grated lemon zest
1 teaspoon lemon juice
2 teaspoons caster (superfine) sugar, extra, to sprinkle
icing (confectioners') sugar, to dust
lemon zest, extra, to garnish

Preheat the oven to 160°C (315°F/Gas 2–3). Grease and flour a deep 18 cm (7 inch) round cake tin, shaking out any excess.

Beat the butter and sugar with electric beaters until pale and creamy. Add the eggs gradually, beating well after each addition. Fold in the flour, lemon zest and juice until combined. When smooth, spoon into the prepared tin and level the surface. Sprinkle the extra caster sugar over the top.

Bake for 1 hour, or until a skewer comes out clean when inserted into the centre of the cake. Allow to cool for 15 minutes in the tin before turning out onto a wire rack. To serve, dust with icing sugar and garnish with lemon zest. Serves 6

Note: This will keep for 4 days wrapped in foil.

72 DEVIL'S FOOD CAKE

165 g (5¾ oz/1⅓ cups) plain (all-purpose) flour
85 g (3 oz/⅔ cup) unsweetened cocoa powder
1 teaspoon bicarbonate of soda (baking soda)
250 g (9 oz/1 cup) sugar
250 ml (9 fl oz/1 cup) buttermilk
2 eggs, lightly beaten
125 g (4½ oz) unsalted butter, softened
125 ml (4 fl oz/½ cup) cream
icing (confectioners') sugar, to dust
fresh berries, to garnish

Preheat the oven to 180°C (350°F/Gas 4). Grease a deep 20 cm (8 inch) round cake tin and line the base with baking paper. Sift the flour, cocoa and bicarbonate of soda into a large bowl.

Add the sugar to the sifted dry ingredients. Combine the buttermilk, eggs and butter, then pour onto the dry ingredients. Beat with electric beaters on low speed for 3 minutes, or until just combined. Increase the speed to high and beat for 3 minutes, or until the mixture is free of lumps and increased in volume. Spoon the mixture into the prepared tin and smooth the surface.

Bake for 40–50 minutes, or until a skewer comes out clean when inserted into the centre of the cake. Leave in the tin for 15 minutes before turning out onto a wire rack to cool completely. Cut the cake in half horizontally and fill with whipped cream. Dust with icing sugar and garnish with fresh berries. Serves 8

73 SPONGE SANDWICH WITH JAM & CREAM

4 eggs
1 teaspoon natural vanilla extract
125 g (4½ oz/½ cup) caster (superfine) sugar
60 g (2¼ oz/½ cup) self-raising flour
60 g (2¼ oz/½ cup) cornflour (cornstarch)
2 tablespoons raspberry jam
300 ml (10½ fl oz/1¼ cups) cream
icing (confectioners') sugar, to dust
coloured cachous, to decorate

Preheat the oven to 180°C (350°F/Gas 4). Grease two shallow 20 cm (8 inch) sponge tins and line each base with baking paper. Beat the eggs, vanilla and sugar with electric beaters for 5 minutes, or until pale and creamy — the beaters should leave a trail in the mixture.

Sift the flours together on a sheet of baking paper. Gently tip the flour into the egg and sugar mixture and fold quickly and lightly using a large metal spoon — do not overmix or it will lose volume. Divide the mixture evenly between the tins. Bake for 20 minutes, or until a skewer comes out clean when inserted into the centre of each cake. Leave in the tins for 5 minutes, then turn out onto a wire rack to cool completely.

Spread one cake with the raspberry jam and whipped cream, then place the other cake on top. Dust with icing sugar to serve, and if desired, decorate with coloured cachous. Serves 8

74 SOUR CHERRY CAKE

125 g (4½ oz) unsalted butter, softened
185 g (6½ oz/¾ cup) caster (superfine) sugar
2 eggs, lightly beaten
95 g (3½ oz/1 cup) ground almonds
125 g (4½ oz/1 cup) self-raising flour
60 g (2¼ oz/½ cup) plain (all-purpose) flour
125 ml (4 fl oz/½ cup) milk
680 g (1 lb 8 oz) jar pitted morello cherries, well drained

Preheat the oven to 180°C (350°F/Gas 4). Grease and flour a 23 cm (9 inch) fluted baba (kugelhopf) tin, shaking out the excess flour.

Beat the butter and sugar with electric beaters until pale but not creamy. Add the egg gradually, beating well after each addition. Stir in the ground almonds, then fold in the sifted flours alternately with the milk. Gently fold in the cherries. Spoon the mixture into the prepared tin and smooth the surface.

Bake for 50 minutes, or until a skewer comes out clean when inserted into the centre of the cake. Leave to cool in the tin for 10 minutes before turning out onto a wire rack to cool. If desired, dust with icing (confectioners') sugar before serving. Serves 8–10

75 LEMON STARS

125 g (4$\frac{1}{2}$ oz) unsalted butter, cubed and softened
125 g (4$\frac{1}{2}$ oz/$\frac{1}{2}$ cup) caster (superfine) sugar
2 egg yolks
2 teaspoons finely grated lemon zest
155 g (5$\frac{1}{2}$ oz/1$\frac{1}{4}$ cups) plain (all-purpose) flour
110 g (3$\frac{3}{4}$ oz/$\frac{3}{4}$ cup) coarse cornmeal
icing (confectioners') sugar, to dust

Preheat the oven to 160°C (315°F/Gas 2–3). Line a baking tray with baking paper. Beat the butter and sugar until creamy. Mix in the egg yolks, lemon zest, flour and cornmeal until they form a ball of soft dough. Roll out on a lightly floured surface to 1 cm ($\frac{1}{2}$ inch) thick.

Cut out stars from the dough using a 3 cm (1$\frac{1}{4}$ inch) star-shaped cutter. Place on the tray and bake for 15–20 minutes, or until lightly golden. Cool on a wire rack and dust with the icing sugar. Makes about 22

77 CRACKLE COOKIES

125 g (4$\frac{1}{2}$ oz) unsalted butter, cubed and softened
370 g (13 oz/2 cups) soft brown sugar
1 teaspoon natural vanilla extract
2 eggs
60 g (2$\frac{1}{4}$ oz) dark chocolate, melted
80 ml (2$\frac{1}{2}$ fl oz/$\frac{1}{3}$ cup) milk
340 g (12 oz/2$\frac{3}{4}$ cups) plain (all-purpose) flour
2 tablespoons unsweetened cocoa powder
2 teaspoons baking powder
$\frac{1}{4}$ teaspoon ground allspice
85 g (3 oz/$\frac{2}{3}$ cup) chopped pecan nuts
icing (confectioners') sugar, to coat

Lightly grease two baking trays. Beat the butter, sugar and vanilla until light and creamy. Beat in the eggs, one at a time. Stir the chocolate and milk into the butter mixture. Sift the flour, cocoa, baking powder, allspice and a pinch of salt into the butter mixture and mix well. Stir the pecans through. Refrigerate for at least 3 hours, or overnight.

Preheat the oven to 180°C (350°F/Gas 4). Roll tablespoons of the mixture into balls and roll each in the icing sugar to coat. Place well apart on the trays. Bake for 20–25 minutes, or until lightly browned. Leave for 3–4 minutes, then cool on a wire rack. Makes about 60

76 SPICED TREACLE GINGERBREADS

140 g (5 oz) unsalted butter, cubed and softened
115 g (4 oz/$\frac{1}{2}$ cup) dark brown sugar
3 tablespoons treacle, preferably black
1 egg
250 g (9 oz/2 cups) plain (all-purpose) flour
3 tablespoons self-raising flour
3 teaspoons ground ginger
2 teaspoons ground cinnamon
$\frac{3}{4}$ teaspoon ground cloves
$\frac{3}{4}$ teaspoon ground nutmeg
1 teaspoon bicarbonate of soda (baking soda)

TINTED ICING (FROSTING)
1 egg white
$\frac{1}{2}$ teaspoon lemon juice
125 g (4$\frac{1}{2}$ oz/1 cup) icing (confectioners') sugar, sifted
assorted food colourings

Lightly grease two baking trays. Beat the butter and sugar until light and creamy, then beat in the treacle and egg. Fold in the combined sifted flours, spices and bicarbonate of soda. Turn out onto a lightly floured surface and knead until smooth. Cover with plastic wrap and chill for 10 minutes.

Divide the dough in half and roll out between two sheets of lightly floured baking paper to a 4 mm ($\frac{1}{4}$ inch) thickness. Lay the dough on the trays and chill for 15 minutes until just firm. Preheat the oven to 180°C (350°F/Gas 4).

Cut out the dough using a 7 cm (2$\frac{3}{4}$ inch) heart-shaped cutter. Using a 1 cm ($\frac{1}{2}$ inch) plain cutter, cut a hole at the top of each heart. (You can thread these with ribbon to hang up the biscuits.) Lay on the trays and bake for 10 minutes. Leave for 5 minutes, then cool on a wire rack.

To make the icing (frosting), whisk the egg white until foamy. Add the lemon juice and sugar and stir until glossy. Tint the icing any colour you want, then spoon into paper piping bags, seal the end and snip off the tip. Decorate the biscuits with the icing. Makes about 36

78

79

80

78 BAKEWELL SLICE

125 g (4¹/₂ oz/1 cup) plain (all-purpose) flour
3 tablespoons icing (confectioners') sugar
170 g (6 oz) unsalted butter, chilled and chopped
1 egg yolk
125 g (4¹/₂ oz/¹/₂ cup) caster (superfine) sugar
4 eggs
125 g (4¹/₂ oz/1¹/₄ cups) ground almonds
2 drops almond essence
160 g (5³/₄ oz/¹/₂ cup) raspberry jam
3 tablespoons flaked almonds

Preheat the oven to 180°C (350°F/Gas 4). Lightly grease a 20 x 30 cm (8 x 12 inch) baking tin and line with baking paper, hanging over the two long sides. Sift the flour and 1 tablespoon of the icing sugar into a bowl, add 50 g (1³/₄ oz) of the butter and rub it in until the mixture resembles breadcrumbs. Add the egg yolk and 2 tablespoons cold water and mix with a flat-bladed knife until the mixture comes together in beads. Gather into a ball, cover with plastic wrap and refrigerate for 30 minutes. Roll out between two sheets of baking paper, remove the paper and put in the tin, pressing into the edges. Bake for 10 minutes. Cool.

Beat the remaining butter and the caster sugar until creamy. Add the eggs and fold in the ground almonds and almond essence. Spread the jam over the pastry base and pour over the filling. Sprinkle with almonds and bake for 30–35 minutes, or until firm. Allow to cool.

Sift the remaining icing sugar into a bowl and mix in 2–3 teaspoons warm water to form a paste. Drizzle over the slice in a zigzag pattern and leave to set. Trim the edges and cut into squares. Makes 15 pieces

80 CHEWY FRUIT & SEED SLICE

200 g (7 oz) unsalted butter
175 g (6 oz/¹/₂ cup) golden syrup or treacle
125 g (4¹/₂ oz/¹/₂ cup) crunchy peanut butter
2 teaspoons natural vanilla extract
3 tablespoons plain (all-purpose) flour
30 g (1 oz/¹/₃ cup) ground almonds
¹/₂ teaspoon mixed spice
300 g (10¹/₂ oz/3 cups) quick-cooking oats
2 teaspoons finely grated orange zest
185 g (6¹/₂ oz/1 cup) soft brown sugar
45 g (1¹/₂ oz/¹/₂ cup) desiccated coconut
50 g (1³/₄ oz/¹/₃ cup) sesame seeds, toasted
90 g (3¹/₄ oz/¹/₂ cup) pepitas (pumpkin seeds)
    or shelled sunflower seeds
80 g (2³/₄ oz/¹/₂ cup) raisins, chopped
3 tablespoons mixed peel (mixed candied citrus peel)

Preheat the oven to 170°C (325°F/Gas 3). Lightly grease a 20 x 30 cm (8 x 12 inch) shallow tin and line with baking paper, leaving it hanging over the two long sides. Place the butter and golden syrup or treacle in a saucepan over low heat, stirring occasionally until melted. Remove from the heat and stir in the peanut butter and vanilla until combined.

Mix together the remaining ingredients, stirring well. Make a well in the centre and add the butter and syrup mixture. Mix with a large metal spoon until combined. Press evenly into the tin and bake for 25 minutes, or until golden and firm. Cool in the tin, then cut into squares. Makes 18 pieces

79 APRICOT & MACAROON SLICE

100 g (3¹/₂ oz) unsalted butter, softened
90 g (3¹/₄ oz/¹/₃ cup) caster (superfine) sugar
1 egg
185 g (6¹/₂ oz/1¹/₂ cups) plain (all-purpose) flour
¹/₂ teaspoon baking powder

FILLING
250 g (9 oz/1¹/₃ cups) dried apricots, roughly chopped
1 tablespoon Grand Marnier
2 tablespoons caster (superfine) sugar

TOPPING
100 g (3¹/₂ oz) unsalted butter
90 g (3¹/₄ oz/¹/₃ cup) caster (superfine) sugar
1 teaspoon natural vanilla extract
2 eggs
270 g (9¹/₂ oz/3 cups) desiccated coconut
40 g (1¹/₂ oz/¹/₃ cup) plain (all-purpose) flour
¹/₂ teaspoon baking powder

Preheat the oven to 180°C (350°F/Gas 4). Lightly grease a 20 x 30 cm (8 x 12 inch) baking tin and line with baking paper. Cream the butter and sugar until light and fluffy. Add the egg and beat well. Sift the flour and baking powder and fold into the butter mixture with a metal spoon. Press firmly into the tin and bake for 20–25 minutes, or until golden brown. Cool.

To make the filling, combine the apricots, Grand Marnier, sugar and 125 ml (4 fl oz/¹/₂ cup) boiling water in a bowl. Set aside for 30 minutes, then purée in a food processor. Spread evenly over the cooled base.

To make the topping, cream the butter, sugar and vanilla until light and fluffy. Gradually add the eggs, beating well after each addition. Fold in the coconut, flour and baking powder with a large metal spoon. Spoon onto the apricot leaving it lumpy and loose — do not press down. Bake for 20–25 minutes, or until lightly golden. Makes 16 pieces

81

82

83

84

81 RICH DARK CHOCOLATE CAKE

185 g (6$^1/_2$ oz) unsalted butter, chopped
250 g (9 oz/1$^1/_2$ cups) dark chocolate bits (chocolate chips)
215 g (1$^1/_2$ oz/1$^3/_4$ cups) self-raising flour
40 g (1$^1/_2$ oz/$^1/_3$ cup) unsweetened cocoa powder
375 g (13 oz/1$^1/_2$ cups) caster (superfine) sugar
3 eggs, lightly beaten

CHOCOLATE TOPPING
20 g ($^3/_4$ oz) unsalted butter, chopped
125 g (4$^1/_2$ oz) dark chocolate, chopped

Preheat the oven to 160°C (315°F/Gas 2–3). Grease a 22 cm (8$^1/_2$ inch) spring-form tin and line the base with baking paper. Place the butter and chocolate bits in a heatproof bowl and melt, stirring frequently, over a saucepan of simmering water. Make sure the base of the bowl doesn't touch the water.

Sift the flour and cocoa into a large bowl. Combine the melted butter and chocolate mixture, sugar and egg, then add 250 ml (9 fl oz/1 cup) water and mix well. Add to the flour and cocoa and stir until well combined. Pour the mixture into the prepared tin and bake for 1 hour 30 minutes, or until a skewer comes out clean when inserted into the centre of the cake. Leave in the tin for 15 minutes before turning out onto a wire rack to cool.

To make the chocolate topping, place the butter and chocolate pieces in a small heatproof bowl and melt, stirring frequently, over a saucepan of simmering water — ensure the base of the bowl doesn't touch the water. Spread the topping over the cooled cake in a swirl pattern. Serves 10–12

82 FIG & RASPBERRY CAKE

185 g (6$^1/_2$ oz) unsalted butter
185 g (6$^1/_2$ oz/$^3/_4$ cup) caster (superfine) sugar
1 egg and 1 egg yolk
335 g (11$^3/_4$ oz/2$^2/_3$ cups) plain (all-purpose) flour
1 teaspoon baking powder
4 figs, quartered
grated zest of 1 orange
200 g (7 oz/1$^2/_3$ cups) raspberries
2 tablespoons sugar

Preheat the oven to 180°C (350°F/Gas 4). Cream the butter and sugar in a bowl until light and pale. Add the eggs and beat again. Sift the flour over the bowl and fold in with the baking powder and a pinch of salt. Chill for 15 minutes until firm enough to roll out.

Lightly grease a 23 cm (9 inch) spring-form tin. Divide the dough in two and roll out one piece large enough to fit the base of the tin. Cover with the figs, orange zest and raspberries. Roll out the remaining dough and fit it over the filling. Lightly brush the dough with water and sprinkle with sugar.

Bake for 30 minutes, or until the top and bottom of the cake are cooked. Poke a skewer into the cake to see if it is ready — there should be no wet cake mixture clinging to the skewer. Serve with cream or mascarpone. Serves 6

Note: If fresh figs are not available, you can use the same amount of dried figs but you need to rehydrate them first. Simmer them in orange juice for 5 minutes until they are plumped up and soft.

83 ORANGE POPPY SEED CAKE WITH CITRUS ICING

50 g (1$^3/_4$ oz/$^1/_3$ cup) poppy seeds
185 ml (6 fl oz/$^3/_4$ cup) warm milk
250 g (9 oz/1 cup) caster (superfine) sugar
3 eggs
250 g (9 oz/2 cups) self-raising flour, sifted
210 g (7$^1/_2$ oz) unsalted butter, softened
1$^1/_2$ tablespoons finely grated orange zest
250 g (9 oz/2 cups) icing (confectioners') sugar
thick (double/heavy) cream, to serve

Preheat the oven to 180°C (350°F/Gas 4). Lightly grease a 23 cm (9 inch) fluted baba tin. Combine the poppy seeds and milk in a bowl and set aside for at least 15 minutes.

Place the caster sugar, eggs, flour, 185 g (6$^1/_2$ oz) of the butter and 3 teaspoons of the orange zest in a large bowl. Add the poppy seed mixture and beat with electric beaters on low speed until combined. Increase to medium speed and beat for 3 minutes, or until the mixture is thick and pale. Pour the mixture evenly into the prepared tin.

Bake for 50 minutes, or until a skewer comes out clean when inserted into the centre of the cake. Leave in the tin for 5 minutes, then turn out onto a wire rack.

To make the icing (frosting), melt the remaining butter, then place the butter in a bowl with the icing sugar, remaining orange zest and 3 tablespoons boiling water. Mix to make a soft icing, then spread over the warm cake and serve with thick cream. Serves 8

84 GLACÉ FRUIT SLICE

480 g (1 lb 1 oz/2 cups) roughly chopped glacé fruit
2 tablespoons rum
100 g (3$^1/_2$ oz) unsalted butter, softened
90 g (3$^1/_4$ oz/$^1/_3$ cup) caster (superfine) sugar
2 eggs
2 teaspoons natural vanilla extract
125 g (4$^1/_2$ oz/1 cup) mixed toasted nuts, roughly chopped
3 tablespoons plain (all-purpose) flour, sifted
3 tablespoons self-raising flour, sifted
3 tablespoons milk powder
80 g (2$^3/_4$ oz/$^2/_3$ cup) icing (confectioners') sugar
1 teaspoon rum, extra

Preheat the oven to 190°C (375°F/Gas 5). Lightly grease an 18 x 27 cm (7 x 10$^3/_4$ inch) shallow baking tin and line with baking paper, hanging over the two long sides. Combine the glacé fruit and rum in a bowl. Beat the butter and sugar with electric beaters until light and fluffy. Add the eggs one at a time, beating well after each addition. Beat in the vanilla, then stir in the fruit mixture, nuts, flours and milk powder.

Spread evenly into the tin. Bake for 15 minutes, then reduce the oven to 180°C (350°F/Gas 4) and bake for 10 minutes, or until golden brown. Cool in the tin until just warm. Combine the icing sugar, extra rum and 1 teaspoon water until smooth and spreadable but not runny. If the icing (frosting) is too thick, add a little more rum or water. Spread over the slice and cool completely. Cut into three lengthways strips, then cut each strip into eight pieces. Makes 24 pieces

85

86

87

85 LEMON MERINGUE MUFFINS

215 g (7^1/$_2$ oz/1^3/$_4$ cups) self-raising flour
185 g (6^1/$_2$ oz/^{3}/$_4$ cup) caster (superfine) sugar
1 egg plus 1 egg yolk
170 ml (5^1/$_2$ fl oz/^{2}/$_3$ cup) milk
^{1}/$_2$ teaspoon natural vanilla extract
90 g (3^1/$_4$ oz) unsalted butter, melted and cooled
200 g (7 oz/^{2}/$_3$ cup) ready-made lemon curd
2 egg whites
1 teaspoon caster (superfine) sugar, extra

Preheat the oven to 200°C (400°F/Gas 6). Grease 12 regular muffin holes. Sift the flour into a large bowl and stir in 3 tablespoons of the sugar. Make a well in the centre. Put a pinch of salt, the egg and egg yolk in a bowl and beat together. Stir in the milk, vanilla and butter. Pour the egg mixture into the well. Fold until just combined.

Divide the muffin mixture among the holes. Bake for 15 minutes — the muffins will only rise a little. (Leave the oven on.) Cool the muffins in the tin for 10 minutes, then loosen with a knife but leave in the tin. Hollow out the centre of each muffin with a melon baller. Fill a piping bag with the lemon curd and fill the centre of each muffin.

Whisk the egg whites in a clean, dry bowl until firm peaks form. Add a quarter of the remaining sugar at a time, beating well after each addition until firm peaks form. Put a heaped tablespoon of meringue on top of each muffin and form peaks with the back of a spoon. Sprinkle over caster sugar and bake for 5 minutes, or until the meringue is golden and crisp. Cool in the tin for 10 minutes, then transfer to a wire rack. Serve warm or at room temperature. Makes 12 muffins

87 CHOCOLATE HAZELNUT FRIANDS

200 g (7 oz/1^1/$_2$ cups) hazelnuts
185 g (6^1/$_2$ oz) unsalted butter
6 egg whites
155 g (5^1/$_2$ oz/1^1/$_4$ cups) plain (all-purpose) flour
3 tablespoons unsweetened cocoa powder
250 g (9 oz/2 cups) icing (confectioners') sugar
icing (confectioners') sugar, extra, to dust

Preheat the oven to 200°C (400°F/Gas 6). Grease twelve 125 ml (4 fl oz/ ^{1}/$_2$ cup) friand or muffin holes. Spread the hazelnuts out on a baking tray and bake for 8–10 minutes, or until fragrant (take care not to burn). Put in a clean cloth and rub vigorously to loosen the skins. Discard the skins. Cool, then process in a food processor until finely ground.

Place the butter in a small pan and melt over medium heat, then cook for 3–4 minutes, or until it turns a deep golden colour. Strain any dark solids and set aside to cool (the colour will become deeper on standing).

Lightly whisk the egg whites in a bowl until frothy but not firm. Sift the flour, cocoa powder and icing sugar into a large bowl and stir in the ground hazelnuts. Make a well in the centre, add the egg whites and butter and mix until combined.

Spoon the mixture into the friand holes until three-quarters filled. Bake for 20–25 minutes, or until a skewer inserted into the centre comes out clean. Leave in the tin for a few minutes, then cool on a wire rack. Dust with icing sugar, to serve. Makes 12

86 STICKY GINGERBREAD MUFFINS

250 g (9 oz/2 cups) self-raising flour, sifted
90 g (3^1/$_4$ oz/^{3}/$_4$ cup) plain (all-purpose) flour, sifted
^{1}/$_2$ teaspoon bicarbonate of soda (baking soda)
3 teaspoons ground ginger
1 teaspoon ground cinnamon
1 teaspoon mixed spice
230 g (8^1/$_4$ oz/1 cup) soft brown sugar
3 tablespoons chopped glacé ginger
235 g (8^1/$_2$ oz/^{2}/$_3$ cup) golden syrup or treacle
100 g (3^1/$_2$ oz) unsalted butter, chopped
250 ml (9 fl oz/1 cup) buttermilk
1 egg, lightly beaten
50 g (1^3/$_4$ oz) dark chocolate, melted

GINGER FROSTING
60 g (2^1/$_4$ oz) unsalted butter, softened
1^1/$_2$ tablespoons golden syrup or treacle
125 g (4^1/$_2$ oz/1 cup) icing (confectioners') sugar
^{1}/$_2$ teaspoon ground ginger

Preheat the oven to 200°C (400°F/Gas 6). Grease 12 regular muffin holes. Put the flours, bicarbonate of soda, ginger, cinnamon and mixed spice into a large bowl and stir in the brown sugar and glacé ginger. Make a well in the centre. Melt the golden syrup or treacle and butter in a pan, stirring until well mixed. Cool. Combine the golden syrup mixture, buttermilk and egg in a large jug, mix together and pour into the well. Fold until just combined — the batter will be lumpy.

Divide the mixture among the muffin holes. Bake for 20–25 minutes, or until the muffins come away from the side of the tin. Cool for 5 minutes in the tin, then transfer to a wire rack.

To make the ginger frosting, beat the butter, golden syrup or treacle, icing sugar and ground ginger together with electric beaters in a bowl until light and fluffy. Spread over the top of the muffins.

Spoon the melted chocolate into the corner of a plastic bag. Snip off the corner to create a nozzle. Pipe the chocolate over the icing in crisscrossing lines. Apply even pressure and move at a steady speed to prevent the chocolate from clumping. Allow to set before serving. Makes 12 muffins

88

89

90

88 PEPPERMINT & CHOCOLATE SLICE

220 g (7^3/$_4$ oz/1^3/$_4$ cups) plain (all-purpose) flour
1 teaspoon baking powder
95 g (3^1/$_2$ oz/^{1}/$_2$ cup) soft brown sugar
180 g (6^1/$_4$ oz) unsalted butter, melted
60 g (2^1/$_4$ oz) copha (white vegetable shortening)
435 g (15^1/$_4$ oz/3^1/$_2$ cups) icing (confectioners') sugar, sifted
1 teaspoon peppermint essence
2 tablespoons milk
2 tablespoons cream
300 g (10^1/$_2$ oz) dark cooking chocolate
70 g (2^1/$_2$ oz) unsalted butter, extra

Preheat the oven to 180°C (350°F/Gas 4). Grease a 20 x 30 cm (8 x 12 inch) baking tin and line with baking paper, leaving the paper hanging over the two long sides of the tin. Sift together the flour and baking powder and add the brown sugar. Stir in the melted butter, press into the tin and bake for 20 minutes. Cool.

Melt the copha in a saucepan over medium heat. Stir in the icing sugar, peppermint essence, milk and cream. Mix well and pour over the pastry base. Leave to set.

Chop the chocolate and extra butter into small even-sized pieces and place in a heatproof bowl. Bring a saucepan of water to the boil and remove from the heat. Sit the bowl over the pan, making sure the bowl doesn't touch the water. Stand, stirring occasionally, until melted and combined. Cool slightly, then spread over the icing. Chill until set, then cut into pieces. Makes 20 pieces

90 CHOCOLATE CARAMEL SLICE

200 g (7 oz) plain chocolate biscuits (cookies), crushed
100 g (3^1/$_2$ oz) unsalted butter, melted
2 tablespoons desiccated coconut
125 g (4^1/$_2$ oz) unsalted butter, extra
400 ml (14 fl oz) sweetened condensed milk
90 g (3^1/$_4$ oz/^{1}/$_3$ cup) caster (superfine) sugar
3 tablespoons maple syrup
250 g (9 oz) dark chocolate, chopped into small even-sized pieces
2 teaspoons oil

Grease a 20 x 30 cm (8 x 12 inch) shallow baking tin and line with baking paper, leaving it hanging over the two long sides. Combine the biscuits, melted butter and coconut in a bowl, then press into the tin and smooth the surface.

Combine the butter, condensed milk, sugar and maple syrup in a small saucepan. Stir over low heat for 15 minutes, or until the sugar has dissolved and the mixture is smooth, thick and lightly coloured. Remove from the heat and cool slightly. Pour over the biscuit base and smooth the surface. Refrigerate for 30 minutes, or until firm.

Place the chopped chocolate pieces in a heatproof bowl. Bring a saucepan of water to the boil and remove from the heat. Sit the bowl over the saucepan, making sure the bowl doesn't touch the water. Allow to stand, stirring occasionally, until the chocolate has melted. Add the oil and stir until smooth. Spread over the caramel and leave until partially set before marking into 24 triangles. Refrigerate until firm. Cut into triangles before serving. Makes 24 triangles

89 PANFORTE

110 g (3^3/$_4$ oz/^{3}/$_4$ cup) hazelnuts
110 g (3^3/$_4$ oz/^{3}/$_4$ cup) almonds
125 g (4^1/$_2$ oz/^{2}/$_3$ cup) mixed peel (mixed candied citrus peel), chopped
100 g (3^1/$_2$ oz/^{2}/$_3$ cup) candied pineapple, chopped
grated zest of 1 lemon
75 g (2^3/$_4$ oz/^{2}/$_3$ cup) plain (all-purpose) flour
1 teaspoon ground cinnamon
^{1}/$_4$ teaspoon ground coriander
^{1}/$_4$ teaspoon ground cloves
^{1}/$_4$ teaspoon grated nutmeg
pinch of white pepper
150 g (5^1/$_2$ oz/^{2}/$_3$ cup) sugar
115 g (4 oz/^{1}/$_3$ cup) honey
50 g (1^3/$_4$ oz) unsalted butter
icing (confectioners') sugar, to dust

Line a 20 cm (8 inch) spring-form tin with rice paper or baking paper and grease well with butter. Toast the nuts under a hot grill (broiler), turning them so they brown on all sides, then leave to cool. Put the nuts in a bowl with the mixed peel, pineapple, lemon zest, flour and spices and toss together. Preheat the oven to 150°C (300°F/Gas 2).

Put the sugar, honey and butter in a saucepan and melt them together. Cook the syrup until it reaches 118°C (245°F) on a sugar thermometer, or a little of it dropped into cold water forms a firm ball when moulded between your fingers.

Pour the syrup into the nut mixture and mix well, working fast before it stiffens too much. Pour straight into the prepared tin, smooth the surface and bake for 35 minutes. (Unlike other cakes, this cake will neither firm up as it cooks nor colour at all, so you need to time it carefully.) Cool in the tin until the cake firms up enough to remove the side of the tin. Peel off the paper and leave to cool completely. Dust the top with icing sugar. Serves 10

91

92

93

94

91 CHOCOLATE PEANUT SQUARES

200 g (7 oz) dark chocolate
125 g (4$\frac{1}{2}$ oz) unsalted butter
230 g (8$\frac{1}{4}$ oz/1 cup) soft brown sugar
3 tablespoons crunchy peanut butter
2 eggs
125 g (4$\frac{1}{2}$ oz/1 cup) plain (all-purpose) flour
3 tablespoons self-raising flour
80 g (2$\frac{3}{4}$ oz/$\frac{1}{2}$ cup) unsalted roasted peanuts, roughly chopped
100 g (3$\frac{1}{2}$ oz) dark chocolate, extra, broken into pieces

Preheat the oven to 170°C (325°F/Gas 3). Lightly grease an 18 x 27 cm (7 x 10$\frac{3}{4}$ inch) baking tin and line with baking paper, hanging over the two long sides. Chop the chocolate into small even-sized pieces and place in a heatproof bowl. Bring a saucepan of water to the boil and remove from the heat. Sit the bowl over the pan — ensure the bowl doesn't touch the water. Allow to stand, stirring occasionally until melted. Allow to cool.

Cream the butter, sugar and peanut butter with electric beaters until thick. Add the eggs one at a time, beating well after each addition. Stir in the chocolate, sifted flours and peanuts. Spread the mixture into the tin and gently press the pieces of dark chocolate evenly into the surface. Bake for 30 minutes, or until a skewer inserted into the centre comes out clean. Cool in the tin. Makes 24 pieces

92 CHOCOLATE MUD CAKE

125 g (4$\frac{1}{2}$ oz/1 cup) plain (all-purpose) flour
125 g (4$\frac{1}{2}$ oz/1 cup) self-raising flour
60 g (2$\frac{1}{4}$ oz/$\frac{1}{2}$ cup) dark unsweetened cocoa powder
$\frac{1}{2}$ teaspoon bicarbonate of soda (baking soda)
625 g (1 lb 6 oz/2$\frac{3}{4}$ cups) sugar
450 g (1 lb) dark chocolate, chopped
450 g (1 lb) unsalted butter
125 ml (4 fl oz/$\frac{1}{2}$ cup) buttermilk
2 tablespoons oil
2 tablespoons instant espresso coffee granules or powder
4 eggs

Preheat the oven to 160°C (315°F/Gas 2–3). Grease or oil a deep 23 cm (9 inch) square cake tin. Line the base and sides with baking paper, extending at least 2 cm ($\frac{3}{4}$ inch) above the rim. Sift the flours, cocoa and bicarbonate of soda into a large bowl. Stir in the sugar and make a well in the centre. Put 250 g (9 oz) of the chocolate and 250 g (9 oz) of the butter in a saucepan. Add 185 ml (6 fl oz/$\frac{3}{4}$ cup) water and stir over low heat until melted. Gradually stir the chocolate mixture into the dry ingredients using a metal spoon.

Whisk together the buttermilk, oil, coffee and eggs and add to the mixture, stirring until smooth. Pour into the tin and bake for 1 hour 40 minutes, or until a skewer comes out clean when inserted in the centre. Cool in the tin, then turn out. Combine the remaining chocolate and butter in a pan and stir over low heat until smooth. Cool to room temperature, stirring often, until thick enough to spread. Turn the cake upside down and spread the icing (frosting) over the entire cake. Allow the icing to set slightly before serving. Serves 12

93 HAZELNUT CREAM SQUARES

4 eggs, separated
125 g (4$\frac{1}{2}$ oz/$\frac{1}{2}$ cup) caster (superfine) sugar
60 g (2$\frac{1}{4}$ oz/$\frac{1}{2}$ cup) self-raising flour
75 g (2$\frac{3}{4}$ oz/$\frac{2}{3}$ cup) ground hazelnuts
150 g (5$\frac{1}{2}$ oz) unsalted butter, softened
170 g (6 oz/$\frac{1}{2}$ cup) chocolate hazelnut spread
60 g (2$\frac{1}{4}$ oz/$\frac{1}{2}$ cup) icing (confectioners') sugar, sifted
unsweetened cocoa powder, to dust

Preheat the oven to 180°C (350°F/Gas 4). Grease a 20 cm (8 inch) shallow square cake tin and line the base with baking paper. Beat the egg whites with electric beaters in a bowl until soft peaks form. Gradually add the sugar, beating until thick and glossy. Beat the egg yolks into the mixture, one at a time.

Sift the flour over the mixture, add the ground hazelnuts and fold in with a metal spoon. Melt 20 g ($\frac{3}{4}$ oz) of the butter with 2 tablespoons boiling water in a small bowl, then fold into the sponge mixture. Pour the mixture into the prepared tin and bake for 25 minutes, or until cooked. Leave in the tin for 5 minutes before turning out onto a wire rack to cool. Cut the sponge in half horizontally through the centre.

Beat the hazelnut spread and the remaining butter with electric beaters until very creamy. Beat in the icing sugar, then gradually add 3 teaspoons of boiling water and beat until smooth. Fill the cake with the icing mixture and refrigerate until the filling is firm. Dust with the cocoa powder then cut into squares. Makes 16

94 PECAN BROWNIES

125 g (4$\frac{1}{2}$ oz) dark chocolate
90 g (3$\frac{1}{4}$ oz) unsalted butter, softened
250 g (9 oz/1 cup) caster (superfine) sugar
1 teaspoon natural vanilla extract
2 eggs
80 g (2$\frac{3}{4}$ oz/$\frac{2}{3}$ cup) plain (all-purpose) flour
3 tablespoons unsweetened cocoa powder
$\frac{1}{2}$ teaspoon baking powder
125 g (4$\frac{1}{2}$ oz/1 cup) roughly chopped pecan nuts

Preheat the oven to 180°C (350°F/Gas 4). Grease a 17 cm (6$\frac{1}{2}$ inch) square tin and line the base with baking paper, hanging over two opposite sides.

Chop the chocolate into small even-sized pieces and place in a heatproof bowl. Bring a saucepan of water to the boil and remove from the heat. Sit the bowl over the pan — ensure the bowl doesn't touch the water. Stand, stirring occasionally, until melted. Cool slightly.

Beat the butter, sugar and vanilla with electric beaters until thick and creamy. Beat in the eggs one at a time, beating well after each addition. Stir in the chocolate.

Fold in the sifted combined flour, cocoa and baking powder with a metal spoon, then fold in the pecans. Spoon into the tin and smooth the surface. Bake for 30–35 minutes, or until firm and it comes away from the sides of the tin. Cool in the tin, remove and cut into squares. Makes 16 pieces

95

96

97

95 ORANGE, PISTACHIO & SEMOLINA SLICE

100 g (3$\frac{1}{2}$ oz/$\frac{2}{3}$ cup) shelled pistachio nuts
200 g (7 oz) unsalted butter, chopped
160 g (5$\frac{3}{4}$ oz/$\frac{2}{3}$ cup) caster (superfine) sugar
1 teaspoon natural vanilla extract
1 tablespoon finely grated orange zest
2 eggs
60 g (2$\frac{1}{4}$ oz/$\frac{1}{2}$ cup) self-raising flour, sifted
125 ml (4 fl oz/$\frac{1}{2}$ cup) orange juice
185 g (6$\frac{1}{2}$ oz/1$\frac{1}{2}$ cups) fine semolina
250 g (9 oz/1 cup) caster (superfine) sugar, extra
125 ml (4 fl oz/$\frac{1}{2}$ cup) orange juice, extra
icing (confectioners') sugar, to dust

Preheat the oven to 180°C (350°F/Gas 4). Lightly grease a 20 x 30 cm (8 x 12 inch) shallow baking tin and line with baking paper, leaving it hanging over on the two long sides. Bake the pistachios for 8–10 minutes, or until they are lightly toasted. Cool, then chop. Beat the butter and sugar with electric beaters until light and fluffy. Add the vanilla, orange zest and eggs, and beat until combined. Add the flour, orange juice, semolina and pistachio nuts, and fold in with a spatula until just combined — do not overmix. Spread into the tin. Bake for 30 minutes, or until golden brown and firm when lightly touched. Cool for 10 minutes in the tin, then on a wire rack placed on a tray.

Mix the extra sugar and orange juice in a small saucepan. Bring to the boil, then simmer for 1 minute. Spoon over the slice. Cool and cut into squares or diamonds. Dust with icing sugar. Makes 18 pieces

97 PEANUT TOFFEE SHORTBREAD

290 g (10$\frac{1}{4}$ oz) unsalted butter
125 g (4$\frac{1}{2}$ oz/$\frac{1}{2}$ cup) caster (superfine) sugar
1 egg
185 g (6$\frac{1}{2}$ oz/1$\frac{1}{2}$ cups) plain (all-purpose) flour, sifted
60 g (2$\frac{1}{4}$ oz/$\frac{1}{2}$ cup) self-raising flour, sifted
185 g (6$\frac{1}{2}$ oz/1 cup) soft brown sugar
2 tablespoons golden syrup
$\frac{1}{2}$ teaspoon lemon juice
400 g (14 oz/2$\frac{1}{2}$ cups) roasted unsalted peanuts

Preheat the oven to 180°C (350°F/Gas 4). Lightly grease an 18 x 27 cm (7 x 10$\frac{3}{4}$ inch) baking tin and line the base and sides with baking paper hanging over the two long sides. Cream 110 g (3$\frac{3}{4}$ oz) of the butter and all the caster sugar with electric beaters until light and fluffy. Add the egg and beat well. Fold in the sifted flours with a large metal spoon until just combined. Press into the tin and bake for 15 minutes, or until firm and lightly coloured. Cool for 10 minutes.

Place the brown sugar, golden syrup, lemon juice and remaining butter in a saucepan. Stir over low heat until the sugar has dissolved. Simmer, stirring, for 5 minutes. Stir in the peanuts. Spread evenly over the base using two spoons — be careful as the mixture is very hot. Bake for a further 5 minutes. Leave to cool in the tin for 15 minutes, then turn out and cut into fingers. Makes 18 pieces

96 POPPY SEED SLICE

125 g (4$\frac{1}{2}$ oz/1 cup) plain (all-purpose) flour
75 g (2$\frac{3}{4}$ oz) unsalted butter, chilled and chopped
3 tablespoons caster (superfine) sugar
1 egg yolk
3 tablespoons poppy seeds
2 tablespoons milk, warmed
125 g (4$\frac{1}{2}$ oz) unsalted butter, extra
90 g (3$\frac{1}{4}$ oz/$\frac{1}{3}$ cup) caster (superfine) sugar, extra
1 teaspoon finely grated lemon zest
1 egg
90 g (3$\frac{1}{4}$ oz/$\frac{3}{4}$ cup) plain (all-purpose) flour, extra, sifted
125 g (4$\frac{1}{2}$ oz/1 cup) icing (confectioners') sugar
$\frac{1}{2}$ teaspoon finely grated lemon zest, extra
1 tablespoon lemon juice

Preheat the oven to 180°C (350°F/Gas 4). Grease an 11 x 35 cm (4$\frac{1}{4}$ x 14 inch) loose-based flan tin. Sift the flour into a bowl and rub in the butter with your fingers until it resembles breadcrumbs. Stir in the sugar. Make a well in the centre and add 2–3 teaspoons water and the egg yolk. Mix with a flat-bladed knife, using a cutting action until it comes together in beads. Press into a ball and flatten slightly. Cover in plastic wrap and chill for 15 minutes.

Roll out the dough to fit the base and sides of the tin. Trim the edges. Line the pastry with baking paper and baking beads or rice and blind bake the pastry for 10 minutes, then remove the paper and beads and bake for 5 minutes, or until the pastry is dry. Cool.

Soak the poppy seeds in the milk for 10 minutes. Beat the extra butter and sugar and the zest until light and fluffy. Beat in the egg and stir in the poppy seed mixture and extra flour. Spread over the pastry and bake for 25 minutes, or until light brown and cooked through. Cool in the tin until just warm.

Combine the icing sugar, extra zest and enough juice to form a paste. Spread over the slice and cool. Makes 14 pieces

98

99

100

98 STRAWBERRY ROULADE

2 eggs
1 egg white
125 g (4$\frac{1}{2}$ oz/$\frac{1}{2}$ cup) caster (superfine) sugar
90 g (3$\frac{1}{4}$ oz/$\frac{3}{4}$ cup) self-raising flour
1 tablespoon caster (superfine) sugar, extra
250 g (9 oz/1 cup) smooth ricotta cheese
1 teaspoon natural vanilla extract
40 g (1$\frac{1}{2}$ oz/$\frac{1}{3}$ cup) icing (confectioners') sugar
250 g (9 oz/1$\frac{2}{3}$ cups) strawberries, hulled and chopped

Preheat the oven to 200°C (400°F/Gas 6). Lightly grease a 26 x 30 cm (10$\frac{1}{2}$ x 12 inch) swiss roll tin and line with baking paper, leaving the paper hanging over the two long sides. Using electric beaters, beat the eggs, egg white and sugar in a large bowl on high speed for 5 minutes, or until light and foamy. Sift the flour into the bowl and fold in quickly and lightly. Pour the mixture into the prepared tin and smooth the surface. Bake for 8–10 minutes, or until the sponge springs back to the light touch. Lay a sheet of baking paper on a clean cloth and sprinkle lightly with the extra caster sugar.

Turn the sponge out onto the sugared paper, remove the lining paper and, starting from a short end, roll up the sponge with the paper, using the cloth as a guide. Cool for 30 minutes.

Mix the ricotta, vanilla and icing sugar together with a wooden spoon. Unroll the sponge and spread with the ricotta mixture, leaving a 2 cm ($\frac{3}{4}$ inch) border at the far end. Scatter over the strawberries, then carefully re-roll the sponge. Trim the ends, and cut into slices. Serves 8

100 MADELEINES

3 eggs
100 g (3$\frac{1}{2}$ oz/$\frac{1}{2}$ cup) caster (superfine) sugar
150 g (5$\frac{1}{2}$ oz/1$\frac{1}{4}$ cups) plain (all-purpose) flour
100 g (3$\frac{1}{2}$ oz) unsalted butter, melted
grated zest of 1 lemon and 1 orange

Preheat the oven to 200°C (400°F/Gas 6). Brush a tray of madeleine moulds with melted butter and coat with flour, then tap the tray to remove the excess flour.

Whisk the eggs and sugar until the mixture is thick and pale and the whisk leaves a trail when lifted. Gently fold in the flour, then the melted butter and grated lemon and orange zest. Spoon into the moulds, leaving a little room for rising. Bake for 12 minutes (small madeleines will only need 7 minutes), or until very lightly golden and springy to the touch. Remove from the tray and cool on a wire rack. Makes 14 (or 30 small ones)

99 COCONUT & PINEAPPLE SLICE

20 g ($\frac{3}{4}$ oz/$\frac{1}{3}$ cup) shredded coconut
90 g (3$\frac{1}{4}$ oz/$\frac{3}{4}$ cup) self-raising flour
50 g (1$\frac{3}{4}$ oz/$\frac{1}{2}$ cup) plain (all-purpose) flour
140 g (5 oz/$\frac{3}{4}$ cup) soft brown sugar
2 tablespoons sunflower seeds
2 tablespoons sesame seeds
70 g (2$\frac{1}{2}$ oz/$\frac{1}{2}$ cup) chopped macadamia nuts
60 g (2$\frac{1}{4}$ oz/$\frac{1}{3}$ cup) chopped dates
1 tablespoon chopped glacé ginger
45 g (1$\frac{1}{2}$ oz/$\frac{1}{2}$ cup) desiccated coconut
230 g (8$\frac{1}{4}$ oz) tin crushed pineapple, drained
100 g (3$\frac{1}{2}$ oz) unsalted butter, melted
2 eggs, lightly beaten

ICING (FROSTING)
250 g (9 oz/2 cups) icing (confectioners') sugar
30 g (1 oz) unsalted butter, melted
1$\frac{1}{2}$ tablespoons lemon juice

Preheat the oven to 170°C (325°F/Gas 3). Spread the coconut evenly on a baking tray and toast for 5–8 minutes, or until lightly golden. Grease a 20 x 30 cm (8 x 12 inch) shallow baking tin and line with enough baking paper to overlap on the longer sides — this will make the slice easier to remove once baked.

Sift the self-raising and plain flours into a large bowl. Add the brown sugar, seeds, macadamia nuts, dates, ginger and desiccated coconut. Stir in the pineapple, melted butter and beaten egg, and mix well.

Spoon the mixture into the prepared tin. Bake for 25–30 minutes, or until golden brown. Cool in the tin, remove and cover with the icing.

To make the icing (frosting), combine the icing sugar, melted butter and lemon juice in a small bowl. Stir in 1–2 teaspoons of boiling water to reach a smooth consistency. Spread evenly over the slice. Sprinkle the top with the toasted shredded coconut and when set, slice and serve. Makes 24 pieces

101

102

103

104

101 CHOC CHIP COOKIES

125 g (4$\frac{1}{2}$ oz) unsalted butter
185 g (6$\frac{1}{2}$ oz/1 cup) soft brown sugar
1 teaspoon natural vanilla extract
1 egg, lightly beaten
1 tablespoon milk
215 g (7$\frac{1}{2}$ oz/1$\frac{3}{4}$ cups) plain (all-purpose) flour
1 teaspoon baking powder
250 g (9 oz/1$\frac{1}{2}$ cups) dark chocolate bits (chocolate chips)

Preheat the oven to 180°C (350°F/Gas 4). Line a large baking tray with baking paper. Cream the butter and sugar with electric beaters in a large bowl. Mix in the vanilla extract and gradually add the egg, beating well. Stir in the milk. Sift the flour and baking powder into a large bowl, then fold into the butter and egg mixture. Stir in the dark chocolate bits.

Drop level tablespoons of the cookie mixture onto the baking tray, leaving about 4 cm (1$\frac{1}{2}$ inches) between each cookie, then lightly press with a floured fork. Bake for 15 minutes, or until lightly golden. Cool on a wire rack. Makes 16

102 ALMOND, ORANGE & CARDAMOM BISCOTTI

2 eggs
155 g (5$\frac{1}{2}$ oz/$\frac{2}{3}$ cup) soft brown sugar
125 g (4$\frac{1}{2}$ oz/1 cup) self-raising flour
90 g (3$\frac{1}{4}$ oz/$\frac{3}{4}$ cup) plain (all-purpose) flour
125 g (4$\frac{1}{2}$ oz/1$\frac{1}{4}$ cups) almonds
1 tablespoon finely grated orange zest
$\frac{1}{4}$ teaspoon ground cardamom

Preheat the oven to 160°C (315°F/Gas 2–3). Line a baking tray with baking paper. Beat the eggs and sugar in a bowl with electric beaters until pale and creamy. Sift the self-raising and plain flours into the bowl, then add the almonds, orange zest and cardamom and mix to a soft dough. Turn out the dough onto a lightly floured work surface. Divide the mixture into two portions, shaping it into two 5 x 20 cm (2 x 8 inch) loaves.

Bake for 35–40 minutes, or until lightly golden. Transfer to a wire rack to cool. Cut the loaves into 1 cm ($\frac{1}{2}$ inch) diagonal slices with a large serrated bread knife. The biscotti will be crumbly on the edges so work slowly and, if possible, try to hold the sides as you cut. Arrange the slices on baking trays in a single layer. Return to the oven for 10 minutes on each side. Don't worry if they don't seem fully dry as they will become crisp on cooling. Allow the biscotti to cool before serving. Makes 40

Notes: Biscotti will store in an airtight container for 2–3 weeks.

103 PECAN & COFFEE BISCOTTI

215 g (7$\frac{1}{2}$ oz/1$\frac{3}{4}$ cups) plain (all-purpose) flour
$\frac{1}{2}$ teaspoon baking powder
160 g (5$\frac{3}{4}$ oz/$\frac{2}{3}$ cup) caster (superfine) sugar
60 g (2$\frac{1}{4}$ oz) unsalted butter
2 eggs
$\frac{1}{2}$ teaspoon natural vanilla extract
2 tablespoons instant coffee granules
135 g (4$\frac{3}{4}$ oz/1$\frac{1}{3}$ cups) pecan nuts
$\frac{1}{2}$ teaspoon caster (superfine) sugar, extra

Preheat the oven to 180°C (350°F/Gas 4) and line two baking trays with baking paper. Put the sifted flour, baking powder, sugar and a pinch of salt in a food processor and mix for 1–2 seconds. Add the butter and mix until the mixture resembles fine breadcrumbs. Add the eggs and vanilla and process until smooth.

Transfer the dough to a well-floured surface and knead in the coffee and pecans. Divide into two equal portions and, using lightly floured hands, shape each into a log about 20 cm (8 inches) long. Place the logs on the baking trays and sprinkle with the extra sugar. Press the top of each log down gently to make an oval. Bake for 35 minutes, or until golden. Remove and set aside to cool for about 20 minutes. Reduce the oven temperature to 170°C (325°F/Gas 3).

Cut the logs into 1 cm ($\frac{1}{2}$ inch) slices. Turn the baking paper over, then spread the biscotti well apart on the tray so that they do not touch. Return to the oven and bake for 30 minutes, or until they just begin to colour. Cool completely before storing in an airtight container. Makes 40

104 PASSIONFRUIT MELTING MOMENTS

250 g (9 oz) unsalted butter
40 g (1$\frac{1}{2}$ oz/$\frac{1}{3}$ cup) icing (confectioners') sugar
1 teaspoon natural vanilla extract
185 g (6$\frac{1}{2}$ oz/1$\frac{1}{2}$ cups) self-raising flour
60 g (2$\frac{1}{4}$ oz/$\frac{1}{2}$ cup) custard powder

PASSIONFRUIT FILLING
60 g (2$\frac{1}{4}$ oz) unsalted butter
60 g (2$\frac{1}{4}$ oz/$\frac{1}{2}$ cup) icing (confectioners') sugar
1$\frac{1}{2}$ tablespoons passionfruit pulp

Preheat the oven to 180°C (350°F/Gas 4). Line two baking trays with baking paper. Beat the butter and sugar until light and creamy. Beat in the vanilla extract. Sift in the flour and custard powder and mix to a soft dough. Roll level tablespoons of the mixture into 28 balls and place on the trays. Flatten slightly with a floured fork. Bake for 20 minutes, or until lightly golden. Cool on a wire rack.

To make the filling, beat the butter and sugar until light and creamy, then beat in the passionfruit pulp. Use the filling to sandwich the biscuits (cookies) together. Leave to firm before serving. Makes 14 filled biscuits

Variation: You can vary the flavour of the filling. To make a coffee filling, for example, dissolve 2 teaspoons of instant coffee in 2 teaspoons water and add to the butter and sugar mixture. Beat until well combined.

105

106

107

105 ALMOND SHORTBREADS

250 g (9 oz) unsalted butter
250 g (9 oz/2 cups) plain (all-purpose) flour
1 teaspoon baking powder
90 g (3¼ oz/¾ cup) icing (confectioners') sugar, sifted
1 egg yolk
1 teaspoon natural vanilla extract
1 tablespoon ouzo
100 g (3½ oz/¾ cup) slivered almonds, ground
    to a medium-fine texture
35 g (1¼ oz/⅓ cup) ground almonds
60 g (2¼ oz/½ cup) icing (confectioners') sugar, extra, to dust

Melt the butter over low heat in a heavy-based saucepan, without stirring or shaking the pan. Carefully pour the clear butter into another container, leaving the white sediment in the pan to be discarded. Refrigerate for 1 hour. Preheat the oven to 170°C (325°F/Gas 3) and line two baking trays with baking paper.

In a bowl, sift the flour and baking powder together. Using electric beaters, beat the chilled butter until light and fluffy. Gradually add the icing sugar and combine well. Add the egg yolk, vanilla and ouzo and beat until just combined. Fold in the flour, the ground slivered almonds and the ground almonds. Shape heaped tablespoons of mixture into crescents, place on the baking trays and bake for 12 minutes, or until lightly coloured. Remove from the oven and dust liberally with icing sugar. Allow to cool a little on the trays. Line a baking tray with baking paper and dust the paper with icing sugar. Lift the warm biscuits onto this and dust again with icing sugar. When the biscuits are cool, dust them once again with icing sugar before storing them in an airtight container. Makes 22

107 ORANGE-SCENTED DATE CRESCENTS

185 g (6½ oz/1 cup) pitted dates, chopped
3 teaspoons finely grated orange zest
2 teaspoons orange flower water or orange juice
125 g (4½ oz) unsalted butter, cubed and softened
125 g (4½ oz/½ cup) caster (superfine) sugar
1 egg
250 g (9 oz/2 cups) plain (all-purpose) flour, sifted
1 teaspoon baking powder
sugar, to sprinkle

Put the dates and 1 tablespoon water in a small pan. Stir over low heat for 2–3 minutes, or until the dates are soft. Remove from the heat and stir in 1 teaspoon of the zest and 1 teaspoon of the orange flower water. Cool.

Line two baking trays with baking paper. Beat the butter, caster sugar, the remaining orange zest and orange flower water until creamy. Add the egg and beat until well combined. Mix in the combined flour and baking powder until a smooth dough forms. Cover with plastic wrap and refrigerate for 30 minutes. Put half the dough between two sheets of baking paper and roll out to 5 mm (¼ inch) thick. Refrigerate again if the dough is too soft. Preheat the oven to 180°C (350°F/Gas 4).

Cut out ten 6.5 cm (2½ inch) circles from the dough with a fluted cutter. Put 1 small teaspoon of filling onto each circle and fold over to form a crescent, pressing the edges to seal. The pastry should be well filled with the mixture. Repeat with the remaining dough. Lay on the trays, brush the tops with water and sprinkle with the sugar. Bake for 10–15 minutes, or until lightly golden. Cool on a wire rack. Makes about 25

106 SHREDDED PASTRIES WITH ALMONDS

250 g (9 oz) unsalted butter, melted
125 g (4½ oz/1 cup) ground pistachios
230 g (8¼ oz/2 cups) ground almonds
625 g (1 lb 6 oz/2½ cups) caster (superfine) sugar
1 teaspoon ground cinnamon
¼ teaspoon ground cloves
1 tablespoon brandy
1 egg white, lightly beaten
500 g (1 lb 2 oz) kataifi pastry (Greek shredded pastry),
    left at room temperature for 2 hours (in its packaging)
1 teaspoon lemon juice
5 cm (2 inch) strip lemon zest
4 cloves
1 cinnamon stick
1 tablespoon honey

Preheat the oven to 170°C (325°F/Gas 3). Brush a 20 x 30 cm (8 x 12 inch) baking tray with some melted butter. Put the nuts in a bowl with 125 g (4½ oz/½ cup) of the caster sugar, cinnamon, cloves and brandy. Add the beaten egg white and stir to make a paste. Divide the mixture into eight portions — form each into a 'sausage' about 18 cm (7 inches) long.

Take a small handful of the pastry strands and spread them out fairly compactly with the strands running lengthways towards you. The pastry should measure 25 x 18 cm (10 x 7 inches). Brush with melted butter. Put one of the nut sausages along the end of the pastry nearest to you and roll up into a neat sausage shape. Repeat with the other pastry portions. Place the rolls close together in the baking tray and brush with melted butter. Bake for 50 minutes, or until golden brown.

Place the remaining sugar in a small saucepan with 500 ml (17 fl oz/2 cups) water and stir over low heat until dissolved. Add the lemon juice, zest, cloves and cinnamon and boil for 10 minutes. Stir in the honey, then set aside until cold.

When the pastries come out of the oven, pour the cold syrup over the top. Leave to cool completely before cutting each roll into 5 pieces. Makes 40 pieces

108

109

110

108 PORTUGUESE CUSTARD TARTS

155 g (5 1/2 oz/1 1/4 cups) plain (all-purpose) flour
25 g (1 oz) vegetable shortening, chopped and softened
30 g (1 oz) butter, chopped and softened
250 g (9 oz/1 cup) sugar
500 ml (17 fl oz/2 cups) milk
3 tablespoons cornflour (cornstarch)
1 tablespoon instant custard powder
4 egg yolks
1 teaspoon natural vanilla extract

Sift the flour and add about 185 ml (6 fl oz/3/4 cup) water, or enough to form a soft dough. Gather into a ball, then roll out on non-stick baking paper to form a 24 x 30 cm (9 1/2 x 12 inch) rectangle. Spread with the vegetable shortening and roll up from the short edge. Roll the dough out into a rectangle again, and spread with the butter. Roll up again into a log and slice into 12 even pieces. Working from the centre outwards, use your fingertips to press each piece out to a circle that is large enough to cover the base and sides of twelve 80 ml (2 1/2 fl oz/1/3 cup) muffin holes. Press into the tin and refrigerate while preparing the filling.

Stir the sugar and 80 ml (2 1/2 fl oz/1/3 cup) water over low heat until the sugar dissolves. Mix a little milk with the cornflour and custard powder to form a smooth paste. Add to the pan with the remaining milk, egg yolks and vanilla. Stir over low heat until the mixture thickens. Put in a bowl, cover and cool. Preheat the oven to 220°C (425°F/ Gas 7). Divide the filling among the pastry bases and bake for 30 minutes, or until the custard is set and the tops have browned. Cool in the tins, then transfer to a wire rack. Makes 12

110 MIXED NUT TARTLETS

300 g (10 1/2 oz) mixed nuts (pecans, macadamia nuts or hazelnuts)
375 g (13 oz/3 cups) plain (all-purpose) flour
230 g (8 1/4 oz) butter, chopped
3 tablespoons soft brown sugar
2 tablespoons white sugar
3 tablespoons light corn syrup
30 g (1 oz) butter, melted
2 eggs, lightly beaten

Preheat the oven to 180°C (350°F/Gas 4). Spread the nuts on a baking tray and bake for 7 minutes. Place the sifted flour and butter in a food processor. Pulse for 10 seconds, or until the mixture resembles fine breadcrumbs. Add about 80 ml (2 1/2 fl oz/1/3 cup) water and process until the mixture just comes together. Add another tablespoon of water if needed. Turn out onto a lightly floured surface and gather into a ball. Refrigerate for 20 minutes.

Divide the pastry into 10 portions. Roll each portion out on a lightly floured surface and line 10 fluted, 8 cm (3 1/4 inch) flan tins. Trim any excess pastry, then refrigerate for 10 minutes. Put the tins on two baking trays. Cut sheets of crumpled baking paper to line the base and side of each tin. Place baking beads or rice in the tins and bake for 10 minutes. Remove the beads and paper and bake for 10–15 minutes.

Divide the nuts among the pastry shells. Whisk together the remaining ingredients and drizzle the mixture over the nuts. Bake for 15–20 minutes, or until just set and golden. Allow to cool completely before serving. Makes 10

109 BAKLAVA

SYRUP
500 g (1 lb 2 oz/2 cups) sugar
2 whole cloves
1 slice lemon
1/2 teaspoon ground cardamom

235 g (8 1/2 oz/1 1/2 cups) finely chopped unblanched almonds
185 g (6 1/2 oz/1 1/2 cups) finely chopped walnuts
1 teaspoon ground cardamom
1 teaspoon mixed spice
125 g (4 1/2 oz/1/2 cup) caster (superfine) sugar
16 sheets filo pastry
160 g (5 3/4 oz) unsalted butter, melted

To make the syrup, put the sugar, cloves, lemon, cardamom and 500 ml (17 fl oz/2 cups) water in a large heavy-based pan and bring to the boil, stirring. Simmer for 12 minutes, remove the cloves and lemon and refrigerate.

Preheat the oven to 180°C (350°F/Gas 4). Grease an 18 x 28 cm (7 x 11 1/4 inch) shallow tin. Mix the almonds, walnuts, cardamom, mixed spice and sugar in a bowl. Take 4 sheets of filo and, layering the pastry, brush each sheet lightly with some of the melted butter. Fold the sheets in half crossways, trim the edges so the pastry fits the base of the tin, then put in the tin.

Sprinkle one-third of the nut mixture over the filo, then top with another 4 sheets of filo, brushing each with some of the melted butter and then layering, folding and trimming. Repeat the layers twice more. Trim the edges of the top layers of filo, brush with melted butter and score into large diamonds. Bake for 30–35 minutes, or until golden brown and crisp. Pour the cold syrup over the hot baklava and refrigerate overnight before cutting into diamonds. Serves 10

111

112

113

114

111 FLORENTINES

55 g (2 oz) unsalted butter
3 tablespoons soft brown sugar
2 teaspoons honey
3 tablespoons flaked almonds, roughly chopped
2 tablespoons chopped dried apricots
2 tablespoons chopped glacé cherries
2 tablespoons mixed peel (mixed candied citrus peel)
40 g (1$\frac{1}{2}$ oz/$\frac{1}{3}$ cup) plain (all-purpose) flour, sifted
120 g (4$\frac{1}{4}$ oz) dark chocolate

Preheat the oven to 180°C (350°F/Gas 4). Melt the butter, brown sugar and honey in a pan until the butter is melted and all the ingredients are combined. Remove from the heat and add the almonds, apricots, glacé cherries, mixed peel and the flour. Mix well.

Grease and line two baking trays with baking paper. Place level tablespoons of the mixture well apart on the trays. Reshape and flatten the biscuits into 5 cm (2 inch) rounds before cooking. Bake for 10 minutes, or until lightly browned. Cool on the tray, then allow to cool completely on a wire rack.

To melt the chocolate, break it up into small pieces and put it in a heatproof bowl. Bring a pan of water to a simmer, remove from the heat and place the bowl over the pan. Stir the chocolate until melted. Spread the melted chocolate on the bottom of each florentine and, using a fork, make a wavy pattern on the chocolate before it sets. Let the chocolate set before serving. Makes 12

112 FENNEL WAFERS

3 tablespoons sugar
2 tablespoons sesame seeds
2 tablespoons fennel seeds
185 g (6$\frac{1}{2}$ oz/1$\frac{1}{2}$ cups) plain (all-purpose) flour
3 tablespoons olive oil
3 tablespoons beer
1 tablespoon anisette liqueur

Preheat the oven to 200°C (400°F/Gas 6). Lightly grease a baking tray and line with baking paper. Combine the sugar, sesame seeds and fennel seeds. Sift the flour and a pinch of salt into a large bowl and make a well in the centre. Add the oil, beer and liqueur, and mix with a large metal spoon until the dough comes together.

Transfer the dough to a lightly floured surface and knead until elastic. Wrap in plastic wrap and refrigerate for 30 minutes. Divide the dough in two and roll each portion out between two sheets of baking paper as thinly as possible. Stamp rounds out of the dough using a 4 cm (1$\frac{1}{2}$ inch) round cutter; you should get about 40 rounds.

Sprinkle the dough rounds with the sugar mixture, then gently roll a rolling pin over the top of them so that the seeds adhere to the dough. Transfer the rounds to a baking tray and cook for 6–8 minutes. Put the wafers under a hot grill for 2 minutes to caramelise the sugar, taking care not to burn them. Transfer to a wire rack and allow to cool. Makes about 40

113 MACADAMIA & WHITE CHOCOLATE COOKIES

180 g (6$\frac{1}{4}$ oz/1$\frac{1}{3}$ cups) macadamia nuts, lightly toasted
1 egg
140 g (5 oz/$\frac{3}{4}$ cup) soft brown sugar
2 tablespoons sugar
1 teaspoon natural vanilla extract
125 ml (4 fl oz/$\frac{1}{2}$ cup) oil
60 g (2$\frac{1}{4}$ oz/$\frac{1}{2}$ cup) plain (all-purpose) flour
3 tablespoons self-raising flour
$\frac{1}{4}$ teaspoon ground cinnamon
30 g (1 oz/$\frac{1}{2}$ cup) shredded coconut
130 g (4$\frac{1}{2}$ oz/$\frac{3}{4}$ cup) white chocolate bits (chocolate chips)

Roughly chop the toasted macadamia nuts and set them aside. Using electric beaters, beat the egg and sugars in a bowl until light and fluffy. Add the vanilla and oil. Using a wooden spoon, stir in the sifted flours, cinnamon, coconut, macadamia nuts and chocolate, and mix well. Refrigerate for 30 minutes. Preheat the oven to 180°C (350°F/Gas 4). Grease and line two baking trays.

Form rounded tablespoons of the mixture into balls and place on the baking trays, pressing the mixture together with your fingertips if it is crumbly. Bake for 12–15 minutes, or until golden. Cool slightly on the trays, then transfer to a wire rack. Makes about 25

114 ITALIAN ORANGE BISCUITS

175 g (6 oz/1$\frac{1}{2}$ cups) plain (all-purpose) flour
200 g (7 oz/1$\frac{2}{3}$ cups) semolina or fine polenta
100 g (3$\frac{1}{2}$ oz/$\frac{1}{2}$ cup) caster (superfine) sugar
100 g (3$\frac{1}{2}$ oz) unsalted butter, softened
2$\frac{1}{2}$ teaspoons grated orange zest
2 eggs

Put the flour, semolina, sugar, butter, orange zest, eggs and a pinch of salt in a food processor and mix until smooth. Chill the mixture in the fridge for 15 minutes.

Preheat the oven to 190°C (375°F/Gas 5). Grease a baking tray and place a teaspoon of the mixture on the tray. Lightly moisten your fingers with a little water and press the mixture down to flatten it. Don't use too much water or it will affect the texture of the biscuits. Leave space between the biscuits as they will expand during cooking.

Bake for about 15 minutes, or until the edge of the biscuit is dark golden brown. Remove from the oven, scoop off the tray with a metal spatula and cool on a wire rack. If you are baking the biscuits in batches, make sure the tray is greased each time you use it. Makes 45

115

116

117

115 COFFEE CUPCAKES

195 g (6³/₄ oz) unsalted butter, softened
125 g (4¹/₂ oz/²/₃ cup) soft brown sugar
2 eggs
1 tablespoon coffee and chicory essence
155 g (5¹/₂ oz/1¹/₄ cups) self-raising flour
100 ml (3¹/₂ fl oz) buttermilk
125 g (4¹/₂ oz/1 cup) icing (confectioners') sugar

Preheat the oven to 150°C (300°F/Gas 2). Line two 50 ml (1³/₄ fl oz) 12-hole cupcake trays with paper patty cases. Beat 185 g (6¹/₂ oz) of the butter and the brown sugar with electric beaters until light and creamy. Add the eggs one at a time, beating well after each addition. Mix in 3 teaspoons of the coffee and chicory essence.

Fold the flour and a pinch of salt alternately with the buttermilk into the creamed mixture until combined. Spoon evenly into the patty cases and bake for 25–30 minutes, or until just springy to the touch. Leave to cool in the tray.

To make the icing (frosting), combine the remaining butter, remaining essence, the icing sugar and 1¹/₂ tablespoons boiling water in a small bowl. Spread a little icing over each cupcake with a palette knife until evenly covered. If desired, decorate with chocolate-coated coffee beans. Makes 24

117 BUTTERFLY CUPCAKES

120 g (4¹/₄ oz) unsalted butter, softened
170 g (6 oz/³/₄ cup) caster (superfine) sugar
185 g (6¹/₂ oz/1¹/₂ cups) self-raising flour
125 ml (4 fl oz/¹/₂ cup) milk
2 eggs
125 ml (4 fl oz/¹/₂ cup) thick (double/heavy) cream
1¹/₂ tablespoons strawberry jam
icing (confectioners') sugar, to dust

Preheat the oven to 180°C (350°F/Gas 4). Line a flat-bottomed 12-hole cupcake tray with paper patty cases.

Beat the butter, sugar, flour, milk and eggs with electric beaters on low speed. Increase the speed and beat until smooth and pale. Divide evenly among the cases and bake for 30 minutes, or until cooked and golden. Transfer to a wire rack to cool.

Cut shallow rounds from the centre of each cake using the point of a sharp knife, then cut in half. Spoon 2 teaspoons cream into each cavity, top with 1 teaspoon jam and position two halves of the cake tops in the jam to resemble butterfly wings. Dust with icing sugar. Makes 12

Note: If using foil patty cases instead of the standard paper cases as suggested, the size and number of butterfly cakes may vary.

116 INDIVIDUAL WHITE CHOCOLATE CHIP CAKES

125 g (4¹/₂ oz) unsalted butter, softened
185 g (6¹/₂ oz/³/₄ cup) caster (superfine) sugar
2 eggs, lightly beaten
1 teaspoon natural vanilla extract
250 g (9 oz/2 cups) self-raising flour, sifted
125 ml (4 fl oz/¹/₂ cup) buttermilk
280 g (10 oz/1²/₃ cups) white chocolate bits (chocolate chips)
white chocolate, shaved, to decorate

WHITE CHOCOLATE CREAM CHEESE ICING

100 g (3¹/₂ oz) white chocolate
3 tablespoons cream
200 g (7 oz/³/₄ cup) cream cheese, softened
40 g (1¹/₂ oz/¹/₃ cup) icing (confectioners') sugar

Preheat the oven to 170°C (325°F/Gas 3). Lightly grease twelve 125 ml (4 fl oz/¹/₂ cup) muffin tins. Beat the butter and sugar in a large bowl with electric beaters until pale and creamy. Gradually add the egg, beating well after each addition. Add the vanilla extract and beat until combined. Fold in the flour alternately with the buttermilk, then fold in the chocolate bits.

Fill each muffin hole three-quarters full with the mixture and bake for 20 minutes, or until a skewer comes out clean when inserted into the centre of each cake. Leave in the tins for 5 minutes before turning out onto a wire rack to cool.

To make the icing (frosting), melt the chocolate and cream in a small saucepan over low heat until completely smooth. Allow to cool slightly, then add to the cream cheese and icing sugar and beat until smooth. Spread the icing over the cakes and garnish with white chocolate shavings. Makes 12

118 BABY COFFEE & WALNUT SOUR CREAM CAKES

75 g (2³/₄ oz/³/₄ cup) walnuts
155 g (5¹/₂ oz/²/₃ cup) soft brown sugar
125 g (4¹/₂ oz) unsalted butter, softened
2 eggs, lightly beaten
125 g (4¹/₂ oz/1 cup) self-raising flour
80 g (2³/₄ oz/¹/₃ cup) sour cream
1 tablespoon coffee and chicory essence

Preheat the oven to 160°C (315°F/Gas 2–3). Lightly grease two 12-hole 60 ml (2 fl oz/¹/₄ cup) baby muffin tins. Process the walnuts and 3 tablespoons of the brown sugar in a food processor until the walnuts are roughly chopped into small pieces. Transfer to a bowl.

Cream the butter and remaining sugar together in the food processor until pale and creamy. With the motor running, gradually add the egg and process until smooth. Add the flour and blend until well mixed. Add the sour cream and essence and process until thoroughly mixed.

Spoon half a teaspoon of the walnut and sugar mixture into the base of each muffin hole, followed by a teaspoon of the cake mixture. Sprinkle a little more walnut mixture over the top, a little more cake mixture and top with the remaining walnut mixture. Bake for 20 minutes, or until risen and springy to the touch. Leave in the tins for 5 minutes. Remove the cakes using the handle of a teaspoon to loosen the side and base, then transfer to a wire rack to cool completely. Makes 24

120 SCOTTISH SHORTBREAD

250 g (9 oz) unsalted butter, softened
160 g (5³/₄ oz/²/₃ cup) caster (superfine) sugar
210 g (7¹/₂ oz/1²/₃ cups) plain (all-purpose) flour
90 g (3¹/₄ oz/¹/₂ cup) rice flour
1 teaspoon sugar

Preheat the oven to 160°C (315°F/Gas 2–3). Brush a 28 cm (11¹/₄ inch) round pizza tray with melted butter or oil and line with baking paper.

Beat the butter and sugar with electric beaters in a small bowl until light and creamy. Transfer to a large bowl and add the sifted flours. Mix to a soft dough with a flat-bladed knife. Lift the dough onto a lightly floured work surface and knead for 30 seconds, or until smooth.

Transfer to the pizza tray and press into a 25 cm (10 inch) round (the tray must be larger than the uncooked shortbread as the mixture will spread during cooking). Pinch and flute around the edge with your fingers to decorate. Prick the surface lightly with a fork and mark into 16 segments with a sharp knife. Sprinkle with sugar and bake on the middle shelf of the oven for 35 minutes, or until firm and lightly golden. Allow the shortbread to cool on the tray. Makes 16 pieces

119 PASSIONFRUIT & LEMON DELICIOUS SLICE

120 g (4¹/₄ oz) unsalted butter, softened
60 g (2¹/₄ oz/¹/₂ cup) icing (confectioners') sugar, sifted
¹/₂ teaspoon natural vanilla extract
185 g (6¹/₂ oz/1¹/₂ cups) plain (all-purpose) flour, sifted
1 teaspoon grated lemon zest
icing (confectioners') sugar, to dust

FILLING
100 g (3¹/₂ oz/³/₄ cup) plain (all-purpose) flour
¹/₂ teaspoon baking powder
65 g (2¹/₄ oz/³/₄ cup) desiccated coconut
3 eggs
250 g (9 oz/1 cup) caster (superfine) sugar
170 g (6 oz) tin passionfruit pulp
2 tablespoons lemon juice
1 teaspoon grated lemon zest

Preheat the oven to 180°C (350°F/Gas 4). Lightly grease an 18 x 27 cm (7 x 10³/₄ inch) baking tin and line with baking paper, leaving the paper hanging over the two long sides.

Cream the butter and icing sugar with electric beaters until pale and creamy, then add the vanilla. Fold in the flour and lemon zest with a large metal spoon. Press into the tin and bake for 15–20 minutes, or until lightly golden.

To make the filling, sift the flour and baking powder together and add the coconut. Lightly beat the eggs and sugar in a bowl, then add the passionfruit pulp, lemon juice and zest. Add the dry ingredients and stir until combined. Pour over the base and bake for 20 minutes, or until firm to touch. Cool in the tin. Dust with icing sugar and cut into pieces. Makes 18 pieces

121

122

123

124

121 CHOCOLATE TRUFFLE MACAROON SLICE

3 egg whites
185 g (6½ oz/¾ cup) caster (superfine) sugar
180 g (6¼ oz/2 cups) desiccated coconut
250 g (9 oz) dark chocolate
300 ml (10½ fl oz/1¼ cups) cream
1 tablespoon unsweetened cocoa powder

Preheat the oven to 180°C (350°F/Gas 4). Lightly grease a 20 x 30 cm (8 x 12 inch) shallow baking tin and line with baking paper, leaving it hanging over the two long sides.

Beat the egg whites in a clean, dry bowl until soft peaks form. Slowly add the sugar, beating well after each addition until stiff and glossy. Fold in the coconut. Spread into the tin and bake for 20 minutes, or until light brown. While still warm, press down lightly but firmly with a palette knife. Cool completely.

Chop the chocolate into small even-sized pieces and place in a heatproof bowl. Bring a saucepan of water to the boil, then remove from the heat. Sit the bowl over the pan — ensure the bowl doesn't touch the water. Stand, stirring occasionally, until the chocolate has melted. Cool slightly.

Beat the cream until thick. Gently fold in the chocolate until well combined — do not overmix or it will curdle. Spread evenly over the base and refrigerate for 3 hours, or until set. Lift from the tin and dust with the cocoa. Makes 24 pieces

122 SESAME & GINGER SLICE

125 g (4½ oz/1 cup) plain (all-purpose) flour
½ teaspoon bicarbonate of soda (baking soda)
1 teaspoon ground ginger
¼ teaspoon mixed spice
2 eggs
140 g (5 oz/¾ cup) soft brown sugar
125 g (4½ oz) unsalted butter, melted
3 tablespoons chopped crystallised ginger
50 g (1¾ oz/⅓ cup) sesame seeds, toasted

Preheat the oven to 180°C (350°F/Gas 4). Lightly grease a 20 x 30 cm (8 x 12 inch) shallow baking tin and line with baking paper, leaving it hanging over the two long sides.

Sift together the flour, bicarbonate of soda, ginger, mixed spice and ¼ teaspoon salt. Beat the eggs and brown sugar in a large bowl for 2 minutes, or until thick and creamy. Mix in the melted butter and gently fold in the flour mixture. Add the crystallised ginger and half the sesame seeds and mix gently.

Spread into the tin and sprinkle evenly with the remaining sesame seeds. Bake for 20 minutes, or until firm to touch and slightly coloured. Cool in the tin for 10 minutes, then cool on a wire rack. Makes 15 pieces

123 LEMON SQUARES

125 g (4½ oz) unsalted butter
75 g (2¾ oz/⅓ cup) caster (superfine) sugar
155 g (5½ oz/1¼ cups) plain (all-purpose) flour, sifted
icing (confectioners') sugar, to dust

TOPPING
4 eggs, lightly beaten
250 g (9 oz/1 cup) caster (superfine) sugar
3 tablespoons lemon juice
1 teaspoon finely grated lemon zest
3 tablespoons plain (all-purpose) flour
½ teaspoon baking powder

Preheat the oven to 180°C (350°F/Gas 4). Lightly grease a 20 x 30 cm (8 x 12 inch) baking tin and line with baking paper, leaving the paper hanging over two opposite sides.

Cream the butter and sugar with electric beaters until pale and fluffy. Fold in the flour with a metal spoon. Press into the tin and bake for 20 minutes, or until golden and firm. Leave to cool.

Beat the eggs and sugar with electric beaters for 2 minutes, or until light and fluffy. Stir in the lemon juice and lemon zest. Sift together the flour and baking powder and gradually whisk into the egg mixture. Pour onto the base. Bake for 25 minutes, or until just firm. Cool in the tin and dust with icing sugar. Makes 30 pieces

124 FIG & CINNAMON SLICE

125 g (4½ oz) unsalted butter, softened
3 tablespoons soft brown sugar
1 teaspoon ground cinnamon
185 g (6½ oz/1½ cups) plain (all-purpose) flour
375 g (13 oz/2⅓ cups) dried figs
1 cinnamon stick
125 g (4½ oz/½ cup) caster (superfine) sugar

Preheat the oven to 180°C (350°F/Gas 4). Lightly grease an 18 x 27 cm (7 x 10¾ inch) baking tin and line with baking paper, hanging over the two long sides.

Beat the butter, brown sugar and cinnamon until light and fluffy, then fold in the flour with a large metal spoon. Press the mixture evenly into the tin and bake for 25 minutes. Cool slightly.

Place the dried figs, cinnamon stick, sugar and 375 ml (13 fl oz/1½ cups) boiling water in a saucepan, mix together and bring to the boil. Reduce the heat and simmer for 20 minutes, or until the figs have softened and the water has reduced by a third. Remove the cinnamon stick and place the mixture in a food processor. Process in short bursts until smooth.

Pour onto the cooked base and bake for 10 minutes, or until set. Cool in the tin, then lift out and cut into squares. Makes 15 squares

125

126

127

128

125 BREAKFAST SHAKE

150 g (5$\frac{1}{2}$ oz) fruit (passionfruit, mango, banana, peaches,
strawberries, blueberries)
250 ml (9 fl oz/1 cup) milk
2 teaspoons wheat germ
1 tablespoon honey
3 tablespoons vanilla yoghurt
1 egg (optional)
1 tablespoon malt powder

Blend all the ingredients in a blender for 30–60 seconds, or until
well combined. Pour into chilled glasses and serve immediately.
Makes 2 x 325 ml (11 fl oz) glasses

126 BANANA DATE SMOOTHIE

250 g (9 oz/1 cup) low-fat plain yoghurt
125 ml (4 fl oz/$\frac{1}{2}$ cup) skim milk
50 g (1$\frac{3}{4}$ oz/$\frac{1}{2}$ cup) fresh dates, stoned and chopped
2 bananas, sliced
8 ice cubes

Put the yoghurt, milk, dates, banana and ice cubes in a blender.
Blend until the mixture is smooth and the ice cubes have been well
incorporated. Serve in chilled glasses. Makes 2 x 350 ml (12 fl oz) glasses

127 BIG BOLD BANANA

750 ml (26 fl oz/3 cups) soy milk, chilled
125 g (4$\frac{1}{2}$ oz) soft silken tofu
4 very ripe bananas, sliced
1 tablespoon honey
1 tablespoon natural vanilla extract
1 tablespoon unsweetened cocoa powder

Combine the soy milk and tofu in a blender. Add the banana, honey,
vanilla extract and cocoa powder. Blend until smooth. Serve in chilled
glasses with a long spoon. Makes 4 x 375 ml (13 fl oz/1$\frac{1}{2}$ cups) glasses

128 PASSIONFRUIT & VANILLA
ICE CREAM WHIP

4 passionfruit
100 g (3$\frac{1}{2}$ oz) passionfruit yoghurt
500 ml (17 fl oz/2 cups) milk
1 tablespoon caster (superfine) sugar
2 scoops vanilla ice cream

Scoop out the pulp from the passionfruit and push through a sieve to
remove the seeds. Place into the blender with the yoghurt, milk, sugar
and ice cream and blend until smooth. Pour into tall glasses and serve
with an extra scoop of ice cream, if desired. Makes 2 x
375 ml (13 fl oz/1$\frac{1}{2}$ cups) glasses

129

130

131

132

129 MELON SHAKE

500 g (1 lb 2 oz) rockmelon, peeled and seeded
2 tablespoons honey
375 ml (13 fl oz/1$\frac{1}{2}$ cups) milk
5 scoops vanilla ice cream
ground nutmeg, to sprinkle

Cut the rockmelon into pieces and place in a blender. Mix for
30 seconds, or until smooth. Add the honey, milk and ice cream
and blend the mixture for a further 10–20 seconds, or until well
combined and smooth. Serve sprinkled with nutmeg. Makes 2 x 375 ml
(13 fl oz/1$\frac{1}{2}$ cups) glasses

130 SUMMER BUTTERMILK SMOOTHIE

350 g (12 oz) rockmelon, peeled and seeded
2 peaches, peeled and sliced
150 g (5$\frac{1}{2}$ oz) strawberries, roughly chopped
4 mint leaves
125 ml (4 fl oz/$\frac{1}{2}$ cup) buttermilk
125 ml (4 fl oz/$\frac{1}{2}$ cup) orange juice
1–2 tablespoons honey

Cut the rockmelon into pieces. Place the rockmelon, peaches,
strawberries and mint leaves in a blender and blend until smooth.
Add the buttermilk, orange juice and 1 tablespoon of the honey and
blend to combine. Taste for sweetness and add more honey if needed.
Makes 2 x 375 ml (13 fl oz/1$\frac{1}{2}$ cups) glasses

Note: This drink should be consumed within 3 hours of being made or
it will lose colour and freshness of flavour.

131 APRICOT WHIP

75 g (2$\frac{3}{4}$ oz) dried apricots
125 g (4$\frac{1}{2}$ oz/$\frac{1}{2}$ cup) apricot yoghurt
170 ml (5$\frac{1}{2}$ fl oz/$\frac{2}{3}$ cup) light coconut milk
310 ml (10$\frac{3}{4}$ fl oz/1$\frac{1}{4}$ cups) milk
1 tablespoon honey
1 scoop vanilla ice cream
flaked coconut, toasted

Cover the apricots with boiling water and soak for 15 minutes. Drain
and roughly chop. Place the apricots, yoghurt, coconut milk, milk,
honey and ice cream in a blender and blend until smooth. Pour
into tall, chilled glasses and sprinkle with the flaked coconut.
Makes 3 x 250 ml (9 fl oz/1 cup) glasses

132 COCONUT & PASSIONFRUIT SMOOTHIE

140 ml (4$\frac{3}{4}$ fl oz) coconut milk
250 ml (9 fl oz/1 cup) milk
3 tablespoons desiccated coconut
$\frac{1}{4}$ teaspoon natural vanilla extract
3 scoops vanilla ice cream
170 g (6 oz) tin passionfruit pulp in syrup

Blend together the coconut milk, milk, coconut, vanilla, ice cream
and half the passionfruit pulp until the mixture is smooth and fluffy.
Stir in the remaining pulp and serve immediately. Makes 2 x 375 ml
(13 fl oz/1$\frac{1}{2}$ cups) glasses

133

134

135

136

133 COCONUT & LIME LASSI

400 ml (14 fl oz) coconut milk
185 g (6$^1/_2$ oz/$^3/_4$ cup) plain yoghurt
3 tablespoons lime juice
3 tablespoons caster (superfine) sugar
8–10 ice cubes
lime slices, to serve

Blend together the coconut milk, yoghurt, lime juice, sugar and ice cubes until the mixture is well combined and the ice cubes are well crushed. Pour into tall glasses and serve immediately, garnished with slices of fresh lime. Makes 2 x 375 ml (13 fl oz/1$^1/_2$ cups) glasses

134 SPORTS SHAKE

500 ml (17 fl oz/2 cups) milk, chilled
2 tablespoons honey
2 eggs
$^1/_2$ teaspoon natural vanilla extract
1 tablespoon wheat germ
1 banana, sliced

Blend the milk, honey, eggs, vanilla, wheat germ and banana until smooth. Chill well and serve. Makes 2 x 250 ml (9 fl oz/1 cup) glasses

135 CINNAMON & CUSTARD SHAKE

375 ml (13 fl oz/1$^1/_2$ cups) milk
185 ml (6 fl oz/$^3/_4$ cup) prepared custard
3 teaspoons honey
1$^1/_2$ teaspoons ground cinnamon
3 scoops vanilla ice cream
ground cinnamon, extra, to sprinkle

Blend together the milk, custard, honey, cinnamon and ice cream until smooth and fluffy. Pour into tall glasses, sprinkle with the extra cinnamon and serve. Makes 2 x 375 ml (13 fl oz/1$^1/_2$ cups) glasses

136 BANANA PASSION

3 passionfruit, halved
1 large banana, chopped
250 ml (9 fl oz/1 cup) skim milk
3 tablespoons low-fat plain yoghurt

Scoop out the passionfruit pulp and place in a blender. Add the banana, milk and yoghurt and blend, turning quickly on and off (or use the pulse button), until smooth and the seeds are finely chopped. (Add more milk if it is too thick.) Don't blend for too long or it will become very bubbly and increase in volume. Makes 2 x 250 ml (9 fl oz/1 cup) glasses

137

138

139 140

137 SMOOTHBERRY

150 g (5$\frac{1}{2}$ oz) strawberries, hulled
60 g (2$\frac{1}{4}$ oz) raspberries
200 g (7 oz) boysenberries
250 ml (9 fl oz/1 cup) milk
3 scoops vanilla ice cream

Place the strawberries, raspberries, boysenberries, milk and ice cream in a blender and blend until smooth, then chill. Pour into chilled glasses and serve. Makes 4 x 200 ml (7 fl oz) glasses

Note: If boysenberries are unavailable, any other berry can be used.

138 SUMMER STRAWBERRY SMOOTHIE

1 tablespoon strawberry flavouring
250 ml (9 fl oz/1 cup) wildberry drinking yoghurt
250 g (9 oz) strawberries, hulled
4 scoops frozen strawberry yoghurt
few drops natural vanilla extract
ice cubes, to serve

Combine the strawberry flavouring, drinking yoghurt, strawberries, frozen yoghurt and vanilla in a blender and process until smooth. Pour over lots of ice to serve. Makes 2 x 300 ml (10$\frac{1}{2}$ fl oz) glasses

139 CHOC CHERRY SMOOTHIE

500 ml (17 fl oz/2 cups) milk
3 tablespoons whole red glacé cherries
3 tablespoons desiccated coconut
1 tablespoon chocolate topping
3 scoops chocolate ice cream

Blend together the milk, cherries, coconut, topping and ice cream until smooth and fluffy. Pour into tall glasses and serve immediately. Makes 2 x 375 ml (13 fl oz/1$\frac{1}{2}$ cups) glasses

140 VERY BERRY

250 g (9 oz/1 cup) low-fat strawberry yoghurt
125 ml (4 fl oz/$\frac{1}{2}$ cup) cranberry juice, chilled
250 g (9 oz) strawberries, hulled and quartered
125 g (4$\frac{1}{2}$ oz) frozen raspberries

Combine the yoghurt and cranberry juice in a blender. Add the quartered strawberries and 80 g (2$\frac{3}{4}$ oz) of the raspberries. Blend until smooth. Pour into chilled glasses and top with the remaining frozen raspberries. Serve with a spoon as it is thick. Makes 4 x 200 ml (7 fl oz) glasses

141

142

143

144

141 MANDARIN & MANGO CHILL

1 mango, cut into slices
500 ml (17 fl oz/2 cups) mandarin juice
125 ml (4 fl oz/$1/2$ cup) lime juice cordial
375 ml (13 fl oz/$1 1/2$ cups) soda water
2 tablespoons caster (superfine) sugar
ice cubes, to serve

Freeze the mango for about 1 hour, or until semi-frozen. Combine the juice, cordial, soda water and sugar in a jug. Place the mango slices and some ice cubes into each glass, then pour in the juice mix. Makes 2 x 375 ml (13 fl oz/$1 1/2$ cups) glasses

142 RASPBERRY LEMONADE

300 g ($10 1/2$ oz) fresh or frozen raspberries, thawed
310 g (11 oz/$1 1/4$ cups) sugar
500 ml (17 fl oz/2 cups) lemon juice
ice cubes, to serve
mint leaves, to serve

Combine the raspberries and sugar in a blender and blend until smooth. Place a strong sieve over a large bowl and push the mixture through to remove the seeds. Discard the seeds. Add the lemon juice and mix well. Pour into a large jug and stir in 1.5 litres (52 fl oz/6 cups) water, then chill. To serve, pour over ice cubes and garnish with mint leaves. Makes 6 x 375 ml (13 fl oz/$1 1/2$ cups) glasses

143 HOMEMADE LEMONADE

685 ml ($23 1/2$ fl oz/$2 3/4$ cups) lemon juice
310 g (11 oz/$1 1/4$ cups) sugar
ice cubes, to serve
mint leaves, to serve

Combine the lemon juice and sugar in a large bowl, stirring until the sugar has dissolved. Pour into a large jug. Add 1.25 litres (44 fl oz/ 5 cups) water to the jug, stirring well to combine. Chill. To serve, pour over ice cubes and garnish with mint leaves. Makes 6 x 375 ml (13 fl oz/$1 1/2$ cups) glasses

144 VIRGIN MARY

750 ml (26 fl oz/3 cups) tomato juice
2 tablespoons lemon juice
1 tablespoon worcestershire sauce
$1/4$ teaspoon ground nutmeg
few drops of Tabasco sauce
12 ice cubes
2 lemon slices, halved

Place the tomato juice, lemon juice, worcestershire sauce, nutmeg and Tabasco sauce in a large jug and stir until combined. Place the ice cubes in a blender and blend for 30 seconds, or until the ice is crushed. Pour the tomato juice mixture into serving glasses and add the crushed ice and lemon slices. Season with salt and pepper before serving. Makes 4 x 200 ml (7 fl oz) glasses

145

146

147

148

145 CRANBERRY & VANILLA ICE CREAM SPIDER

500 ml (17 fl oz/2 cups) cranberry juice
500 ml (17 fl oz/2 cups) soda water
4 scoops vanilla ice cream
185 ml (6 fl oz/³/₄ cup) cream
1 tablespoon caster (superfine) sugar
20 g (³/₄ oz) flaked almonds, toasted

Combine the juice and soda water in a jug. Add a scoop of ice cream to each tall glass. Pour the juice and soda over the ice cream. Whip the cream and sugar until soft peaks form. Spoon over the juice and soda and top with almonds. Makes 4 x 250 ml (9 fl oz/1 cup) glasses

146 CHOCOHOLIC THICKSHAKE

125 ml (4 fl oz/¹/₂ cup) cold milk
50 g (1³/₄ oz) dark chocolate, grated
2 tablespoons chocolate syrup
2 tablespoons cream
4 scoops chocolate ice cream
2 scoops chocolate ice cream, extra
grated dark chocolate, to sprinkle

Blend the milk, chocolate, syrup, cream and ice cream in a blender until smooth. Pour into chilled glasses. Top each glass with a scoop of ice cream and sprinkle with grated chocolate. Makes 2 x 250 ml (9 fl oz/1 cup) glasses

147 ICED CHOCOLATE

2 tablespoons rich chocolate topping
375 ml (13 fl oz/1¹/₂ cups) ice-cold milk
1 scoop vanilla ice cream
whipped cream, to serve
drinking chocolate, to dust

Pour the chocolate topping into a glass and swirl it around the sides. Fill with the cold milk and add the ice cream. Serve with a big swirl of whipped cream and dust with drinking chocolate. Makes 1 x 375 ml (13 fl oz/1¹/₂ cups) glass

148 BLACKCURRANT CRUSH

750 ml (26 fl oz/3 cups) apple and blackcurrant juice
500 ml (17 fl oz/2 cups) soda water
1 tablespoon caster (superfine) sugar
150 g (5¹/₂ oz) blueberries
ice cubes, to serve

Place the apple and blackcurrant juice, soda water, sugar and blueberries into a blender and blend until smooth. Serve in chilled glasses over ice. Makes 4 x 300 ml (10¹/₂ fl oz) glasses

Note: If you have a really good blender, you may wish to add the ice cubes when blending the other ingredients to make a slushy.

149

150

151

152

149 LEMONGRASS TEA

3 lemongrass stems
2 lemon slices
3 teaspoons honey, or to taste
lemon slices, to serve

Prepare the lemongrass by removing the first two tough outer layers. For maximum flavour, only use the bottom one-third of the stalk (the white part). Slice thinly into rings. (You could use the remaining stalks as a garnish, if you like.)

Place the lemongrass in a jug and cover with 625 ml ($21\frac{1}{2}$ fl oz/ $2\frac{1}{2}$ cups) boiling water. Add the lemon slices and cover. Allow to infuse and cool. When cooled to room temperature, strain. Add the honey, to taste. Place the tea in the refrigerator to chill. To serve, pour the tea into two glasses with extra slices of lemon. Add ice, if desired. Makes 2 x 310 ml ($10\frac{3}{4}$ fl oz/$1\frac{1}{4}$ cups) glasses

150 ORANGE & GINGER TEA COOLER

1 small orange
$\frac{1}{2}$–1 tablespoon darjeeling tea leaves
250 ml (9 fl oz/1 cup) ginger beer
8 thin slices glacé ginger
2 tablespoons sugar
4–6 ice cubes
mint leaves

Remove the peel from the orange using a vegetable peeler, avoiding the white pith, and cut into long thin strips. Place half the peel and the tea leaves in a bowl and pour in 500 ml (17 fl oz/2 cups) boiling water. Cover and leave to steep for 5 minutes, then strain through a fine strainer.

Pour into a jug, add the ginger beer and chill for 6 hours, or overnight if possible. One hour before serving, add the ginger, sugar and remaining orange peel. Stir well. Pour into tall glasses, add 2–3 ice cubes per glass and garnish with mint leaves. Makes 2 x 375 ml (13 fl oz/$1\frac{1}{2}$ cups) glasses

151 EARL GREY SUMMER TEA

1 cinnamon stick
1 tablespoon earl grey tea leaves
250 ml (9 fl oz/1 cup) orange juice
2 teaspoons finely grated orange zest
2 tablespoons sugar, to taste
ice cubes, to serve
1 orange, sliced into thin rounds
4 cinnamon sticks, extra, to serve

Place the cinnamon stick, tea leaves, orange juice, orange zest and 750 ml (26 fl oz/3 cups) water in a saucepan.

Slowly bring to a simmer over gentle heat. Once simmering, stir in the sugar, to taste, and stir until dissolved. Remove from the heat and allow to cool. Once the mixture has cooled, strain the liquid into a jug and refrigerate until cold.

Serve in a jug with lots of ice cubes, and garnish with the orange slices and extra cinnamon stick. Makes 4 x 250 ml (9 fl oz/1 cup) glasses

152 LEMON BARLEY WATER

110 g ($3\frac{3}{4}$ oz/$\frac{1}{2}$ cup) pearl barley
3 lemons
125 g ($4\frac{1}{2}$ oz/$\frac{1}{2}$ cup) caster (superfine) sugar
crushed ice, to serve
lemon slices, to serve

Wash the barley well and place in a saucepan. Using a sharp vegetable peeler, remove the peel from the lemons, avoiding the bitter white pith. Squeeze out the juice and set aside. Add the peel and 1.75 litres (60 fl oz/7 cups) cold water to the barley and bring to the boil. Simmer briskly for 30 minutes. Add the sugar and mix to dissolve. Allow to cool.

Strain the liquid into a jug and add the lemon juice. Serve over crushed ice and garnish with lemon slices. Makes 4 x 250 ml (9 fl oz/1 cup) glasses

153

154

155

156

153 LEMON, LIME & SODA WITH CITRUS ICE CUBES

1 lemon
1 lime
2$\frac{1}{2}$ tablespoons lemon juice
170 ml (5$\frac{1}{2}$ fl oz/$\frac{2}{3}$ cup) lime juice cordial
625 ml (21$\frac{1}{2}$ fl oz/2$\frac{1}{2}$ cups) soda water, chilled

Using a sharp knife, remove the peel and white pith from the lemon and lime. On a chopping board, cut between the membranes to release the segments. Place a lemon and lime segment in each hole of an ice cube tray and cover with water. Freeze for 2–3 hours or overnight until firm.

Combine the lemon juice, lime juice cordial and soda water. Pour into long, chilled glasses with the ice cubes. Makes 2 x 375 ml (13 fl oz/ 1$\frac{1}{2}$ cups) glasses and 8 ice cubes

154 ORANGE & CARDAMOM HERBAL TEA

3 cardamom pods
250 ml (9 fl oz/1 cup) orange juice
3 strips orange zest
2 tablespoons caster (superfine) sugar

Place the cardamom pods on a chopping board and press with the side of a large knife to crack them open. Place the cardamom, orange juice, zest, sugar and 500 ml (17 fl oz/2 cups) water in a pan and stir over medium heat for 10 minutes, or until the sugar has dissolved. Bring to the boil then remove from the heat.

Leave to infuse for 2–3 hours, or until cold. Chill in the refrigerator. Strain and serve over ice. Makes 2 x 275 ml (9$\frac{1}{2}$ fl oz) glasses

155 AMERICAN ICED TEA

4 ceylon tea bags
2 tablespoons sugar
2 tablespoons lemon juice
375 ml (13 fl oz/1$\frac{1}{2}$ cups) dark grape juice
500 ml (17 fl oz/2 cups) orange juice
375 ml (13 fl oz/1$\frac{1}{2}$ cups) ginger ale
ice cubes, to serve
lemon slices, to serve

Place the tea bags in a heatproof bowl with 1 litre (35 fl oz/4 cups) boiling water. Leave for 3 minutes. Remove the bags and stir in the sugar. Cool.

Stir in the juices. Refrigerate until cold, then add the ginger ale. Serve over ice cubes with a lemon slice. Makes 8 x 250 ml (9 fl oz/1 cup) glasses

156 ICED MINT TEA

4 peppermint tea bags
115 g (4 oz/$\frac{1}{3}$ cup) honey
500 ml (17 fl oz/2 cups) grapefruit juice
250 ml (9 fl oz/1 cup) orange juice
mint sprigs, to serve

Place the tea bags in a large heatproof jug and pour in 750 ml (26 fl oz/ 3 cups) boiling water. Allow to steep for 3 minutes, then remove and discard the bags. Stir in the honey and allow to cool.

Add the grapefruit and orange juice. Cover and chill in the fridge. Serve in glasses, garnished with mint. Makes 6 x 250 ml (9 fl oz/1 cup) glasses

NOON

157

158

159

157 PRAWN, POTATO & CORN CHOWDER

600 g (1 lb 5 oz) raw prawns (shrimp)
3 corn cobs, husks removed
1 tablespoon olive oil
2 leeks, white part only, finely chopped
2 garlic cloves, crushed
650 g (1 lb 7 oz) potatoes, cut into 1.5 cm ($^5/_8$ inch) cubes
750 ml (26 fl oz/3 cups) fish or chicken stock
375 ml (13 fl oz/$1^1/_2$ cups) milk
250 ml (9 fl oz/1 cup) cream
pinch of cayenne pepper
3 tablespoons finely chopped flat-leaf (Italian) parsley

Peel and devein the prawns, then chop them into 1.5 cm ($^5/_8$ inch) pieces. Cut the kernels from the corn cobs. Heat the oil in a large saucepan and add the leek. Cook over medium–low heat for about 5 minutes, or until soft and lightly golden. Add the garlic and cook for 30 seconds, then add the corn, potato, stock and milk.

Bring to the boil, then reduce the heat and simmer, partially covered, for about 20 minutes, or until the potato is soft but still holds its shape (it will break down slightly). Remove the lid and simmer for a further 10 minutes to allow the soup to thicken. Reduce the heat to low.

Put 500 ml (17 fl oz/2 cups) of the soup in a blender and blend until very smooth. Return the blended soup to the saucepan and add the prawns. Increase the heat to medium and simmer for 2 minutes, or until the prawns are pink and cooked through. Stir in the cream, cayenne pepper and 2 tablespoons of the parsley. Season to taste with salt, then serve garnished with the remaining parsley. Serves 4–6

159 CREAMY CHICKEN & CORN SOUP

20 g ($^3/_4$ oz) butter
1 tablespoon olive oil
500 g (1 lb 2 oz) chicken thigh fillets, trimmed and thinly sliced
2 garlic cloves, chopped
1 leek, chopped
1 large celery stalk, chopped
1 bay leaf
$^1/_2$ teaspoon thyme
1 litre (35 fl oz/4 cups) chicken stock
3 tablespoons sherry
550 g (1 lb 4 oz) corn kernels (fresh, tinned or frozen)
1 large floury potato (russet), cut into 1 cm ($^1/_2$ inch) cubes
185 ml (6 fl oz/$^3/_4$ cup) cream, plus extra, to drizzle
chives, to garnish

Melt the butter and oil in a large saucepan over high heat. Cook the chicken in batches for 3 minutes, or until just cooked through. Place in a bowl, cover and refrigerate until needed. Reduce the heat to medium and stir in the garlic, leek, celery, bay leaf and thyme. Cook for 2 minutes, or until the leek softens. Add the stock, sherry and 500 ml (17 fl oz/2 cups) water and stir. Add the corn and potato and bring to the boil. Reduce the heat and simmer for 1 hour, skimming any scum off the surface. Cool slightly.

Remove the bay leaf and purée the soup. Return to the cleaned pan, add the cream and chicken and stir over medium–low heat for 2–3 minutes, or until heated through — do not boil. Season. Drizzle with extra cream and garnish with chives. Serves 4–6

158 CHICKPEA SOUP WITH SPICED PITTA BREAD

1 tablespoon olive oil
1 large onion, chopped
5 garlic cloves, chopped
1 large carrot, chopped
1 bay leaf
2 celery stalks, chopped
1 teaspoon ground cumin
$^1/_2$ teaspoon ground cinnamon
3 x 425 g (15 oz) tins chickpeas, drained and rinsed
1.25 litres (44 fl oz/5 cups) chicken stock
1 tablespoon finely chopped flat-leaf (Italian) parsley,
    plus extra, to garnish
1 tablespoon finely chopped coriander (cilantro) leaves
2 tablespoons lemon juice
extra virgin olive oil, to drizzle

SPICED PITTA BREAD
40 g ($1^1/_2$ oz) butter
2 tablespoons olive oil
2 garlic cloves, crushed
$^1/_8$ teaspoon ground cumin
$^1/_8$ teaspoon ground cinnamon
$^1/_8$ teaspoon cayenne pepper
$^1/_2$ teaspoon sea salt
4 small pitta breads, split

Heat the oil in a large saucepan and cook the onion over medium heat for 3–4 minutes, or until soft. Add the garlic, carrot, bay leaf and celery and cook for 4 minutes, or until the vegetables start to caramelise.

Stir in the cumin and cinnamon and cook for 1 minute. Add the chickpeas, stock and 1 litre (35 fl oz/4 cups) water and bring to the boil. Reduce the heat and simmer for 1 hour. Allow to cool.

Remove the bay leaf and purée the soup. Return to the cleaned pan and stir over medium heat until warmed. Stir in the herbs and lemon juice. Season. Drizzle with oil and garnish with parsley.

To make the spiced pitta bread, melt the butter and oil in a saucepan over medium heat. Add the garlic, spices and salt and cook for 1 minute. Place the pitta (smooth side up) on a lined tray and grill (broil) for 1–2 minutes, or until golden. Turn and brush with the spiced butter. Grill until golden and serve with the soup. Serves 4–6

160

161

162

160 RED LENTIL, BURGHUL & MINT SOUP

2 tablespoons olive oil
1 large red onion, finely chopped
2 garlic cloves, crushed
2 tablespoons tomato paste (concentrated purée)
2 tomatoes, finely chopped
2 teaspoons paprika
1 teaspoon cayenne pepper
500 g (1 lb 2 oz/2 cups) red lentils
3 tablespoons long-grain rice
2.125 litres (74 fl oz/8$\frac{1}{2}$ cups) chicken stock
3 tablespoons fine burghul (bulgur)
2 tablespoons chopped mint
2 tablespoons chopped flat-leaf (Italian) parsley
90 g (3$\frac{1}{4}$ oz/$\frac{1}{3}$ cup) Greek-style yoghurt
$\frac{1}{4}$ preserved lemon, pulp removed, zest washed and julienned

Heat the oil in a saucepan over medium heat. Add the onion and garlic and cook for 2–3 minutes, or until soft. Stir in the tomato paste, tomato and spices and cook for 1 minute. Add the lentils, rice and chicken stock, then cover and bring to the boil over high heat. Reduce the heat and simmer for 30–35 minutes, or until the rice is cooked.

Stir in the burghul and herbs, then season to taste. Divide the soup among serving bowls, garnish with yoghurt and preserved lemon and serve immediately. Serves 4–6

Note: This soup will thicken on standing, so if reheating you may need to add more liquid.

162 ORANGE SWEET POTATO SOUP

40 g (1$\frac{1}{2}$ oz) butter
2 onions, chopped
2 garlic cloves, crushed
1 kg (2 lb 4 oz) orange sweet potato, peeled and chopped
1 large celery stalk, chopped
1 large green apple, peeled, cored and chopped
1$\frac{1}{2}$ teaspoons ground cumin
2 litres (70 fl oz/8 cups) chicken stock
125 g (4$\frac{1}{2}$ oz/$\frac{1}{2}$ cup) Greek-style yoghurt
lavash bread, to serve (optional)

Melt the butter in a large pan over low heat. Add the onion and cook, stirring occasionally, for 10 minutes, or until soft. Add the garlic, sweet potato, celery, apple and 1 teaspoon of the cumin and continue to cook for 5–7 minutes, or until well coated. Add the chicken stock and the remaining cumin and bring to the boil over high heat. Reduce the heat and simmer for 25–30 minutes, or until the sweet potato is very soft.

Cool the soup slightly and blend in batches until smooth. Return to the cleaned pan and gently stir over medium heat until warmed through. Season with salt and freshly ground black pepper. Divide among serving bowls and top each serve with a dollop of yoghurt.

Cut the lavash bread into rectangular strips, brush lightly with oil and place on a baking tray. Bake in a 190°C (375°F/Gas 5) oven for 15–20 minutes, or until crisp and lightly golden. Serve with the soup. Serves 4–6

161 SPICY SEAFOOD & ROASTED CORN SOUP WITH QUESADILLAS

2 corn cobs (about 700 g/1 lb 9 oz)
1 tablespoon olive oil
1 red onion, finely chopped
1 small red chilli, finely chopped
$\frac{1}{2}$ teaspoon ground allspice
4 vine-ripened tomatoes, peeled and finely diced
1.5 litres (52 fl oz/6 cups) fish stock or light chicken stock
300 g (10$\frac{1}{2}$ oz) boneless firm white fish fillets (such as ling or perch), diced
200 g (7 oz) fresh crabmeat
200 g (7 oz) peeled raw prawns (shrimp), roughly chopped
1 tablespoon lime juice

QUESADILLAS
4 flour tortillas (19 cm/7$\frac{1}{2}$ inch)
85 g (3 oz/$\frac{2}{3}$ cup) grated cheddar cheese
4 tablespoons coriander (cilantro) leaves
2 tablespoons olive oil

Preheat the oven to 200°C (400°F/Gas 6). Peel back the husks on the corn cobs (making sure they stay intact at the base) and remove the silks. Fold the husks back over the corn, place in a baking dish and bake for 1 hour, or until the corn is tender.

Heat the oil in a large saucepan over medium heat. Add the onion and cook until soft. Add the chilli and allspice and cook for 1 minute, then add the tomato and stock and bring to the boil. Reduce the heat and simmer, covered, for 45 minutes.

Slice off the kernels from the corn cobs with a sharp knife, add to the soup and simmer, uncovered, for 15 minutes. Add the fish, crab and prawn meat to the soup and simmer for 5 minutes, or until the seafood is cooked. Stir in the lime juice and serve with the quesadillas, if desired.

To make the quesadillas, top one tortilla with half the cheese and half the coriander. Season, then top with another tortilla. Heat 1 tablespoon of the oil in a frying pan and cook the quesadilla for 30 seconds on each side, or until the cheese just begins to melt. Repeat to make the other quesadilla. Cut into wedges. Serves 4

163

164

165

163 PEA & ROCKET SOUP

1 tablespoon olive oil
1 red onion, finely chopped
700 g (1 lb 9 oz) frozen peas
100 g (3½ oz) rocket (arugula) leaves
750 ml (26 fl oz/3 cups) hot vegetable stock
shaved parmesan cheese, to garnish
rocket (arugula) leaves, extra, to garnish

Heat the oil in a large saucepan over medium heat. Add the onion and cook for 5 minutes, or until soft. Add the peas and rocket, and cook for a further 2 minutes. Add the stock and 250 ml (9 fl oz/1 cup) water, bring to the boil, then reduce the heat and simmer for 20 minutes.

Cool slightly then place in a food processor or blender in batches and process until almost smooth. Return to the cleaned saucepan and heat through. Serve garnished with shaved parmesan and the extra rocket. Serves 4

165 SPICY PUMPKIN & COCONUT SOUP

1 small red chilli, seeded and chopped
1 lemongrass stem, white part only, sliced
1 teaspoon ground coriander
1 tablespoon chopped fresh ginger
500 ml (17 fl oz/2 cups) vegetable stock
2 tablespoons oil
1 onion, finely chopped
800 g (1 lb 12 oz) pumpkin (winter squash) flesh, cubed (see Note)
375 ml (13 fl oz/1½ cups) coconut milk
3 tablespoons chopped coriander (cilantro) leaves
2 teaspoons shaved palm sugar or soft brown sugar
extra coriander (cilantro) leaves, to garnish

Place the chilli, lemongrass, ground coriander, ginger and 2 tablespoons vegetable stock in a food processor, and process until smooth. Heat the oil in a large saucepan, add the onion and cook over medium heat for 5 minutes. Add the spice paste and cook, stirring, for 1 minute.

Add the pumpkin and remaining vegetable stock. Bring to the boil, then reduce the heat and simmer, covered, for 15–20 minutes, or until the pumpkin is tender. Cool slightly then process in a food processor or blender until smooth. Return to the cleaned pan, stir in the coconut milk, coriander and palm sugar, and simmer until hot. Garnish with the extra coriander leaves. Serves 4

Note: You will need to buy 1.5 kg (3 lb 5 oz) pumpkin with the skin on to yield 800 g (1 lb 12 oz) flesh.

164 DUCK, SHIITAKE & NOODLE BROTH

3 dried shiitake mushrooms
1 Chinese roast duck (1.5 kg/3 lb 5 oz)
500 ml (17 fl oz/2 cups) chicken stock
2 tablespoons light soy sauce
1 tablespoon Chinese rice wine
2 teaspoons sugar
400 g (14 oz) fresh flat rice noodles
2 tablespoons oil
3 spring onions (scallions), thinly sliced
1 teaspoon finely chopped ginger
400 g (14 oz) bok choy (pak choy), trimmed and leaves separated
¼ teaspoon sesame oil

Place the shiitake mushrooms in a heatproof bowl, cover with 250 ml (9 fl oz/1 cup) boiling water and soak for 20 minutes. Drain, reserving the liquid and squeezing the excess liquid from the mushrooms. Discard the woody stems and thinly slice the caps.

Remove the skin and flesh from the roast duck. Discard the fat and carcass. Finely slice the duck meat and the skin. Place the chicken stock, soy sauce, rice wine, sugar and the reserved mushroom liquid in a saucepan over medium heat. Bring to a simmer and cook for 5 minutes. Meanwhile, place the rice noodles in a heatproof bowl, cover with boiling water and soak briefly. Gently separate the noodles with your hands and drain well. Divide evenly among large soup bowls.

Heat the oil in a wok over high heat. Add the spring onion, ginger and shiitake mushrooms and cook for several seconds. Transfer to the broth with the bok choy and duck meat and simmer for 1 minute, or until the duck has warmed through and the bok choy has wilted. Ladle the soup over the noodles and drizzle sesame oil on each serving. Serve immediately. Serves 4–6

166

167

168

166 SPRING VEGETABLE SOUP WITH BASIL PESTO

1.25 litres (44 fl oz/5 cups) vegetable or chicken stock
1 tablespoon extra virgin olive oil
8 spring onions (scallions), finely sliced
2 celery stalks, finely sliced
12 baby carrots, sliced
310 g (11 oz/2 bunches) asparagus, woody ends removed,
    cut into 3 cm (1¼ inch) lengths
150 g (5½ oz) baby corn, cut into 3 cm (1¼ inch) lengths
3 tablespoons fresh or bottled pesto
extra virgin olive oil, to thin pesto (see Note)
shaved parmesan cheese, to garnish

Bring the stock to the boil in a large saucepan. Meanwhile, heat the oil in a large heavy-based saucepan and add the spring onion and celery. Cover and cook over medium heat for 5 minutes, or until softened.

Add the stock to the spring onion mixture and mix well. Add the carrot, asparagus and corn to the pan. Return the mixture to the boil, then reduce the heat and simmer for 10 minutes. Spoon into warmed soup bowls. Top with a dollop of pesto, season to taste with salt and pepper, and garnish with shaved parmesan. Serves 4

Note: Home-made pesto or fresh pesto from a deli will give a better flavour than bottled pesto. If you prefer a thinner pesto, mix it with a little olive oil to give it a runnier consistency.

168 GAZPACHO

1 kg (2 lb 4 oz) vine-ripened tomatoes, chopped
1 Lebanese (short) cucumber, chopped
1 small red capsicum (pepper), seeded and chopped
1 red onion, chopped
3 garlic cloves
80 g (2¾ oz) sourdough bread, crusts removed
2 tablespoons sherry vinegar
Tabasco sauce

DRESSING
2 teaspoons each finely diced tomato, red capsicum (pepper),
    red onion and Lebanese (short) cucumber
2 teaspoons finely chopped flat-leaf (Italian) parsley
1 tablespoon extra virgin olive oil
1 teaspoon lemon juice

In a blender, place the tomatoes, cucumber, capsicum, onion, garlic, sourdough and 250 ml (9 fl oz/1 cup) cold water, and blend until smooth. Pass through a strainer into a bowl, and add the sherry vinegar. Season to taste with salt and Tabasco, then cover and refrigerate for at least 2 hours or overnight to allow the flavours to develop.

To make the dressing, combine all the ingredients in a small bowl. Season. Stir the gazpacho well, then ladle into bowls. Spoon the dressing over the top before serving. Serves 4

167 MINESTRONE

400 g (14 oz/2 cups) dried cannellini or borlotti (cranberry) beans
1 tablespoon olive oil
100 g (3½ oz) mild pancetta, finely diced
1 onion, chopped
1 carrot, diced
2 celery stalks, diced
1 large potato, diced
2 garlic cloves, crushed
3 tablespoons tomato paste (concentrated purée)
2 x 425 g (15 oz) tins crushed tomatoes
750 ml (26 fl oz/3 cups) beef stock
155 g (5½ oz/1 cup) elbow macaroni or ditalini
1 cup (75 g) shredded cabbage
2 tablespoons shredded basil
shaved parmesan cheese, to serve
extra virgin olive oil, to serve

Place the beans in a large bowl, cover with cold water and leave to soak overnight. Heat the oil in a large saucepan, add the pancetta and cook over medium heat, stirring, for 1–2 minutes, or until slightly crisp. Add the onion, carrot, celery, potato and garlic and cook for 1–2 minutes.

Add the tomato paste, tomato, beef stock and drained beans. Bring to the boil, then reduce the heat and simmer, covered, for 40 minutes or until the beans are tender. (Do not add salt prior to this stage as it will toughen the beans.)

Add the pasta and cabbage, and cook for a further 15 minutes. Season with salt and freshly ground black pepper. Serve in deep bowls with the basil, shaved parmesan, a drizzle of extra virgin olive oil and wood-fired bread. Serves 6

169

170

171

169 HEARTY BEAN & PASTA SOUP

1 tablespoon olive oil
1 onion, finely chopped
3 garlic cloves, crushed
2 x 290 g (10¼ oz) tins mixed beans, drained
1.75 litres (60 fl oz/7 cups) chicken stock (see Note)
100 g (3½ oz) conchigliette pasta
1 tablespoon chopped tarragon

Heat the oil in a saucepan over low heat. Add the onion and cook for 5 minutes, then add the garlic and cook for a further 1 minute, stirring frequently. Add the beans and chicken stock, cover the pan with a lid, increase the heat and bring to the boil. Add the pasta and cook until *al dente*. Stir in the tarragon, then season with salt and black pepper. Serve with crusty bread. Serves 4

Note: The flavour of this soup is enhanced by using a good-quality stock. Either make your own or use the tetra packs of liquid stock that are available at the supermarket.

171 MOROCCAN LAMB, CHICKPEA & CORIANDER SOUP

165 g (5¾ oz/¾ cup) dried chickpeas
1 tablespoon olive oil
850 g (1 lb 14 oz) boned lamb leg, cut into 1 cm (½ inch) cubes
1 onion, chopped
2 garlic cloves, crushed
½ teaspoon ground cinnamon
½ teaspoon ground turmeric
½ teaspoon ground ginger
4 tablespoons chopped coriander (cilantro) leaves
2 x 400 g (14 oz) tins chopped tomatoes
1 litre (35 fl oz/4 cups) chicken stock
160 g (5¾ oz/⅔ cup) dried red lentils, rinsed
coriander (cilantro) leaves, to garnish

Soak the chickpeas in cold water overnight. Drain and rinse well. Heat the oil in a large saucepan over high heat and brown the lamb in batches for 2–3 minutes. Reduce the heat to medium, return the lamb to the pan with the onion and garlic and cook for 5 minutes. Add the spices, season and cook for 2 minutes. Add the coriander, tomato, stock and 500 ml (17 fl oz/2 cups) water and bring to the boil over high heat.

Add the lentils and chickpeas and simmer, covered, over low heat for 1½ hours. Uncover and cook for 30 minutes, or until the lamb is tender and the soup is thick. Season with salt and pepper. Garnish with coriander. Serves 4–6

170 WINTER LAMB SHANK SOUP

1 tablespoon olive oil
1.25 kg (2 lb 12 oz) lamb shanks
2 onions, chopped
4 garlic cloves, chopped
250 ml (9 fl oz/1 cup) red wine
2 bay leaves
1 tablespoon chopped rosemary
2.5 litres (85 fl oz/10 cups) beef stock
425 g (15 oz) tin crushed tomatoes
165 g (5¾ oz/¾ cup) pearl barley, rinsed and drained
1 large carrot, diced
1 potato, diced
1 turnip, diced
1 parsnip, diced
2 tablespoons redcurrant jelly (optional)

Heat the oil in a large saucepan over high heat. Cook the lamb shanks for 2–3 minutes, or until brown. Remove from the pan and set aside. Add the onion to the pan and cook over low heat for 8 minutes, or until soft. Add the garlic and cook for 30 seconds, then add the wine and simmer for 5 minutes.

Add the shanks, bay leaves, half the rosemary and 1.5 litres (52 fl oz/ 6 cups) of the stock to the pan. Season. Bring to the boil over high heat. Reduce the heat and simmer, covered, for 2 hours, or until the meat falls off the bone. Remove the shanks and cool slightly.

Take the meat off the bone and roughly chop. Add to the broth with the tomato, barley, the remaining rosemary and stock and simmer for 30 minutes. Add the vegetables and cook for 1 hour, or until the barley is tender. Remove the bay leaves, then stir in the redcurrant jelly. Serves 4

172

173

174

172 CARAMELISED ONION & PARSNIP SOUP

30 g (1 oz) butter
3 large onions, halved and thinly sliced
2 tablespoons soft brown sugar
250 ml (9 fl oz/1 cup) dry white wine
3 large parsnips, peeled, chopped
1.25 litres (44 fl oz/5 cups) vegetable stock
3 tablespoons cream
thyme leaves, to garnish

Melt the butter in a large saucepan. Add the onion and sugar, and cook over low heat for 10 minutes. Add the wine and parsnip, and simmer, covered, for 20 minutes, or until the onion and parsnip are golden and tender.

Pour in the stock, bring to the boil, then reduce the heat and simmer, covered, for 10 minutes. Cool slightly, then place in a blender or food processor and blend in batches until smooth. Season. Drizzle with a little cream and sprinkle thyme leaves over the top. Serve with toasted crusty bread slices. Serves 4

174 CREAMY JERUSALEM ARTICHOKE & ROAST GARLIC SOUP

1 garlic head
40 g (1 1/2 oz) butter
1 tablespoon olive oil
1 onion, chopped
1 leek, white part only, washed and chopped
1 celery stalk, chopped
700 g (1 lb 9 oz) jerusalem artichokes, peeled and chopped
1 small potato, chopped
1.5 litres (52 fl oz/6 cups) vegetable or chicken stock
olive oil, to serve
finely chopped chives, to serve

Preheat the oven to 200°C (400°F/Gas 6). Slice the base from the head of garlic, wrap it in foil and roast for 30 minutes, or until soft. When cool enough to handle, remove from the foil and slip the cloves from the skin. Set aside.

In a large heavy-based saucepan, heat the butter and oil. Add the onion, leek and celery and a large pinch of salt, and cook for 10 minutes, or until soft. Add the jerusalem artichokes, potato and garlic and cook for a further 10 minutes. Pour in the stock, bring the mixture to the boil, then reduce the heat and simmer for 30 minutes, or until the vegetables are soft.

Purée in a blender until smooth, and season well. Serve with a drizzle of olive oil and some chives. Delicious with warm crusty bread. Serves 4

173 LONG & SHORT NOODLE SOUP

300 g (10 1/2 oz) minced (ground) pork
4 spring onions (scallions), sliced
3 garlic cloves, roughly chopped
2 teaspoons grated ginger
2 teaspoons cornflour (cornstarch)
125 ml (4 fl oz/1/2 cup) light soy sauce
3 tablespoons Chinese rice wine
30 won ton wrappers
3 litres (104 fl oz/12 cups) ready-made Chinese chicken broth, or home-made or ready-made chicken stock
200 g (7 oz) dried flat egg noodles
2 spring onions (scallions), extra, sliced on the diagonal
1 teaspoon sesame oil

Put the minced pork, spring onion, garlic, grated ginger, cornflour, 1 1/2 tablespoons of the soy sauce and 1 tablespoon of the rice wine in a food processor and process until well combined. Place 2 teaspoons of the mixture in the centre of a won ton wrapper and lightly brush the edges with water. Lift the sides up tightly and pinch around the filling to form a pouch. Repeat this process to make 30 won tons.

Put the chicken broth in a large saucepan and bring to a simmer over medium–high heat. Stir in the remaining soy sauce and rice wine. Meanwhile, bring a large pan of water to the boil. Reduce the heat, add the won tons and simmer for 1 minute, or until they float to the surface and are cooked through, then remove with a slotted spoon. Return the water to the boil, add the egg noodles and cook for 3 minutes, or until tender. Drain and add to the broth along with the cooked won tons. Simmer for 2 minutes, or until heated through.

Divide the broth, noodles and won tons among six large serving bowls, sprinkle with extra spring onion and drizzle each with a little sesame oil. Serves 6

175

176

177

175 FRENCH ONION SOUP

50 g (1³/₄ oz) butter
750 g (1 lb 10 oz) onions, finely sliced
2 garlic cloves, finely chopped
45 g (1¹/₂ oz/¹/₃ cup) plain (all-purpose) flour
2 litres (70 fl oz/8 cups) beef or chicken stock
250 ml (9 fl oz/1 cup) white wine
1 bay leaf
2 thyme sprigs
12 slices stale baguette
100 g (3¹/₂ oz) gruyère cheese, finely grated

Melt the butter in a heavy-based saucepan and add the onion. Cook over low heat, stirring occasionally, for 25 minutes, or until the onion is deep golden brown and beginning to caramelize.

Add the garlic and flour and stir continuously for 2 minutes. Gradually blend in the stock and the wine, stirring all the time, and bring to the boil. Add the bay leaf and thyme and season. Cover the pan and simmer for 25 minutes. Remove the bay leaf and thyme and check the seasoning. Preheat the grill (broiler).

Toast the baguette slices, then divide among six warmed soup bowls and ladle the soup over the top. Sprinkle with the grated cheese and grill (broil) until the cheese melts and turns light golden brown. Serve immediately. Serves 6

177 PORK & GLASS NOODLE SOUP

150 g (5¹/₂ oz) cellophane noodles
2 teaspoons peanut oil
2 teaspoons grated fresh ginger
1.25 litres (44 fl oz/5 cups) chicken stock
80 ml (2¹/₂ fl oz/¹/₃ cup) Chinese rice wine
1 tablespoon hoisin sauce
1 tablespoon soy sauce
4 spring onions (scallions), thinly sliced on the diagonal,
    plus extra, to garnish
300 g (10¹/₂ oz) Chinese roast pork, sliced

Soak the noodles in a large bowl with enough boiling water to cover for 3–4 minutes. Drain. Heat the oil in a large saucepan. Add the ginger and stir-fry for 1 minute. Add the stock, Chinese rice wine, hoisin and soy sauces and simmer for 10 minutes. Add the spring onion and roast pork, then cook for a further 5 minutes.

Divide the noodles among four large bowls. Ladle in the soup and arrange the pork on top. Garnish with extra spring onion. Serves 4

176 CAULIFLOWER & ALMOND SOUP WITH HOT CHEESE ROLLS

75 g (2³/₄ oz/¹/₂ cup) blanched almonds
1 tablespoon olive oil
1 large leek, white part only, chopped
2 garlic cloves, crushed
1 kg (2 lb 4 oz) cauliflower, cut into small florets
2 desiree potatoes, (about 370 g/13 oz), cut into 1.5 cm
    (⁵/₈ inch) pieces
1.75 litres (60 fl oz/7 cups) chicken stock

CHEESE ROLLS
4 round bread rolls
40 g (1¹/₂ oz) softened butter
125 g (4¹/₂ oz/1 cup) grated cheddar cheese
50 g (1³/₄ oz/¹/₂ cup) grated parmesan cheese

Preheat the oven to 180°C (350°F/Gas 4). Place the almonds on a baking tray and toast for 5 minutes, or until golden. Heat the oil in a large saucepan over medium heat and cook the leek for 2–3 minutes, or until softened. Add the garlic and cook for 30 seconds, then add the cauliflower, potato and stock. Bring to the boil, then reduce the heat and simmer for 15 minutes, or until the vegetables are very tender. Cool for 5 minutes.

Blend the soup with the almonds in batches in a blender until smooth. Season to taste with salt and pepper. Return to the cleaned pan and stir over medium heat until heated through. Serve with the cheese rolls, if desired.

To make the cheese rolls, split the rolls and butter both sides. Combine the grated cheeses and divide evenly among the rolls. Sandwich together and wrap in foil. Bake in the oven for 15–20 minutes, or until the cheese has melted. Serves 4

178 MISO SOUP WITH CHICKEN & UDON NOODLES

8 dried shiitake mushrooms
600 g (1 lb 5 oz) chicken breast fillets, cut into 1.5 cm
 (⅝ inch) strips
3 tablespoons white miso paste
2 teaspoons dashi granules
1 tablespoon wakame flakes or other seaweed (see Note)
300 g (10½ oz) baby bok choy (pak choy), halved lengthways
400 g (14 oz) fresh udon noodles
150 g (5½ oz) silken firm tofu, cut into 1 cm (½ inch) cubes
3 spring onions (scallions), sliced diagonally

Soak the mushrooms in 250 ml (9 fl oz/1 cup) boiling water for
20 minutes. Drain, reserving the liquid; discard the stalks and thinly
slice the caps. Pour 2 litres (70 fl oz/8 cups) water into a saucepan and
bring to the boil, then reduce the heat and simmer. Add the chicken
and cook for 2–3 minutes, or until almost cooked through.

Add the mushrooms and cook for 1 minute, then add the miso paste,
dashi granules, wakame and reserved mushroom liquid. Stir to dissolve
the dashi and miso paste. Do not boil. Add the bok choy halves and
simmer for 1 minute, or until beginning to wilt, then add the noodles
and simmer for a further 2 minutes. Gently stir in the tofu and ladle
the hot soup into large serving bowls. Garnish with the sliced spring
onion. Serves 4–6

Note: Wakame is a curly-leafed, brown algae with a mild vegetable
taste and a soft texture. It can be used in salads or can be boiled and
served like a vegetable. Use a small amount as it swells by about ten
times after being cooked.

180 EIGHT TREASURE NOODLE SOUP

10 g (¼ oz) dried shiitake mushrooms
375 g (13 oz) thick fresh egg noodles
1.25 litres (44 fl oz/5 cups) good-quality chicken stock
3 tablespoons light soy sauce
2 teaspoons Chinese rice wine
200 g (7 oz) chicken breast fillet, cut into 1 cm (½ inch) strips
200 g (7 oz) Chinese barbecued pork, cut into 5 mm (¼ inch) slices
¼ onion, finely chopped
1 carrot, cut into 1 cm (½ inch) slices on the diagonal
125 g (4½ oz) snow peas (mangetout), cut in half on the diagonal
4 spring onions (scallions), thinly sliced

Place the shiitake mushrooms in a heatproof bowl, cover with boiling
water and soak for 20 minutes, or until soft. Drain and squeeze out
any excess liquid. Discard the woody stems and thinly slice the caps.
Bring a large saucepan of water to the boil and cook the noodles for
1 minute, or until cooked through. Drain, then rinse with cold water.
Divide evenly into four deep warmed serving bowls.

Meanwhile, bring the chicken stock to the boil in a large saucepan over
high heat. Reduce the heat to medium and add the soy sauce and rice
wine, stirring to combine. Simmer for 2 minutes. Add the chicken and
pork and cook for another 2 minutes, or until the chicken is cooked
through and the pork is heated. Add the onion, carrot, snow peas,
shiitake mushrooms and half the spring onion and cook for a further
1 minute, or until the carrot is tender. Divide the vegetables and meat
among the serving bowls and ladle on the hot broth. Garnish each
bowl with the remaining spring onion. Serves 4

179 VEGETABLE RAMEN

375 g (13 oz) fresh ramen noodles
1 tablespoon oil
1 tablespoon finely chopped fresh ginger
2 garlic cloves, crushed
150 g (5½ oz) oyster mushrooms, halved
1 small zucchini (courgette), sliced into thin rounds
1 leek, white and light green part, halved lengthways
 and thinly sliced
100 g (3½ oz) snow peas (mangetout), halved diagonally
100 g (3½ oz) fried tofu puffs, cut into matchsticks
1.25 litres (44 fl oz/5 cups) vegetable stock
1½ tablespoons white miso paste
2 tablespoons light soy sauce
1 tablespoon mirin
90 g (3¼ oz/1 cup) bean sprouts
1 teaspoon sesame oil
4 spring onions (scallions), thinly sliced
100 g (3½ oz) enoki mushrooms

Bring a large saucepan of lightly salted water to the boil. Add the
noodles and cook, stirring to prevent sticking, for 4 minutes, or until
just tender. Drain and rinse under cold running water.

Heat the oil in a large saucepan over medium heat, add the ginger,
crushed garlic, oyster mushrooms, zucchini, leek, snow peas and tofu
puffs, and stir-fry for 2 minutes. Add the stock and 300 ml (10½ fl oz)
water and bring to the boil, then reduce the heat and simmer. Stir in
the miso, soy sauce and mirin until heated through. Do not boil. Stir
in the bean sprouts and sesame oil.

Place the noodles in the bottom of six serving bowls, then pour in the
soup. Garnish with the spring onion and enoki mushrooms. Serves 6

181

182

183

181 PORK CONGEE

300 g (10½ oz/1½ cups) long-grain rice, thoroughly rinsed
½ star anise
2 spring onions (scallions), white part only
4 x 4 cm (1½ x 1½ inch) piece ginger, cut into slices
3.5 litres (120 fl oz/14 cups) chicken stock
1 tablespoon peanut oil
2 garlic cloves, crushed
1 teaspoon grated ginger, extra
400 g (14 oz) minced (ground) pork
ground white pepper
3 tablespoons light soy sauce
sesame oil, to drizzle
6 fried dough sticks (see Note)

Put the rice in a large saucepan with the star anise, spring onion, sliced ginger and chicken stock. Bring to the boil, then reduce the heat to low and simmer for 1½ hours, stirring occasionally.

Heat the oil in a frying pan over high heat. Cook the garlic and grated ginger for 30 seconds. Add the mince and cook for 5 minutes, or until browned, breaking up any lumps with the back of a spoon. Remove the star anise, spring onion and ginger from the soup and discard them. Add the mince mixture and simmer for 10 minutes. Season with white pepper and stir in the soy sauce. Serve with a drizzle of sesame oil and the dough sticks. Serves 4–6

Note: Fried dough sticks are available at Chinese bakeries and speciality shops and are best eaten soon after purchasing.

183 PUMPKIN SOUP

2 kg (4 lb 8 oz) butternut pumpkin (squash)
40 g (1½ oz) butter
2 onions, chopped
½ teaspoon cumin seeds
1 litre (35 fl oz/4 cups) chicken stock
1 bay leaf
80 ml (2½ fl oz/⅓ cup) cream
pinch of nutmeg

Peel the pumpkin and chop into small chunks. Melt the butter in a large saucepan, add the onion and cook over low heat for 5–7 minutes, or until soft. Add the cumin and cook for 1 minute, then add the pumpkin, stock and bay leaf. Increase the heat to high and bring to the boil, then reduce the heat and simmer for 20 minutes, or until the pumpkin is soft. Remove the bay leaf and allow the soup to cool slightly.

Blend the soup in batches until it is smooth. Return to the cleaned pan and stir in the cream and nutmeg. Simmer gently until warmed through and season with salt and freshly ground black pepper before serving. Serves 4

182 TOMATO & CAPSICUM SOUP WITH POLENTA & OLIVE STICKS

2 tablespoons vegetable oil
2 tablespoons olive oil
2 red onions, finely chopped
2 garlic cloves, crushed
1 tablespoon ground cumin
¼ teaspoon ground cayenne pepper
2 teaspoons paprika
2 red capsicums (peppers), diced
90 g (3¼ oz/⅓ cup) tomato paste (concentrated purée)
250 ml (9 fl oz/1 cup) dry white wine
2 x 400 g (14 oz) tins chopped tomatoes
2 long red chillies, seeded and chopped
500 ml (17 fl oz/2 cups) chicken or vegetable stock
3 tablespoons chopped flat-leaf (Italian) parsley
4 tablespoons chopped coriander (cilantro) leaves

POLENTA AND OLIVE STICKS
500 ml (17 fl oz/2 cups) chicken or vegetable stock
185 g (6½ oz/1¼ cups) coarse polenta (cornmeal)
100 g (3½ oz) pitted kalamata olives, chopped
125 ml (4 fl oz/½ cup) olive oil, to deep-fry

Heat the oils in a large saucepan over medium heat and cook the onion and garlic for 2–3 minutes, or until soft. Reduce the heat to low, add the spices and cook for 1–2 minutes. Add the capsicum and cook for 5 minutes. Stir in the tomato paste and wine, simmer for 2 minutes, or until reduced slightly. Add the tomato, chilli, stock and 500 ml (17 fl oz/2 cups) water. Season. Simmer for 20 minutes. Purée the soup with the herbs.

To make the polenta and olive sticks, grease a 20 x 30 cm (8 x 12 inch) shallow baking tray. Bring the stock and 500 ml (17 fl oz/2 cups) water to the boil in a saucepan. Slowly add the polenta in a fine stream, whisking until smooth. Reduce the heat to low. Cook, stirring constantly, for 15–20 minutes, or until it starts to come away from the side. Stir in the olives, then spoon into the tray, smoothing the surface. Cover and chill for 30 minutes, or until firm. Cut into sticks.

Heat the oil in a large deep frying pan to 190°C (375°F), or until a cube of bread browns in 10 seconds. Cook the sticks in batches on each side for 1–2 minutes, or until crisp. Drain well, and serve with the soup. Serves 4–6

184

185

186

184 WATERCRESS SOUP

30 g (1 oz) butter
1 onion, finely chopped
250 g (9 oz) potatoes, diced
625 ml (21^1/$_2$ fl oz/2^1/$_2$ cups) chicken stock
1 kg (2 lb 4 oz) watercress, trimmed and chopped
125 ml (4 fl oz/^{1}/$_2$ cup) cream
125 ml (4 fl oz/^{1}/$_2$ cup) milk
freshly grated nutmeg
2 tablespoons chopped chives

Melt the butter in a large saucepan and add the onion. Cover the pan and cook over low heat until the onion is softened but not brown. Add the potato and chicken stock and simmer for 12 minutes, or until the potato is tender. Add the watercress and cook for 1 minute.

Remove from the heat and leave the soup to cool a little before pouring into a blender or food processor. Blend until smooth and return to the cleaned saucepan. Bring the soup gently back to the boil and stir in the cream and milk. Season with nutmeg, salt and pepper and reheat without boiling. Serve garnished with chives. Serves 4

186 SPLIT PEA & VEGETABLE SOUP

1 tablespoon peanut or vegetable oil
1 onion, chopped
2 garlic cloves, chopped
1^1/$_2$ teaspoons chopped fresh ginger
1^1/$_2$ tablespoons Madras curry paste
100 g (3^1/$_2$ oz) yellow split peas, rinsed and drained
1 large zucchini (courgette), peeled and chopped
1 large carrot, roughly chopped
170 g (6 oz) button mushrooms, roughly chopped
1 celery stalk, roughly chopped
1 litre (35 fl oz/4 cups) vegetable stock
125 ml (4 fl oz/^{1}/$_2$ cup) cream

Heat the oil in a saucepan, add the onion and cook over low heat for 5 minutes, or until soft. Add the garlic, ginger and curry paste and cook over medium heat for 2 minutes. Stir in the split peas until well coated with paste, then add the zucchini, carrot, mushroom and celery and cook for 2 minutes.

Add the stock, bring to the boil, then reduce the heat and simmer, partly covered, for 1 hour. Remove from the heat and allow to cool slightly. Transfer the soup to a blender or food processor and process in batches until smooth. Return to the pan, stir in the cream and gently heat until warmed through. Delicious served with naan bread. Serves 4

185 GOULASH SOUP WITH DUMPLINGS

3 tablespoons olive oil
1 kg (2 lb 4 oz) chuck or round steak, cut into 1 cm (^{1}/$_2$ inch) cubes
2 large onions, chopped
3 garlic cloves, crushed
1 green capsicum (pepper), chopped
1^1/$_2$ teaspoons caraway seeds, ground
3 tablespoons sweet paprika
^{1}/$_4$ teaspoon ground nutmeg
pinch cayenne pepper
^{1}/$_2$ teaspoon sea salt
400 g (14 oz) tin chopped tomatoes
2 litres (70 fl oz/8 cups) chicken stock
350 g (12 oz) potatoes, cut into 2 cm (^{3}/$_4$ inch) cubes
1 green capsicum (pepper), julienned
2 tablespoons sour cream

DUMPLINGS
1 egg
3 tablespoons finely grated parmesan cheese
85 g (3 oz/^{2}/$_3$ cup) self-raising flour
pinch cayenne pepper

Heat half the oil in a saucepan and brown the cubed beef in batches for 1–2 minutes. Remove and set aside. Heat the remaining oil in the same pan over low heat. Add the onion, garlic and chopped capsicum and cook for 5–6 minutes, or until softened. Stir in the spices and salt for 1 minute.

Return the beef to the pan and stir to coat. Stir in the tomato and stock and bring to the boil. Reduce the heat to low and simmer, covered, for 1^1/$_4$ hours. Add the potato and cook for 30 minutes. Stir in the julienned capsicum and sour cream. Season.

To make the dumplings, mix together all the ingredients and a pinch of salt with a fork to form a soft dough (add 1–2 tablespoons water if necessary). Turn onto a lightly floured surface and knead for 5 minutes, or until smooth. Roll ^{1}/$_2$ teaspoonfuls of the dough into balls, drop into the simmering soup and cook for 6 minutes, or until cooked. Serves 4–6

187

188

189

187 SOUTH AMERICAN BLACK BEAN SOUP

330 g (11$\frac{1}{2}$ oz/1$\frac{1}{2}$ cups) black turtle beans (black kidney beans)
1 tablespoon vegetable oil
1 onion, finely chopped
1 leek, finely chopped
2 garlic cloves, crushed
2 teaspoons ground cumin
4 bacon slices, diced
1 litre (35 fl oz/4 cups) chicken stock
90 g (3$\frac{1}{4}$ oz/$\frac{1}{3}$ cup) sour cream
1$\frac{1}{2}$ tablespoons snipped chives

Soak the black beans in a bowl of cold water overnight. Drain. Heat the oil in a large saucepan over medium heat and cook the onion, leek, garlic and cumin for about 3 minutes, or until soft. Add the bacon and cook for 2–3 minutes, or until lightly browned.

Add the black beans, chicken stock and 500 ml (17 fl oz/2 cups) water to the saucepan and bring to the boil over high heat. Reduce the heat and simmer for 1 hour, or until the black beans are tender. Season with salt and freshly ground black pepper.

Cool slightly and blend half the soup in batches in a blender until smooth. Return to the saucepan and stir through the unblended soup. Spoon into bowls, dollop with sour cream and garnish with the chives. Serves 4

189 CURRIED CHICKEN NOODLE SOUP

175 g (6 oz) dried thin egg noodles
2 tablespoons peanut oil
2 chicken breasts (about 250 g/9 oz each)
1 onion, sliced
1 small red chilli, seeded and finely chopped
1 tablespoon finely chopped fresh ginger
2 tablespoons Indian curry powder
750 ml (26 fl oz/3 cups) chicken stock
800 ml (28 fl oz) coconut milk
300 g (10$\frac{1}{2}$ oz) baby bok choy (pak choy), cut into long strips
4 tablespoons torn basil

Cook the noodles in a large saucepan of boiling water for 3–4 minutes, or until cooked. Drain well and set aside. Wipe the saucepan clean and dry. Heat the oil in the dry pan and add the chicken. Cook on each side for 5 minutes, or until cooked through. Remove the chicken and keep warm.

Place the onion in the pan and cook over low heat for 8 minutes, or until softened but not browned. Add the chilli, ginger and curry powder and cook for a further 2 minutes. Add the chicken stock and bring to the boil. Reduce the heat and simmer for 20 minutes. Thinly slice the chicken on the diagonal.

Add the coconut milk to the saucepan and simmer for 10 minutes. Add the bok choy and cook for 3 minutes, then stir in the basil. To serve, divide the noodles among four deep serving bowls. Top with slices of chicken and ladle in the soup. Serve immediately. Serves 4

188 OXTAIL SOUP WITH STOUT & VEGETABLES

2 kg (4 lb 8 oz) oxtails, trimmed
2 tablespoons vegetable oil
2 onions, finely chopped
1 leek, finely chopped
2 carrots, diced
1 celery stalk, diced
2 garlic cloves, crushed
2 bay leaves
2 tablespoons tomato paste (concentrated purée)
1 thyme sprig
2 flat-leaf (Italian) parsley sprigs
3.5 litres (120 fl oz/14 cups) chicken stock
375 ml (13 fl oz/1$\frac{1}{2}$ cups) stout
2 tomatoes, seeded and diced
100 g (3$\frac{1}{2}$ oz) cauliflower florets
100 g (3$\frac{1}{2}$ oz) green beans
100 g (3$\frac{1}{2}$ oz) broccoli florets
100 g (3$\frac{1}{2}$ oz) asparagus, cut into 3 cm (1$\frac{1}{4}$ inch) lengths

Preheat the oven to 200ºC (400°F/Gas 6). Place the oxtails in a baking dish and bake for 1 hour, turning occasionally, or until dark golden. Leave to cool. Heat the oil in a large saucepan over medium heat and cook the onion, leek, carrot and celery for 3–4 minutes, or until soft. Stir in the garlic, bay leaves and tomato paste, then add the oxtails, thyme and parsley.

Add the stock and bring to the boil over high heat. Reduce the heat and simmer for 3 hours, or until the oxtails are tender and the meat falls off the bone. Skim off any scum that rises to the surface. Remove the oxtails and cool slightly.

Take the meat off the bones and discard any fat or sinew. Roughly chop and add to the soup with the stout, tomato and 500 ml (17 fl oz/ 2 cups) water. Add the vegetables and simmer for 5 minutes, or until the vegetables are tender. Season. Serves 4

190

191

192

190 TOMATO & BREAD SOUP

750 g (1 lb 10 oz) vine-ripened tomatoes
1 loaf (450 g/1 lb) day-old crusty Italian bread
1 tablespoon olive oil
3 garlic cloves, crushed
1 tablespoon tomato paste (concentrated purée)
1.25 litres (44 fl oz/5 cups) hot vegetable stock
4 tablespoons torn basil
2–3 tablespoons extra virgin olive oil, plus extra, to serve

Score a cross in the base of each tomato. Place in a bowl of boiling water for 1 minute, then plunge into cold water and peel the skin away from the cross. Cut the tomatoes in half and scoop out the seeds with a teaspoon. Chop the tomato flesh. Remove most of the crust from the bread and discard. Cut the bread into 3 cm (1 1/4 inch) pieces.

Heat the oil in a large saucepan. Add the garlic, tomato and tomato paste, then reduce the heat and simmer, stirring occasionally, for 15 minutes until thickened. Add the stock and bring to the boil, stirring for 2 minutes. Reduce the heat to medium, add the bread pieces and cook, stirring, for 5 minutes, or until the bread softens and absorbs most of the liquid. Add more stock or water if necessary.

Stir in the torn basil leaves and extra virgin olive oil, and leave for 5 minutes so the flavours have time to develop. Drizzle with a little of the extra oil. Serves 4

Note: This soup is popular in Italy in the summer months when tomatoes are at their tastiest, and as a way of using up leftover bread.

192 ZUCCHINI SOUP

60 g (2 1/4 oz) butter
2 large leeks, white part only, thinly sliced
4 garlic cloves, crushed
1.25 kg (2 lb 12 oz) zucchini (courgettes), coarsely grated
1.75 litres (60 fl oz/7 cups) chicken stock
80 ml (2 1/2 fl oz/1/3 cup) cream
bacon and onion bread, to serve (optional)

Melt the butter in a saucepan over medium heat. Cook the leek, stirring once or twice, for 2–3 minutes, or until it starts to soften. Reduce the heat to low, add the garlic and cook, covered, stirring once or twice, for 10 minutes, or until the leek is really soft — do not allow it to brown.

Add the zucchini to the pan and cook, uncovered, for 4–5 minutes. Pour in the chicken stock and bring to the boil over high heat. Reduce the heat to medium-low and simmer for 20 minutes, or until soft.

Let the soup cool slightly and blend half in a blender until smooth. Return to the pan, stir in the cream and gently reheat over medium heat until warmed through. Season to taste with salt and freshly ground black pepper. Serve the soup with bacon and onion bread or crusty fresh bread, if desired. Serves 4

191 GRILLED ITALIAN SAUSAGE & VEGETABLE SOUP

500 g (1 lb 2 oz) Italian pork sausages
200 g (7 oz) speck (see Note)
1 tablespoon olive oil
1 large onion, chopped
3 garlic cloves, crushed
1 celery stalk, cut in half and sliced
1 large carrot, cut into 1 cm (1/2 inch) cubes
bouquet garni (1 flat-leaf (Italian) parsley sprig, 1 oregano sprig, 2 bay leaves)
1 small red chilli, halved lengthways
400 g (14 oz) tin chopped tomatoes
1.75 litres (60 fl oz/7 cups) chicken stock
300 g (10 1/2 oz) brussels sprouts, cut in half from top to base
300 g (10 1/2 oz) green beans, cut into 3 cm (1 1/4 inch) lengths
300 g (10 1/2 oz) shelled broad beans, fresh or frozen
2 tablespoons chopped flat-leaf (Italian) parsley

Grill (broil) the sausages under a hot grill (broiler) for 8–10 minutes, turning occasionally, or until brown. Remove and cut into 3 cm (1 1/4 inch) lengths. Trim and reserve the fat, then dice the speck.

Heat the oil in a large saucepan over medium heat. Add the speck and reserved speck fat and cook for 2–3 minutes, or until golden. Add the onion, garlic, celery and carrot, reduce the heat to low and cook for 6–8 minutes, or until softened. Discard the remains of the speck fat.

Stir in the sausages, bouquet garni, chilli and chopped tomato and cook for 5 minutes. Add the stock, bring to the boil, then reduce the heat and simmer for 1 hour. Add the brussels sprouts, green beans and broad beans and simmer for 30 minutes. Discard the bouquet garni, then stir in the parsley. Season to taste. Divide among four bowls and serve. Serves 4

Note: Speck is cured smoked ham or pork belly. It has a strong taste and is usually cut into small pieces and used as a flavour base.

193

194

195

193 HOT & SOUR PRAWN SOUP

350 g (12 oz) raw prawns (shrimp)
1 tablespoon oil
3 lemongrass stems, white part only
3 thin slices fresh galangal
3–5 small red chillies
5 kaffir lime leaves, finely shredded
2 tablespoons fish sauce
2 spring onions (scallions), sliced
70 g (2½ oz/½ cup) tinned straw mushrooms, drained,
    or quartered button mushrooms
3 tablespoons lime juice
1–2 tablespoons chilli paste, or to taste
coriander (cilantro) leaves, to garnish (optional)

Peel and devein the prawns, leaving the tail intact and reserving the heads and shells. Heat the oil in a large saucepan or wok and add the prawn heads and shells. Cook for 5 minutes, or until the shells turn bright orange. Bruise 1 lemongrass stem with the back of a knife. Add to the pan with the galangal and 2 litres (70 fl oz/8 cups) water. Bring to the boil, then reduce the heat and simmer for 20 minutes. Strain the stock and return to the pan. Discard the shells and herbs.

Finely slice the chillies and remaining lemongrass. Add to the liquid with the lime leaves, fish sauce, spring onion and mushrooms. Cook gently for 2 minutes. Add the prawns and cook for 3 minutes, or until the prawns are tender. Add the lime juice and chilli paste (adjust to taste with extra lime juice or fish sauce). If desired, garnish with coriander leaves. Serves 4–6

195 PORK & BUTTERED CORN RAMEN SOUP

200 g (7 oz) Chinese barbecued pork (char sui) fillet in one piece
2 small corn cobs (550 g/1 lb 4 oz)
200 g (7 oz) dried ramen noodles
2 teaspoons peanut oil
1 teaspoon grated ginger
1.5 litres (52 fl oz/6 cups) chicken stock
2 tablespoons mirin
2 spring onions (scallions), sliced on the diagonal
20 g (¾ oz) unsalted butter
1 spring onion (scallion), extra, sliced on the diagonal

Cut the pork into thin slices and remove the corn kernels from the cob using a sharp knife. Bring a large saucepan of water to the boil, add the ramen noodles and cook or 4 minutes, or until tender. Drain, then rinse in cold water.

Heat the oil in a large saucepan over high heat. Stir-fry the grated ginger for 1 minute. Add the chicken stock and mirin and bring to the boil. Reduce the heat and simmer for 8 minutes. Add the pork slices to the liquid and cook for 5 minutes, then add the corn kernels and spring onion and cook for a further 4–5 minutes, or until the kernels are tender.

Separate the noodles by running them under hot water, then divide among four deep bowls. Ladle on the soup, then place 1 teaspoon butter on each serving. Garnish with the extra spring onion and serve at once. Serves 4

194 BEEF PHO

200 g (7 oz) rice noodle sticks
1.5 litres (52 fl oz/6 cups) beef stock
1 star anise
4 cm (1½ inch) piece of fresh ginger, sliced
2 pigs trotters (ask your butcher to cut them in half)
½ onion, studded with 2 cloves
2 lemongrass stems, pounded
2 garlic cloves, pounded
¼ teaspoon white pepper
1 tablespoon fish sauce
400 g (14 oz) beef fillet, partially frozen, and thinly sliced
90 g (3¼ oz/1 cup) bean sprouts
2 spring onions (scallions), thinly sliced on the diagonal
1 handful coriander (cilantro) leaves, chopped
1 handful Vietnamese mint, chopped
1 red chilli, thinly sliced
red chillies, extra, to serve
Vietnamese mint, extra, to serve
coriander (cilantro) leaves, extra, to serve
2 limes, cut into quarters
fish sauce, extra, to serve

Soak the noodles in boiling water for 15–20 minutes. Drain. Bring the stock, star anise, ginger, trotters, onion, lemongrass, garlic and white pepper to the boil in a large saucepan. Reduce the heat and simmer for 30 minutes. Strain, return to the same pan and stir in the fish sauce.

Divide the noodles among bowls, then top with beef strips, sprouts, spring onion, coriander, mint and chilli. Ladle on the broth.

Place the extra chilli, mint, coriander, lime quarters and fish sauce in small bowls on a platter, serve with the soup and allow your guests to help themselves. Serves 4

196

197

198

196 CHICKEN, MUSHROOM & MADEIRA SOUP

10 g (1/4 oz) dried porcini mushrooms
25 g (1 oz) butter
1 leek, white part only, thinly sliced
250 g (9 oz) pancetta or bacon, chopped
200 g (7 oz) Swiss brown mushrooms, roughly chopped
300 g (10 1/2 oz) large field mushrooms, roughly chopped
2 tablespoons plain (all-purpose) flour
125 ml (4 fl oz/1/2 cup) Madeira
1.25 litres (44 fl oz/5 cups) chicken stock
1 tablespoon olive oil
2 chicken breast fillets (about 200 g/7 oz each)
80 g (2 3/4 oz/1/3 cup) light sour cream
2 teaspoons chopped marjoram, plus whole leaves, to garnish

Soak the porcini in 250 ml (9 fl oz/1 cup) boiling water for 20 minutes. Melt the butter in a large saucepan over medium heat and cook the leek and pancetta for 5 minutes, or until the leek is softened. Add all the mushrooms and the porcini soaking liquid and cook for 10 minutes.

Stir in the flour and cook for 1 minute. Add the Madeira and cook, stirring, for 10 minutes. Stir in the stock, bring to the boil, then reduce the heat and simmer for 45 minutes. Cool slightly.

Heat the oil in a frying pan and cook the chicken fillets for 4–5 minutes each side, or until cooked through. Remove from the pan and thinly slice. Blend the soup until smooth. Return to the cleaned saucepan, add the sour cream and chopped marjoram and stir over medium heat for about 1–2 minutes to warm through. Season. Top with the chicken and garnish with marjoram. Serves 4

198 PEA, LETTUCE & BACON SOUP

2 tablespoons vegetable oil
2 onions, finely chopped
200 g (7 oz) bacon slices, chopped
1 kg (2 lb 4 oz) frozen baby peas, defrosted
1.5 litres (52 fl oz/6 cups) chicken stock
1.2 kg (2 lb 11 oz) iceberg lettuce, finely shredded
watercress sprigs, to garnish

Heat the oil in large saucepan over medium heat. Add the onion and bacon and cook for 2–3 minutes, or until soft, but not browned. Add the peas, stock and half the lettuce to the pan, then simmer for 5 minutes, or until the peas are tender. Season.

Allow the soup to cool slightly, then blend in batches until smooth. Return to the pan with the remaining lettuce and stir over medium–low heat until warmed through. Serve, garnished with the watercress. Serves 4

197 BEEF & BEET BORSCHT

2 tablespoons olive oil
1 onion, chopped
2 garlic cloves, crushed
500 g (1 lb 2 oz) beef chuck steak, cut into 2 cm (3/4 inch) cubes
1 litre (35 fl oz/4 cups) beef stock
2 small beetroot (250 g/9 oz)
200 g (7 oz) tinned crushed tomatoes
1 carrot, diced
2 potatoes (280 g/10 oz), diced
190 g (6 3/4 oz/2 1/2 cups) finely shredded cabbage
2 teaspoons lemon juice
2 teaspoons sugar
2 tablespoons chopped flat-leaf (Italian) parsley
2 tablespoons chopped dill
90 g (3 1/4 oz/1/3 cup) sour cream

Preheat the oven to 200°C (400°F/Gas 6). Heat the oil in a saucepan, and cook the onion and garlic over medium heat for 3–5 minutes. Add the beef, stock and 1 litre (35 fl oz/4 cups) water, and bring to the boil. Reduce the heat and simmer, covered, for 1 hour 15 minutes, or until the meat is tender. Remove the meat. Trim the beetroot just above the end of the leaf stalks. Wrap in foil and bake for 30–40 minutes, or until tender. Unwrap and leave to cool.

Return the stock to the boil and add the tomato, carrot and potato, and season with salt. Cook over medium heat for 10 minutes. Add the cabbage and cook for 5 minutes. Peel and dice the beetroot. Return the meat to the pan and add the beetroot, lemon juice, sugar and 1 1/2 tablespoons each of parsley and dill. Cook for 2 minutes, or until heated through. Season to taste.

Remove from the heat and leave for 10 minutes. Serve with a dollop of sour cream and garnish with the remaining dill and parsley. Serves 4

199

200

201

199 PEA & HAM SOUP

500 g (1 lb 2 oz) yellow or green split peas
1½ tablespoons olive oil
2 onions, chopped
1 carrot, diced
3 celery stalks, finely chopped
1 kg (2 lb 4 oz) ham bones or a smoked hock, chopped
1 bay leaf
2 thyme sprigs
lemon juice, to taste (optional)

Place the peas in a large bowl, cover with cold water and soak for 6 hours. Drain well. Heat the oil in a large saucepan, add the onion, carrot and celery, and cook over low heat for 6–7 minutes, or until vegetables are soft but not brown.

Add the split peas, ham bones, bay leaf, thyme and 2.5 litres (85 fl oz/ 10 cups) cold water, and bring to the boil. Reduce the heat and simmer, stirring occasionally, for 2 hours, or until the peas are tender. Discard the bay leaf and the thyme sprigs.

Remove the ham bones from the soup and cool slightly. Remove the meat from the bone, discard the bones and chop the meat. Return the ham to the soup and reheat. Season to taste with freshly ground pepper and lemon juice, if desired. Serves 6–8

Note: For a finer texture, the soup can be cooled and processed before returning the meat to the pan.

201 LEEK & POTATO SOUP

50 g (1¾ oz) butter
1 onion, finely chopped
3 leeks, white part only, sliced
1 celery stalk, finely chopped
1 garlic clove, finely chopped
200 g (7 oz) potatoes, chopped
750 ml (26 fl oz/3 cups) chicken stock
220 ml (7½ fl oz) cream
2 tablespoons chopped chives

Melt the butter in a large saucepan and add the onion, leek, celery and garlic. Cover the pan and cook, stirring occasionally, over low heat for 15 minutes, or until the vegetables are softened but not browned. Add the potato and stock and bring to the boil.

Reduce the heat and leave to simmer, covered, for 20 minutes. Allow the soup to cool a little before puréeing in a blender or food processor. Return to the cleaned saucepan. Bring the soup gently back to the boil and stir in the cream. Season with salt and white pepper and reheat without boiling. Serve hot or well chilled, garnished with chives. Serves 6

200 CHICKPEA SOUP

330 g (11½ oz/1½ cups) dried chickpeas
½ brown onion
1 bay leaf
½ head garlic, unpeeled (8 cloves)
2 tablespoons olive oil
1 celery stalk, chopped
1 large onion, extra, finely chopped
3 garlic cloves, extra, chopped
1 teaspoon ground cumin
1 teaspoon paprika
¼ teaspoon dried chilli powder
3 teaspoons chopped oregano
1 litre (35 fl oz/4 cups) vegetable stock
2 tablespoons lemon juice
olive oil, extra to drizzle

Place the chickpeas in a bowl and cover with water. Soak overnight, then drain. Transfer to a saucepan and add the onion, bay leaf, garlic and 1.5 litres (52 fl oz/6 cups) water. Bring to the boil, then reduce the heat and simmer for 1 hour, or until the chickpeas are tender. Drain, reserving 500 ml (17 fl oz/2 cups) cooking liquid. Discard the onion, bay leaf and garlic.

Heat the oil in the same saucepan, add the celery and extra onion, and cook over medium heat for 5 minutes, or until golden. Add the extra garlic and cook for a further 1 minute. Add the ground cumin, paprika, chilli powder and 2 teaspoons of the chopped oregano, and cook, stirring, for 1 minute. Return the chickpeas to the pan and stir to coat with the spices.

Pour in the vegetable stock and reserved cooking liquid, bring to the boil, then reduce the heat and simmer for 20 minutes. Stir in the lemon juice and remaining oregano and serve drizzled with olive oil. Serves 4

202

203

204

202 FRESH BEETROOT & GOAT'S CHEESE SALAD

4 bulbs (about 1 kg/2 lb 4 oz) beetroot, with leaves
200 g (7 oz) green beans
1 tablespoon red wine vinegar
2 tablespoons extra virgin olive oil
1 garlic clove, crushed
1 tablespoon capers in brine, rinsed, drained
    and coarsely chopped
100 g (3½ oz) goat's cheese

Trim the leaves from the beetroot. Scrub the bulbs and wash the leaves well. Bring a large saucepan of water to the boil, add the beetroot, then reduce the heat and simmer, covered, for 30 minutes, or until tender when pierced with the point of a knife. (The cooking time may vary depending on the size of the bulbs.) Drain and cool. Peel the skins off the beetroot and cut the bulbs into wedges.

Meanwhile, bring a saucepan of water to the boil, add the beans and cook for 3 minutes, or until just tender. Remove with tongs and plunge into a bowl of cold water. Drain well. Add the beetroot leaves to the boiling water and cook for 3–5 minutes, or until the leaves and stems are tender. Drain, plunge into a bowl of cold water, then drain again well.

To make the dressing, put the vinegar, oil, garlic, capers, ½ teaspoon salt and ½ teaspoon freshly ground black pepper in a jar and shake well. Divide the beans and beetroot wedges and leaves among four plates. Crumble the goat's cheese over the top and drizzle with the dressing. Serves 4

204 ROASTED FENNEL & ORANGE SALAD

8 baby fennel bulbs
100 ml (3½ fl oz) olive oil
1 teaspoon sea salt
2 oranges
1 tablespoon lemon juice
1 red onion, halved and thinly sliced
100 g (3½ oz) kalamata olives
2 tablespoons chopped mint
1 tablespoon roughly chopped flat-leaf (Italian) parsley

Preheat the oven to 200°C (400°F/Gas 6). Trim and reserve the fennel fronds. Remove the stalks and cut a 5 mm (¼ inch) slice off the base of each fennel. Cut each bulb into 6 wedges. Place in an ovenproof dish and drizzle with 3 tablespoons oil. Add the salt and plenty of pepper. Bake for 40–60 minutes, or until the fennel is tender and slightly caramelised. Cool.

Cut a slice off the top and bottom of each orange. Using a small, sharp knife, carefully remove the skin and as much pith as possible. Working over a bowl, cut down each side of a segment between the flesh and the membrane, and lift the segment out. Repeat with all the segments. Squeeze out any remaining juice from the membrane.

Whisk the remaining olive oil into the orange and lemon juice until emulsified. Season. Combine the orange segments, onion and olives, pour on half the dressing and mix in half the mint. Transfer to a serving dish and top with the roasted fennel. Drizzle with the remaining dressing, and scatter with the parsley and the remaining mint. Roughly chop the fronds and scatter over the salad. Serves 4

203 INDIAN MARINATED CHICKEN SALAD

3 tablespoons lemon juice
1½ teaspoons garam masala
1 teaspoon ground turmeric
1 tablespoon finely grated fresh ginger
2 garlic cloves, finely chopped
3½ tablespoons vegetable oil
3 chicken breast fillets (about 650 g/1 lb 7 oz)
1 onion, thinly sliced
2 zucchini (courgettes), thinly sliced on the diagonal
100 g (3½ oz) watercress leaves
150 g (5½ oz) freshly shelled peas
2 ripe tomatoes, finely chopped
1 large handful coriander (cilantro) leaves

DRESSING
1 teaspoon cumin seeds
½ teaspoon coriander seeds
90 g (3¼ oz/⅓ cup) plain yoghurt
2 tablespoons chopped mint
2 tablespoons lemon juice

Combine the lemon juice, garam masala, turmeric, ginger, garlic and 2 teaspoons oil in a large bowl. Add the chicken fillets and onion, toss to coat in the marinade, cover, and refrigerate for 1 hour.

Remove and discard the onion then heat 2 tablespoons of oil in a large, frying pan. Cook the chicken for about 4–5 minutes on each side or until it is cooked through. Remove the chicken from the pan and leave for 5 minutes. Cut each breast across the grain into 1 cm (½ inch) slices.

Heat the remaining oil in the pan and cook the zucchini for 2 minutes, or until lightly golden and tender. Toss with the watercress in a large bowl. Cook the peas in boiling water for 5 minutes, or until tender, then drain. Rinse under cold water to cool. Add to the salad with the tomato, chicken and coriander.

For the dressing, gently roast the cumin and coriander seeds in a dry frying pan for 1–2 minutes, or until fragrant. Remove, then pound the seeds to a powder. Mix with the yoghurt, mint and lemon juice, then gently fold through the salad. Serves 4

205

206

207

208

205 WATERCRESS, FETA & WATERMELON SALAD

2 tablespoons sunflower seeds
475 g (1 lb 1 oz) rindless watermelon, cut into 1 cm
   ($\frac{1}{2}$ inch) cubes
180 g ($6\frac{1}{4}$ oz) feta cheese, cut into 1 cm ($\frac{1}{2}$ inch) cubes
75 g ($2\frac{3}{4}$ oz/$2\frac{1}{2}$ cups) watercress sprigs
2 tablespoons olive oil
1 tablespoon lemon juice
2 teaspoons chopped oregano

Heat a small frying pan over high heat. Add the sunflower seeds and, shaking the pan continuously, dry-fry for 2 minutes, or until they are toasted and lightly golden.

Place the watermelon, feta and watercress leaves in a large serving dish and toss gently to combine. Combine the olive oil, lemon juice and chopped oregano in a small jug, and season to taste with a little salt and freshly ground black pepper (don't add too much salt as the feta is already quite salty). Pour the dressing over the salad and toss together well. Scatter with the toasted sunflower seeds, and serve. Serves 4

206 MUSHROOM & GOAT'S CHEESE SALAD

DRESSING
2 tablespoons lemon juice
3 tablespoons olive oil
1 teaspoon grated lemon zest

8 large cap mushrooms, stems removed
1 tablespoon chopped thyme
4 garlic cloves, finely chopped
2 tablespoons olive oil
50 g ($1\frac{3}{4}$ oz/4 cups) baby rocket (arugula)
100 g ($3\frac{1}{2}$ oz) goat's cheese
2 tablespoons chopped flat-leaf (Italian) parsley

Preheat the oven to 200°C (400°F/Gas 6). For the dressing, combine the juice, oil and zest in a small bowl. Place the mushrooms on a large baking tray, sprinkle with thyme and garlic, then drizzle with olive oil. Cover with foil and roast for 20 minutes. Remove the mushrooms from the oven and toss to combine the flavours. Re-cover and roast for a further 10 minutes or until cooked. Remove the mushrooms from the oven and cut in half.

Place the rocket on a serving platter, top with the mushrooms and crumble the goat's cheese over the top. Whisk the dressing to ensure it is well combined and drizzle over the salad. Serve sprinkled with parsley. Serves 4–6

207 PRAWN SALAD WITH ASIAN DRESSING

DRESSING
80 ml ($2\frac{1}{2}$ fl oz/$\frac{1}{3}$ cup) rice vinegar
3 tablespoons soy sauce
2 tablespoons honey
1 teaspoon sesame oil
1–2 teaspoons grated fresh ginger
2 garlic cloves, crushed

2 carrots (150 g/$5\frac{1}{2}$ oz), cut into 5 cm (2 inch) long strips
1 red capsicum (pepper), thinly sliced
$\frac{1}{2}$ daikon radish (75 g/$2\frac{3}{4}$ oz), peeled and cut into 5 cm
   (2 inch) long strips
10 g ($\frac{1}{4}$ oz) garlic chives, cut into 5 cm (2 inch) lengths
750 g (1 lb 10 oz) cooked prawns (shrimp), peeled and deveined,
   tails intact
200 g (7 oz) baby English spinach leaves

Place all the dressing ingredients in a small saucepan and warm over medium heat for 2–3 minutes, or until the honey dissolves; do not boil. Remove the pan from the heat.

Place the thin strips of carrot, capsicum, radish and garlic chives in a bowl and toss with tongs to evenly distribute. Add the prawns to the vegetables, pour on half the dressing, then toss thoroughly again.

To assemble the salad, make a bed of spinach on four plates (or a platter), place the mixed vegetable strips and prawns on the spinach and drizzle with the remaining dressing. Serve immediately. Serves 4

208 GREEK SALAD

4 tomatoes, cut into wedges
1 telegraph (long) cucumber, peeled, halved, seeded,
   cut into small cubes
2 green capsicums (peppers), seeded, halved lengthways,
   cut into strips
1 red onion, finely sliced
16 kalamata olives
250 g (9 oz) firm feta cheese, cut into cubes
3 tablespoons flat-leaf (Italian) parsley
12 mint leaves
125 ml (4 fl oz/$\frac{1}{2}$ cup) olive oil
2 tablespoons lemon juice
1 garlic clove, crushed

Place the tomato wedges, cucumber, capsicum strips, onion, olives, feta and half of the parsley and mint leaves in a large serving bowl, and toss together gently.

Place the oil, lemon juice and garlic in a screw-top jar, season, and shake until well combined. Pour the dressing over the salad and toss. Garnish with the remaining parsley and mint. Serves 4

209

210

211

209 CHICKPEA & FLATBREAD SALAD

3 large pitta breads
6 firm, ripe tomatoes, chopped
1 1/2 red capsicums (peppers), seeded and sliced
9 spring onions (scallions), sliced
600 g (1 lb 5 oz) tinned chickpeas, rinsed and drained
125 ml (4 fl oz/1/2 cup) olive oil
2 teaspoons grated lemon zest
3 tablespoons lemon juice
1 1/2 teaspoons ground cumin
4 tablespoons chopped flat-leaf (Italian) parsley

Preheat the oven to 200°C (400°F/Gas 6). Place the bread on a baking tray and bake for 8 minutes, or until crisp. Cool, then break up into pieces.

Place the tomato, capsicum, spring onion, chickpeas and bread pieces in a large bowl, and toss gently. Combine the oil, lemon zest and juice and cumin, and pour over the salad. Scatter the parsley over the top, mix well and serve. Serves 4

Note: This salad can be made in advance, but don't add the flat bread pieces until just prior to serving or they will become soggy.

211 TUSCAN BREAD SALAD

200 g (7 oz) ciabatta bread
8 vine-ripened tomatoes
80 ml (2 1/2 fl oz/1/3 cup) olive oil
1 tablespoon lemon juice
1 1/2 tablespoons red wine vinegar
6 anchovy fillets, finely chopped
1 tablespoon baby capers, rinsed, drained and finely chopped
1 garlic clove, crushed
1 large handful basil

Preheat the oven to 220°C (425°F/Gas 7). Tear the bread into 2 cm (3/4 inch) pieces, spread on a baking tray and bake for 5–7 minutes, or until golden on the outside. Leave the toasted bread on a rack to cool.

Score a cross in the base of each tomato. Place in a heatproof bowl and cover with boiling water. Leave for 30 seconds then transfer to cold water and peel the skin away from the cross. Cut four of the tomatoes in half and squeeze the juice and seeds into a bowl, reserving and chopping the flesh. Add the oil, juice, vinegar, anchovies, capers and garlic to the tomato juice, and season.

Seed and slice the remaining tomatoes, and place in a large bowl with the reserved tomato and most of the basil. Add the dressing and toasted bread, and toss. Garnish with the remaining basil, season, and leave for at least 15 minutes. Serve at room temperature. Serves 6

210 WHITE BEAN SALAD WITH TUNA

200 g (7 oz/1 cup) dried cannellini beans (see Note)
2 bay leaves
1 large garlic clove, smashed
350 g (12 oz) green beans, trimmed
2 baby fennel bulbs, thinly sliced
1/2 small red onion, very thinly sliced
1 large handful flat-leaf (Italian) parsley, roughly chopped
1 tablespoon olive oil
2 fresh tuna fillets (400 g/14 oz)
80 ml (2 1/2 fl oz/1/3 cup) lemon juice
1 garlic clove, extra, finely chopped
1 red chilli, seeds removed, finely chopped
1 teaspoon sugar
1 tablespoon lemon zest
125 ml (4 fl oz/1/2 cup) extra virgin olive oil

Put the beans in a bowl, cover with cold water, allowing room for the beans to expand, and leave for at least 8 hours. Rinse the beans well and transfer them to a saucepan. Cover with cold water, add the torn bay leaves and smashed garlic, and simmer for 20–25 minutes, or until tender. Drain.

Cook the green beans in boiling water for 1–2 minutes, or until tender, and refresh under cold water. Mix with the fennel, onion and parsley.

Heat the oil in a large, heavy-based frying pan and cook the tuna fillets over high heat for 2 minutes on each side or until still pink in the centre. Remove, rest for 2–3 minutes, then cut into 3 cm (1 1/4 inch) chunks. Add to the green bean mixture with the cannellini beans and toss to combine.

Combine the lemon juice, garlic, chilli, sugar and lemon zest. Whisk in the olive oil and season with salt and pepper. Toss gently through the salad. Serves 4–6

Note: You may substitute a 425 g (15 oz) tin of cooked cannellini beans for the dried beans. Rinse and drain well before using — they will not require any further preparation.

212

213

214

215

212 EGGPLANT, TOMATO & SUMAC SALAD

2 eggplants (aubergines), cut into 1 cm (1/2 inch) thick rounds
100 ml (3 1/2 fl oz) olive oil
5 large ripe tomatoes
1 small red onion, finely sliced
4 tablespoons roughly chopped mint
4 tablespoons roughly chopped flat-leaf (Italian) parsley
2 teaspoons sumac (see Note)
2 tablespoons lemon juice

Put the eggplant slices in a colander, and sprinkle them with salt. Leave the eggplant for 30 minutes to allow some of the bitter juices to drain away, then rinse the slices and pat them dry with paper towels. Using 2 tablespoons of the olive oil, brush both sides of each slice, then chargrill them for 5 minutes on each side or until they are cooked through. Let the slices cool slightly and cut them in half.

Cut the tomatoes into wedges and arrange them in a serving bowl with the eggplant and onion. Scatter the mint, parsley and sumac over the top, then put the lemon juice and remaining olive oil in a small, screw-top jar, season, and shake it up. Drizzle the dressing over the salad and toss it gently. Serves 6

Note: Sumac is a spice made from crushing the dried sumac berry. It has a mild lemony flavour and is used extensively in many cuisines, from North Africa and the Middle East, to India and Asia.

213 PRAWN, MANGO & MACADAMIA SALAD

1 radicchio heart
1 handful basil, torn
30 g (1 oz/1 cup) watercress sprigs
24 cooked king prawns (shrimp), peeled and deveined, with tails intact
3 tablespoons macadamia oil
3 tablespoons extra virgin olive oil
150 g (5 1/2 oz/1 cup) macadamia nuts, coarsely chopped
2 garlic cloves, crushed
3 tablespoons lemon juice
1 ripe mango, cut into small dice

Remove the outer green leaves from the radicchio, leaving only the tender pink leaves. Tear any large leaves in half and arrange in a shallow serving bowl. Scatter with half of the basil leaves and the watercress, and toss lightly. Arrange the prawns over the salad leaves.

Heat the oils in a small, frying pan over medium heat. Add the nuts and cook for 5 minutes, or until golden. Add the garlic and cook for a further 30 seconds, then remove from the heat and add the lemon juice and mango. Season to taste, pour over the salad and scatter with the remaining basil leaves. Serves 4–6

214 FENNEL SALAD

2 large fennel bulbs
1 tablespoon lemon juice
1 tablespoon extra virgin olive oil
2 teaspoons red wine vinegar
150 g (5 1/2 oz) niçoise olives, pitted

Trim the fennel bulbs, reserving the fronds, and discard the tough outer layers. Using a very sharp knife, slice the fennel lengthways as thinly as possible and put it in a bowl of very cold water with the lemon juice.

Just before you are ready to serve the main meal, drain the fennel well, pat it dry with paper towels and toss it in a bowl with the olive oil and red wine vinegar. Finely chop the fennel fronds, add them to the fennel with the olives and season to taste with freshly ground black pepper. Serves 4

215 WARM MARINATED MUSHROOM SALAD

750 g (1 lb 10 oz) mixed mushrooms (such as baby button, oyster, Swiss brown, shiitake and enoki)
2 garlic cloves, finely chopped
1/2 teaspoon green peppercorns, crushed
80 ml (2 1/2 fl oz/1/3 cup) olive oil
80 ml (2 1/2 fl oz/1/3 cup) orange juice
250 g (9 oz) salad leaves, watercress or baby spinach leaves
1 teaspoon finely grated orange zest

Trim the mushroom stems and wipe the mushrooms with a damp paper towel. Cut any large mushrooms in half. Mix together the garlic, peppercorns, olive oil and orange juice. Pour over the mushrooms and marinate for about 20 minutes.

Arrange the salad leaves in a large serving dish. Drain the mushrooms, reserving the marinade. Cook the flat and button mushrooms on a hot, lightly oiled barbecue grill or flat plate for about 2 minutes. Add the softer mushrooms and cook for 1 minute, or until they just soften. Scatter the mushrooms over the salad leaves and drizzle with the marinade. Sprinkle with orange zest and season well with salt and pepper. Serves 4

216

217

218

216 SNOW PEA SALAD WITH JAPANESE DRESSING

250 g (9 oz) snow peas (mangetout), trimmed
50 g (1¾ oz) snow pea (mangetout) sprouts
1 small red capsicum (pepper), julienned
½ teaspoon dashi granules
1 tablespoon soy sauce
1 tablespoon mirin
1 teaspoon soft brown sugar
1 garlic clove, crushed
1 teaspoon very finely chopped ginger
¼ teaspoon sesame oil
1 tablespoon vegetable oil
1 tablespoon toasted sesame seeds

Bring a saucepan of water to the boil, add the snow peas and cook for 1 minute. Drain, then plunge into a bowl of iced water for 2 minutes. Drain well and combine with the sprouts and capsicum in a serving bowl.

Dissolve the dashi granules in 1½ tablespoons hot water and whisk in a small bowl with the soy sauce, mirin, sugar, garlic, ginger, sesame oil, vegetable oil and half of the toasted sesame seeds. Pour over the snow pea mixture and toss well. Season to taste, and serve sprinkled with the remaining sesame seeds. Serves 4–6

218 COLESLAW

½ green cabbage
¼ red cabbage
3 carrots, coarsely grated
6 radishes, coarsely grated
1 red capsicum (pepper), chopped
4 spring onions (scallions), sliced
3 tablespoons chopped flat-leaf (Italian) parsley
250 g (9 oz/1 cup) whole-egg mayonnaise

Remove the hard core from the cabbages and shred the leaves with a sharp knife. Place in a large bowl and add the grated carrot, grated radish, red capsicum, spring onion and parsley to the bowl.

Add the mayonnaise, season to taste with salt and freshly ground black pepper and toss until well combined. Serves 8–10

Note: Cover and refrigerate the chopped vegetables for up to 3 hours before serving. Add the mayonnaise just before serving.

217 MINCED PORK & NOODLE SALAD

1 tablespoon peanut oil
500 g (1 lb 2 oz) minced (ground) pork
2 garlic cloves, finely chopped
1 lemongrass stem, finely chopped
2–3 red Asian shallots, thinly sliced
3 teaspoons finely grated fresh ginger
1 small red chilli, finely chopped
5 kaffir lime leaves, very finely shredded
170 g (6 oz) glass (mung bean) noodles
60 g (2¼ oz) baby English spinach leaves
1 large handful roughly chopped coriander (cilantro) leaves
170 g (6 oz) peeled, finely chopped fresh pineapple
1 handful mint
1½ tablespoons shaved palm sugar (jaggery) or soft brown sugar
2 tablespoons fish sauce
80 ml (2½ fl oz/⅓ cup) lime juice
2 teaspoons sesame oil
2 teaspoons peanut oil, extra

Heat a wok until very hot, add the peanut oil and swirl to coat the wok. Add the pork and stir-fry in batches over high heat for 5 minutes, or until lightly golden. Add the garlic, lemongrass, shallots, ginger, chilli and lime leaves, and stir-fry for a further 1–2 minutes, or until fragrant.

Place the noodles in a bowl and cover with boiling water for 30 seconds, or until softened. Rinse under cold water and drain well. Toss in a bowl with the spinach, coriander, pineapple, mint and pork mixture.

To make the dressing, mix together the palm sugar, fish sauce and lime juice. Add the sesame oil and extra peanut oil, and whisk to combine. Toss through the salad and season with freshly ground black pepper. Serves 4

219

220

221

222

219 ASIAN PORK SALAD

2 teaspoons rice vinegar
1 small red chilli, finely chopped
2 tablespoons light soy sauce
1 teaspoon julienned fresh ginger
$\frac{1}{4}$ teaspoon sesame oil
1 star anise
2 teaspoons lime juice
250 g (9 oz) Chinese roasted pork (char siu)
100 g ($3\frac{1}{2}$ oz) snow pea (mangetout) sprouts
2 spring onions (scallions), thinly sliced on the diagonal
$\frac{1}{2}$ red capsicum (pepper), thinly sliced

For the dressing, combine the vinegar, chilli, soy sauce, ginger, sesame oil, star anise and lime juice in a small saucepan. Gently warm for 2 minutes, or until just about to come to the boil, then set aside to cool. Once it is cool, remove the star anise.

Thinly slice the pork and place in a serving bowl. Pick over the sprouts, discarding any brown or broken ones, and add to the pork. Add the spring onion and capsicum, pour on the dressing, and toss well. Serves 4

220 ROASTED TOMATO & BOCCONCINI SALAD

8 roma (plum) tomatoes, halved
pinch of sugar
125 ml (4 fl oz/$\frac{1}{2}$ cup) olive oil
3 tablespoons torn basil
2 tablespoons balsamic vinegar
350 g (12 oz) cherry bocconcini or baby fresh mozzarella
160 g ($5\frac{3}{4}$ oz) mizuna lettuce
sea salt

Preheat the oven to 150°C (300°F/Gas 2). Place the tomato, cut side up, on a rack over a baking tray lined with baking paper. Sprinkle with salt, freshly ground black pepper, and a pinch of sugar. Roast for 2 hours, then remove from the oven and allow to cool.

Combine the oil and basil in a saucepan, and stir gently over medium heat for 3–5 minutes, or until it is very hot, but not smoking. Remove from the heat and discard the basil from the pan. Mix 2 tablespoons of the oil with the vinegar.

Toss together the tomato, bocconcini and lettuce. Arrange the salad in a shallow serving bowl and drizzle with the dressing. Sprinkle with sea salt and freshly ground black pepper. Serves 6

Notes: If cherry bocconcini are unavailable, use regular bocconcini cut into quarters. Leftover basil oil can be stored in a clean jar in the refrigerator, and is great in pasta sauces.

221 PEAR & WALNUT SALAD WITH LIME VINAIGRETTE

1 small baguette, cut into 16 thin slices
oil, for brushing
1 garlic clove, cut in half
100 g ($3\frac{1}{2}$ oz/1 cup) walnuts
200 g (7 oz) ricotta cheese
400 g (14 oz) mixed salad leaves
2 pears, cut into 2 cm ($\frac{3}{4}$ inch) cubes, mixed with
    2 tablespoons lime juice

LIME VINAIGRETTE
3 tablespoons lime juice
3 tablespoons oil
2 tablespoons raspberry vinegar

Preheat the oven to 180°C (350°F/Gas 4). Brush the baguette slices with a little oil, rub with the cut side of the garlic, then place on a baking tray. Bake for 10 minutes, or until crisp and golden. Place the walnuts on a baking tray and roast for 5–8 minutes, or until slightly browned – shake the tray to ensure even colouring. Allow to cool for 5 minutes.

To make the lime vinaigrette, whisk together the lime juice, oil, vinegar, 1 teaspoon salt and $\frac{1}{2}$ teaspoon freshly ground black pepper in a small bowl. Set aside until ready to use.

Spread some of the ricotta cheese on each crouton, then cook under a hot grill (broiler) for 2–3 minutes, or until hot. Place the mixed salad, pears and walnuts in a bowl, add the vinaigrette and toss through. Divide the salad among four serving bowls and serve with the ricotta cheese croutons. Serves 4

222 ORANGE, GOAT'S CHEESE & HAZELNUT SALAD

20 g ($\frac{3}{4}$ oz) hazelnuts
1 tablespoon orange juice
1 tablespoon lemon juice
125 ml (4 fl oz/$\frac{1}{2}$ cup) olive oil
250 g (9 oz) watercress, well rinsed and dried
50 g ($1\frac{3}{4}$ oz) baby English spinach leaves, well rinsed and dried
24 orange segments
300 g ($10\frac{1}{2}$ oz) firm goat's cheese, sliced into 4 equal portions

Preheat the oven to 180°C (350°F/Gas 4). Put the hazelnuts on a tray and roast for 5–6 minutes, or until the skin turns dark brown. Wrap the hazelnuts in a clean tea towel and rub them together to remove the skins.

Combine the nuts, orange juice, lemon juice and a pinch of salt in a food processor. With the motor running, gradually add the oil a few drops at a time. When about half the oil has been added, pour in the remainder in a steady stream.

Remove the stems from the watercress and place the leaves in a bowl with the spinach, orange segments and 2 tablespoons of the dressing. Toss to combine and season with pepper. Arrange the salad on plates.

Heat a small, non-stick frying pan over medium–high heat and brush lightly with olive oil. When hot, carefully press each slice of goat's cheese firmly into the pan and cook for 1–2 minutes, or until a crust has formed on the cheese. Carefully remove the cheese from the pan and arrange over the salads, crust side up. Drizzle the remaining dressing over the salads. Serves 4

223

224

223 JAPANESE-STYLE STEAK SALAD

750 g (1 lb 10 oz) rump steak
3 teaspoons oil
3 teaspoons wasabi paste
1/2 teaspoon dijon mustard
1 teaspoon grated fresh ginger
2 tablespoons rice wine vinegar
3 tablespoons pickled ginger, plus 1 tablespoon pickling liquid
2 tablespoons sesame oil
3 tablespoons oil, extra
100 g (3 1/2 oz) baby spinach leaves
100 g (3 1/2 oz) mizuna or watercress, trimmed
4 radishes, thinly sliced
1 Lebanese (short) cucumber, peeled and cut into ribbons
    with a vegetable peeler
3 tablespoons sesame seeds, toasted

Generously season the steak with salt and freshly ground black pepper. Heat the oil in a large frying pan or heat a barbecue plate to very hot. Add the steak and cook for 2–3 minutes on each side, or until browned. Remove and leave to rest, covered, for 5 minutes.

Put the wasabi paste, mustard, ginger, rice wine vinegar, pickled ginger, pickling liquid and 1/2 teaspoon salt in a large bowl and whisk together. Whisk in the oils, then add the spinach, mizuna, radish and cucumber to the bowl and toss well.

Slice the steak across the grain into thin strips. Divide the salad among four serving plates, top with the beef slices and sprinkle with sesame seeds. Serve immediately. Serves 4

225 SMOKED SALMON & ROCKET SALAD

DRESSING
1 tablespoon extra virgin olive oil
2 tablespoons balsamic vinegar

150 g (5 1/2 oz) rocket (arugula)
1 avocado
250 g (9 oz) smoked salmon
325 g (11 1/2 oz) jar marinated goat's cheese, drained
    and crumbled
2 tablespoons roasted hazelnuts, coarsely chopped

For the dressing, thoroughly whisk together the oil and vinegar in a bowl. Season, to taste. Trim any long stems from the rocket, rinse, pat dry and gently toss in a bowl with the dressing.

Cut the avocado in half lengthways, then cut each half lengthways into six wedges. Discard the skin and place three wedges on each serving plate and arrange a pile of rocket over the top. Drape pieces of salmon over the rocket. Scatter the cheese and nuts over the top and season with ground black pepper. Serve immediately. Serves 4

Note: A whole smoked trout can be used instead of the salmon. Peel, remove the bones, then break the flesh into bite-sized pieces.

224 ARTICHOKE, PROSCIUTTO & ROCKET SALAD

4 artichokes
2 eggs, lightly beaten
3 tablespoons fresh breadcrumbs
3 tablespoons grated parmesan cheese
olive oil for frying, plus 1 tablespoon extra
8 slices prosciutto
3 teaspoons white wine vinegar
1 garlic clove, crushed
150 g (5 1/2 oz) rocket (arugula), long stalks trimmed
shaved parmesan cheese (optional)
sea salt

Bring a large saucepan of water to the boil. Remove the hard, outer leaves of each artichoke, trim the stem and cut 2–3 cm (3/4–1 1/4 inches) off the top. Cut into quarters and remove the furry 'choke'. Boil the pieces for 2 minutes, then drain.

Whisk the eggs in a bowl and combine the seasoned breadcrumbs and grated parmesan in another bowl. Dip each artichoke quarter into the egg, then roll in the crumb mixture to coat. Fill a frying pan with olive oil to a depth of 2 cm (3/4 inch) and heat over medium–high heat. Add the artichokes in batches and fry for 2–3 minutes, or until golden. Remove from the pan and drain on paper towels.

Heat 1 tablespoon of olive oil in a non-stick frying pan over medium–high heat. Cook the prosciutto in two batches for 2 minutes, or until crisp and golden. Remove from the pan, reserving the oil.

Combine the reserved oil, vinegar and garlic with a little salt and pepper. Place the rocket in a bowl, add half of the salad dressing and toss well. Divide the rocket, artichokes and prosciutto among four plates, and drizzle with the remaining dressing. Garnish with shaved parmesan, if desired, and sprinkle with sea salt. Serves 4

226

227

228

229

226 EGG SALAD WITH CREAMY DRESSING

10 large eggs, at room temperature
1 egg yolk
3 teaspoons lemon juice
2 teaspoons dijon mustard
70 ml (2 1/4 fl oz) olive oil
70 ml (2 1/4 fl oz) oil
2 tablespoons chopped dill
1 1/2 tablespoons crème frâiche or sour cream
2 tablespoons baby capers, rinsed and drained
20 g (3/4 oz/1/3 cup) mustard cress

Place the eggs in a large saucepan of cold water. Bring to the boil and simmer gently for 10 minutes. Drain, then cool the eggs under cold running water. Remove the shells. Place the egg yolk, lemon juice and dijon mustard in a food processor or blender and season with salt and freshly ground black pepper. With the motor running, slowly add the combined olive oil and safflower oil, drop by drop at first, then slowly increasing the amount to a thin, steady stream as the mixture thickens. When all of the oil has been added, place the mayonnaise in a large bowl, and gently stir in the dill, crème frâiche and capers.

Roughly chop the eggs and fold into the mayonnaise. Transfer the salad to a serving bowl and use scissors to cut the green tips from the mustard cress. Scatter them over the salad and serve. Serves 4

Note: If you prefer, serve the salad on slices of toasted bruschetta, draped with smoked salmon and topped with the mustard cress and extra black pepper.

227 DILL POTATO SALAD

600 g (1 lb 5 oz) desiree potatoes
2 eggs
2 tablespoons finely chopped dill
1 1/2 tablespoons finely chopped French shallots
1 egg yolk
2 teaspoons lemon juice
1 teaspoon dijon mustard
100 ml (3 1/2 fl oz) light olive oil

Bring a large saucepan of water to the boil. Cook the potatoes for 20 minutes, or until tender. Add the eggs for the last 10 minutes. Remove the potatoes and eggs, and allow to cool. Peel the potatoes, then cut into 2–3 cm (3/4–1 1/4 inch) cubes. Peel and chop the eggs. Place in a large bowl with the dill, eggs and shallots. Toss to combine, then season.

Place the egg yolk, lemon juice, mustard and a pinch of salt in the bowl of a food processor. With the motor running, gradually add the olive oil a few drops at a time. When about half the oil has been added, pour in the remaining oil in a steady stream until it has all been incorporated. Use a large metal spoon to gently combine the potato and mayonnaise, then serve. Serves 4

228 ROAST DUCK SALAD WITH CHILLI DRESSING

1/2 teaspoon chilli flakes
2 1/2 tablespoons fish sauce
1 tablespoon lime juice
2 teaspoons grated palm sugar (jaggery)
1 Chinese roasted duck
1 small red onion, thinly sliced
1 tablespoon julienned fresh ginger
4 tablespoons roughly chopped coriander (cilantro) leaves
4 tablespoons roughly chopped mint
80 g (2 3/4 oz/1/2 cup) roasted cashews
90 g (3 1/4 oz) butter lettuce

Dry-fry the chilli flakes in a frying pan for 30 seconds, then grind to a powder in a mortar and pestle or spice grinder. Combine the chilli with the fish sauce, lime juice and palm sugar in a bowl, and set aside.

Remove the flesh from the duck and cut it into bite-sized pieces. Place the duck in a bowl with the onion, ginger, coriander, mint and cashews. Pour in the dressing and toss gently. Place the lettuce on a serving platter. Top with the duck salad and serve. Serves 4–6

229 CHICKEN WALDORF SALAD

750 ml (26 fl oz/3 cups) chicken stock
2 chicken breast fillets
2 red apples
2 green apples
2 celery stalks, sliced
100 g (3 1/2 oz) toasted walnuts
125 g (4 1/2 oz/1/2 cup) whole-egg mayonnaise
3 tablespoons sour cream
1/2 teaspoon chopped tarragon
1 baby cos (romaine) lettuce

Bring the stock to the boil in a saucepan. Remove from the heat, add the chicken to the stock, then cover and allow to cool in the liquid for 10 minutes, by which time the chicken should be cooked. Test by touching with your finger — the chicken should feel quite springy.

Cut the apples into bite-sized pieces. Shred the chicken breasts and place in a large bowl with the apple, celery, walnuts, mayonnaise, sour cream and tarragon. Season with salt and freshly ground black pepper, and toss well to combine. Separate the lettuce leaves and arrange them in a serving bowl. Pile the waldorf salad over the lettuce and serve. Serves 4

230

231

232

230 CHILLI CHICKEN & CASHEW SALAD

3 tablespoons sweet chilli sauce
2 tablespoons lime juice
2 teaspoons fish sauce
2 tablespoons chopped coriander (cilantro) leaves
1 garlic clove, crushed
1 small red chilli, finely chopped
1 1/2 teaspoons grated fresh ginger
2 tablespoons olive oil
600 g (1 lb 5 oz) chicken breast fillets
100 g (3 1/2 oz) salad leaves
250 g (9 oz) cherry tomatoes, halved
100 g (3 1/2 oz) Lebanese (short) cucumber, cut into
    bite-sized chunks
50 g (1 3/4 oz) snow pea (mangetout) sprouts, trimmed
80 g (2 3/4 oz/1/2 cup) cashew nuts, roughly chopped

Combine the chilli sauce, lime juice, fish sauce, coriander, garlic, chilli, ginger and 1 tablespoon of the oil in a large bowl. Heat the remaining oil in a frying or chargrill pan over medium heat until hot, and cook the chicken for 5–8 minutes on each side or until cooked through. While still hot, slice each breast widthways into 1 cm (1/2 inch) slices and toss in the bowl with the dressing. Leave to cool slightly.

Combine the salad leaves, cherry tomatoes, cucumber chunks and snow pea sprouts in a serving bowl. Add the chicken and all of the dressing, and toss gently until the leaves are lightly coated. Scatter with chopped cashews and serve. Serves 4

232 ASIAN TOFU SALAD

1 large red capsicum (pepper)
1 large green capsicum (pepper)
180 g (6 1/4 oz/2 cups) bean sprouts
4 spring onions (scallions), sliced diagonally
3 tablespoons chopped coriander (cilantro) leaves
450 g (1 lb/3 cups) shredded Chinese cabbage
3 tablespoons chopped roasted peanuts
450 g (1 lb) firm tofu
3 tablespoons peanut oil

DRESSING

2 tablespoons sweet chilli sauce
2 tablespoons lime juice
1/2 teaspoon sesame oil
1 1/2 tablespoons light soy sauce
1 garlic clove, finely chopped
3 teaspoons finely grated fresh ginger
3 tablespoons peanut oil

Thinly slice the capsicums, and combine with the bean sprouts, spring onion, coriander, cabbage and peanuts. Drain the liquid from the tofu and cut into 8 x 2 cm (3 1/4 x 3/4 inch) wide slices. Heat the oil in a large, frying pan. Cook the tofu for 2–3 minutes on each side, or until it is golden with a crispy edge, and add to the salad.

To make the dressing, mix together the chilli sauce, lime juice, oil, soy, garlic and ginger. Whisk in the peanut oil, then toss through the salad and serve immediately. Serves 4–6

231 ROAST DUCK & NOODLE SALAD

400 g (14 oz) fresh flat Chinese egg noodles
1 teaspoon sesame oil, plus 1 tablespoon extra
1 tablespoon grated fresh ginger
1/2–1 teaspoon sambal oelek, or to taste
2 tablespoons fish sauce
2 tablespoons rice wine vinegar
1 tablespoon lime juice
1/4 teaspoon Chinese five-spice
1 tablespoon soft brown sugar
2 tablespoons peanut oil
1 large handful roughly chopped coriander (cilantro) leaves,
    plus extra leaves, to garnish
1 Chinese roast duck, meat removed from bones and sliced
    into bite-sized pieces
180 g (6 1/4 oz/2 cups) bean sprouts
3 spring onions (scallions), thinly sliced
80 g (2 3/4 oz/1/2 cup) roasted peanuts, chopped

Bring a large saucepan of lightly salted water to the boil. Add the noodles and cook for 3–4 minutes, or until just tender. Rinse under cold water, drain and toss with 1 teaspoon sesame oil.

Place the ginger, sambal oelek, fish sauce, vinegar, lime juice, five-spice and sugar in a small bowl and stir to dissolve the sugar. Whisk in the extra sesame oil and the peanut oil, then stir in the coriander. Season to taste with salt.

Place the noodles, duck, bean sprouts and spring onion in a large bowl. Pour on the dressing and toss to coat. Season to taste. Garnish with the chopped peanuts and extra coriander leaves. Serves 4

233

234

235

236

233 FRISÉE & GARLIC CROUTON SALAD

VINAIGRETTE
1 French shallot, finely chopped
1 tablespoon dijon mustard
3 tablespoons tarragon vinegar
170 ml (5$\frac{1}{2}$ fl oz/$\frac{2}{3}$ cup) extra virgin olive oil

1 tablespoon olive oil
250 g (9 oz) speck, rind removed, cut into 0.5 x 2 cm
 ($\frac{1}{4}$ x $\frac{3}{4}$ inch) pieces
$\frac{1}{2}$ baguette, sliced
4 garlic cloves
1 baby frisée (curly endive), washed and dried
100 g (3$\frac{1}{2}$ oz/$\frac{1}{2}$ cup) walnuts, toasted

For the vinaigrette, whisk together in a bowl the shallot, mustard and vinegar. Slowly add the oil, whisking constantly until thickened. Set aside.

Heat the oil in a large frying pan, add the speck, bread and garlic cloves and cook over medium–high heat for 5–8 minutes, until the bread and speck are both crisp. Remove the garlic from the pan.

Place the frisée, bread, speck, walnuts and vinaigrette in a large bowl. Toss together well and serve. Serves 4–6

234 LAMB, CAPSICUM & CUCUMBER SALAD

1 red onion, very thinly sliced
1 red capsicum (pepper), very thinly sliced
1 green capsicum (pepper), very thinly sliced
2 large Lebanese (short) cucumbers, cut into batons
4 tablespoons shredded mint
3 tablespoons chopped dill
3 tablespoons olive oil
600 g (1 lb 5 oz) lamb backstraps or fillets
80 ml (2$\frac{1}{2}$ fl oz/$\frac{1}{3}$ cup) lemon juice
2 small garlic cloves, crushed
100 ml (3$\frac{1}{2}$ fl oz) extra virgin olive oil

Combine the onion, red and green capsicum, cucumber, mint and dill in a large bowl. Heat a chargrill pan or frying pan until hot. Drizzle with the oil and cook the lamb for 2–3 minutes on each side, or until it is tender but still a little pink. Remove from the pan and allow to rest for 5 minutes. Thinly slice the lamb and add to the salad, tossing to mix.

Combine the lemon juice and garlic in a small jug, then whisk in the extra virgin olive oil with a fork until well combined. Season with salt and freshly ground black pepper, then toss the dressing gently through the salad. Serves 4

Note: This salad is delicious served on fresh or toasted Turkish bread spread with hummus.

235 MOROCCAN SPICED CARROT SALAD

4 large carrots
2 cardamom pods
1 teaspoon black mustard seeds
$\frac{1}{2}$ teaspoon ground cumin
$\frac{1}{2}$ teaspoon ground ginger
1 teaspoon paprika
$\frac{1}{2}$ teaspoon ground coriander
80 ml (2$\frac{1}{2}$ fl oz/$\frac{1}{3}$ cup) olive oil
1 tablespoon lemon juice
2 tablespoons orange juice
3 tablespoons currants
1 handful finely chopped coriander (cilantro) leaves
2 tablespoons finely chopped pistachio nuts
1 teaspoon orange flower water
250 g (9 oz/1 cup) Greek-style yoghurt

Peel and coarsely grate the carrots, and place in a large bowl. Crush the cardamom pods to extract the seeds. Discard the pods. Heat a frying pan over low heat, and cook the mustard seeds for a few seconds, or until they start to pop. Add the cumin, ginger, paprika, cardamom and ground coriander, and heat for 5 seconds, or until fragrant. Remove from the heat and stir in the oil, juices and currants until combined.

Pour the dressing over the carrot and leave for 30 minutes. Add the coriander and toss to combine. Pile the salad onto a serving dish and garnish with the chopped pistachios. Mix the orange flower water and yoghurt, and serve separately. Serves 4–6

236 SCALLOP SALAD WITH SAFFRON DRESSING

pinch of saffron threads
3 tablespoons mayonnaise
1$\frac{1}{2}$ tablespoons cream
1 teaspoon lemon juice
20 scallops (about 500 g/1 lb 2 oz), with roe attached
25 g (1 oz) butter
1 tablespoon olive oil
100 g (3$\frac{1}{2}$ oz) mixed salad leaves
1 handful chervil leaves

To make the dressing, place the saffron threads in a bowl and soak in 2 teaspoons of hot water for 10 minutes. Add the mayonnaise, mixing well, until it is a rich yellow in colour. Stir in the cream, then the lemon juice. Refrigerate until needed.

Make sure the scallops are clean of digestive tract before cooking. Heat the butter and olive oil in a large frying pan over high heat and sear the scallops in small batches for 1 minute on each side.

Divide the mixed salad leaves and chervil among four serving plates, then top each with five scallops. Drizzle the dressing over the scallops and the salad leaves before serving. Serves 4

237

238

239

237 GRILLED HALOUMI & ROAST VEGETABLE SALAD

4 slender eggplants (aubergines), cut in half, halved lengthways
1 red capsicum (pepper), halved, thickly sliced
4 small zucchini (courgettes), cut in half, halved lengthways
80 ml (2½ fl oz/⅓ cup) olive oil
2 garlic cloves, crushed
200 g (7 oz) haloumi cheese, cut into 5 mm (¼ inch) thick slices
150 g (5½ oz) baby English spinach leaves, trimmed
1 tablespoon balsamic vinegar

Preheat the oven to 220°C (425°F/Gas 7). Place the vegetables in a large bowl, add 3 tablespoons olive oil and the garlic, season and toss well to combine. Place the vegetables in an ovenproof dish in a single layer and roast for 20–30 minutes, or until tender and browned around the edges.

Meanwhile, lightly brush a chargrill or heavy-based frying pan with oil and cook the haloumi slices for 1–2 minutes each side. Place the spinach leaves on four serving plates. Top with the roast vegetables and haloumi. Place the remaining oil in a small jug, add the vinegar and whisk to combine, then pour over the vegetables and haloumi. Serve immediately, warm or at room temperature, with lots of crusty bread. Serves 4

Note: You can use any roasted vegetable, such as orange sweet potatoes, leeks and roma (plum) tomatoes.

239 TUNA, TOMATO & ROCKET PASTA SALAD

350 g (12 oz) fettucine
350 g (12 oz) tuna steaks
75 g (2¾ oz/½ cup) sun-dried tomatoes, drained, roughly chopped, reserving 2 tablespoons oil
2 garlic cloves, crushed
115 g (4 oz/½ cup) sun-dried capsicums (peppers), drained and roughly chopped
100 g (3½ oz) capers, drained
175 g (6 oz/1 cup) black olives, pitted and quartered
100 g (3½ oz) baby rocket (arugula) leaves

Bring a large saucepan of lightly salted water to the boil. Add the pasta and cook until al dente. Drain. Meanwhile, lightly brush a chargrill plate with oil and cook the tuna for 1–2 minutes each side (it should be rare in the centre), or until cooked to your liking. Cut the tuna into 2.5 cm (1 inch) cubes. Keep warm.

Heat the reserved sun-dried tomato oil in a saucepan over medium heat. Add the tomato, garlic, capsicum, capers and olives, and cook, stirring, for 5–6 minutes, or until the mixture is heated through.

Place the pasta, tomato mixture and rocket in a large bowl, season and toss to combine. Divide among serving plates and top with the tuna. Serve with lemon wedges and shaved parmesan, if desired. Serves 4

Note: If you prefer the tuna rare, use very fresh sashimi tuna. If baby rocket leaves are not available, use larger rocket leaves and tear them into pieces.

238 SEAFOOD SALAD

500 g (1 lb 2 oz) small squid
1 kg (2 lb 4 oz) large clams
1 kg (2 lb 4 oz) black mussels
500 g (1 lb 2 oz) raw prawns (shrimp), peeled, deveined, tails intact
5 tablespoons finely chopped flat-leaf (Italian) parsley

DRESSING
2 tablespoons lemon juice
80 ml (2½ fl oz/⅓ cup) olive oil
1 garlic clove, crushed

Gently pull apart the body and tentacles of the squid to separate. Remove the head by cutting below the eyes. Push out the beak and discard. Pull the quill from the body of the squid and discard. Under cold running water, pull away all the skin (the flaps can be used). Rinse well, then slice the squid into rings.

Scrub the clams and mussels and remove the beards. Discard any that are cracked or don't close when tapped. Rinse under running water. Fill a saucepan with 2 cm (¾ inch) water, add the clams and mussels, cover, and boil for 4–5 minutes, or until the shells open. Remove, reserving the liquid. Discard any that do not open. Remove the mussels and clams from their shells and place in a bowl.

Bring 1 litre (35 fl oz/4 cups) water to the boil and add the prawns and squid. Cook for 3–4 minutes, or until the prawns turn pink and the squid is tender. Drain and add to the clams and mussels.

To make the dressing, whisk all of the ingredients together. Season. Pour over the seafood, add 4 tablespoons of the parsley and toss to coat. Cover and refrigerate for 30–40 minutes. Sprinkle with the remaining parsley and serve with fresh bread. Serves 4

240

241

242

243

240 RED POTATO SALAD WITH DILL & MUSTARD DRESSING

6 waxy, red-skinned potatoes (about 1.1 kg/2 lb 8 oz), such as desiree

DILL AND MUSTARD DRESSING
1 tablespoon seeded mustard
1¹⁄₂ tablespoons chopped dill
2 teaspoons soft brown sugar
3 tablespoons red wine vinegar
80 ml (2¹⁄₂ fl oz/¹⁄₃ cup) olive oil

Steam or boil the potatoes for 20 minutes, or until tender. Remove, and when cool enough to handle, cut into 3 cm (1¹⁄₄ inch) chunks.

For the dill and mustard dressing, mix the mustard, dill, brown sugar and vinegar together in a jug. Whisk in the oil with a fork until combined. Toss through the warm potatoes, and season with salt and pepper. Serves 4

241 MOROCCAN CARROT SALAD WITH GREEN OLIVES & MINT

1¹⁄₂ teaspoons cumin seeds
¹⁄₂ teaspoon coriander seeds
1 tablespoon red wine vinegar
2 tablespoons olive oil
1 garlic clove, crushed
2 teaspoons harissa
¹⁄₄ teaspoon orange flower water
600 g (1 lb 5 oz) baby carrots, tops trimmed, well scrubbed
40 g (1¹⁄₂ oz/¹⁄₃ cup) large green olives, pitted and finely sliced
2 tablespoons shredded mint
30 g (1 oz/1 cup) picked watercress leaves

In a small frying pan, dry-fry the cumin and coriander seeds for 30 seconds or until fragrant. Cool and then grind in a mortar and pestle or spice grinder. Place into a large bowl with the red wine vinegar, olive oil, garlic, harissa and orange flower water. Whisk to combine.

Blanch the carrots in boiling salted water for 5 minutes, until almost tender. Drain into a colander and allow to sit for a few minutes until they dry. While still hot, add to the red wine vinegar dressing, and toss gently to coat. Allow to cool to room temperature, for the dressing to infuse into the carrots. Add the green olives and mint. Season well and toss gently to combine. Serve on the watercress leaves. Serves 4

242 SMOKED TROUT CAESAR SALAD

350 g (12 oz) skinless smoked trout fillets
300 g (10¹⁄₂ oz) green beans, halved
6 tinned artichokes, drained, rinsed and quartered
2 eggs
1 small garlic clove, chopped
2 teaspoons dijon mustard
2 tablespoons white wine vinegar
80 ml (2¹⁄₂ fl oz/¹⁄₃ cup) olive oil
6 slices (200 g/7 oz) day-old Italian-style bread (ciabatta), cut into 2 cm (³⁄₄ inch) cubes
2 tablespoons capers, drained
1 baby cos (romaine) lettuce, leaves separated
40 g (1¹⁄₂ oz/¹⁄₂ cup) freshly shaved parmesan cheese

Flake the trout into 4 cm (1¹⁄₂ inch) shards and place in a bowl. Cook the beans in boiling water for 3 minutes, or until tender and still bright green. Refresh under cold water. Add to the bowl, with the artichoke.

Poach the eggs in simmering water for 40 seconds, or until just cooked. Place in a food processor with the garlic, mustard and vinegar, and process until smooth. With the motor running, add 2 tablespoons oil in a thin stream, processing until thick and creamy. Season to taste.

Heat the remaining oil in a frying pan, add the bread and capers, and cook over high heat for 3–5 minutes, or until golden. Line four bowls with the cos leaves. Divide the trout mixture among the bowls, drizzle with the dressing and top with the croutons, capers and parmesan. Serves 4

243 GREEN PAWPAW SALAD

370 g (13 oz) green pawpaw, peeled and seeded
90 g (3¹⁄₄ oz) snake beans, cut into 2 cm (³⁄₄ inch) lengths
2 garlic cloves
2 small red chillies, chopped
5 teaspoons dried shrimp
8 cherry tomatoes, halved
50 g (1³⁄₄ oz/1 bunch) coriander (cilantro) sprigs
3 tablespoons chopped roasted peanuts

DRESSING
3 tablespoons fish sauce
2 tablespoons tamarind purée
1 tablespoon lime juice
3 tablespoons grated palm sugar (jaggery) or soft brown sugar

Grate the pawpaw, sprinkle with salt and stand for 30 minutes. Rinse well. Cook the beans in boiling water for 3 minutes, or until tender. Plunge into cold water, then drain.

To make the dressing, combine the fish sauce, tamarind purée, lime juice and palm sugar in a small bowl. Pound the garlic and chilli in a mortar and pestle until fine. Add the dried shrimp and pound until puréed. Add the pawpaw and snake beans and lightly pound for 1 minute. Add the tomato and pound briefly to bruise.

Combine the coriander with the pawpaw mixture and spoon onto serving plates. Pour the dressing over the top. Sprinkle with the peanuts and, if desired, sliced red chilli. Serves 6

244

245

246

244 EGGPLANT & LENTIL SALAD

3 tablespoons olive oil
300 g (10½ oz) eggplant (aubergine), diced into 5 mm
    (¼ inch) cubes
1 small red onion, finely diced
¼ teaspoon ground cumin
3 garlic cloves, chopped
200 g (7 oz) puy lentils
375 ml (13 fl oz/1½ cups) vegetable stock
2 tablespoons chopped flat-leaf (Italian) parsley
1 tablespoon red wine vinegar
1 tablespoon extra virgin olive oil

Heat 2 tablespoons of olive oil in a large frying pan over medium heat. Add the eggplant and cook, stirring constantly, for 5 minutes, or until soft. Add the onion and cumin and cook for another 2–3 minutes, or until the onion has softened. Place the mixture in a bowl and season.

Heat the remaining olive oil in the frying pan over medium heat. Add the garlic and cook for 1 minute. Add the lentils and stock and cook, stirring regularly, over low heat for 40 minutes, or until the liquid has evaporated and the lentils are tender.

Add the lentils to the bowl with the eggplant and stir in the parsley and red wine vinegar. Season well with salt and black pepper, drizzle with the extra virgin olive oil and serve warm. Serves 4–6

246 WILD RICE SALAD

95 g (3½ oz/½ cup) wild rice
250 ml (9 fl oz/1 cup) chicken stock
1 tablespoon butter
100 g (3½ oz/½ cup) basmati rice
2 bacon slices, rind removed, chopped and cooked
110 g (3¾ oz/¾ cup) currants
60 g (2¼ oz/½ cup) slivered almonds, toasted
1 large handful chopped flat-leaf (Italian) parsley
6 spring onions (scallions), finely sliced
grated zest and juice of 1 lemon
olive oil, to drizzle
lemon wedges, to serve

Put the wild rice and stock in a saucepan, add the butter, bring to the boil, then cook, covered, over low heat for 1 hour. Drain.

Put the basmati rice in a separate saucepan with cold water and bring to the boil. Cook at a simmer for 12 minutes, then drain. Mix with the cooked wild rice and cool. Combine the rice with the bacon, currants, almonds, parsley, spring onion and lemon zest and juice. Season, drizzle with olive oil and serve with lemon wedges. Serves 4

245 PORK, PRAWN & VERMICELLI SALAD IN LETTUCE CUPS

vegetable oil, for frying
100 g (3½ oz) dried rice vermicelli
3 tablespoons peanut oil
1 garlic clove, crushed
1 tablespoon finely chopped fresh ginger
3 spring onions (scallions), finely sliced and green ends
    reserved for garnish
150 g (5½ oz) minced (ground) pork
500 g (1 lb 2 oz) raw prawns (shrimp), peeled, deveined
    and roughly chopped
2 tablespoons Chinese rice wine
2 tablespoons soy sauce
2 tablespoons hoisin sauce
1 tablespoon brown bean sauce
½ teaspoon sugar
3 tablespoons chicken stock
12 iceberg lettuce leaves, trimmed into cups

Fill a deep, heavy-based saucepan one-third full of oil and heat to 170°C (325°F), or until a cube of bread browns in 20 seconds. Add the vermicelli in batches and deep-fry until puffed up but not browned – this will only take a few seconds. Remove with a slotted spoon and drain on crumpled paper towels.

Heat the peanut oil in a wok over high heat and swirl to coat the side. Add the garlic, ginger and spring onion, and stir-fry for 1 minute, being careful not to burn the garlic.

Add the minced pork to the wok, breaking up the lumps, and cook for a further 4 minutes. Add the prawns and stir-fry for 2 minutes, or until they begin to change colour.

Add the Chinese rice wine, soy sauce, hoisin sauce, brown bean sauce, sugar, chicken stock and ½ teaspoon salt and stir until combined. Cook over high heat for 2 minutes, or until the mixture thickens slightly. Divide the noodles among the lettuce cups, top with the pork and prawn mixture and garnish with the reserved spring onion. Serve immediately. Serves 6

247

248

249

250

247 TABBOULEH

175 g (6 oz/1 cup) burghul (bulgur)
200 g (7 oz) flat-leaf (Italian) parsley, or 100 g (3½ oz) each
    flat-leaf (Italian) parsley and rocket (arugula)
80 g (2¾ oz) mint
6 spring onions (scallions), finely sliced
2 tomatoes, finely chopped
2 large garlic cloves, finely chopped
80 ml (2½ fl oz/⅓ cup) lemon juice
125 ml (4 fl oz/½ cup) extra virgin olive oil

Place the burghul in a large bowl and add enough hot water to cover. Leave to soak for 15–20 minutes, or until tender. Drain well. Finely chop the parsley and mint, and combine in a large bowl with the drained burghul, spring onion and chopped tomato.

Mix the garlic and lemon juice together in a small jug. Whisk in the oil until it is well combined, and season to taste with salt and black pepper. Toss the dressing through the salad before serving. Serves 6–8

Note: For variation, add 3 tablespoons toasted pine nuts with the burghul.

248 BROAD BEAN, MINT & BACON SALAD

600 g (1 lb 5 oz) frozen broad beans (see Notes)
150 g (5½ oz) shredded butter or cos (romaine) lettuce
1 large handful shredded mint
250 g (9 oz) kasseler or pancetta
1 tablespoon olive oil
1½ teaspoons dijon mustard
1 teaspoon sugar
2 tablespoons white wine vinegar
3 tablespoons extra virgin olive oil
4 flatbreads, such as pitta, to serve

Blanch the beans, according to packet instructions. Drain, rinse under cold water, and peel. Place in a large bowl with the lettuce and mint. Slice the kasseler into thick slices, then into 2 cm (¾ inch) chunks. Heat the oil in a heavy-based frying pan and cook the kasseler for 3–4 minutes, or until golden. Add to the bean mixture.

Combine the mustard, sugar and vinegar in a jug. Whisk in the extra virgin oil until well combined and season with salt and freshly ground black pepper. Pile the salad onto fresh or lightly toasted flatbread to serve. Serves 4

Notes: If they are in season, you may like to use fresh broad beans. You will need about 1.8 kg (4 lb) of beans in the pod to give 600 g (1 lb 5 oz) of beans. Boil the beans for 2 minutes and peel before using them. Kasseler is a traditional German speciality. It is a cured and smoked loin of pork that comes in a single piece and should be available at good delicatessens.

249 THAI BEEF SALAD

600 g (1 lb 5 oz) beef fillet, trimmed
125 ml (4 fl oz/½ cup) fish sauce
1 tablespoon peanut oil
1 small dried red chilli, roughly chopped
4 Asian shallots, finely sliced
2 spring onions (scallions), thinly sliced on an angle
4 tablespoons mint
4 tablespoons coriander (cilantro) leaves
1 garlic clove, crushed
100 ml (3½ fl oz) lime juice
2 teaspoons grated palm sugar (jaggery) or soft brown sugar
2 vine-ripened tomatoes, each cut into 8 wedges
100 g (3½ oz) butter lettuce, washed and trimmed

Place the beef fillet in a bowl with 2 tablespoons of fish sauce. Cover and chill for 3 hours, turning the meat several times. Place a baking tray in the oven and preheat to 220°C (425°F/Gas 7). Heat the oil in a frying pan over high heat and cook the beef fillet for 1 minute on each side, or until browned, then roast for 15 minutes, or until medium–rare. Remove from the oven and rest for 10 minutes.

Meanwhile, dry-fry the chilli in a non-stick frying pan over medium-high heat for 1–2 minutes, or until the chilli is dark but not burnt. Transfer to a mortar and pestle or spice mill, and grind until fine. Mix the ground chilli in a bowl with the shallots, spring onion, mint, coriander, garlic, lime juice, palm sugar and remaining fish sauce, stirring to dissolve the sugar. Cut the beef into thin strips and place in a bowl with the dressing and tomato. Toss well. Arrange the lettuce on a serving platter and pile the beef salad on top. Serves 4

250 CHARGRILLED BABY OCTOPUS SALAD

1 kg (2 lb 4 oz) baby octopus
1 teaspoon sesame oil
2 tablespoons lime juice
2 tablespoons fish sauce
3 tablespoons sweet chilli sauce
200 g (7 oz) mixed salad leaves
1 red capsicum (pepper), very thinly sliced
2 small Lebanese (short) cucumbers, seeded and cut into ribbons
4 red Asian shallots, chopped
100 g (3½ oz) toasted unsalted peanuts, chopped

To clean the octopus, remove the head from the tentacles by cutting just underneath the eyes. To clean the head, carefully slit the head open and remove the gut. Cut it in half. Push out the beak from the centre of the tentacles, then cut the tentacles into sets of four or two, depending on their size. Pull the skin away from the head and tentacles if it comes away easily. The eyes will come off as you pull off the skin.

To make the marinade, combine the sesame oil, lime juice, fish sauce and chilli sauce in a shallow, non-metallic bowl. Add the octopus, and stir to coat. Cover and chill for 2 hours.

Heat a chargrill pan or barbecue to very hot. Drain the octopus, reserving the marinade, then cook in batches for 3–5 minutes, turning occasionally. Pour the reserved marinade into a small saucepan, bring to the boil and cook for 2 minutes, or until it has slightly thickened. Divide the salad leaves among four plates, scatter with capsicum and cucumber, then top with the octopus. Drizzle with the marinade and top with the Asian shallots and peanuts. Serves 4

251

252

253

251 CAESAR SALAD

3 eggs
3 garlic cloves, crushed
2–3 anchovy fillets
1 teaspoon worcestershire sauce
2 tablespoons lime juice
1 teaspoon dijon mustard
185 ml (6 fl oz/^{3}/$_4$ cup) olive oil
3 slices white bread
20 g (^{3}/$_4$ oz) butter
1 tablespoon oil, extra
3 back bacon slices
1 large or 4 baby cos (romaine) lettuces
75 g (2^3/$_4$ oz/^{3}/$_4$ cup) shaved parmesan cheese

Process the eggs, garlic, anchovies, worcestershire sauce, lime juice and mustard in a food processor until smooth. With the motor running, add the oil in a thin, continuous stream to produce a creamy dressing. Season to taste with salt and freshly ground black pepper.

Cut the crusts off the bread, then cut the bread into 1.5 cm (^{5}/$_8$ inch) cubes. Heat the butter and extra olive oil in a frying pan over medium heat, add the bread and cook for 5–8 minutes, or until crisp, then remove from the pan. Cook the bacon in the same pan for 3 minutes, or until it is crispy, then break into bite-sized pieces. Toss the lettuce leaves with the dressing, then stir in the croutons and bacon, and top with parmesan. Serves 4–6

253 VIETNAMESE PRAWN & CABBAGE SALAD

80 ml (2^1/$_2$ fl oz/^{1}/$_3$ cup) rice vinegar
2 tablespoons fish sauce
2 tablespoons lime juice
2 tablespoons grated palm sugar (jaggery) or soft brown sugar
1 small red chilli, seeded and finely chopped
2 tablespoons peanut oil
1 garlic clove, crushed
20 raw prawns (shrimp), peeled and deveined with tails intact
150 g (5^1/$_2$ oz/2 cups) thinly sliced cabbage
150 g (5^1/$_2$ oz/2 cups) thinly sliced red cabbage
200 g (7 oz) sliced drained bamboo shoots
1 handful mint
1 handful coriander (cilantro) leaves
2 long green chillies, seeded and thinly sliced on the diagonal
lime wedges, to serve

To make the salad dressing, combine the rice vinegar, fish sauce, lime juice, palm sugar and red chilli in a small bowl and stir together until the sugar has dissolved.

Heat the peanut oil in a non-stick frying pan or wok over medium heat. When hot, add the garlic and cook for 10 seconds, stirring constantly. Add the prawns in two batches and cook for about 2 minutes each side, or until pink and cooked through, then remove from the pan. Place the cabbages, bamboo shoots, herbs and green chilli in a serving bowl and mix together well. Add the prawns to the bowl, drizzle the dressing over the salad, season with pepper and toss well. Serve with lime wedges. Serves 4

252 CRAB SALAD WITH GREEN MANGO & COCONUT

2 garlic cloves
2 small red chillies
2 tablespoons dried shrimp
2 tablespoons fish sauce
3 tablespoons lime juice
3 teaspoons palm sugar (jaggery) or soft brown sugar
30 g (1 oz/^{1}/$_2$ cup) shredded coconut (see Notes)
300 g (10^1/$_2$ oz/1^1/$_2$ cups) shredded green mango
1 handful mint, torn if very big
1 handful coriander (cilantro) leaves
3 kaffir lime leaves, shredded
2 teaspoons thinly shredded, pickled ginger
500 g (1 lb 2 oz) fresh crabmeat
banana leaves (optional)
crushed toasted peanuts
lime wedges

Preheat the oven to 180°C (350°F/Gas 4). Place the garlic, chillies, dried shrimp and ^{1}/$_2$ teaspoon salt in a mortar and pestle. Pound to a paste, then whisk in the fish sauce, lime juice and palm sugar with a fork.

Place the shredded coconut on a baking tray and bake for 3–5 minutes, shaking the tray occasionally to ensure even toasting. Watch the coconut closely, as it will burn easily.

Place the shredded mango in a large bowl and add the mint, coriander, kaffir lime leaves, ginger, coconut and crabmeat. Pour on the dressing and toss together gently.

Place a piece of banana leaf (if using) in each serving bowl. Mound some crab salad on top, sprinkle with the peanuts and serve immediately with lime wedges. Serves 4–6

Notes: Freshly shredded coconut is delicious, so if you have the time, remove the skin from a coconut and shred using a vegetable peeler. The banana leaves are for presentation only, and are not edible.

254

255

256

254 PORK SAUSAGE BURGERS WITH MUSTARD CREAM

800 g (1 lb 12 oz) minced (ground) pork
1 small onion, finely chopped
80 g (2³/₄ oz/1 cup) fresh breadcrumbs
2 garlic cloves, crushed
1 egg, lightly beaten
1 teaspoon dried sage
6 long bread rolls

MUSTARD CREAM
125 g (4¹/₂ oz/¹/₂ cup) sour cream
1 tablespoon wholegrain mustard
2 teaspoons lemon juice

Mix together the pork, onion, breadcrumbs, garlic, egg and sage with your hands. Season well. Divide the mixture into six portions and shape into sausages. Cook the sausages on a hot, lightly oiled barbecue flat plate or grill for 5–10 minutes, turning occasionally.

To make the mustard cream, put the sour cream, mustard and juice in a small bowl and stir together. Spread each cut side of the rolls with a little mustard cream, then sandwich the sausage burgers in the middle. Serve with the remaining mustard cream. Serves 6

256 LEMON PEPPER TUNA BURGER

2 x 185 g (6¹/₂ oz) tins lemon pepper tuna, drained
1 large onion, chopped
65 g (2¹/₄ oz/²/₃ cup) dry breadcrumbs
1 egg, lightly beaten
2 tablespoons chopped lemon thyme
1 tablespoon chopped flat-leaf (Italian) parsley
2 teaspoons grated lemon zest
2 tablespoons oil
1 loaf Turkish bread
80 g (2³/₄ oz/¹/₃ cup) whole-egg mayonnaise
150 g (5¹/₂ oz) rocket (arugula)
4 slices cheddar cheese
2 tomatoes, sliced
1 cucumber, sliced
¹/₂ red onion, sliced

Mix the tuna, onion, breadcrumbs, egg, thyme, parsley and lemon zest in a bowl. Form into four even-sized patties and flatten slightly. Heat a non-stick frying pan with the oil. Cook the patties over medium heat on both sides for 5 minutes, or until browned.

Cut the bread into 4 portions. Cut each portion in half horizontally and place under a grill (broiler) to lightly brown. Spread both cut sides of the bread with mayonnaise. Top with some rocket and layer with a patty, a slice of cheese and slices of tomato, cucumber and onion. Place the other half of the Turkish bread on top, cut in half and serve. Serves 4

255 BEEF FAJITAS

800 g (1 lb 12 oz) rump steak
2 teaspoons ground cumin
1 teaspoon dried oregano
1 teaspoon paprika
2 tablespoons worcestershire sauce
1 tablespoon soy sauce
3 garlic cloves
3 tablespoons lime juice
1 large onion, thinly sliced
1 red capsicum (pepper), cut into 5 mm (¹/₄ inch) strips
1 green capsicum (pepper), cut into 5 mm (¹/₄ inch) strips
1 tablespoon olive oil
8 flour tortillas
1 ripe avocado, diced
2 ripe roma (plum) tomatoes, diced
60 g (2¹/₄ oz/¹/₂ cup) grated cheddar cheese
90 g (3¹/₄ oz/¹/₃ cup) sour cream

Trim the steak of any fat and give it a good pounding with a meat mallet on both sides. Mix the cumin, oregano, paprika, worcestershire sauce, soy sauce, garlic and lime juice in a shallow, non-metallic dish and add the beef. Turn until well coated in the marinade, then cover and refrigerate for at least 4 hours, or overnight.

Drain the steak, reserving the marinade, and pat it dry with paper towels. Simmer the marinade in a small saucepan over medium heat for 5 minutes, or until it is reduced by about half, and keep it warm.

Preheat a barbecue to high direct heat. Toss the onion and capsicum with the oil then spread them across the flat plate, turning every so often, for 10 minutes, or until cooked through and caramelised. While the vegetables are cooking, grill the steak on the chargrill plate for 3 minutes each side, or until cooked to your liking. Remove it from the heat and let it rest, covered, for 5 minutes. Thinly slice the steak and arrange it on a plate with the onion and capsicum strips and serve with the tortillas, avocado, tomato, cheese, sour cream and marinade sauce. Let everyone fill their own tortillas. Serves 4–6

257

258

259

257 LAMB SOUVLAKI ROLL

500 g (1 lb 2 oz) lamb backstrap or loin fillet
100 ml (3$\frac{1}{2}$ fl oz) olive oil
3 tablespoons dry white wine
1 tablespoon chopped oregano
3 tablespoons roughly chopped basil
3 garlic cloves, crushed
2 bay leaves, crushed
2$\frac{1}{2}$ tablespoons lemon juice
1 large loaf Turkish bread
250 g (9 oz/1 cup) baba ganouj dip
1 tablespoon roughly chopped flat-leaf (Italian) parsley

Place the lamb fillet in a shallow non-metallic dish. Mix together the oil, wine, oregano, basil, garlic, bay leaves and 2 tablespoons of the lemon juice and pour over the lamb, turning to coat well. Cover with plastic wrap and marinate for 4 hours.

Remove the lamb fillet from the marinade and cook on a hot, lightly oiled barbecue grill or flat plate for 6–8 minutes, or until seared but still pink in the centre. Remove from the heat and rest for 10 minutes, then cut into slices.

Split the Turkish bread lengthways and spread the bottom thickly with baba ganouj. Top with the lamb slices, sprinkle with the parsley and remaining lemon juice, then season with salt and pepper. Replace the top of the loaf, then cut into quarters to serve. Serves 4

259 HERB BURGERS

750 g (1 lb 10 oz) minced (ground) lamb
2 tablespoons chopped basil
1 tablespoon chopped chives
1 tablespoon chopped rosemary
1 tablespoon chopped thyme
2 tablespoons lemon juice
80 g (2$\frac{3}{4}$ oz/1 cup) fresh breadcrumbs
1 egg
2 long crusty bread sticks
lettuce leaves, rinsed and dried
2 tomatoes, sliced
tomato sauce (ketchup), to serve

Combine the lamb with the herbs, juice, breadcrumbs, egg and season well with salt and pepper. Mix well with your hands. Divide the mixture into eight portions and shape into thick rectangular patties. Place the burgers on a hot, lightly oiled barbecue grill or flat plate. Cook for 5–10 minutes each side until well browned and just cooked through.

Cut the bread sticks in half and sandwich with the burgers, lettuce, tomato and tomato sauce. Makes 8 burgers

258 MEDITERRANEAN BURGERS

1 large red capsicum (pepper)
500 g (1 lb 2 oz) minced (ground) lamb
1 egg, lightly beaten
1 small onion, grated
3 garlic cloves, crushed
2 tablespoons pine nuts, chopped
1 tablespoon finely chopped mint
1 tablespoon finely chopped flat-leaf (Italian) parsley
1 teaspoon ground cumin
2 teaspoons chilli sauce
1 tablespoon olive oil
4 Turkish or pide bread rolls
220 g (7$\frac{3}{4}$ oz/1 cup) ready-made hummus
100 g (3$\frac{1}{2}$ oz) baby rocket (arugula)
1 small Lebanese (short) cucumber, cut into ribbons
chilli sauce, to serve (optional)

Cut the capsicum into large pieces, removing the seeds and membrane. Place the capsicum pieces, skin side up, under a hot grill (broiler) until the skin blackens and blisters. Cool in a plastic bag, then peel and cut into thick strips.

Combine the minced lamb, egg, onion, garlic, pine nuts, herbs, cumin and chilli sauce in a large bowl. Mix with your hands and roll into four even-sized balls. Press the balls into large patties about 9 cm (3$\frac{1}{2}$ inches) in diameter. Heat the oil in a large, heavy-based frying pan and cook the lamb patties over medium heat for 6 minutes each side, or until well browned and completely cooked through, then drain on paper towels.

Halve the rolls and toast both sides. Spread the cut sides of the rolls with hummus, then lay rocket leaves, roasted capsicum and cucumber ribbons over the base. Place a patty on the salad and top with the other half of the roll. Serve with chilli sauce. Serves 4

260

261

262

260 CHICKEN & TZATZIKI WRAP

$^1/_2$ telegraph (long) cucumber, seeded and grated
100 g (3$^1/_2$ oz) low-fat plain yoghurt
$^1/_4$ teaspoon lemon juice
1 tablespoon chopped mint
4 skinless chicken thigh fillets
pinch of paprika
4 sheets lavash or other flat bread (see Note)
4 large butter lettuce leaves

Sprinkle the grated cucumber with $^1/_2$ teaspoon salt. Leave the cucumber for 10 minutes, then drain and mix with the yoghurt, lemon juice and mint. Season.

Flatten the chicken thigh fillets with a meat mallet or rolling pin, season and sprinkle with the paprika. Grill the fillets for 5–7 minutes on each side, or until cooked through.

Lay out the lavash breads and place a large butter lettuce leaf on each. Spread each with one quarter of the tzatziki, then top with a sliced chicken fillet. Roll up, folding one end closed. Wrap in baking paper to serve. Makes 4

Note: If you can't find lavash bread, use any thin, flat bread that will roll up easily.

262 PAN BAGNAT

4 crusty bread rolls, or 1 baguette sliced into 4 chunks
1 garlic clove
3 tablespoons olive oil
1 tablespoon red wine vinegar
3 tablespoons torn basil
2 tomatoes, sliced
2 hard-boiled eggs, sliced
75 g (2$^3/_4$ oz) tin tuna
8 anchovy fillets
1 small cucumber, sliced
$^1/_2$ green capsicum (pepper), thinly sliced
1 French shallot, thinly sliced

Slice the bread rolls in half and remove some of the soft centre from the tops. Cut the garlic clove in half and rub the insides of the rolls with the cut sides. Sprinkle both sides of the bread with olive oil, vinegar, salt and pepper.

Place all the salad ingredients on the base of the rolls, cover with the other half and wrap each sandwich in foil. Press firmly with a light weight, such as a tin of food, and leave in a cool place for 1 hour before serving. Serves 4

261 TOFU FAJITAS

80 ml (2$^1/_2$ fl oz/$^1/_3$ cup) light soy sauce
2 garlic cloves, crushed
400 g (14 oz) smoked tofu, cut into 5 cm (2 inch) strips
200 g (7 oz) tinned tomatoes
1 small onion, roughly chopped
1 small red chilli, seeded and finely chopped
3 tablespoons chopped coriander (cilantro) leaves
1 large ripe avocado
2 teaspoons lemon juice
250 g (9 oz/1 cup) sour cream
2 tablespoons oil
1 red capsicum (pepper), seeded and sliced
1 yellow capsicum (pepper), seeded and sliced
8 spring onions (scallions), cut into 5 cm (2 inch) lengths
8 large (15 cm/6 inch) flour tortillas

Place the soy sauce, garlic and 1 teaspoon pepper in a shallow dish. Add the tofu and toss together well. Cover and leave to marinate.

Combine the tomatoes, onion, chilli and coriander in a food processor until smooth. Season with salt and pepper. Transfer to a small saucepan, and bring to the boil. Reduce the heat and simmer for 10 minutes. Cool.

Halve the avocado and remove the stone. Scoop out the flesh and add the lemon juice and 2 tablespoons of the sour cream. Season and mash well with a fork.

Heat 1 tablespoon oil in a frying pan. Add the tofu and remaining marinade and cook, stirring, over high heat for 4–5 minutes. Remove from the pan. Heat the remaining oil in the pan. Add the capsicum and spring onion, season and cook for 3–4 minutes.

Dry-fry the tortillas over high heat for 5 seconds on each side. To serve, spread a tortilla with a little avocado mixture, tomato salsa and sour cream. Top with some tofu and vegetables, fold in one end and roll. Repeat with the remaining tortillas and fillings. Serves 4

263

264

265

263 LAMB PIDE WITH GARLIC & CHICKPEA PURÉE

1 tablespoon lemon juice
1 teaspoon ground cumin
1 tablespoon olive oil
4 trimmed lamb fillets
1 bulb of garlic
100 g (3½ oz/½ cup) tinned chickpeas, drained
2 teaspoons lemon juice, extra
1 tablespoon low-fat plain yoghurt
4 x 100 g (3½ oz) pieces Turkish bread

Mix the lemon juice, cumin, olive oil and some salt and pepper. Add the lamb fillets and leave to marinate for at least 1 hour. Preheat the oven to 210°C (415°F/Gas 6–7). Wrap the bulb of garlic in foil, then roast for 20 minutes, or until soft. Cool, then squeeze out the pulp from each clove. Purée the pulp with the chickpeas, extra lemon juice and low-fat yoghurt in a food processor — add a little water to achieve a spreading consistency, if needed. Season.

Grill or barbecue the lamb for 3 minutes on each side, or until done to your liking. Grill or toast the Turkish bread, then slice through the middle and spread with the chickpea spread. Top with thin slices of the lamb, tomato and rocket leaves. Serves 4

265 CHICKEN SANDWICH

2 chicken breast fillets, cut in half horizontally
2 tablespoons olive oil
2 tablespoons lemon juice
4 large pieces ciabatta or Turkish bread, cut in half horizontally
1 garlic clove, cut in half
mayonnaise
1 avocado, sliced
2 tomatoes, sliced
1 large handful rocket (arugula) leaves, long stems snapped off

Flatten out each piece of chicken by hitting it either with your fist, the flat side of a knife blade or cleaver, or with a meat mallet. Don't break the flesh, just thin it out a bit. Trim off any fat or sinew.

Heat the oil in a frying pan, add the chicken pieces and fry them on both sides for a couple of minutes, or until they turn brown and are cooked through (you can check by cutting into the middle of one). Sprinkle with the lemon juice, then take the chicken out of the pan. Add the bread to the pan with the cut side down and cook for a minute, pressing down on it to flatten it and help soak up any juices.

Take the bread out of the pan, rub the cut side of the garlic over the surface, then spread all the pieces with a generous amount of mayonnaise. Put a piece of chicken on four of the pieces, season and then layer with the avocado and tomato, seasoning as you go. Finish with the rocket and the tops of the bread, then serve. Serves 4

264 GRILLED LAMB PITTAS WITH FRESH MINT SALAD

1 kg (2 lb 4 oz) lean minced (ground) lamb
1 large handful finely chopped flat-leaf (Italian) parsley
1 handful finely chopped mint
1 onion, finely chopped
1 garlic clove, crushed
1 egg
1 teaspoon chilli sauce
4 small wholemeal (whole-wheat) pitta pockets

MINT SALAD
3 small vine-ripened tomatoes
1 small red onion, finely sliced
1 large handful mint
1 tablespoon olive oil
2 tablespoons lemon juice
plain yoghurt (optional)

Place the lamb, parsley, mint, onion, garlic, egg and chilli sauce in a bowl and mix together. Shape into eight small patties. Chill for 30 minutes. Preheat the oven to 160°C (315°F/Gas 2–3).

To make the mint salad, slice the tomatoes into thin rings and place in a bowl with the onion, mint, olive oil and lemon juice. Season well with salt and pepper. Gently toss to coat.

Wrap the pitta breads in foil and warm in the oven for 5–10 minutes. Heat a chargrill or hot plate and brush with a little oil. When very hot, cook the patties for 3 minutes on each side. Do not turn until a nice crust has formed on the base or they will fall apart.

Remove the pitta breads from the oven. Cut the pockets in half, fill each half with some mint salad and a lamb patty. Serve with some plain yoghurt, if desired. Serves 4

266

267

268

266 YAKITORI CHICKEN BURGERS

4 chicken thigh fillets, trimmed
185 ml (6 fl oz/^{3}/$_4$ cup) yakitori sauce
1 teaspoon cornflour (cornstarch)
oil, for brushing
4 soft hamburger buns, halved
80 g (2^3/$_4$ oz/^{1}/$_3$ cup) Japanese or whole-egg mayonnaise
80 g (2^3/$_4$ oz/2 handfuls) mizuna lettuce
1 Lebanese (short) cucumber, ends trimmed and shaved
    into ribbons with a vegetable peeler

Toss the chicken and yakitori sauce together in a bowl until the chicken fillets are well coated, then cover and refrigerate for 4 hours. Drain the yakitori sauce from the chicken into a small saucepan and sprinkle it with the cornflour. Stir the cornflour into the marinade, bring the mixture to the boil and simmer, stirring frequently, for 5 minutes, or until it is thickened, then keep it warm.

Lightly brush the chargrill with oil, preheat it to low-medium direct heat and cook the chicken on the chargrill for 6–7 minutes on each side, or until it is cooked through. Toast the burger buns for about 1 minute on each side, or until they are marked and golden.

Spread some mayonnaise on the inside surface of each bun, cover the base with mizuna and cucumber ribbons, and top with the chicken. Spread some of the thickened marinade over the chicken and top with the other half of the bun. Serves 4

268 CHILLI BEEF BURGERS

500 g (1 lb 2 oz) minced (ground) beef
6 red Asian shallots, finely chopped
3 tablespoons crisp fried onion flakes (see Notes)
3 garlic cloves, finely chopped
2 long red chillies, seeded and finely chopped
4 tablespoons finely chopped coriander (cilantro) leaves
    and stems
2–2^1/$_2$ tablespoons chilli garlic sauce (see Notes)
1 egg, lightly beaten
160 g (5^3/$_4$ oz/2 cups) fresh breadcrumbs
olive oil, for brushing
1 loaf Turkish bread, cut into 4 pieces, or 4 round Turkish rolls
100 g (3^1/$_2$ oz/3 handfuls) mignonette or green oak lettuce leaves

Put the beef, shallots, onion flakes, garlic, chilli, coriander, chilli garlic sauce, egg, breadcrumbs and 1^1/$_2$ teaspoons of salt in a large bowl, and knead well with your hands until the ingredients are thoroughly combined. Cover the bowl and refrigerate for 2 hours.

Using wet hands, divide the beef mixture into four equal portions, roll each portion into a ball, then flatten it slightly to form patties. Preheat a chargrill plate to medium direct heat. Brush the patties with oil and grill them for 5–6 minutes, turn and cook for another 5–6 minutes, or until well browned and cooked through. Toast the bread, cut side down, on the chargrill plate for 1–2 minutes, or until golden. Divide the lettuce among four of the toasted bread slices. Add a patty, season, then top with the remaining toasted bread. Serves 4

Notes: Crisp fried onion flakes and chilli garlic sauce are available from Asian grocery stores.

267 TUNA BURGERS WITH HERBED MAYONNAISE

4 garlic cloves, crushed
2 egg yolks
250 ml (9 fl oz/1 cup) light olive oil
3 tablespoons chopped flat-leaf (Italian) parsley
1 tablespoon chopped dill
2 teaspoons dijon mustard
1 tablespoon lemon juice
1 tablespoon red wine vinegar
1 tablespoon baby capers in brine, drained
4 anchovy fillets in oil, drained
4 x 150 g (5^1/$_2$ oz) tuna steaks
2 tablespoons olive oil
2 red onions, thinly sliced
4 large round bread rolls, halved and buttered
100 g (3^1/$_2$ oz) mixed lettuce leaves

Put the garlic and egg yolks in a food processor and process them together for 10 seconds. With the motor running, add the oil in a very thin, slow stream. When the mixture starts to thicken start pouring the oil a little faster until all of the oil has been added and the mixture is thick and creamy. Add the parsley, dill, mustard, lemon juice, vinegar, capers and anchovies, and process until the mixture is smooth. Refrigerate the mayonnaise until you need it.

Preheat the chargrill plate to high direct heat. Brush the tuna steaks with 1 tablespoon of olive oil and cook them for 2 minutes on each side, or until they are almost cooked through. Add the remaining olive oil to the onion, toss to separate and coat the rings, and cook on the flat plate for 2 minutes, or until the onion is soft and caramelised. Toast the rolls, buttered side down, on the chargrill plate for 1 minute, or until they are marked and golden.

Put some lettuce, a tuna steak, some of the onion and a dollop of herbed mayonnaise on one half of each roll. Season with salt and pepper and top with the other half of the roll. Serves 4

269

270

271

269 STEAK BAGUETTE WITH ROCKET & MUSTARDY MAYO

3 tablespoons olive oil, plus extra for frying
1 red onion, sliced
1 teaspoon soft brown sugar
2 teaspoons balsamic vinegar
1 teaspoon thyme leaves
1 tablespoon dijon mustard
3 tablespoons mayonnaise
100 g (3½ oz) rocket (arugula)
500 g (1 lb 2 oz) beef fillet, cut into 4 thin slices
2 thick baguettes, cut in half, or 8 thick slices
    of good-quality bread
2 tomatoes, sliced

Heat 2 tablespoons of the oil in a saucepan. Add the onion and cook slowly, with the lid on, stirring occasionally, until the onion is soft but not brown. This could take up to 15 minutes. Remove the lid, add the sugar and vinegar and cook for a further 10 minutes, or until the onion is soft and just browned. Take the pan off the stove and stir in the thyme.

Meanwhile, make the mustardy mayo by mixing together well the mustard and mayonnaise in a small bowl. Drizzle the rocket with the remaining olive oil and season with salt and freshly ground black pepper.

Heat 1 tablespoon of the extra oil in a frying pan over high heat and cook the steaks for 2 minutes on each side, adding more oil if necessary. Season to taste. To serve, put out the bread, along with separate bowls containing the onion, mustardy mayo, rocket leaves, steak and sliced tomatoes. Let everyone make their own baguette so they can get the perfect mix of all the flavours. Serves 4

271 TOASTED CHEESE, AÏOLI & HAM SANDWICH

1 loaf ciabatta or Turkish bread
1 garlic clove, crushed
125 g (4½ oz/½ cup) mayonnaise
4 slices ham
100 g (3½ oz) semi-dried (sun-blushed) tomatoes, chopped
2 tablespoons capers, chopped
6–8 slices cheddar cheese

Turn on the grill (broiler). Cut the bread in half horizontally and then into four equal pieces. Toast all the pieces. To make the aïoli, mix the garlic into the mayonnaise and season it well with salt and pepper.

Spread the aïoli over the insides of each sandwich. Put a slice of ham on four of the pieces and then divide the semi-dried tomatoes and capers among them. Top with enough cheese slices to make a good layer and put them on a baking tray.

Grill the sandwiches until the cheese melts and starts to bubble and then put the tops back on and press them down firmly. Cut each sandwich in half diagonally and enjoy. Serves 4

270 CHEESEBURGERS WITH CAPSICUM SALSA

CAPSICUM SALSA
2 red capsicums (peppers)
1 ripe tomato, finely chopped
1 small red onion, finely chopped
1 tablespoon olive oil
2 teaspoons red wine vinegar

1 kg (2 lb 4 oz) minced (ground) beef
1 small onion, finely chopped
2 tablespoons chopped flat-leaf (Italian) parsley
1 teaspoon dried oregano
1 tablespoon tomato paste (concentrated purée)
70 g (2½ oz) cheddar cheese
6 bread rolls
salad leaves, to serve

To make the salsa, quarter the capsicums, remove the seeds and membranes and cook on a hot, lightly oiled barbecue grill, skin side down, until the skin blackens and blisters. Place in a plastic bag and leave to cool. Peel away the skin and dice the flesh. Combine with the tomato, onion, olive oil and vinegar and leave for at least 1 hour to let the flavours develop. Serve at room temperature.

Mix together the minced beef, onion, herbs and tomato paste with your hands and season well. Divide into six portions and shape into six patties. Cut the cheese into small squares. Make a cavity in the top of each patty with your thumb. Place a piece of cheese in the cavity and smooth the mince over to enclose the cheese completely.

Cook the patties on a hot, lightly oiled barbecue grill or flat plate for 4–5 minutes each side, turning once. Serve in rolls with salad leaves and capsicum salsa. Serves 6

Note: As a variation, try using camembert, brie or any blue cheese instead of the cheddar.

272

273

274

272 THAI FISH CAKES WITH DIPPING SAUCE

500 g (1 lb 2 oz) firm white fish fillets, skin removed
1½ tablespoons red curry paste
3 tablespoons sugar
3 tablespoons fish sauce
1 egg
100 g (3½ oz) snake beans, thinly sliced
10 kaffir lime leaves, finely chopped
oil, for deep-frying

DIPPING SAUCE
125 g (4½ oz/½ cup) sugar
3 tablespoons white vinegar
1 tablespoon fish sauce
1 small red chilli, chopped
2 tablespoons each finely chopped carrot and cucumber
1 tablespoon roasted peanuts, chopped

Place the fish in a food processor and process until smooth. Add the curry paste, sugar, fish sauce and egg. Process for 10 seconds, or until combined. Stir in the beans and lime leaves. Shape the mixture into walnut-size balls, then flatten them into patties. Fill a wok one-third full of oil and heat to 180°C (350°F), or until a cube of bread dropped into the oil browns in 15 seconds. Cook in batches for 3–5 minutes, turning occasionally. Drain on crumpled paper towels.

To make the dipping sauce, place the sugar, vinegar, fish sauce, chilli and 125 ml (4 fl oz/½ cup) water in a saucepan. Simmer for 5 minutes, or until thickened slightly. Cool. Stir in the chopped carrot, cucumber and peanuts. Serve the dipping sauce with the fish cakes. Makes 24

274 VIETNAMESE RICE PAPER ROLLS

NUOC CHAM DIPPING SAUCE
185 ml (6 fl oz/¾ cup) fish sauce
3 tablespoons lime juice
2 tablespoons grated palm sugar (jaggery) or soft brown sugar
2 bird's eye chillies, seeded and finely chopped

150 g (5½ oz) dried rice vermicelli
48 round 15 cm (6 inch) rice paper wrappers
48 cooked king prawns (shrimp), peeled, deveined,
   halved lengthways
150 g (5½ oz) bean sprouts
3 large handfuls mint
2 large handfuls coriander (cilantro) leaves

To make the dipping sauce, combine all the ingredients and 125 ml (4 fl oz/½ cup) water and stir until the sugar dissolves. Set aside. Place the noodles in a heatproof bowl, cover with boiling water and soak for 10 minutes, then drain.

Assemble the rolls one at a time. Dip a rice paper wrapper in a bowl of warm water for 30 seconds, or until it softens. Place the wrapper on a work surface and put 2 prawn halves on the bottom third of the wrapper. Top with a few noodles, bean sprouts, 3 mint leaves and 6 coriander leaves, in that order. Ensure that the filling is neat and compact, then turn up the bottom of the wrapper to cover the filling. Holding the filling in place, fold in the two sides, then roll up. Arrange on a platter, folded side down. Cover with a damp tea towel or plastic wrap until ready to serve. Serve with the dipping sauce. Makes 48

273 DOLMADES

200 g (7 oz) packet vine leaves in brine
250 g (9 oz/1 cup) medium-grain rice
1 small onion, finely chopped
1 tablespoon olive oil
50 g (1¾ oz) pine nuts, toasted
2 tablespoons currants
2 tablespoons chopped dill
2 tablespoons finely chopped mint
2 tablespoons finely chopped flat-leaf (Italian) parsley
80 ml (2½ fl oz/⅓ cup) olive oil, extra
2 tablespoons lemon juice
500 ml (17 fl oz/2 cups) chicken or vegetable stock

Cover the vine leaves with cold water and soak for 15 minutes. Pat dry and cut off any stems. Reserve 5–6 leaves; discard any with holes. Meanwhile, pour boiling water over the rice and soak for 10 minutes, then drain.

Place the rice, onion, oil, pine nuts, currants, herbs and salt and pepper in a large bowl, and mix well. Lay some leaves, vein side down, on a flat surface. Place ½ tablespoon of filling in the middle of each leaf, fold the stalk end over the filling, then the left and right sides into the middle, and finally roll firmly towards the tip. The dolmade should resemble a small cigar. Repeat to make 48 dolmades.

Line the base of a large, heavy-based saucepan or flameproof casserole dish with the reserved leaves. Drizzle with 1 tablespoon of the extra oil. Put the dolmades in the pan, packing them tightly in one layer. Pour the remaining oil and lemon juice over them.

Pour the stock over the dolmades and cover with an inverted plate to stop them moving while cooking. Bring to the boil, then reduce the heat and simmer gently, covered, for 45 minutes. Remove with a slotted spoon. Serve warm or cold. Makes 48

275

276

277

278

275 HUMMUS

220 g (7³/₄ oz/1 cup) dried chickpeas
2 tablespoons tahini
4 garlic cloves, crushed
2 teaspoons ground cumin
80 ml (2¹/₂ fl oz/¹/₃ cup) lemon juice
3 tablespoons olive oil
large pinch of cayenne pepper
extra lemon juice (optional)
extra olive oil, to garnish
paprika, to garnish
chopped flat-leaf (Italian) parsley, to garnish

Soak the chickpeas in 1 litre (35 fl oz/4 cups) water overnight. Drain and place in a large saucepan with 2 litres (70 fl oz/8 cups) fresh water (enough to cover the chickpeas by 5 cm/2 inches). Bring to the boil, then reduce the heat and simmer for 1 hour 15 minutes, or until the chickpeas are very tender. Skim any scum from the surface. Drain well, reserve the cooking liquid and leave until cool enough to handle. Pick over for any loose skins and discard.

Process the chickpeas, tahini, garlic, cumin, lemon juice, olive oil, cayenne pepper and 1¹/₂ teaspoons salt in a food processor until thick and smooth. With the motor still running, gradually add enough reserved cooking liquid, about 185 ml (6 fl oz/³/₄ cup) to form a smooth creamy purée. Season with salt or extra lemon juice.

Spread onto a flat bowl or plate, drizzle with oil, sprinkle with paprika and scatter the parsley over the top. Serve with pitta bread or pide. Makes 750 ml (26 fl oz/3 cups)

276 BABA GHANNOUJ

2 eggplants (aubergine) (1 kg/2 lb 4 oz)
3 garlic cloves, crushed
¹/₂ teaspoon ground cumin
80 ml (2¹/₂ fl oz/¹/₃ cup) lemon juice
2 tablespoons tahini
pinch of cayenne pepper
1¹/₂ tablespoons olive oil
1 tablespoon finely chopped flat-leaf (Italian) parsley
black olives, to garnish

Preheat the oven to 200°C (400°F/Gas 6). Pierce the eggplants several times with a fork, then cook over an open flame for about 5 minutes, or until the skin is black and blistering, then place in a roasting tin and bake for 45 minutes, or until the eggplants are very soft and wrinkled. Place in a colander over a bowl to drain off any bitter juices and leave to stand for 30 minutes, or until cool.

Carefully peel the skin from the eggplant, chop the flesh and place in a food processor with the garlic, cumin, lemon, tahini, cayenne and olive oil. Process until smooth and creamy. Alternatively, use a potato masher or fork. Season with salt and stir in the parsley. Spread onto a flat bowl or plate and garnish with the olives. Serve with flatbread or pide. Makes 435 ml (15¹/₄ fl oz/1³/₄ cups)

Note: If you prefer, you can roast the eggplant in a 200°C (400°F/Gas 6) oven for 1 hour, or until very soft and wrinkled.

277 OLIVE TAPENADE

400 g (14 oz) kalamata olives, pitted
2 garlic cloves, crushed
2 anchovy fillets in oil, drained
2 tablespoons capers in brine, rinsed, squeezed dry
2 teaspoons chopped thyme
2 teaspoons dijon mustard
1 tablespoon lemon juice
3 tablespoons olive oil
1 tablespoon brandy (optional)

Place the kalamata olives, crushed garlic, anchovies, capers, chopped thyme, dijon mustard, lemon juice, olive oil and brandy in a food processor and process until smooth. Season to taste with salt and freshly ground black pepper. Spoon into a clean, warm jar, cover with a layer of olive oil, seal and refrigerate for up to 1 week. Serve on bruschetta or with a meze plate. Makes 375 ml (13 fl oz/1¹/₂ cups)

Note: When refrigerated, the olive oil may solidify, making it an opaque white colour. This is a property of olive oil and will not affect the flavour of the dish. Simply bring the dish to room temperature before serving and the olive oil with return to a liquid state.

278 BROAD BEAN DIP

200 g (7 oz/1 cup) dried broad beans (fava or ful nabed — see Note)
2 garlic cloves, crushed
¹/₄ teaspoon ground cumin
1¹/₂ tablespoons lemon juice
80 ml (2¹/₂ fl oz/¹/₃ cup) olive oil
2 tablespoons chopped flat-leaf (Italian) parsley
flatbread, for serving

Rinse the beans well, then place in a bowl and cover with 500 ml (17 fl oz/2 cups) water and leave to soak overnight. If using peeled beans (see Note), transfer them and their soaking water to a large heavy-based saucepan. If using unpeeled beans, drain, then add to the pan with 500 ml (17 fl oz/2 cups) fresh water. Bring to the boil, cover, and simmer for 5–6 hours. Check the water level from time to time and add a little boiling water, as necessary, to keep the beans moist. Do not stir, but shake the pan occasionally to prevent sticking. Set aside to cool slightly.

Purée the contents of the pan in a food processor, then transfer to a bowl and stir in the garlic, cumin and lemon juice. Gradually stir in enough olive oil to give a dipping consistency (you may not need to add all the oil). As the mixture cools it may become thick, in which case you can stir in a little warm water to return the mixture to dipping consistency. Spread over a large dish and sprinkle with the parsley. Serve with the flatbread, cut into triangles. Serves 6

Note: The fava beans can be the ready-peeled white ones or the small brown ones.

279

280

281

282

279 POTATO SKINS

6 large potatoes, unpeeled
oil, for deep-frying

Preheat the oven to 210°C (415°F/Gas 6–7). Prick each potato with a fork and bake for 1 hour, or until the skins are crisp and the flesh is soft. Turn once during cooking. Leave the potatoes to cool, then halve them and scoop out the flesh, leaving a thin layer of potato in each shell. Cut each half into 3 wedges.

Fill a deep heavy-based pan one-third full of oil and heat to 190°C (375°F), or until a cube of bread dropped in the oil browns in 10 seconds. Cook the potato skins in batches for 2–3 minutes, or until crisp. Drain on paper towels. Sprinkle with salt and pepper. Makes 36

280 ORANGE SWEET POTATO WEDGES

1.3 kg (3 lb) orange sweet potato, peeled and sliced into 6 x 2 cm (2$\frac{1}{2}$ x $\frac{3}{4}$ inch) wedges
2 tablespoons olive oil
1 tablespoon fennel seeds
1 tablespoon coriander seeds
$\frac{1}{2}$ teaspoon cayenne pepper
1 teaspoon sea salt flakes

Preheat the oven to 200°C (400°F/Gas 6). Place the sweet potato in a large baking dish and toss with the oil. In a mortar and pestle, pound together the fennel and coriander seeds until they are roughly crushed. Add to the orange sweet potato along with the cayenne and sea salt flakes. Toss well and bake for about 30 minutes, or until browned and crisp. Serve warm. Serves 6–8

281 SPICY CHICKEN GOUJONS

3 chicken breast fillets
plain (all-purpose) flour, for coating
oil, for deep-frying
$\frac{1}{2}$ teaspoon ground turmeric
$\frac{1}{2}$ teaspoon ground coriander
$\frac{1}{2}$ teaspoon ground cumin
$\frac{1}{2}$ teaspoon chilli powder

Cut the chicken breasts into thin strips and toss in plain flour, shaking off the excess. Fill a deep heavy-based saucepan one-third full of oil and heat to 180°C (350F), or until a cube of bread dropped into the oil browns in 15 seconds. Cook the goujons in batches for 3 minutes, or until golden. Drain on crumpled paper towels and keep warm.

Mix together the turmeric, coriander, cumin, chilli powder and 1 teaspoon salt. Toss the goujons in the mixture, shaking off the excess. Makes about 30

282 CHEESE STICKS

155 g (5$\frac{1}{2}$ oz/1$\frac{1}{4}$ cups) plain (all-purpose) flour
100 g (3$\frac{1}{2}$ oz) unsalted butter, chilled and chopped
100 g (3$\frac{1}{2}$ oz/$\frac{3}{4}$ cup) grated gruyère cheese
1 tablespoon finely chopped oregano
1 egg yolk
1 tablespoon sea salt flakes

Line two baking trays with baking paper. Put the flour and butter in a food processor and process in short bursts until the mixture resembles fine breadcrumbs. Add the gruyère and oregano and process for 10 seconds, or until just combined. Add the egg yolk and about 1 tablespoon water, and process until the dough just comes together.

Turn the dough out onto a lightly floured surface and gather into a ball. Form 2 teaspoons of dough into a ball, then roll out into a stick about 12 cm (5 inches) long and place on the baking trays. Repeat with the remaining dough, then cover with plastic wrap and refrigerate for 15–20 minutes. Preheat the oven to 200°C (400°F/Gas 6).

Lightly brush the sticks with water and sprinkle with the sea salt flakes. Bake for 10 minutes, or until golden. Cool on a wire rack and serve with dips or as part of an antipasto platter. Makes 30

Note: Cheese sticks will keep for up to 1 week in an airtight container.

283

284

285

283 MEXICAN BITES

740 g (1 lb 10 oz) tin kidney beans, drained
1 teaspoon ground cumin
2 tablespoons olive oil
$^1/_4$ teaspoon cayenne pepper
1 avocado
1 small garlic clove, crushed
2 tablespoons sour cream
2 tablespoons lime juice
1 vine-ripened tomato, seeded and finely chopped
2 tablespoons finely chopped coriander (cilantro) leaves
250 g (9 oz) packet round tortilla chips

To make the refried beans, put the kidney beans in a bowl and mash well with a potato masher, then add the cumin. Heat $1^1/_2$ tablespoons of oil in a large non-stick frying pan and add the cayenne pepper and mashed kidney beans. Cook over medium– high heat for 2–3 minutes, stirring constantly. Allow to cool, then refrigerate for about 30 minutes, or until cold.

Scoop the avocado flesh into a food processor and add the garlic, sour cream and 1 tablespoon of the lime juice. Process for a few minutes until it is a thick creamy paste, then add salt to taste. Refrigerate. To make the salsa, mix together the tomato, coriander and the remaining olive oil and lime juice in a bowl. Refrigerate until needed.

To assemble, lay out 36 round tortilla chips. Put a heaped teaspoon of refried beans in the centre of each chip, add a teaspoon of the avocado cream and lastly $^1/_2$ teaspoon of tomato salsa. Makes 36

285 SALMON CAKES WITH HERB MAYONNAISE

500 g (1 lb 2 oz) salmon fillet, skin and bones removed,
    cut into 5 mm ($^1/_4$ inch) cubes
3 tablespoons dry breadcrumbs
1 tablespoon lightly beaten egg
$^1/_2$ teaspoon finely grated lime zest
$3^1/_2$ teaspoons lime juice
3 teaspoons dill, chopped
125 g ($4^1/_2$ oz/$^1/_2$ cup) whole-egg mayonnaise
1 garlic clove, crushed
2 tablespoons light olive oil

Place the salmon, breadcrumbs, egg, lime zest, 3 teaspoons lime juice and 2 teaspoons dill in a bowl. Stir until the mixture comes together and the ingredients are evenly distributed. Season well with salt and freshly ground black pepper. With wet hands, using 2 heaped teaspoons of mixture at a time, shape into 36 small round cakes. Place on a baking tray lined with baking paper. Refrigerate until ready to use.

For the herb mayonnaise, mix the remaining lime juice and dill with the mayonnaise and garlic in a bowl. Heat the olive oil in a large non-stick frying pan. Cook the salmon cakes in batches over medium heat for 2 minutes each side, or until golden and cooked through. Do not overcook. Drain on paper towels. Top each with a little of the herb mayonnaise and season well. Serve immediately, garnished with lime strips if desired. Makes 36

Note: You can also top these with 125 g ($4^1/_2$ oz/$^1/_2$ cup) crème fraîche and $1^1/_2$ tablespoons salmon roe.

284 CHERRY TOMATO & BOCCONCINI TARTLETS

250 g (9 oz/2 cups) plain (all-purpose) flour
125 g ($4^1/_2$ oz) chilled butter, chopped
1 egg

FILLING
300 g ($10^1/_2$ oz) cherry tomatoes, quartered
2 tablespoons olive oil
1 garlic clove, crushed
200 g (7 oz) bocconcini, quartered
80 g ($2^3/_4$ oz) chopped kalamata olives
1 tablespoon extra virgin olive oil
1 tablespoon torn basil
oil, for deep-frying
30 small basil leaves

Preheat the oven to 200°C (400°F/Gas 6). Grease 30 mini muffin holes. Sift the flour and rub the butter in with your fingertips until the mixture resembles fine breadcrumbs. Make a well, add the egg and mix with a flat-bladed knife, using a cutting action, until it gathers in beads. Add a little cold water if necessary. Press the dough into a ball, wrap in plastic wrap and chill for 30 minutes.

Roll out the dough between two sheets of baking paper to 2 mm ($^1/_{16}$ inch) thick and cut 30 rounds with a 6 cm ($2^1/_2$ inch) cutter. Press a round into each muffin hole. Prick each base with a fork and bake for 6 minutes, or until dry and golden. If they puff up, use a clean tea towel to press back. Cool.

To make the filling, preheat the oven to 200°C (400°F/Gas 6). Combine the tomatoes, olive oil and garlic in a roasting tin and bake for 15 minutes, or until golden. Cool, add the bocconcini, olives, extra virgin olive oil and basil, season, and toss. Fill a saucepan one-third full of oil and heat to 180°C (350°F), or until a cube of bread dropped in the oil browns in 15 seconds. Deep-fry the basil in batches for 30 seconds, or until crisp. Drain. Spoon the vegetable mixture into the pastry cases and top with a basil leaf. Makes 30

286

287

288

289

286 WHITE BEAN DIP

2 x 400 g (14 oz) tins lima or cannellini beans, drained and rinsed
125 ml (4 fl oz/$\frac{1}{2}$ cup) olive oil
80 ml (2$\frac{1}{2}$ fl oz/$\frac{1}{3}$ cup) lemon juice
3 garlic cloves, finely chopped
1 tablespoon finely chopped rosemary

Place the beans in a food processor with the oil, lemon juice, garlic and rosemary and 1 teaspoon salt. Process until smooth, then season with freshly ground black pepper. Makes 750 ml (26 fl oz/3 cups)

Note: This dip improves with age, so you can make it up to 2 days ahead of time.

287 WARM CRAB & LEMON DIP

80 g (2$\frac{3}{4}$ oz) butter
2 garlic cloves, crushed
3 French shallots, thinly sliced
1 teaspoon mustard powder
$\frac{1}{2}$ teaspoon cayenne pepper
125 ml (4 fl oz/$\frac{1}{2}$ cup) cream
150 g (5$\frac{1}{2}$ oz) cream cheese
60 g (2$\frac{1}{4}$ oz/$\frac{1}{2}$ cup) grated cheddar cheese
350 g (12 oz) tin crabmeat, drained
2 tablespoons lemon juice
2 teaspoons worcestershire sauce
3 teaspoons chopped tarragon
40 g (1$\frac{1}{2}$ oz/$\frac{1}{2}$ cup) fresh breadcrumbs
1 tablespoon chopped flat-leaf (Italian) parsley

Preheat the oven to 170°C (325°F/Gas 3). Melt half the butter in a saucepan, then cook the garlic and shallots for 2–3 minutes, or until just softened. Add the mustard powder, cayenne and cream. Bring to a simmer and slowly whisk in the cream cheese, a little at a time. When completely incorporated, whisk in the cheddar and allow to cook, stirring constantly, over very low heat for 1–2 minutes, or until smooth. Remove from the heat and add the crab meat, lemon juice, worcestershire sauce and 2 teaspoons of the tarragon. Season to taste. Mix, then transfer to a small baking dish.

Melt the remaining butter in a saucepan, add the breadcrumbs, parsley and remaining tarragon and stir until just combined. Sprinkle over the crab mixture and bake for 15 minutes. Serve warm. Makes 625 ml (21$\frac{1}{2}$ fl oz/ 2$\frac{1}{2}$ cups)

288 GUACAMOLE

2 large ripe avocados
2 tablespoons lime juice
1 tomato, seeded and finely diced
1 red chilli, finely chopped
2 tablespoons finely diced red onion
1$\frac{1}{2}$ tablespoons chopped coriander (cilantro) leaves
1$\frac{1}{2}$ tablespoons sour cream
1 tablespoon olive oil
$\frac{1}{2}$ teaspoon ground cumin
pinch of cayenne pepper

Put the avocado and lime juice in a large bowl, then mash. Stir in the tomato, chilli, onion, coriander, sour cream, olive oil and cumin. Season with cayenne pepper and some salt and pepper. Spoon into a serving bowl and sprinkle with cayenne pepper. Makes 500 ml (17 fl oz/2 cups)

289 GREEK-STYLE FETA & YOGHURT DIP

250 g (9 oz) mild feta cheese
250 g (9 oz) ricotta cheese
2 tablespoons olive oil
3 garlic cloves, crushed
1 tablespoon lemon juice
$\frac{1}{4}$ teaspoon cayenne pepper
185 g (6$\frac{1}{2}$ oz/$\frac{3}{4}$ cup) Greek-style yoghurt
4 tablespoons chopped mint
1 teaspoon chopped oregano
3 tablespoons pitted black olives, diced
1 small tomato, finely diced
1–2 teaspoons lemon zest, thinly sliced

Purée the feta, ricotta, oil, garlic, lemon juice, cayenne pepper and half the yoghurt in a blender or food processor until smooth. Stir in the remaining yoghurt, mint and oregano. Transfer the dip to a serving bowl and top with the olives, tomato and lemon zest. Makes 1 litre (35 fl oz/4 cups)

290 MACADAMIA-CRUSTED CHICKEN STRIPS

12 chicken tenderloins (700 g/1 lb 9 oz), larger ones cut in half
seasoned plain (all-purpose) flour, to dust
2 eggs, lightly beaten
250 g (9 oz) macadamia nuts, finely chopped
160 g (5¾ oz/2 cups) fresh breadcrumbs
oil, to deep-fry

Cut the chicken into strips. First, dust the chicken strips with the flour, then dip them in the egg and, finally, coat them in the combined nuts and breadcrumbs. Refrigerate for at least 30 minutes to firm up.

Fill a large heavy-based saucepan or deep-fryer one-third full of oil and heat to 180°C (350°F), or until a cube of bread dropped in the oil browns in 15 seconds. Cook the chicken in batches for 2–3 minutes, or until golden brown all over, taking care not to burn the nuts. Drain on crumpled paper towels. Serve warm. Makes 24

291 STUFFED BLACK OLIVES

36 pitted large black or large kalamata olives
100 g (3½ oz) goat's cheese
1 teaspoon capers, drained and finely chopped
1 garlic clove, crushed
1 tablespoon chopped flat-leaf (Italian) parsley
1½ tablespoons plain (all-purpose) flour
2 eggs, lightly beaten
100 g (3½ oz/1 cup) dry breadcrumbs
1 tablespoon finely chopped flat-leaf (Italian) parsley, extra
oil, for deep-frying

Carefully cut the olives along the open cavity so they are opened out, but still in one piece. Mash the goat's cheese, capers, garlic and parsley together in a small bowl, then season. Push an even amount of the mixture into the cavity of the olives, then press them closed.

Put the flour in one small bowl, the egg in another and combine the breadcrumbs and extra parsley in a third. Dip each olive first into the flour, then into the egg and, finally, into the breadcrumbs. Put the crumbed olives on a plate and refrigerate for at least 2 hours.

Fill a deep heavy-based saucepan or deep-fryer one-third full of oil and heat to 180°C (350°F), or until a cube of bread dropped into the oil browns in 15 seconds. Cook the olives in batches for 1–2 minutes, or until golden brown; you may need to turn them with tongs or a long-handled metal spoon. Drain on crumpled paper towels and season. Serve warm or at room temperature with lemon wedges. Makes 36

292 FALAFEL

440 g (15½ oz/2 cups) dried chickpeas
1 onion, finely chopped
2 garlic cloves, crushed
2 tablespoons chopped flat-leaf (Italian) parsley
1 tablespoon chopped coriander (cilantro) leaves
2 teaspoons ground cumin
½ teaspoon baking powder
oil, for deep-frying

Soak the chickpeas in 750 ml (26 fl oz/3 cups) water for 4 hours or overnight. Drain and place in a food processor, and process for 30 seconds, or until finely ground. Add the onion, garlic, parsley, coriander, cumin, baking powder, 1 tablespoon of water, salt and pepper and process for 10 seconds, or until the mixture forms a rough paste. Cover and leave for 30 minutes.

Using your hands, shape heaped tablespoons of the falafel mixture into balls and squeeze out any excess liquid. Fill a deep heavy-based pan one-third full of oil to 180°C (350°F), or until a cube of bread dropped in the oil browns in 15 seconds. Gently lower the falafel balls into the oil. Cook in batches of five at a time, for 3–4 minutes each batch. When the balls are browned, remove with a large slotted spoon. Drain well. Serve with pitta bread, tabbouleh and hummus. Makes 30

293 HONEY MUSTARD CHICKEN DRUMETTES

80 ml (2½ fl oz/⅓ cup) oil
3 tablespoons honey
3 tablespoons soy sauce
3 tablespoons dijon mustard
3 tablespoons lemon juice
4 garlic cloves, crushed
24 chicken drumettes (see Note)

To make the marinade, place the oil, honey, soy sauce, mustard, lemon juice and garlic in a large non-metallic dish and mix together thoroughly.

Trim the chicken of excess fat, then place in the dish with the marinade and toss until well coated. Cover and refrigerate for at least 2 hours, or preferably overnight, turning 2–3 times.

Preheat the oven to 200°C (400°F/Gas 6). Place the drumettes on a wire rack over a foil-lined baking tray. Bake, turning and brushing with the marinade 3–4 times, for 45 minutes, or until golden brown and cooked. Serve immediately with napkins for sticky fingers. Makes 24

Note: Drumettes are the chicken wing with the wing tip removed.

294

295

296

294 PIZZA WHEELS

1/2 small red capsicum (pepper), finely chopped
3 tablespoons chopped flat-leaf (Italian) parsley
2 tablespoons chopped oregano
100 g (3 1/2 oz) finely chopped ham or salami
60 g (2 1/4 oz/1/2 cup) grated cheddar cheese
3 tablespoons tomato paste (concentrated purée)
2 sheets ready-rolled puff pastry, thawed

Preheat the oven to 200°C (400°F/Gas 6). Combine the capsicum, parsley, oregano, ham and cheese in a bowl. Spread the tomato paste onto each sheet of pastry, leaving a 2 cm (3/4 inch) border along one side, and sprinkle the capsicum mixture over the top. Roll up the pastry to enclose the filling, leaving the plain edge until last. Brush the edge lightly with water and fold over to seal. Cut each roll into 1 cm (1/2 inch) rounds and place onto greased oven trays. Bake for 20 minutes, or until golden. Makes 48

296 HERB CHEESE LOG

500 g (1 lb 2 oz) cream cheese, softened
1 tablespoon lemon juice
1 garlic clove, crushed
2 teaspoons chopped thyme
2 teaspoons chopped tarragon
1 tablespoon chopped flat-leaf (Italian) parsley
50 g (1 3/4 oz/1 cup) snipped chives

Put the cream cheese in a large bowl and beat with electric beaters until soft and creamy. Mix in the lemon juice and garlic. In a separate bowl, combine the thyme, tarragon and chopped parsley.

Line a 20 x 30 cm (8 x 12 inch) tin with foil. Spread the chives over the base of the tin, then spoon the cream cheese mixture over the chives. Using a palette knife, gently spread the mixture into the tin, pushing it into any gaps. Sprinkle the combined herbs evenly over the top.

Lift the foil from the tin and place on a work surface. Roll the cheese into a log, starting from the longest edge, then cover and place on a baking tray. Refrigerate for at least 3 hours, or preferably overnight. Makes a 30 cm (12 inch) log

295 MAKI ZUSHI

275 g (9 3/4 oz/1 1/4 cups) sushi rice
2 1/2 tablespoons rice vinegar
1 tablespoon sugar
1/2 tablespoon mirin
250 g (9 oz) sashimi tuna
1 small Lebanese (short) cucumber
1/2 avocado
8 sheets nori
3 teaspoons wasabi paste

Rinse the rice under running water until the water runs clear, then drain thoroughly. Place in a large saucepan with 375 ml (13 fl oz/ 1 1/2 cups) water and simmer for 20–25 minutes, or until tender. Cover with a clean tea towel and leave for 15 minutes.

Combine the vinegar, sugar, mirin, and 1 teaspoon salt, and stir until the sugar dissolves. Spread the rice over a non-metallic tray and pour the dressing on top. Mix with a spatula, gently separating the grains of rice. Allow to cool to body temperature.

Cut the tuna, cucumber and avocado into thin strips. Place a sheet of nori on a bamboo mat (available at Asian grocery stores), shiny side down, with a short end towards you. Spread the rice 1 cm (1/2 inch) thick over the nori, leaving a 1 cm (1/2 inch) border. Make a shallow groove down the centre of the rice towards the short end closest to you. Spread some wasabi along the groove. Place a selection of strips of your filling ingredients on top of the wasabi.

Lift the edge of the bamboo mat and roll the sushi, starting from the edge nearest to you. When you've finished rolling, press the mat to make either a round or square roll. Wet a sharp knife, trim the ends and cut the roll into six pieces. Makes 48

297

298

299

300

297 THAI CHICKEN SAUSAGE ROLLS

200 g (7 oz) chicken breast fillet, roughly chopped
150 g (5$^1/_2$ oz) mild pancetta, chopped
1 garlic clove, crushed
3 spring onions (scallions), chopped
2 tablespoons chopped coriander (cilantro) leaves,
    plus extra, to serve
2 bird's eye chillies, seeded and finely chopped
1 teaspoon fish sauce
1 egg
1 teaspoon grated fresh ginger
375 g (13 oz) block frozen puff pastry
1 egg yolk
2 tablespoons sesame seeds
sweet chilli sauce, to serve

Preheat the oven to 180°C (350°F/Gas 4). Put the chicken, pancetta, garlic, spring onion, coriander, chilli, fish sauce, whole egg and ginger in a food processor and process until just combined.

Roll out the pastry to an oblong 30 x 40 cm (12 x 16 inches). Cut in half lengthways. Take half the filling and, using floured hands, roll it into a long sausage shape and place along the long edge of one piece of pastry. Brush the edges with a little water and fold over, pressing down to seal. Place the sealed edge underneath. Repeat with the remaining pastry and filling.

Using a sharp knife, cut the sausage rolls into 3 cm (1$^1/_4$ inch) lengths on the diagonal; discard the end pieces. Brush the tops with egg yolk, then sprinkle with sesame seeds. Bake for 15 minutes, or until golden. Serve with sweet chilli sauce and garnished with coriander. Makes 24

298 CARAMELISED RED ONION & FETA TARTLETS

1$^1/_2$ tablespoons olive oil
2 large red onions, finely chopped
2 teaspoons chopped thyme
3 sheets ready-rolled shortcrust pastry
70 g (2$^1/_2$ oz) feta cheese, crumbled
2 eggs, lightly beaten
125 ml (4 fl oz/$^1/_2$ cup) cream

Preheat the oven to 180°C (350°F/Gas 4). Heat the oil in a frying pan (do not use a non-stick one or the onion won't caramelise). Add the onion and cook, stirring occasionally, over medium–low heat for 30 minutes, or until dark gold. Add the thyme, stir well and transfer to a bowl to cool.

Grease 24 shallow patty tin holes. Using an 8 cm (3$^1/_4$ inch) cutter, cut out 24 pastry rounds and line the tins with the rounds. Divide the onion among the patty cases, then spoon the feta over the onion. Combine the eggs with the cream, season and pour into the pastry cases. Bake for 10–15 minutes, or until puffed and golden. Leave in the tins for 5 minutes before transferring to a wire rack to cool. Makes 24

Note: These can be made a day in advance and reheated in a 150°C (300°F/Gas 2) oven for 10 minutes before serving.

299 SPICY CORN PUFFS

2 corn cobs
3 tablespoons chopped coriander (cilantro) leaves
6 spring onions (scallions), finely chopped
1 small red chilli, seeded and finely chopped
1 large egg
2 teaspoons ground cumin
$^1/_2$ teaspoon ground coriander
125 g (4$^1/_2$ oz/1 cup) plain (all-purpose) flour
oil, for deep-frying
sweet chilli sauce, to serve

Cut down the side of the corn with a sharp knife to release the kernels. Roughly chop the kernels, then place them in a large bowl. Holding the cobs over the bowl, scrape down the sides of the cobs with a knife to release any corn juice from the cob into the bowl.

Add the coriander, spring onion, chilli, egg, cumin, ground coriander, 1 teaspoon salt and some pepper to the bowl and stir well. Add the flour and mix well. If the mixture is too dry, add 1 tablespoon water, but no more than that as the batter should be quite dry. Stand for 10 minutes.

Fill a large heavy-based saucepan or deep-fryer one-third full of oil and heat to 180°C (350°F), or until a cube of bread dropped in the oil browns in 15 seconds. Drop slightly heaped teaspoons of the corn batter into the oil and cook for about 1$^1/_2$ minutes, or until puffed and golden. Drain on crumpled paper towels and serve immediately with a bowl of the sweet chilli sauce to dip the puffs into. Makes about 36

300 PESTO PALMIERS

1 large handful basil
1 garlic clove, crushed
3 tablespoons grated parmesan cheese
1 tablespoon pine nuts, toasted
2 tablespoons olive oil
4 sheets ready-rolled puff pastry, thawed

Preheat the oven to 220°C (425°F/Gas 7). Roughly chop the basil leaves in a food processor with the garlic, parmesan and pine nuts. With the motor running, gradually add the oil in a thin stream and process until the mixture is smooth.

Spread each pastry sheet with a quarter of the basil mixture. Roll up one side until you reach the middle then repeat with the other side. Place on a baking tray. Repeat with the remaining pastry and basil mixture. Freeze for 30 minutes.

Slice each roll into 1.5 cm ($^5/_8$ inch) slices. Curl each slice into a semi-circle and place on a lightly greased baking tray. Allow room for the palmiers to expand during cooking. Bake in batches for 15–20 minutes, or until golden brown. Makes 60

301

302

303

304

301 CURRIED NUTS

500 g (1 lb 2 oz) mixed nuts, such as almonds, brazil nuts, pecans, macadamias, cashew nuts
1 egg white
2 tablespoons curry powder
1 teaspoon ground cumin

Preheat the oven to 150°C (300°F/Gas 2). Spread the nuts in a single layer on a baking tray and roast for 10 minutes. Whisk the egg white until frothy, then add the nuts, curry powder, cumin and 1 teaspoon salt. Toss together and return to the oven for a further 10–15 minutes, then allow to cool. Makes 500 g (1 lb 2 oz)

302 VEGETABLE CHIPS

500 g (1 lb 2 oz) orange sweet potato
500 g (1 lb 2 oz) beetroot
500 g (1 lb 2 oz) parsnip
oil, for deep-frying

Preheat the oven to 180°C (350°F/Gas 4). Run a vegetable peeler along the length of the sweet potato and beetroot to make thin ribbons. Cut the parsnip into thin slices.

Fill a deep, heavy-based saucepan one-third full of oil and heat to 190°C (375°F), or until a cube of bread dropped into the oil browns in 10 seconds. Cook the vegetables in batches for about 30 seconds, or until golden and crisp, turning with tongs, if necessary. Drain on crumpled paper towels and season with salt. Keep warm on a baking tray in the oven and cook the remaining chips. Makes a large bowl

303 SEASONED POPCORN

3 tablespoons oil
150 g (5$\frac{1}{2}$ oz/$\frac{2}{3}$ cup) popping corn
40 g (1$\frac{1}{2}$ oz) butter
125 g (4$\frac{1}{2}$ oz/$\frac{2}{3}$ cup) finely chopped kalamata olives
1 bird's eye chilli, finely chopped
1 garlic clove, crushed
1 tablespoon chopped flat-leaf (Italian) parsley
1 tablespoon chopped oregano
1 teaspoon grated lemon zest

Heat the oil in a large saucepan, add the popping corn and cover. Cook over medium heat, shaking occasionally, until the popping stops. Transfer to a large bowl and discard any unpopped corn.

Melt the butter in a large frying pan and add the remaining ingredients. Mix, then toss through the popcorn. Serve warm. Makes a large bowl

304 MARINATED OLIVES

150 g (5$\frac{1}{2}$ oz) kalamata olives
150 g (5$\frac{1}{2}$ oz) good-quality green olives
185 ml (6 fl oz/$\frac{3}{4}$ cup) extra virgin olive oil
2 sprigs rosemary
$\frac{1}{2}$ tablespoon thyme leaves
2 small red chillies, seeded
several strips lemon zest
2 garlic cloves, bruised
$\frac{1}{2}$ teaspoon fennel seeds
2 thyme sprigs, extra

Place the olives, oil, rosemary, thyme, chillies, lemon peel, garlic and fennel in a large saucepan and warm over low heat. Transfer to a bowl and marinate overnight at room temperature.

Remove the olives from the oil with a slotted spoon and discard the herbs, reserving the oil. Add the extra thyme to the olives before serving. Makes 300 g (10$\frac{1}{2}$ fl oz) olives

Note: Serve the oil with bread.

305

306

307

305 EMPANADAS

2 eggs
40 g (1¼ oz) stuffed green olives, chopped
95 g (3 oz) ham, finely chopped
3 tablespoons grated cheddar cheese
3 sheets ready-rolled puff pastry, thawed
1 egg yolk, lightly beaten

Place the eggs in a small saucepan, cover with water and bring to the boil. Boil for 10 minutes, then drain and cool for 5 minutes in cold water. Peel and chop.

Preheat the oven to 220°C (425°F/ Gas 7). Lightly grease two baking trays. Combine the egg, olives, ham and cheddar in a large bowl. Cut five 10 cm (4 inch) rounds from each pastry sheet. Place a tablespoon of the filling into the centre of each round, fold the pastry over and crimp the edges to seal.

Place the pastries on the trays, about 2 cm (³⁄₄ inch) apart. Brush with the egg yolk and bake in the centre or top half of the oven for 15 minutes, or until well browned and puffed. Swap the trays around after 10 minutes and cover loosely with foil if the empanadas start to brown too much. Serve hot. Makes 15

307 MINI LEEK PIES

60 g (2¼ oz) butter
2 tablespoons olive oil
1 onion, finely chopped
3 leeks, finely sliced
1 garlic clove, chopped
1 tablespoon plain (all-purpose) flour
2 tablespoons sour cream
100 g (3½ oz/1 cup) grated parmesan cheese
1 teaspoon chopped thyme
4 sheets frozen puff pastry, thawed
1 egg, lightly beaten

Heat the butter and oil in a large frying pan over medium heat. Add the onion and cook, stirring occasionally, for 2 minutes. Add the leek and garlic and cook for 5 minutes, or until the leek is softened and lightly coloured. Add the flour and stir into the mixture for 1 minute. Add the sour cream and stir until slightly thickened. Transfer to a bowl and add the parmesan and thyme. Season with salt and freshly ground black pepper and allow to cool.

Preheat the oven to 200°C (400°F/Gas 6). Place a lightly greased baking tray in the oven to heat. Using a 6 cm (2½ inch) cutter, cut the pastry into 64 circles. Place 2 heaped teaspoons of filling on half the pastry circles, leaving a small border. Lightly brush the edges with egg, then place a pastry circle on top of each. Seal the edges well with a fork. Lightly brush the tops with egg. Place the pies on the heated tray and bake for 25 minutes, or until the pies are puffed and golden. Makes 32

306 SPINACH & FETA TRIANGLES

1 kg (2 lb 4 oz) English spinach
3 tablespoons olive oil
1 onion, chopped
10 spring onions (scallions), sliced
4 tablespoons chopped flat-leaf (Italian) parsley
1 tablespoon chopped dill
large pinch of ground nutmeg
35 g (1¼ oz/⅓ cup) grated parmesan cheese
150 g (5½ oz) crumbled feta cheese
90 g (3¼ oz) ricotta cheese
4 eggs, lightly beaten
40 g (1½ oz) butter, melted
1 tablespoon olive oil, extra
12 sheets filo pastry

Trim any stems from the spinach. Wash the leaves, roughly chop and place in a saucepan with a little water clinging to the leaves. Cover and cook over low heat for 5 minutes, or until the leaves have wilted. Drain and allow to cool slightly before squeezing to remove the excess water.

Heat the oil in a heavy-based frying pan. Add the onion and cook over low heat for 10 minutes, or until tender and golden. Add the spring onion and cook for a further 3 minutes. Remove from the heat. Stir in the spinach, parsley, dill, nutmeg, parmesan, feta, ricotta and egg. Season well.

Preheat the oven to 180°C (350°F/Gas 4). Grease two baking trays. Combine the butter with the extra oil. Work with three sheets of pastry at a time, covering the rest with a damp cloth. Brush each sheet with butter mixture and lay them on top of each other. Halve lengthways.

Place 4 tablespoons of filling on an angle at the end of each strip. Fold the pastry to enclose the filling and form a triangle. Continue folding the triangle over until you reach the end. Brush with the remaining butter mixture and bake for 20 minutes, or until golden brown. Makes 8

NIGHT

308
309

310
311

308 BUCKWHEAT NOODLES WITH SWEET & SOUR CAPSICUM

3 capsicums (peppers), preferably red, green and yellow
2 tablespoons vegetable oil
5 teaspoons sesame oil
2 star anise
3 tablespoons red wine vinegar
1 tablespoon fish sauce
125 g (4^1/$_2$ oz/^{1}/$_2$ cup) sugar
300 g (10^1/$_2$ oz) buckwheat noodles
2 teaspoons balsamic vinegar
^{1}/$_2$ teaspoon sugar, extra
2 spring onions (scallions), finely sliced
2 tablespoons sesame seeds, lightly toasted

Thinly slice the capsicums. Heat the oil and 1 teaspoon sesame oil in a saucepan over medium heat. Cook the star anise for 1 minute, or until the oil begins to smoke. Add the capsicum and stir for 2 minutes. Reduce the heat to low and cook, covered, for 5 minutes, stirring occasionally. Increase to medium heat and add the vinegar, fish sauce and sugar, stirring until dissolved. Boil for 2 minutes, then remove from the heat and cool. Remove the star anise. Drain and place the capsicum in a bowl.

Cook the noodles in a large saucepan of rapidly boiling water for 5 minutes. Drain and rinse. Combine the balsamic vinegar, remaining sesame oil, extra sugar and ^{1}/$_2$ teaspoon salt, stirring until the sugar dissolves. Add the noodles and toss to coat, then combine with the capsicum and spring onion. Sprinkle with the sesame seeds and serve. Serves 4

309 NOODLES WITH CHICKEN, PORK & PRAWNS

900 g (2 lb) flat rice noodle sheets, cut into 2 cm (^{3}/$_4$ inch) slices
100 ml (3^1/$_2$ fl oz) oil
2 garlic cloves, finely chopped
1 tablespoon grated fresh ginger
70 g (2^1/$_2$ oz) garlic chives, cut into 5 cm (2 inch) lengths
^{1}/$_2$ barbecue chicken, flesh cut into 1 cm (^{1}/$_2$ inch) slices
300 g (10^1/$_2$ oz) Chinese barbecue pork, cut into 1 cm (^{1}/$_2$ inch) slices
1 small red chilli, chopped
12 large cooked prawns (shrimp), peeled and deveined
180 g (6^1/$_4$ oz/2 cups) bean sprouts
100 g (3^1/$_2$ oz) English spinach
2 eggs, beaten
2 teaspoons caster (superfine) sugar
125 ml (4 fl oz/^{1}/$_2$ cup) light soy sauce
2 tablespoons dark soy sauce
2 tablespoons fish sauce

Rinse the rice noodles under warm water and separate. Drain. Heat a wok over high heat, add 3 tablespoons of the oil and swirl to coat. Add the garlic and ginger, and cook, stirring, for 30 seconds. Then add the chives and cook, stirring, for 10 seconds. Add the barbecue chicken, barbecue pork, chilli and prawns, and cook, stirring, for 2 minutes, then add the bean sprouts and spinach, and cook, stirring, for 1 minute.

Make a well in the centre of the mixture, add the egg and scramble for 1 minute, or until firm but not hard. Stir in the remaining oil, then add the rice noodles. Stir to combine. Add the combined caster sugar, light and dark soy sauce, and fish sauce, and stir-fry for 2–3 minutes, or until heated through. Season with pepper. Serves 4

310 CHIANG MAI NOODLES

250 g (9 oz) fresh thin egg noodles
2 tablespoons oil
6 red Asian shallots, finely chopped
3 garlic cloves, crushed
1–2 small red chillies, seeded and finely chopped
2–3 tablespoons red curry paste
375 g (13 oz) chicken breast fillet, cut into thin strips
2 tablespoons fish sauce
1 tablespoon grated palm sugar (jaggery)
750 ml (26 fl oz/3 cups) coconut milk
1 tablespoon lime juice
250 ml (9 fl oz/1 cup) chicken stock
4 spring onions (scallions), sliced, to garnish
4 tablespoons coriander (cilantro) leaves, to garnish
fried red Asian shallot flakes, to garnish
purchased fried noodles, to garnish
red chilli, finely diced, to garnish

Cook the noodles according to the packet instructions. Drain, cover and set aside. Heat a large wok over high heat, add the oil and swirl to coat. Add the shallots, garlic and chilli, and stir-fry for 3 minutes. Stir in the curry paste and stir-fry for 2 minutes. Add the chicken and stir-fry for 3 minutes, or until it changes colour.

Stir in the fish sauce, palm sugar, coconut milk, lime juice and stock. Reduce the heat and simmer over low heat for 5 minutes — do not boil. To serve, divide the noodles among bowls and spoon in the chicken mixture. Garnish with the spring onion, coriander, shallot flakes, noodles and chilli. Serves 4

311 RISI E BISI

1.25 litres (44 fl oz/5 cups) chicken stock
bouquet garni (1 sprig thyme, 1 bay leaf, 2 stalks flat-leaf (Italian) parsley)
2 tablespoons olive oil
1 onion, chopped
^{1}/$_2$ celery stalk, chopped
60 g (2^1/$_4$ oz) pancetta, chopped
250 g (9 oz) arborio rice
300 g (10^1/$_2$ oz) frozen baby peas
60 g (2^1/$_4$ oz) unsalted butter
80 g (2^3/$_4$ oz) grated parmesan cheese
shaved parmesan cheese, to serve

Place the stock and bouquet garni in a large saucepan with 750 ml (26 fl oz/3 cups) water. Bring to the boil, then reduce the heat and simmer. Heat the oil in a large frying pan, add the onion, celery and pancetta, and cook for 3–5 minutes, or until the onion is soft.

Add the rice and stir for 1 minute, or until coated. Remove the bouquet garni and add 125 ml (4 fl oz/^{1}/$_2$ cup) hot stock to the rice, stirring constantly until all the stock is absorbed. Add another 125 ml (4 fl oz/^{1}/$_2$ cup) stock and stir until all the stock is absorbed. Add the peas. Continue adding stock, 125 ml (4 fl oz/^{1}/$_2$ cup) at a time, stirring, for 20–25 minutes, or until the rice is tender. The texture should be a little wetter than risotto, but not too soupy. Remove from the heat and stir in the butter and grated parmesan. Season. Garnish with shaved parmesan. Serves 4

312

313

314

312 GREEN PILAU WITH CASHEWS

200 g (7 oz) baby English spinach leaves
100 g (3 1/2 oz/2/3 cup) cashew nuts, chopped
2 tablespoons olive oil
6 spring onions (scallions), chopped
300 g (10 1/2 oz/1 1/2 cups) long-grain brown rice
2 garlic cloves, finely chopped
1 teaspoon fennel seeds
2 tablespoons lemon juice
625 ml (21 1/2 fl oz/2 1/2 cups) vegetable stock
3 tablespoons chopped mint
3 tablespoons chopped flat-leaf (Italian) parsley

Preheat the oven to 180°C (350°F/Gas 4). Shred the spinach into 1 cm (1/2 inch) slices. Place the cashew nuts on a baking tray and roast for 5–10 minutes, or until golden brown — watch carefully or they will burn.

Heat the oil in a large frying pan and cook the spring onion over medium heat for 2 minutes, or until soft. Add the rice, garlic and fennel seeds and cook, stirring frequently, for 1–2 minutes, or until the rice is evenly coated. Increase the heat to high, add the lemon juice, stock and 1 teaspoon salt and bring to the boil. Reduce to low, cover and cook for 45 minutes without lifting the lid.

Remove from the heat and sprinkle with the spinach and herbs. Stand, covered, for 8 minutes, then fork the spinach and herbs through the rice. Season. Serve sprinkled with cashews. Serves 6

314 BAKED CHICKEN & LEEK RISOTTO

60 g (2 1/4 oz) butter
1 leek, thinly sliced
2 chicken breast fillets, cut into small cubes
440 g (15 1/2 oz/2 cups) risotto rice
3 tablespoons white wine
1.25 litres (44 fl oz/5 cups) chicken stock
35 g (1 1/4 oz/1/3 cup) grated parmesan cheese
2 tablespoons thyme leaves, plus extra to garnish
freshly grated parmesan cheese, extra

Preheat the oven to 150°C (300°F/Gas 2) and put a 5 litre (170 fl oz/ 20 cup) ovenproof dish with a lid in the oven. Heat the butter in a saucepan over medium heat, stir in the leek and cook for about 2 minutes, then add the chicken and stir for 3 minutes. Toss in the rice and stir for 1 minute. Add the wine and stock, and bring to the boil.

Pour into the ovenproof dish and cover. Cook in the oven for 30 minutes, stirring halfway through. Remove from the oven and stir in the cheese and thyme. Season, then sprinkle with extra thyme and cheese. Serves 4

313 RISOTTO WITH SCALLOPS & MINTED PRAWNS

1 litre (35 fl oz/4 cups) chicken, fish or vegetable stock
360 g (12 3/4 oz/2 3/4 cups) fresh or frozen baby peas
2 tablespoons light sour cream
2 tablespoons finely shredded mint
1 tablespoon olive oil
1 small onion, finely chopped
2 garlic cloves, finely chopped
150 g (5 1/2 oz) arborio rice
16 large scallops (without roe)
1 tablespoon grated parmesan cheese
4 mint leaves, to garnish
lemon wedges, to serve

Bring the stock to the boil, and add the peas. Simmer for 1–2 minutes, or until the peas are tender, then remove, keeping the stock at a low simmer. Blend 230 g (8 1/4 oz/1 3/4 cups) of the peas with the sour cream in a food processor until smooth. Season, then stir in 1 tablespoon of the mint.

Place the oil in a shallow saucepan and cook the onion over low heat for 4–5 minutes, or until soft. Add the garlic and cook for 30 seconds. Stir in the rice to coat. Increase the heat to medium.

Add 250 ml (9 fl oz/1 cup) stock to the rice mixture and cook, stirring constantly, until the liquid has evaporated. Add the stock, 125 ml (4 fl oz/1/2 cup) at a time until the rice is tender and creamy. This will take about 20 minutes. Meanwhile, season the scallops and heat a chargrill pan or hotplate. Add the scallops and sear on both sides until cooked to your liking.

Fold the pea purée through the risotto with the reserved whole peas and parmesan. Divide the risotto among the serving bowls and top with the scallops. Sprinkle with the remaining mint, garnish with a mint leaf and serve with a wedge of lemon. Serves 4–6

315 PENNE WITH MUSHROOM & HERB SAUCE

2 tablespoons olive oil
500 g (1 lb 2 oz) button mushrooms, sliced
2 garlic cloves, crushed
2 teaspoons chopped marjoram
125 ml (4 fl oz/^{1}/$_2$ cup) dry white wine
80 ml (2^1/$_2$ fl oz/^{1}/$_3$ cup) cream
375 g (13 oz) penne
1 tablespoon lemon juice
1 teaspoon finely grated lemon zest
2 tablespoons chopped flat-leaf (Italian) parsley
50 g (1^3/$_4$ oz/^{1}/$_2$ cup) grated parmesan cheese

Heat the oil in a large heavy-based frying pan over high heat. Add the mushrooms and cook for 3 minutes, stirring constantly to prevent the mushrooms from burning. Add the garlic and marjoram and cook for a further 2 minutes.

Add the white wine to the pan, reduce the heat and simmer for 5 minutes, or until nearly all the liquid has evaporated. Stir in the cream and cook over low heat for 5 minutes, or until the sauce has thickened.

Meanwhile, cook the penne in a large saucepan of boiling salted water until *al dente*. Drain. Add the lemon juice, zest, parsley and half the parmesan to the sauce. Season to taste with salt and freshly ground black pepper. Toss the penne through the sauce and sprinkle with the remaining parmesan. Serves 4

316 PASTA CARBONARA

400 g (14 oz) penne
1 tablespoon olive oil
200 g (7 oz) piece pancetta or bacon, cut into long thin strips
6 egg yolks
185 ml (6 fl oz/^{3}/$_4$ cup) thick (double/heavy) cream
75 g (2^3/$_4$ oz/^{3}/$_4$ cup) grated parmesan cheese

Cook the pasta in a saucepan of boiling salted water until *al dente*. Meanwhile, heat the oil in a frying pan and cook the pancetta over high heat for 6 minutes, or until crisp and golden. Remove with a slotted spoon and drain on paper towels.

Beat the egg yolks, cream and the parmesan together in a bowl and season generously. Return the freshly cooked and drained pasta to its saucepan and pour the egg mixture over the pasta, tossing gently. Add the pancetta, then return the pan to very low heat and cook for 30–60 seconds, or until the sauce thickens and coats the pasta. Season with pepper and serve immediately. Serves 4–6

Note: Be careful not to cook the pasta over high heat once you have added the egg mixture, or the sauce risks being scrambled by the heat.

317 PENNE WITH VEAL RAGOUT

2 onions, sliced
2 bay leaves, crushed
1.5 kg (3 lb 5 oz) veal shin, cut into osso buco pieces
    (about 4 cm/1^1/$_2$ inches thick)
250 ml (9 fl oz/1 cup) red wine
2 x 400 g (14 oz) tins crushed tomatoes
375 ml (13 fl oz/1^1/$_2$ cups) beef stock
2 teaspoons chopped rosemary
400 g (14 oz) penne
150 g (5^1/$_2$ oz/1 cup) frozen peas

Preheat the oven to 220°C (425°F/Gas 7). Scatter the onion over the bottom of a large roasting tin, lightly spray with oil and put the bay leaves and veal pieces on top. Season with salt and pepper. Roast for 10–15 minutes, or until the veal is browned.

Pour the wine over the veal and return to the oven for a further 5 minutes. Reduce the oven to 180°C (350°F/Gas 4), remove the tin from the oven and pour on the tomato, stock and 1 teaspoon of the rosemary. Cover with foil and return to the oven. Cook for 2 hours, or until the veal is starting to fall from the bone. Remove the foil and cook for a further 15 minutes.

Cook the pasta in a large saucepan of boiling salted water until *al dente*. Meanwhile, remove the veal from the oven and cool slightly. Add the peas and remaining rosemary, place over a hotplate and cook over medium heat for 5 minutes, or until the peas are cooked. Drain the pasta, divide among four bowls and top with the ragout. Serves 4

318 PENNE WITH PUMPKIN, BAKED RICOTTA & PROSCIUTTO

500 g (1 lb 2 oz) penne
450 g (1 lb) butternut pumpkin (squash), cut into 1 cm
    (^{1}/$_2$ inch) cubes
3 tablespoons extra virgin olive oil
2 garlic cloves, crushed
100 g (3^1/$_2$ oz) semi-dried tomatoes, chopped
4 slices prosciutto, chopped
250 g (9 oz) baked ricotta, cut into 1 cm (^{1}/$_2$ inch) cubes
3 tablespoons shredded basil

Cook the penne in a large saucepan of rapidly boiling salted water until *al dente*. Drain. Meanwhile, cook the pumpkin in a saucepan of boiling water for 10–12 minutes, or until just tender, then drain.

Heat the oil in a large saucepan, add the garlic and cook over medium heat for 30 seconds. Add the tomato, prosciutto, pumpkin and penne and toss gently over low heat for 1–2 minutes, or until heated through. Add the baked ricotta and the basil, season with salt and freshly ground black pepper and serve immediately. Serves 4

319

320

321

319 THAI CHICKEN WITH GLASS NOODLES

90 g (3¼ oz/⅓ cup) coconut cream
1 tablespoon fish sauce
1 tablespoon palm sugar (jaggery)
2 chicken breast fillets, cut into shreds
120 g (4½ oz) glass noodles
2 lemongrass stems, white part only, finely sliced
4 kaffir lime leaves, finely sliced
1 red onion, finely chopped
1 large handful each coriander (cilantro) and mint leaves, chopped
1–2 red chillies, sliced
3 green bird's eye chillies, finely sliced
2 tablespoons roasted peanuts, chopped
1–2 limes, cut in halves or quarters

Mix the coconut cream in a small saucepan or a wok with the fish sauce and palm sugar and bring to the boil, then add the chicken and simmer until the chicken is cooked through. This should only take a minute if you stir it a couple of times. Leave the chicken to cool in the sauce. Soak the noodles in boiling water for a minute or two — they should turn translucent and soft when they are ready. Drain them, then, using a pair of scissors, cut them into shorter lengths.

Put all the ingredients, except the lime, in a bowl with the noodles and chicken, with its sauce, and toss everything together. Now squeeze the lime pieces over the dish and toss again. Serves 4

321 BEEF & HOKKIEN NOODLE STIR-FRY

600 g (1 lb 5 oz) fresh hokkien (egg) noodles
350 g (12 oz) beef fillet, partially frozen, thinly sliced
1 tablespoon peanut oil
1 large onion, cut into thin wedges
1 large carrot, thinly sliced on the diagonal
1 red capsicum (pepper), cut into thin strips
2 garlic cloves, crushed
1 teaspoon grated fresh ginger
100 g (3½ oz) snow peas (mangetout), sliced in half diagonally
200 g (7 oz) fresh shiitake mushrooms, sliced
3 tablespoons oyster sauce
2 tablespoons light soy sauce
1 tablespoon soft brown sugar
½ teaspoon Chinese five-spice

Soak the noodles in a large bowl with enough boiling water to cover for 10 minutes. Spray a large wok with oil spray and when very hot, cook the steak in batches until brown. Remove and keep warm.

Heat the peanut oil in the wok, and when very hot, stir-fry the onion, carrot and capsicum for 2–3 minutes, or until tender. Add the garlic, ginger, snow peas and shiitake mushrooms, and cook for another minute before returning the steak to the wok.

Separate the noodles with a fork, then drain. Add to the wok, tossing well. Combine the oyster sauce with the soy sauce, brown sugar, five-spice and 1 tablespoon water and pour over the noodles. Toss until warmed through, then serve. Serves 4

320 INDONESIAN-STYLE FRIED NOODLES

400 g (14 oz) fresh flat egg noodles (5 mm/¼ inch wide)
2 tablespoons peanut oil
4 red Asian shallots, thinly sliced
2 garlic cloves, chopped
1 small red chilli, finely diced
200 g (7 oz) pork fillet, thinly sliced across the grain
200 g (7 oz) chicken breast fillet, thinly sliced
200 g (7 oz) small raw prawns (shrimp), peeled and deveined, with tails intact
2 Chinese cabbage leaves, shredded
2 carrots, cut in half lengthways and thinly sliced
100 g (3½ oz) snake beans, cut into 3 cm (1¼ inch) lengths
3 tablespoons kecap manis
1 tablespoon light soy sauce
2 tomatoes, peeled, seeded and chopped
4 spring onions (scallions), sliced on the diagonal
1 tablespoon crisp fried onion flakes
flat-leaf (Italian) parsley, to garnish

Cook the noodles in a large saucepan of boiling water for 1 minute, or until tender. Drain and rinse them under cold water. Heat a wok over high heat, add the oil and swirl to coat. Stir-fry the Asian shallots for 30 seconds. Add the garlic, chilli and pork and stir-fry for 2 minutes, then add the chicken and cook a further 2 minutes, or until the meat is golden and tender.

Add the prawns and stir-fry for another 2 minutes, or until pink and just cooked. Stir in the cabbage, carrot and beans and cook for 3 minutes, then add the noodles and gently stir-fry for 4 minutes, or until heated through — taking care not to break up the noodles.

Stir in the kecap manis, soy sauce, chopped tomato and spring onion and stir-fry for 1–2 minutes. Season with salt and freshly ground black pepper. Garnish with the fried onion flakes and parsley. Serves 4

Note: This dish, called bahmi goreng in Indonesian, is traditionally eaten with chopped roasted peanuts and sambal oelek on the side. It is also delicious with satay sauce.

322 SPAGHETTI WITH OLIVE, CAPER & ANCHOVY SAUCE

375 g (13 oz) spaghetti
80 ml (2¹/₂ fl oz/¹/₃ cup) olive oil
2 onions, finely chopped
3 garlic cloves, finely chopped
¹/₂ teaspoon chilli flakes
6 large ripe tomatoes, diced
4 tablespoons capers in brine, rinsed, drained
7–8 anchovies in oil, drained, minced
150 g (5¹/₂ oz) kalamata olives
3 tablespoons chopped flat-leaf (Italian) parsley

Bring a large saucepan of salted water to the boil, add the spaghetti and cook until *al dente*. Drain. Meanwhile, heat the oil in a large saucepan, add the onion and cook over medium heat for 5 minutes. Add the garlic and chilli flakes, and cook for 30 seconds, then add the tomato, capers and anchovies. Simmer over low heat for 5–10 minutes, or until thick and pulpy, then stir in the olives and parsley.

Stir the pasta through the sauce. Season with salt and freshly ground black pepper and serve immediately with crusty bread. Serves 6

323 SPAGHETTI BOLOGNESE

60 g (2¹/₄ oz) butter
1 onion, finely chopped
2 garlic cloves, crushed
1 celery stalk, finely chopped
1 carrot, diced
50 g (1³/₄ oz) piece pancetta, diced
500 g (1 lb 2 oz) minced (ground) beef
1 tablespoon chopped oregano
250 ml (9 fl oz/1 cup) red wine
500 ml (17 fl oz/2 cups) beef stock
2 tablespoons tomato paste (concentrated purée)
2 x 400 g (14 oz) tins crushed tomatoes
400 g (14 oz) spaghetti
3 tablespoons grated parmesan cheese

Melt the butter in a large saucepan, add the onion and cook over medium heat for 2–3 minutes, or until it starts to soften. Add the garlic, celery and carrot, and cook, stirring, over low heat, for 5 minutes. Increase the heat to high, add the pancetta, beef and oregano, and cook for 4–5 minutes, or until browned. Use a fork to break up any lumps.

Pour in the wine, reduce the heat and simmer for 4–5 minutes, or until it is absorbed. Add the stock, tomato paste and tomato, and season well. Cover with a lid and simmer for 1¹/₂ hours, stirring occasionally to prevent the sauce from catching on the bottom of the saucepan. Uncover and simmer for another hour, stirring occasionally.

Cook the spaghetti in a large saucepan of boiling water until *al dente*. Drain, divide among four serving plates and top with the sauce. Sprinkle with the parmesan and serve. Serves 4

324 SPAGHETTI VONGOLE

1 kg (2 lb 4 oz) baby clams (vongole)
375 g (13 oz) spaghetti
125 ml (4 fl oz/¹/₂ cup) virgin olive oil
40 g (1¹/₂ oz) butter
1 small onion, very finely chopped
6 large garlic cloves, finely chopped
125 ml (4 fl oz/¹/₂ cup) dry white wine
1 small red chilli, seeded and finely chopped
1 handful chopped flat-leaf (Italian) parsley

Scrub the clams with a small stiff brush to remove any grit, discarding any that are open or cracked. Then soak and rinse the clams in several changes of water over an hour or so until the water is clean and free of grit. Drain and set aside.

Cook the pasta in a saucepan of boiling salted water until *al dente*. Heat the oil and 1 tablespoon of the butter in a large saucepan over medium heat. Add the onion and half the garlic and cook for 10 minutes, or until lightly golden — ensure the garlic doesn't start to burn. Add the wine and cook for 2 minutes. Then add the clams, chilli and the remaining butter and garlic and cook, covered, for 8 minutes, shaking regularly, until the clams pop open — discard any that are still closed. Stir in the parsley and season. Add the hot pasta and toss well. Serves 4

325 CHILLI LINGUINE WITH CHERMOULA CHICKEN

600 g (1 lb 5 oz) chicken breast fillets
500 g (1 lb 2 oz) chilli linguine

CHERMOULA
2 large handfuls coriander (cilantro) leaves, chopped
2 large handfuls flat-leaf (Italian) parsley, chopped
4 garlic cloves, crushed
2 teaspoons ground cumin
2 teaspoons ground paprika
125 ml (4 fl oz/¹/₂ cup) lemon juice
2 teaspoons lemon zest
100 ml (3¹/₂ fl oz) olive oil

Heat a large non-stick frying pan over medium heat. Add the chicken breasts and cook until tender. Remove from the pan and leave for 5 minutes before cutting into thin slices.

Cook the pasta in a large saucepan of rapidly boiling salted water until al dente, then drain. Meanwhile, combine the chermoula ingredients in a glass bowl and add the sliced chicken. Leave to stand until the pasta has finished cooking. Serve the pasta topped with the chermoula chicken. Serves 4

326

327

328

329

326 CHICKEN, BROCCOLI & PASTA BAKE

300 g (10½ oz) fusilli
425 g (15 oz) tin cream of mushroom soup
2 eggs
185 g (6½ oz/¾ cup) whole-egg mayonnaise
1 tablespoon dijon mustard
210 g (7½ oz/1⅔ cups) grated cheddar cheese
600 g (1 lb 5 oz) chicken breast fillets, thinly sliced
400 g (14 oz) frozen broccoli pieces, thawed
40 g (1½ oz/½ cup) fresh breadcrumbs

Preheat the oven to 180°C (350°F/Gas 4). Cook the pasta in a large saucepan of boiling water until al dente, then drain and return to the pan. Combine the soup, eggs, mayonnaise, mustard and half the cheese in a bowl.

Heat a lightly greased non-stick frying pan over medium heat, add the chicken pieces and cook for 5–6 minutes, or until cooked through. Season with salt and pepper, then set aside to cool.

Add the chicken and broccoli to the pasta, pour the soup mixture over the top and stir until well combined. Transfer the mixture to a 3 litre (100 fl oz/12 cup) ovenproof dish. Sprinkle with the combined breadcrumbs and remaining cheese. Bake for 20 minutes, or until the top is golden brown. Serves 6–8

327 ROASTED VEGETABLE CANNELLONI

60 g (2¼ oz) butter
1 large leek, cut into 1 cm (½ inch) pieces
200 g (7 oz) purchased chargrilled eggplant (aubergine) in oil
200 g (7 oz) purchased chargrilled orange sweet potato in oil
125 g (4½ oz/1 cup) grated cheddar cheese
40 g (1½ oz/⅓ cup) plain (all-purpose) flour
1 litre (35 fl oz/4 cups) milk
6 fresh lasagne sheets

Preheat the oven to 200°C (400°F/Gas 6) and lightly grease a ceramic dish (28 x 18 x 5 cm/11¼ x 7 x 2 inches). Melt 20 g (¾ oz) butter in a saucepan, add the leek and stir over medium heat for 8 minutes, or until soft. Chop the eggplant and sweet potato into 1 cm (½ inch) pieces and place in a bowl. Mix in the leek and 40 g (1½ oz/⅓ cup) of the cheddar.

Melt the remaining butter in a saucepan over medium heat. Stir in the flour and cook for 1 minute, or until foaming. Remove from the heat and gradually stir in the milk. Return to the heat and stir until the sauce boils and thickens. Reduce the heat and simmer for 2 minutes. Season with salt and pepper. Stir 375 ml (13 fl oz/1½ cups) of the sauce into the vegetable mixture, adding extra if necessary to bind it together.

Cut the rectangular lasagne sheets in half widthways to make two smaller rectangles. Spoon vegetable mixture along the centre of one sheet and roll up. Repeat to make 12 tubes in total. Place the tubes, seam-side-down, in the dish and spoon the remaining white sauce over the top until they are covered. Sprinkle with the remaining cheese and bake for about 20 minutes, or until the cheese is golden. Serves 4

328 BEETROOT RAVIOLI WITH SAGE BURNT BUTTER SAUCE

340 g (12 oz) jar baby beetroots in sweet vinegar
40 g (1½ oz) grated parmesan cheese
250 g (9 oz) fresh ricotta cheese
750 g (1 lb 10 oz) fresh lasagne sheets (4 sheets)
fine cornmeal, for sprinkling
200 g (7 oz) butter, chopped
3 tablespoons sage leaves, torn
2 garlic cloves, crushed
shaved parmesan cheese, to garnish

Drain the beetroot, then grate it into a bowl. Add the parmesan and ricotta and mix well. Lay a sheet of pasta on a flat surface and place evenly spaced tablespoons of the ricotta mixture on the pasta to give 12 mounds. Flatten the mounds of filling slightly. Lightly brush the edges of the pasta sheet and around each pile of filling with water.

Place a second sheet of pasta over the top and gently press around each mound to seal and enclose the filling. Using a pasta wheel or sharp knife, cut the pasta into 12 ravioli. Lay them out separately on a lined tray that has been sprinkled with cornmeal. Repeat with the remaining filling and lasagne sheets to make 24 ravioli. Gently remove any air bubbles after cutting so that they are completely sealed.

Cook the pasta in a large saucepan of boiling water until al dente. Drain, divide among four serving plates and keep warm. Melt the butter in a saucepan and cook for 3–4 minutes, or until golden brown. Remove from the heat, stir in the sage and garlic and spoon over the ravioli. Sprinkle with parmesan and season with pepper. Serves 4

329 FREEFORM PUMPKIN, SPINACH & RICOTTA LASAGNE

3 tablespoons olive oil
1.5 kg (3 lb 5 oz) butternut pumpkin (squash), cut into 1.5 cm (⅝ inch) dice
500 g (1 lb 2 oz) English spinach leaves, thoroughly washed
4 fresh lasagne sheets (12 x 20 cm/4½ x 8 inches)
500 g (1 lb 2 oz/2 cups) ricotta cheese
2 tablespoons cream
3 tablespoons grated parmesan cheese
pinch of ground nutmeg

Heat the oil in a non-stick frying pan over medium heat. Add the pumpkin and toss. Cook, stirring occasionally, for 15 minutes, or until tender. Season and keep warm. Cook the spinach in a large saucepan of boiling water for 30 seconds, or until wilted. Using a slotted spoon, transfer to a bowl of cold water. Drain well and squeeze out as much excess water as possible. Finely chop the spinach. Add the lasagne sheets to the pan of boiling water and cook, stirring occasionally, until al dente. Drain and lay the sheets, side by side, on a clean cloth. Cut each sheet widthways into thirds.

Put the ricotta, cream, parmesan, spinach and nutmeg in a small pan. Stir over low heat for 2–3 minutes, or until warmed through. Work quickly to assemble. Place a piece of lasagne on the base of each plate. Using half the pumpkin, top each of the sheets, then cover with another piece of lasagne. Use half the ricotta mixture to spread over the lasagne sheets, then add another lasagne piece. Top with the remaining pumpkin, then remaining ricotta mixture. Season well and serve immediately. Serves 4

330

331

332

330 NOODLES WITH BEEF & BLACK BEAN SAUCE

300 g (10^1/$_2$ oz) rump steak
1 garlic clove, crushed
3 tablespoons oyster sauce
2 teaspoons sugar
2 tablespoons soy sauce
100 ml (3^1/$_2$ fl oz) black bean sauce
2 teaspoons cornflour (cornstarch)
^{3}/$_4$ teaspoon sesame oil
1.2 kg (2 lb 11 oz) fresh or 600 g (1 lb 5 oz) dried flat rice noodles
1^1/$_2$ tablespoons oil
2 red capsicums (peppers), sliced
1 green capsicum (pepper), sliced
1 handful coriander (cilantro) leaves

Cut the steak across the grain into thin slices and put it in a bowl with the garlic, oyster sauce, sugar, soy sauce, black bean sauce, cornflour and sesame oil. Mix everything together, making sure the slices are all well coated. If you are using dried rice noodles, soak them in boiling water for 10 minutes, or until they are opaque and soft. If your noodles are particularly dry, they may need a little longer. Drain the noodles.

Heat the oil in a wok or frying pan and, when it is hot, add the capsicums. Stir-fry the capsicums for a minute or two until they are starting to soften, then add the meat mixture and cook for a minute. Add the noodles and toss everything together well. Keep cooking until the meat is cooked through and everything is hot, then toss in the coriander leaves and stir once before turning off the heat. Serve straight away. Serves 4

332 SPICY CELLOPHANE NOODLES WITH PORK

200 g (7 oz) minced (ground) pork
1 teaspoon cornflour (cornstarch)
1^1/$_2$ tablespoons light soy sauce
2 tablespoons Chinese rice wine
1 teaspoon sesame oil
150 g (5^1/$_2$ oz) cellophane noodles (mung bean vermicelli)
2 tablespoons oil
4 spring onions (scallions), finely chopped
1 garlic clove, crushed
1 tablespoon finely chopped ginger
2 teaspoons chilli bean sauce
185 ml (6 fl oz/^{3}/$_4$ cup) chicken stock
^{1}/$_2$ teaspoon sugar
2 spring onions (scallions), green part only, extra, thinly sliced

Combine the pork, cornflour, 1 tablespoon each of the soy sauce and rice wine and ^{1}/$_2$ teaspoon of the sesame oil in a bowl, using a fork or your fingers. Cover with plastic wrap and marinate for 10–15 minutes. Meanwhile, place the noodles in a heatproof bowl, cover with boiling water and soak for 3–4 minutes, or until softened. Drain well.

Heat a wok over high heat, add the oil and swirl to coat. Cook the spring onion, garlic, ginger and chilli bean sauce for 10 seconds, add the pork mixture and cook for 2 minutes, stirring to break up any lumps. Stir in the stock, sugar, ^{1}/$_2$ teaspoon salt, and the remaining soy sauce, rice wine and sesame oil. Add the noodles to the wok and toss to combine. Bring to the boil, then reduce the heat to low and simmer, stirring occasionally, for 7–8 minutes, or until the liquid is almost absorbed. Garnish with the extra spring onion and serve. Serves 4

331 MEE GROB

4 Chinese dried mushrooms
oil, for deep-frying
100 g (3^1/$_2$ oz) dried rice vermicelli
100 g (3^1/$_2$ oz) fried tofu, cut into matchsticks
4 garlic cloves, crushed
1 onion, chopped
1 chicken breast fillet, thinly sliced
8 green beans, sliced on the diagonal
6 spring onions (scallions), thinly sliced on the diagonal
8 raw prawns (shrimp), peeled and deveined, with tails intact
30 g (1 oz/^{1}/$_3$ cup) bean sprouts
coriander (cilantro) leaves, to garnish

SAUCE
1 tablespoon soy sauce
3 tablespoons white vinegar
5 tablespoons sugar
3 tablespoons fish sauce
1 tablespoon sweet chilli sauce

Soak the mushrooms in boiling water for 20 minutes. Drain, discard the stems and thinly slice. Fill a wok one-third full of oil and heat to 180°C (350°F), or until a cube of bread dropped in the oil browns in 15 seconds. Cook the vermicelli in small batches for 5 seconds, or until puffed and crispy. Drain. Add the tofu to the wok in batches and deep-fry for 1 minute, or until crisp. Drain. Carefully remove all but 2 tablespoons of oil.

Reheat the wok until very hot and add the garlic and onion and stir-fry for 1 minute. Add the chicken pieces, mushrooms, beans and half the spring onion. Stir-fry for 2 minutes, or until the chicken has almost cooked through. Add the prawns and stir-fry for a further 2 minutes, or until they just turn pink.

Combine all the sauce ingredients and add to the wok. Stir-fry for 2 minutes, or until the meat and prawns are tender and the sauce is syrupy. Remove from the heat and stir in the vermicelli, tofu and bean sprouts. Garnish with the coriander and remaining sliced spring onion. Serves 4–6

333

334

335

333 PRAWN PILAU

400 g (14 oz/2 cups) basmati rice
60 g (2¼ oz) butter
1 onion, finely chopped
2 garlic cloves, finely chopped
1 x 4 cm (½ x 1½ inch) piece fresh ginger, peeled and grated
1 green chilli, finely chopped
3 teaspoons coriander seeds
1 teaspoon ground turmeric
2 cardamom pods, bruised
1 kg (2 lb 4 oz) raw prawns (shrimp), peeled and deveined, tails intact
80 g (2¾ oz/½ cup) raw cashew nuts
80 ml (2½ fl oz/⅓ cup) lemon juice
1 handful chopped coriander (cilantro) leaves

Rinse the rice under cold water until the water runs clear. Drain well. Melt half the butter over low heat in a large saucepan; add the onion and cook for 3 minutes, or until soft. Add the garlic, ginger, chilli, coriander seeds and turmeric, and cook for 2 minutes.

Add the rice to the saucepan and cook for 1 minute, then add the cardamom pods and 1 litre (35 fl oz/4 cups) water. Bring to the boil, then reduce the heat and simmer, covered, for 10 minutes, or until the rice is tender. Remove from the heat and leave, covered, for 5 minutes to steam.

Melt the remaining butter in a frying pan, and cook the prawns and cashew nuts over high heat for 3–4 minutes, or until the prawns are pink and cooked through. Add both to the pan with the rice, then add the lemon juice and coriander and stir everything together. Season to taste with salt and pepper, and serve. Serves 4–6

335 SPANISH SAFFRON CHICKEN & RICE

3 tablespoons olive oil
4 chicken thighs and 6 drumsticks
1 large red onion, finely chopped
1 large green capsicum (pepper), two-thirds diced and one-third julienned
3 teaspoons sweet paprika
400 g (14 oz) tin diced tomatoes
275 g (9¾ oz/1¼ cups) paella or arborio rice
½ teaspoon ground saffron

Heat 2 tablespoons of the oil in a large deep frying pan over high heat. Season the chicken pieces well and brown in batches. Remove the chicken from the pan.

Reduce the pan to medium heat and add the remaining oil. Add the onion and the diced capsicum and cook gently for 5 minutes. Stir in the paprika and cook for 30 seconds. Add the tomato and simmer for 1–3 minutes, or until it thickens.

Stir 875 ml (30 fl oz/3½ cups) boiling water into the pan, then add the rice and saffron. Return the chicken to the pan and stir to combine. Season, to taste. Bring to the boil, then cover, reduce the heat to medium–low and simmer for 20–30 minutes, or until all the liquid has been absorbed and the chicken is tender. Stir in the julienned capsicum, then allow to stand, covered, for 3–4 minutes before serving. Serves 4

334 PAELLA

500 g (1 lb 2 oz) black mussels
3 tablespoons olive oil
600 g (1 lb 5 oz) chicken drumettes or thigh fillets, halved
1 onion, chopped
2 large garlic cloves, chopped
3 vine-ripened tomatoes, peeled, seeded and finely chopped
1 small red capsicum (pepper), diced
1 small green capsicum (pepper), diced
¼ teaspoon chilli flakes
1 teaspoon paprika
¼ teaspoon saffron threads soaked in 3 tablespoons warm water
290 g (10¼ oz/1⅓ cups) short-grain rice
1 litre (35 fl oz/4 cups) vegetable stock
12 raw prawns (shrimp), peeled, deveined, tails intact
155 g (5½ oz/1 cup) peas
3 tablespoons dry sherry
1 handful chopped flat-leaf (Italian) parsley
1 lemon, cut into wedges

Scrub the mussels and remove the beards. Discard any open mussels that don't close when tapped. Heat 2 tablespoons oil in a large frying pan, add the chicken and cook over medium heat for 5–7 minutes, or until browned. Remove. Add the remaining oil to the pan, then add the onion, garlic and tomato, and cook over low heat for 5 minutes, or until soft. Do not brown.

Add the capsicum and cook for 1 minute, then stir in the chilli flakes, paprika and saffron and its soaking liquid. Pour in the rice and return the chicken to the pan. Add the stock, bring to the boil, then reduce the heat and simmer for 10 minutes.

Stir in the prawns, peas, sherry and mussels. Cover for 2 minutes, or until the mussels open. Discard any that do not open. Stir for 2 minutes, or until the prawns are pink and cooked through. Stir in the parsley. Serve immediately with the lemon wedges. Serves 4

336

337

338

339

336 CREAMY CHICKEN & PEPPERCORN PAPPARDELLE

2 chicken breast fillets (425 g/15 oz in total)
30 g (1 oz) butter
1 onion, halved and thinly sliced
2 tablespoons drained green peppercorns, slightly crushed
125 ml (4 fl oz/½ cup) white wine
300 ml (10½ fl oz) cream
400 g (14 oz) fresh pappardelle pasta
80 g (2¾ oz/⅓ cup) sour cream (optional)
2 tablespoons chopped chives

Cut the chicken in half so that you have four flat fillets and season with salt and pepper. Melt the butter in a frying pan, add the chicken and cook for 3 minutes each side, or until lightly browned and cooked through. Remove from the pan, cut into slices and keep warm. Add the onion and peppercorns to the same pan and cook over medium heat for 3 minutes, or until the onion has softened slightly. Add the wine and cook for 1 minute, or until reduced by half. Stir in the cream and cook for 4–5 minutes, or until thickened slightly, then season with salt and freshly ground black pepper.

Meanwhile, cook the pasta in a large saucepan of boiling water until *al dente*, then drain. Mix together the pasta, chicken and any juices and cream sauce. Divide the pasta among serving bowls, top with a dollop of sour cream and sprinkle with chives. Serves 4

337 ANGEL-HAIR PASTA WITH GARLIC, SCALLOPS & ROCKET

20 large scallops with roe
250 g (9 oz) angel-hair pasta
150 ml (5 fl oz) extra virgin olive oil
2 garlic cloves, finely chopped
3 tablespoons white wine
1 tablespoon lemon juice
100 g (3½ oz) baby rocket (arugula) leaves
1 handful chopped coriander (cilantro) leaves

Trim any veins, membrane or hard white muscle from the scallops. Pat dry with paper towels. Bring a large saucepan of water to the boil, add the pasta and cook until *al dente*. Drain the pasta well and toss with 1 tablespoon oil.

Meanwhile, heat 1 tablespoon oil in a frying pan, add the garlic and cook for a few seconds, or until fragrant. Do not brown. Add the combined wine and lemon juice, and remove from the heat.

Heat a chargrill plate over high heat and brush with a little oil. Season the scallops with salt and pepper and cook for 1 minute each side, or until just cooked. Gently reheat the garlic mixture, add the rocket and stir over medium heat for 1–2 minutes, or until wilted. Toss through the pasta then add the remaining oil and half the coriander, and mix well. Divide the pasta among four serving bowls, arrange the scallops over the top and garnish with the remaining coriander. Serves 4

Note: Add ½ teaspoon chilli flakes just before the wine and lemon juice for an added kick.

338 CHICKEN & MUSHROOM RISOTTO

1.25 litres (44 fl oz/5 cups) vegetable or chicken stock
2 tablespoons olive oil
300 g (10½ oz) chicken breast fillets, cut into 1.5 cm (⅝ inch) strips
250 g (9 oz) small button mushrooms, halved
pinch of nutmeg
2 garlic cloves, crushed
20 g (¾ oz) butter
1 small onion, finely chopped
375 g (13 oz) arborio rice
170 ml (5½ fl oz/⅔ cup) dry white wine
3 tablespoons sour cream
3 tablespoons finely chopped flat-leaf (Italian) parsley
45 g (1½ oz) freshly grated parmesan cheese

Bring the stock to the boil, reduce the heat and keep at a simmer. Heat the oil in a saucepan. Cook the chicken over high heat for 3–4 minutes or until golden. Add the mushrooms and cook for 1–2 minutes more, or until starting to brown. Stir in the nutmeg and garlic, and season. Cook for 30 seconds then remove from the pan and set aside.

Melt the butter in the same pan and cook the onion over low heat for 5–6 minutes. Add the rice, stir to coat, then add the wine. Once the wine is absorbed, reduce the heat and add 125 ml (4 fl oz/½ cup) of the stock. When it is absorbed, add another 125 ml (4 fl oz/½ cup). Continue adding stock for 20–25 minutes, or until all the stock has been used and the rice is creamy. Add the mushrooms and the chicken with the last of the stock. Remove the pan from the heat, and stir in the sour cream, parsley and parmesan. Check the seasoning then cover and leave for 2 minutes before serving. Serves 4

339 SPAGHETTI MARINARA

1 tablespoon olive oil
1 onion, chopped
3 garlic cloves, crushed
2 x 400 g (14 oz) tins crushed tomatoes
2 tablespoons tomato paste (concentrated purée)
170 ml (5½ fl oz/⅔ cup) dry white wine
2 teaspoons soft brown sugar
1 teaspoon finely grated lemon zest
2 tablespoons chopped basil
12 raw prawns (shrimp), peeled and deveined
12 large white scallops, without roe
2 calamari tubes (300 g/10½ oz), cleaned and cut into 1 cm (½ inch) rings
300 g (10½ oz) spaghetti
2 tablespoons finely chopped flat-leaf (Italian) parsley
shaved parmesan cheese, to serve

Heat the oil in a large saucepan, add the onion and cook over medium heat for 5–8 minutes, or until golden. Add the garlic, tomato, tomato paste, wine, sugar, lemon zest, half the basil and 250 ml (9 fl oz/1 cup) water. Cook for 1 hour, stirring occasionally, or until the sauce is reduced and thickened. Season with salt and pepper.

Add the prawns and cook for 1 minute, then add the scallops and cook for 2 minutes. Stir in the calamari and cook for 1 minute more, or until all of the seafood is cooked through and tender. Meanwhile, cook the spaghetti in lightly salted boiling water until *al dente*. Drain and toss with the sauce, parsley and remaining basil. Serve topped with shaved parmesan. Serves 4

340

341

342

340 PORCINI & WALNUT PASTA

20 g ($^3/_4$ oz) dried porcini mushrooms
400 g (14 oz) penne
2 tablespoons olive oil
1 onion, finely chopped
2 garlic cloves, crushed
24 button mushrooms, sliced
3 thyme sprigs
90 g ($3^1/_4$ oz) walnuts
2 tablespoons sour cream
parmesan cheese, grated

Put the porcini in a bowl with just enough boiling water to cover them and leave to soak for half an hour. Meanwhile, cook the penne in a saucepan of boiling water until *al dente.*

Heat the oil in a deep frying pan and fry the onion and garlic together until translucent but not browned. Add the porcini and any soaking liquid, mushrooms and thyme, and keep frying. The mushrooms will give off liquid as they cook so keep cooking until they soak it back up again.

In a separate pan, fry the walnuts without any oil until they start to brown and smell toasted. When they have cooled down a bit, roughly chop and add them to the frying pan. Toss with the drained penne, stir the sour cream through and season well. Serve with the parmesan. Serves 4

342 CHEESE TORTELLINI WITH CAPSICUM & ALMOND SAUCE

1 red capsicum (pepper)
1 yellow capsicum (pepper)
60 g ($2^1/_4$ oz/$^2/_3$ cup) flaked almonds
8 spring onions (scallions)
2 garlic cloves, crushed
500 g (1 lb 2 oz) cheese tortellini
170 ml ($5^1/_2$ fl oz/$^2/_3$ cup) olive oil
30 g (1 oz/$^1/_3$ cup) finely grated pecorino cheese

Cut the capsicums into large pieces, removing the seeds and membrane. Place, skin side up, under a hot grill (broiler) until the skin blackens and blisters. Cool in a plastic bag, then peel away the skin. Spread the almonds on a grill tray and grill for 1–2 minutes, or until lightly toasted.

Roughly chop the white part of the spring onions and slice the green tops, reserving for garnish. Put the capsicum, almonds, garlic and white part of the spring onion in a food processor and pulse until chopped.

Cook the pasta in a large saucepan of boiling water until *al dente.* Drain and return to the pan. Toss the capsicum mixture through the pasta, then add the oil and cheese. Season to taste. Serve garnished with the reserved green spring onion. Serves 4

341 SWEET POTATO GNOCCHI WITH WILTED GREENS

500 g (1 lb 2 oz) russet or sebago potatoes, chopped
250 g (9 oz) orange sweet potato, chopped
1 egg yolk
2 tablespoons milk
$^1/_4$ teaspoon ground nutmeg
155 g ($5^1/_2$ oz/$1^1/_4$ cups) plain (all-purpose) flour
1 tablespoon olive oil
4 bacon slices, thinly sliced
1 small onion, chopped
80 ml ($2^1/_2$ fl oz/$^1/_3$ cup) sweet sherry
500 g (1 lb 2 oz) English spinach
40 g ($1^1/_2$ oz) butter
2 tablespoons toasted pine nuts

Preheat the oven to 220°C (425°F/Gas 7). Bake the potato and sweet potato in a roasting tin for 40–60 minutes, or until soft. Cut in half and leave for 10 minutes. While still warm, press through a sieve into a large bowl. Add the egg yolk and milk, then the nutmeg, 125 g ($4^1/_2$ oz/1 cup) flour and $1^1/_4$ teaspoons salt, and mix well to combine.

Lightly knead the mixture until it is smooth, adding more flour if it gets sticky. Roll into 2 cm ($^3/_4$ inch) cylinders, then cut into 2 cm ($^3/_4$ inch) diagonal lengths. Indent on one side with a fork.

Heat the oil in a large frying pan, add the bacon and onion, and cook over medium heat for 5 minutes, or until the onion is just golden. Add the sherry, stir well and cook for 2 minutes, or until reduced slightly. Add the spinach and cook, stirring, for 2 minutes, or until wilted, but still bright green. Stir in the butter and season. Keep warm.

Cook the gnocchi in boiling water in batches for 2–3 minutes, or until they rise to the surface. Drain and toss through the sauce. Scatter the pine nuts over the top. Serves 4

343

344

345

343 HOKKIEN NOODLES WITH ASIAN GREENS & GLAZED TOFU

300 g (10½ oz) firm tofu, cut into 1 cm (½ inch) slices
3 tablespoons kecap manis
1 tablespoon mushroom soy sauce
1 tablespoon vegetarian oyster sauce
1 teaspoon sesame oil
1 tablespoon peanut oil
2 garlic cloves, crushed
1 tablespoon grated fresh ginger
1 onion, cut into wedges
450 g (1 lb/1 bunch) choy sum, roughly chopped
500 g (1 lb 2 oz/1 bunch) baby bok choy (pak choy),
   roughly chopped
450 g (1 lb) fresh hokkien (egg) noodles, separated
2 tablespoons peanut oil, extra

Place the tofu in a shallow, non-metallic dish. Mix together the kecap manis, soy and oyster sauces and pour over the tofu. Leave to marinate for about 15 minutes, then drain and reserve the marinade.

Heat the oils in a wok over medium heat, add the garlic, ginger and onion and stir-fry until the onion is soft. Remove. Add the green vegetables to the wok and stir-fry until just wilted. Remove. Add the separated noodles and the reserved marinade and stir-fry until heated through. Remove from the wok and divide among four plates.

Fry the tofu in the extra oil until it is browned on both sides. Serve the noodles topped with the tofu, green vegetables and onion mixture. Serves 4

345 UDON NOODLE STIR-FRY WITH MISO DRESSING

1 tablespoon white miso
1 tablespoon Japanese soy sauce
2 tablespoons sake
½ teaspoon sugar
400 g (14 oz) fresh udon noodles
1 tablespoon peanut oil
5 spring onions (scallions), cut into 5 cm (2 inch) lengths
1 red capsicum (pepper), thinly sliced
100 g (3½ oz) fresh shiitake mushrooms, sliced
150 g (5½ oz) snow peas (mangetout), sliced lengthways
   into strips

Combine the miso with the soy sauce to form a smooth paste. Add the sake and sugar and mix well. Cook the udon noodles in a large saucepan of boiling salted water for 1–2 minutes, or until tender and plump. Drain and rinse under cold water.

Heat the oil in a wok over high heat and swirl to coat. Add the spring onion and capsicum and toss frequently for 1–2 minutes, or until softened slightly. Add the mushrooms and snow peas and stir-fry for 2–3 minutes, or until tender. Add the noodles and miso mixture to the wok and toss until well combined. Serve immediately. Serves 4

344 SINGAPORE NOODLES

375 g (13 oz) thin fresh egg noodles
10 g (¼ oz) dried Chinese mushrooms
2½ teaspoons sugar
1½ tablespoons soy sauce
2 tablespoons Chinese rice wine
1½ tablespoons Indian madras curry powder
150 ml (5 fl oz) coconut milk
125 ml (4 fl oz/½ cup) chicken stock
2 eggs
1 tablespoon sesame oil
3 tablespoons vegetable oil
2 garlic cloves, finely chopped
1 tablespoon finely chopped fresh ginger
2 small red chillies, seeded and finely chopped
3 spring onions (scallions), sliced
300 g (10½ oz) small raw prawns (shrimp), peeled, deveined
   and halved
150 g (5½ oz) Chinese roast pork, thinly sliced
120 g (4¼ oz) frozen peas
coriander (cilantro) leaves, to garnish

Cook the noodles in boiling salted water for 1 minute. Drain and rinse in cold water. Soak the mushrooms in a bowl with 125 ml (4 fl oz/ ½ cup) hot water for 10 minutes. Drain and reserve the liquid, then discard the hard stalks and finely slice the caps. Combine the reserved liquid with the sugar, soy sauce, rice wine, curry powder, coconut milk and stock. Lightly beat the eggs and sesame oil together.

Heat a wok and add 2 tablespoons of the oil. Cook the garlic, ginger, chilli and mushrooms for 30 seconds. Add the spring onion, prawns, roast pork, peas and noodles. Stir in the mushroom liquid mixture. Add the egg mixture in a thin stream and toss until warmed through. Serve in deep bowls, garnished with coriander leaves. Serves 4

346

347

348

349

346 LEMON & ZUCCHINI RISOTTO

1.25 litres (44 fl oz/5 cups) hot vegetable or chicken stock
2 tablespoons olive oil
1 onion, finely chopped
360 g (12³/₄ oz/1²/₃ cups) arborio rice
80 ml (2¹/₂ fl oz/¹/₃ cup) dry sherry
3 teaspoons grated lemon zest
2 tablespoons lemon juice
350 g (12 oz) zucchini (courgettes), diced
2 tablespoons chopped flat-leaf (Italian) parsley
50 g (1³/₄ oz/¹/₂ cup) freshly grated parmesan cheese
lemon zest, to garnish

Place the stock in a large saucepan, bring to the boil, then reduce the heat, cover, and keep at a low simmer. Heat the oil in a large saucepan, add the onion and cook over medium heat for 5 minutes, or until softened. Reduce the heat, stir in the rice and cook for 1 minute, stirring constantly.

Add 125 ml (4 fl oz/¹/₂ cup) hot stock, stirring until all the stock is absorbed. Continue adding the stock, 125 ml (4 fl oz/¹/₂ cup) at a time, stirring constantly, for 20 minutes, or until all the liquid is absorbed. If the risotto gets too dry add a little extra stock or water. Stir in the sherry, lemon zest, lemon juice and zucchini. Cook over low heat for a further 5 minutes, or until the risotto is tender, with a slight bite to the inside of the grain. Season with salt and freshly ground black pepper, and stir in the parsley and half the parmesan. Garnish with the lemon zest and remaining parmesan. Serves 4

347 ASPARAGUS & PISTACHIO RISOTTO

1 litre (35 fl oz/4 cups) vegetable stock
250 ml (9 fl oz/1 cup) white wine
80 ml (2¹/₂ fl oz/¹/₃ cup) extra virgin olive oil
1 red onion, finely chopped
440 g (15¹/₂ oz/2 cups) arborio rice
310 g (11 oz) asparagus spears, trimmed and cut into 3 cm (1¹/₄ inch) pieces
125 ml (4 fl oz/¹/₂ cup) cream
100 g (3¹/₂ oz/1 cup) grated parmesan cheese
40 g (1¹/₂ oz/¹/₂ cup) shelled pistachio nuts, toasted and roughly chopped

Heat the stock and wine in a large saucepan, bring to the boil, then reduce the heat, cover and keep at a low simmer. Heat the oil in another saucepan. Add the onion and cook over medium heat for 3 minutes, or until soft. Add the rice and stir for 1 minute, or until the rice is translucent.

Add 125 ml (4 fl oz/¹/₂ cup) hot stock, stirring constantly over medium heat until the liquid is absorbed. Continue adding stock, 125 ml (4 fl oz/ ¹/₂ cup) at a time, stirring constantly for 20–25 minutes, or until all the stock is absorbed and the rice is tender and creamy. Add the asparagus pieces during the final 5 minutes of cooking. Remove from the heat. Stand for 2 minutes, stir in the cream and parmesan and season to taste with salt and black pepper. Serve sprinkled with pistachios. Serves 4–6

348 CHINESE FRIED RICE

3 tablespoons oil
2 eggs, lightly beaten
1 carrot, thinly sliced
1 red capsicum (pepper), diced
6 fresh baby corn, sliced
2 garlic cloves, crushed
100 g (3¹/₂ oz) lap cheong sausages, sliced on the diagonal
80 g (2³/₄ oz/¹/₂ cup) frozen peas
1.5 kg (3 lb 5 oz) frozen cooked long-grain rice, thawed (see Note)
3 spring onions (scallions), thinly sliced
3¹/₂ tablespoons soy sauce
2 teaspoons sugar
2 teaspoons sesame oil

Heat a wok or large frying pan over high heat, add 1 tablespoon of the oil and swirl to coat. Add the egg and swirl to distribute evenly. Cook for 1–2 minutes, or until golden, then turn and cook the other side. Remove, leave until cool enough to handle, then roll up and thinly slice.

Heat the remaining oil over high heat, add the carrot and stir-fry for 1 minute, then add the capsicum and cook for another minute. Finally, add the corn, garlic, sausage and peas, and stir-fry for 1 minute. Add the rice, spring onion and omelette, and mix, separating the rice grains. Stir over medium heat for 3–4 minutes, or until the rice is warmed through. Stir in the soy sauce, sugar and sesame oil, and toss. Serve hot. Serves 4–6

Note: If you are not using frozen rice, you will need to cook 600 g (1 lb 5 oz/3 cups) rice, then cool.

349 MACARONI & CHEESE WITH PANCETTA

390 g (13³/₄ oz/2¹/₂ cups) macaroni
75 g (2³/₄ oz) pancetta, diced
500 ml (17 fl oz/2 cups) cream
125 g (4¹/₂ oz/1 cup) grated cheddar cheese
260 g (9¹/₄ oz/2 cups) grated gruyère cheese
100 g (3¹/₂ oz/1 cup) grated parmesan cheese
1 garlic clove, crushed
2 teaspoons dijon mustard
¹/₂ teaspoon paprika
2 tablespoons snipped chives
chives, extra, to garnish

Bring a large saucepan of lightly salted water to the boil. Add the macaroni and cook until al dente. Drain, cover and keep warm.

Meanwhile, place the pancetta in a large saucepan and cook over high heat, stirring, for 4 minutes, or until well browned and slightly crisp. Drain on paper towels. Reduce the heat to medium, stir in the cream and simmer. Add the cheeses, garlic, mustard and paprika, and stir for 5 minutes, or until the cheeses have melted and the sauce has thickened. Season. Add the macaroni and pancetta and stir for 1 minute, or until heated through. Stir in the chives, garnish with the extra chives and serve. Serves 4

350

351

352

350 RICE & RED LENTIL PILAU

GARAM MASALA
1 tablespoon coriander seeds
1 tablespoon cardamom pods
1 tablespoon cumin seeds
1 teaspoon whole black peppercorns
1 teaspoon whole cloves
1 small cinnamon stick, crushed

3 tablespoons oil
1 onion, chopped
3 garlic cloves, chopped
200 g (7 oz/1 cup) basmati rice
250 g (9 oz/1 cup) red lentils
750 ml (26 fl oz/3 cups) hot vegetable stock
spring onions (scallions), sliced on the diagonal, to garnish

To make the garam masala, place all the spices in a dry frying pan and shake over medium heat for 1 minute, or until fragrant. Blend in a spice grinder or blender to a fine powder. Heat the oil in a saucepan. Add the onion, garlic and 3 teaspoons garam masala. Cook over medium heat for 3 minutes, or until the onion is soft.

Stir in the rice and lentils and cook for 2 minutes. Add the stock and stir well. Slowly bring to the boil, then reduce the heat and simmer, covered, for 15–20 minutes, or until the rice is cooked and all the stock has been absorbed. Gently fluff the rice with a fork. Garnish with spring onion. Serves 4–6

352 JAMBALAYA

1 tablespoon olive oil
2 chicken breast fillets, cut into 1.5 x 6 cm ($5/8$ x $2^1/2$ inch) strips
1 red onion, sliced
3 bacon slices, chopped
2 chorizo sausages, cut into 1 cm ($1/2$ inch) diagonal slices
1 small red capsicum (pepper) and small green capsicum (pepper), sliced
2 garlic cloves, finely chopped
1–2 teaspoons seeded, finely chopped fresh jalapeño chilli
1 teaspoon smoked paprika
3 teaspoons Cajun spice mix
400 g (14 oz/2 cups) long-grain rice, washed
250 ml (9 fl oz/1 cup) beer
4 vine-ripened tomatoes, peeled and quartered
750 ml (26 fl oz/3 cups) chicken stock
$1/2$ teaspoon saffron threads, soaked in 1 tablespoon warm water
16 raw prawns (shrimp), peeled, deveined, tails intact

Heat the oil in a large saucepan. Cook the chicken in batches over medium heat for 4 minutes, or until lightly browned. Remove. Cook the onion for 3 minutes, then add the bacon and sausage, and cook for 4–5 minutes, or until browned. Add the capsicum and cook for 2 minutes, then add the garlic, chilli, paprika and Cajun spice mix, and cook for a further 2 minutes.

Add the rice and stir to coat. Add the beer and stir for 30 seconds. Stir in the tomato, stock, saffron and soaking liquid. Bring to the boil, reduce the heat and simmer, covered, for 10–12 minutes. Add the prawns and chicken, and cook, covered, for 3–5 minutes, or until the rice is creamy and tender. Serves 6

351 VEGETARIAN PAELLA

200 g (7 oz/1 cup) dried haricot beans
$1/4$ teaspoon saffron threads
2 tablespoons olive oil
1 onion, diced
1 red capsicum (pepper), cut into 1 x 4 cm ($1/2$ x $1^1/2$ inch) strips
5 garlic cloves, crushed
275 g ($9^3/4$ oz/$1^1/4$ cups) paella or arborio rice
1 tablespoon sweet paprika
$1/2$ teaspoon mixed spice
750 ml (26 fl oz/3 cups) vegetable stock
400 g (14 oz) tin chopped tomatoes
$1^1/2$ tablespoons tomato paste (concentrated purée)
150 g ($5^1/2$ oz) fresh or frozen soy beans (see Note)
100 g ($3^1/2$ oz) silverbeet (Swiss chard) leaves (no stems), shredded
400 g (14 oz) tin artichoke hearts, drained and quartered
4 tablespoons chopped coriander (cilantro) leaves

Put the haricot beans in a bowl, cover with cold water and soak overnight. Drain and rinse well. Place the saffron threads in a small frying pan over medium–low heat. Dry-fry, shaking the pan, for 1 minute, or until darkened. Remove from the heat and, when cool, crumble into a small bowl. Pour in 125 ml (4 fl oz/$1/2$ cup) warm water and allow to steep.

Heat the oil in a large paella or frying pan. Add the onion and capsicum and cook over medium–high heat for 4–5 minutes, or until the onion is soft. Stir in the garlic and cook for 1 minute. Reduce the heat and add the beans, rice, paprika, mixed spice and $1/2$ teaspoon salt. Stir to coat. Add the saffron water, stock, tomato and tomato paste and bring to the boil. Cover, reduce the heat and simmer for 20 minutes.

Stir in the soy beans, silverbeet and artichoke hearts and cook, covered, for 8 minutes, or until all the liquid is absorbed and the rice and beans are tender. Turn off the heat and leave for 5 minutes. Stir in the coriander just before serving. Serves 6

Note: Fresh or frozen soy beans are available from Asian grocery stores.

353

354

355

353 JAPANESE PORK & NOODLE STIR-FRY

80 ml (2¹/₂ fl oz/¹/₃ cup) soy sauce
3 tablespoons mirin
2 teaspoons grated fresh ginger
2 garlic cloves, crushed
1¹/₂ tablespoons soft brown sugar
350 g (12 oz) pork fillet, thinly sliced
500 g (1 lb 2 oz) hokkien (egg) noodles
2 tablespoons peanut oil
1 onion, cut into thin wedges
1 red capsicum (pepper), cut into thin strips
2 carrots, finely sliced on the diagonal
4 spring onions (scallions), finely sliced on the diagonal
200 g (7 oz) fresh shiitake mushrooms, sliced

Combine the soy sauce, mirin, ginger, garlic and sugar in a large non-metallic bowl, add the pork and coat. Cover with plastic wrap and refrigerate for 10 minutes. Meanwhile, place the noodles in a bowl of hot water for 5 minutes to separate and soften.

Heat a large wok over high heat, add 1 tablespoon oil and swirl to coat. Drain the pork, reserving the marinade, and stir-fry in batches for 3 minutes, or until browned. Remove and keep warm.

Reheat the wok over high heat, add the remaining oil and swirl to coat. Add the onion, capsicum and carrot, and stir-fry for 2–3 minutes, or until just tender, then add the spring onion and shiitake mushrooms. Cook for another 2 minutes, then return the pork to the wok. Drain the noodles and add to the wok with the reserved marinade. Toss to combine and cook for another 1 minute, then serve. Serves 4

355 SEARED SALMON WITH SESAME & CUCUMBER NOODLES

250 g (9 oz) buckwheat soba noodles
1¹/₂ tablespoons sesame oil
2 tablespoons kecap manis
1 tablespoon Chinese black vinegar
2 Lebanese (short) cucumbers, julienned
6 spring onions (scallions), trimmed and sliced on the diagonal into 4 cm (1¹/₂ inch) lengths
2 tablespoons black sesame seeds
600 g (1 lb 5 oz) salmon fillet pieces, skinned and boned

Cook the noodles in a large saucepan of boiling water until tender — this should take about 5 minutes. Drain well. Place in a large bowl and mix in 2 teaspoons of the sesame oil, then set aside to cool. Combine the kecap manis, vinegar and the remaining sesame oil, then toss 1 tablespoon of the mixture through the noodles. Cover the noodles and refrigerate for about 2 hours. About 20 minutes before serving, gently mix the noodles with the cucumber, spring onion and black sesame seeds.

Heat a large frying pan over medium–high heat. Brush the salmon pieces lightly with oil and season with salt and freshly ground black pepper. Cook for 1–2 minutes on each side, or until cooked to your liking. Remove from the heat and allow to cool until cool enough to handle. Flake the fish into large pieces and gently incorporate it into the noodles, along with the rest of the dressing — be careful not to over-handle or the salmon will flake into small pieces. Serve immediately. Serves 4

354 PHAD THAI

250 g (9 oz) dried flat rice stick noodles
1 tablespoon tamarind purée
1 small red chilli, chopped
2 garlic cloves, chopped
2 spring onions (scallions), sliced
1¹/₂ tablespoons soft brown sugar
2 tablespoons fish sauce
2 tablespoons lime juice
2 tablespoons oil
2 eggs, beaten
150 g (5¹/₂ oz) pork fillet, thinly sliced
8 large raw prawns (shrimp), peeled and deveined, with tails intact
100 g (3¹/₂ oz) fried tofu puffs, julienned
90 g (3¹/₄ oz/1 cup) bean sprouts
3 tablespoons chopped roasted peanuts
3 tablespoons coriander (cilantro) leaves
1 lime, cut into wedges

Place the noodles in a heatproof bowl, cover with warm water and soak for 15–20 minutes, or until the noodles are *al dente*. Drain well.

Combine the tamarind purée with 1 tablespoon water. Place the chilli, garlic and spring onion in a spice grinder (or use a mortar and pestle) and grind to a smooth paste. Transfer the mixture to a bowl and stir in the tamarind mixture along with the sugar, fish sauce and lime juice, stirring until the ingredients are combined.

Heat a wok until very hot, add 1 tablespoon of the oil and swirl to coat the side. Add the egg, swirl to coat and cook for 1–2 minutes, or until set. Remove the egg, roll it up and cut into thin slices.

Heat the remaining oil in the wok, stir in the chilli mixture and stir-fry for 30 seconds. Add the pork and stir-fry for 2 minutes, or until tender. Add the prawns and stir-fry for a further minute, or until pink and curled.

Stir in the noodles, egg, tofu puffs and the bean sprouts and gently toss together until heated through. Serve immediately topped with the peanuts, coriander and lime wedges. Serves 4–6

356

357

358

359

356 TAGLIATELLE WITH TUNA, CAPERS & ROCKET

350 g (12 oz) fresh tagliatelle
3 garlic cloves, crushed
1 teaspoon finely grated lemon zest
80 ml (2½ fl oz/⅓ cup) extra virgin olive oil
500 g (1 lb 2 oz) tuna, cut into 1.5 cm (⅝ inch) cubes
200 g (7 oz) rocket (arugula) leaves, roughly chopped
4 tablespoons baby capers in salt, rinsed and squeezed dry
3 tablespoons lemon juice
2 tablespoons finely chopped flat-leaf (Italian) parsley

Cook the pasta in a saucepan of boiling salted water until *al dente*. Meanwhile, put the garlic, lemon zest and 1 tablespoon of the oil in a bowl with the tuna and gently mix. Season.

Heat a frying pan over high heat and sear the tuna for 30 seconds on each side. Add the rocket and capers and gently stir for 1 minute, or until the rocket has just wilted. Pour in the lemon juice and then remove from the heat. Add the remaining oil to the hot pasta along with the tuna mixture and parsley. Season to taste and gently toss. Serve immediately. Serves 4

357 GENOVESE PESTO SAUCE

PESTO
2 garlic cloves
50 g (1¾ oz/⅓ cup) pine nuts
125 g (4½ oz/1 bunch) basil, stems removed
150–185 ml (5–6 fl oz) extra virgin olive oil
50 g (1¾ oz/½ cup) finely grated parmesan cheese, plus extra, to serve

500 g (1 lb 2 oz) trenette or spaghetti (see Note)
175 g (6 oz) green beans, trimmed
175 g (6 oz) small potatoes, very thinly sliced

Put the garlic and pine nuts in a food processor and process until finely ground (or use a mortar and pestle to do this). Add the basil and then drizzle in the olive oil a little at a time while pounding or processing. When you have a thick purée, stop adding the oil. Season and mix in the parmesan.

Bring a large saucepan of salted water to the boil. Add the pasta, green beans and potatoes, stirring well to prevent the pasta from sticking together. Cook until the pasta is *al dente* (the vegetables should be cooked by this time), then drain, reserving a little of the water.

Return the pasta and vegetables to the saucepan, add the pesto, and mix well. If necessary, add some of the reserved water to loosen the pasta. Season and serve immediately with the extra parmesan. Serves 4

Note: Traditionally, pesto sauce is served with trenette pasta, green beans and potatoes, but you can leave out the vegetables if you prefer or use spaghetti.

358 FETTUCINE WITH SPINACH & ROASTED TOMATOES

6 roma (plum) tomatoes
40 g (1½ oz) butter
2 garlic cloves, crushed
1 onion, chopped
500 g (1 lb 2 oz) English spinach, trimmed
250 ml (9 fl oz/1 cup) vegetable stock
125 ml (4 fl oz/½ cup) thick (double/heavy) cream
500 g (1 lb 2 oz) fresh spinach fettucine
50 g (1¾ oz) shaved parmesan cheese

Preheat the oven to 220°C (425°F/Gas 7). Cut the tomatoes in half lengthways, then cut each half into three wedges. Place the wedges on a lightly greased baking tray and bake for 30–35 minutes, or until softened and slightly golden. Meanwhile, heat the butter in a large frying pan. Add the garlic and onion and cook over medium heat for 5 minutes, or until the onion is soft. Add the spinach, stock and cream, increase the heat to high and bring to the boil. Simmer rapidly for 5 minutes.

While the spinach mixture is cooking, cook the pasta in a large saucepan of boiling water until *al dente*. Drain and return to the pan. Remove the spinach from the heat and season well. Cool slightly, then process in a food processor until smooth. Toss through the pasta until well coated. Divide among serving bowls, top with the roasted tomatoes and parmesan. Serves 4–6

359 PASTA PRIMAVERA

120 g (4¼ oz) broad beans, fresh or frozen
150 g (5½ oz) asparagus, cut into short lengths
350 g (12 oz) fresh tagliatelle
100 g (3½ oz) green beans, cut into short lengths
120 g (4¼ oz/¾ cup) peas, fresh or frozen
30 g (1 oz) butter
1 small fennel bulb, thinly sliced
375 ml (13 fl oz/1½ cups) thick (double/heavy) cream
2 tablespoons grated parmesan cheese, plus extra, to serve

Bring a large saucepan of water to the boil. Add 1 teaspoon of salt, the broad beans and asparagus and simmer for 3 minutes. Remove the vegetables with a slotted spoon and set them aside. Add the tagliatelle to the saucepan and, when it has softened, stir in the beans and the peas (if you're using frozen peas, add them a few minutes later). Cook for about 4 minutes, or until the pasta is *al dente*.

Meanwhile, heat the butter in a large frying pan. Add the fennel and cook over moderately low heat without colouring for 5 minutes. Add the cream, season with salt and pepper and cook at a low simmer.

Peel the skins from the broad beans. Drain the pasta, green beans and peas and add them to the frying pan. Add 2 tablespoons of parmesan and the broad beans and asparagus. Toss lightly to coat. Serve immediately with extra parmesan. Serves 4

360 STIR-FRIED MIXED VEGETABLES

2 tablespoons oil
4 spring onions (scallions), cut into 3 cm (1¼ inch) lengths
3 garlic cloves, crushed
1 red chilli, seeded and sliced
75 g (2¾ oz) button mushrooms, quartered
100 g (3½ oz) Chinese cabbage, roughly chopped
2 tablespoons soy sauce
1 teaspoon fish sauce
1 tablespoon oyster sauce
3 tablespoons vegetable stock
½ teaspoon grated palm sugar (jaggery)
150 g (5½ oz) snow peas (mangetout)
150 g (5½ oz) cauliflower, cut into small florets
150 g (5½ oz) broccoli, cut into small florets
coriander (cilantro) leaves, chopped, to garnish

Heat a wok until very hot, add the oil and swirl to coat. Add the spring onion, garlic and chilli. Stir-fry for 20 seconds. Add the mushrooms and cabbage and stir-fry for 1 minute. Stir in the sauces, stock, palm sugar, snow peas, cauliflower and broccoli. Cook for 2 minutes, or until tender. Garnish with the coriander leaves. Serves 6

362 BALTI EGGPLANT & TOFU STIR-FRY

2 tablespoons oil
1 onion, finely chopped
3 tablespoons balti curry paste
300 g (10½ oz) slender eggplant (aubergine), cut diagonally into 1 cm (½ inch) slices
300 g (10½ oz) firm tofu, cut into 1.5 cm (⅝ inch) cubes
3 ripe tomatoes, cut into wedges
3 tablespoons vegetable stock
75 g (2¾ oz) baby English spinach leaves
50 g (1¾ oz/⅓ cup) toasted cashews
saffron rice, to serve

Heat a wok or deep frying pan until very hot. Add the oil and swirl to coat. Add the onion and stir-fry over high heat for 3–4 minutes, or until softened and golden. Stir in the balti curry paste and cook for 1 minute. Add the eggplant and cook for 5 minutes. Stir in the tofu, gently tossing for 3–4 minutes, or until golden.

Add the tomato and stock and cook for 3 minutes, or until the tomato is soft. Stir in the spinach and cook for 1–2 minutes, or until wilted. Season. Sprinkle the cashews over the top and serve with saffron rice. Serves 4

361 TOFU WITH CHILLI RELISH & CASHEWS

CHILLI RELISH
80 ml (2½ fl oz/⅓ cup) peanut oil
12 red Asian shallots, chopped
8 garlic cloves, chopped
8 long red chillies, chopped
2 red capsicums (peppers), chopped
1 tablespoon tamarind concentrate
1 tablespoon soy sauce
100 g (3½ oz) palm sugar (jaggery), grated

2 tablespoons kecap manis
1 tablespoon peanut oil
6 spring onions (scallions), cut into 3 cm (1¼ inch) lengths
750 g (1 lb 10 oz) silken firm tofu, cut into 3 cm (1¼ inch) cubes
1 handful Thai basil
100 g (3½ oz/⅔ cup) roasted salted cashews

To make the relish, heat half the oil in a frying pan. Add the Asian shallots and garlic and cook over medium heat for 2 minutes. Transfer to a food processor, add the chilli and capsicum and process until smooth. Heat the remaining oil in the pan, add the shallot mixture and cook over medium heat for 2 minutes. Stir in the tamarind, soy sauce and sugar and cook for 20 minutes.

Place 2–3 tablespoons of the relish with the kecap manis in a bowl and mix. Heat the oil in a wok over high heat and swirl to coat. Add the spring onion, cook for 30 seconds, then remove. Add the tofu and stir-fry for 1 minute, then add the relish and kecap manis mixture. Cook for about 3 minutes, or until the tofu is coated and heated through. Return the spring onion to the wok, add the basil and cashews and cook until the basil has wilted. Serves 4

363

364

365

366

363 PUMPKIN & FETA PIE

700 g (1 lb 9 oz) butternut pumpkin (squash), cut into 2 cm
(3/4 inch) pieces
4 garlic cloves, unpeeled
100 ml (3 1/2 fl oz) olive oil
2 small red onions, halved and sliced
1 tablespoon balsamic vinegar
1 tablespoon soft brown sugar
100 g (3 1/2 oz) good-quality feta cheese, broken into small pieces
1 tablespoon chopped rosemary
1 large sheet ready-rolled shortcrust pastry

Preheat the oven to 200°C (400°F/Gas 6). Place the pumpkin and garlic cloves on a baking tray, drizzle with 2 tablespoons olive oil and bake for 25–30 minutes, or until the pumpkin is tender. Transfer the pumpkin to a large bowl and the garlic to a plate. Leave the pumpkin to cool.

Meanwhile, heat 2 tablespoons oil in a pan, add the onion and cook over medium heat, stirring occasionally, for 10 minutes. Add the vinegar and sugar and cook for 15 minutes, or until the onion is caramelised. Remove from the heat and add to the pumpkin. Cool completely. Add the feta and rosemary to the pumpkin. Squeeze out the garlic flesh and mix it through the vegetables. Season with salt and freshly ground black pepper.

Roll out the pastry between two sheets of baking paper to a 35 cm (14 inch) circle. Remove the top sheet of paper and place the bottom paper with the pastry on a tray. Arrange the pumpkin and feta mixture on top, leaving a 4 cm (1 1/2 inch) border. Fold over the edges, pleating as you fold, and bake for 30 minutes, or until crisp and golden. Serves 6

364 VEGETARIAN GRILLED NACHOS

2 x 300 g (10 1/2 oz) packets corn chips
4 tomatoes, chopped
1 red onion, finely chopped
3 jalapeño chillies, thinly sliced
2 tablespoons lime juice
4 tablespoons chopped coriander (cilantro) leaves
220 g (7 3/4 oz/1 1/2 cups) crumbled feta cheese

Turn on the grill (broiler). Arrange the corn chips on four ovenproof plates. Scatter the tomato, onion and chilli on top of the corn chips, then drizzle with the lime juice and season with some salt. Scatter the coriander and feta cheese over the top, making sure the corn chips are well covered.

Grill the nachos until they start to brown around the edges and the cheese starts to melt. Serve hot but be careful of the plates — they will be very hot too. Serves 4

365 SALAD PIZZA

4 ready-made individual thick pizza bases
2 tablespoons tomato paste (concentrated purée)
2 teaspoons chopped oregano
60 g (2 1/4 oz) feta cheese, crumbled
100 g (3 1/2 oz/2/3 cup) grated mozzarella cheese
60 g (2 1/4 oz) parmesan cheese, grated
100 g (3 1/2 oz) baby rocket (arugula) leaves, trimmed
3 tablespoons flat-leaf (Italian) parsley
1/4 small red onion, thinly sliced
3 tablespoons olive oil
1 tablespoon lemon juice
1 teaspoon dijon mustard
50 g (1 3/4 oz) parmesan cheese, extra, shaved

Preheat the oven to 200°C (400°F/Gas 6). Place the pizza bases on baking trays. Spread with tomato paste and sprinkle with oregano, feta and the grated cheeses. Bake for 12 minutes, or until bubbling.

Meanwhile, combine the rocket, parsley and onion in a bowl. Whisk together the oil, lemon juice and mustard, and toss through the salad. Top the pizzas with salad and sprinkle with shaved parmesan. Season with ground pepper and serve immediately. Serves 4

366 ARTICHOKE, OLIVE & GOAT'S CHEESE PIZZA

25 cm (10 inch) purchased pizza base
80 ml (2 1/2 fl oz/1/3 cup) Italian tomato pasta sauce
150 g (5 1/2 oz) marinated artichokes, quartered
70 g (2 1/2 oz) pitted kalamata olives
1 garlic clove, thinly sliced
50 g (1 3/4 oz) goat's cheese, crumbled
good-quality olive oil, to drizzle
2 tablespoons chopped oregano

Preheat the oven to 220°C (425°F/Gas 7). Place the pizza base on a baking tray, then spread with the tomato pasta sauce. Evenly scatter the artichoke pieces, olives and the garlic over the pasta sauce, then top with the crumbled goat's cheese.

Lightly drizzle the surface of the pizza with olive oil and bake for 20 minutes, or until golden. Sprinkle with oregano and season with salt and freshly ground black pepper. Cut into wedges and serve. Serves 4

367

368

369

367 VEGETABLE SKEWERS WITH BASIL COUSCOUS

5 thin zucchini (courgettes), cut into 2 cm ($^3/_4$ inch) cubes
5 slender eggplants (aubergines), cut into 2 cm ($^3/_4$ inch) cubes
12 button mushrooms, halved
2 red capsicums (peppers), cut into 1.5 cm ($^5/_8$ inch) cubes
250 g (9 oz) kefalotyri cheese, cut into 2 cm ($^3/_4$ inch) pieces
80 ml ($2^1/_2$ fl oz/$^1/_3$ cup) lemon juice
2 garlic cloves, finely chopped
5 tablespoons finely chopped basil
145 ml ($4^3/_4$ fl oz) extra virgin olive oil
185 g ($6^1/_2$ oz/1 cup) couscous
1 teaspoon grated lemon zest

Soak 12 wooden skewers in water for 30 minutes. Thread alternate pieces of vegetables and kefalotyri, starting and finishing with a piece of capsicum and using two pieces of kefalotyri per skewer. Place in a non-metallic dish which will hold them in one layer. Combine the lemon juice, garlic, 4 tablespoons basil and 125 ml (4 fl oz/$^1/_2$ cup) oil. Season. Pour two thirds of the marinade over the skewers, reserving the remainder. Turn to coat, cover and marinate for at least 5 minutes.

Place the couscous, lemon zest and 375 ml (13 fl oz/$1^1/_2$ cups) boiling water in a large heatproof bowl. Stand for 5 minutes, or until all the water has been absorbed. Add the remaining oil and basil, then fluff gently with a fork to separate the grains. Cover. Heat a chargrill pan or barbecue plate to medium–high. Cook the skewers, brushing often with the leftover marinade, for 4–5 minutes on each side, or until the vegetables are cooked and the cheese browns. Divide the couscous and skewers among serving plates. Season, then drizzle with the reserved marinade to taste. Serve with lemon wedges. Serves 4

369 TOFU KEBABS WITH MISO PESTO

1 large red capsicum (pepper), cubed
12 button mushrooms, halved
6 baby onions, quartered
3 zucchini (courgettes), cut into chunks
450 g (1 lb) firm tofu, cubed
125 ml (4 fl oz/$^1/_2$ cup) light olive oil
3 tablespoons light soy sauce
2 garlic cloves, crushed
2 teaspoons grated fresh ginger

MISO PESTO
90 g ($3^1/_4$ oz/$^1/_2$ cup) unsalted roasted peanuts
2 large handfuls coriander (cilantro) leaves
2 tablespoons white miso paste
2 garlic cloves
100 ml ($3^1/_2$ fl oz) olive oil

If using wooden skewers, soak them in water for 30 minutes to prevent scorching. Thread the vegetables and tofu alternately onto 12 skewers, then place in a large non-metallic dish. Mix together the olive oil, soy sauce, garlic and ginger, then pour half over the kebabs. Cover and leave to marinate for 1 hour.

To make the miso pesto, finely chop the peanuts, coriander leaves, miso paste and garlic in a food processor. Slowly add the olive oil while the machine is still running and blend to a smooth paste. Cook the kebabs on a hot, lightly oiled barbecue flat plate or grill, turning and brushing with the remaining marinade, for 4–6 minutes, or until the edges are slightly brown. Serve with the miso pesto. Serves 4

368 EGGPLANT, TOMATO & GOAT'S CHEESE STACKS

125 ml (4 fl oz/$^1/_2$ cup) olive oil
2 large garlic cloves, crushed
2 small eggplants (aubergines)
2 ripe tomatoes
150 g ($5^1/_2$ oz) goat's cheese
8 basil leaves
small rocket (arugula) leaves, to garnish

DRESSING
285 g (10 oz) jar sun-dried tomatoes, drained, reserving 1 tablespoon oil
1 garlic clove, crushed
2 tablespoons white wine vinegar
2 tablespoons whole-egg mayonnaise

Place the oil and garlic in a bowl and mix together. Cut each eggplant into six 1 cm ($^1/_2$ inch) slices, then cut each tomato into four 1 cm ($^1/_2$ inch) slices. Using a sharp knife dipped in hot water, cut the cheese into eight 1 cm ($^1/_2$ inch) slices.

Brush both sides of the eggplant with half of the oil mixture. Heat a frying pan and cook the eggplant in batches over high heat for 3–4 minutes each side, or until golden. Remove and keep warm. Brush both sides of the tomato with the remaining oil mixture and cook for 1 minute each side, or until sealed and warmed through.

To make the dressing, blend the sun-dried tomatoes, reserved oil and the garlic in a food processor until smooth. Add the vinegar and process until combined. Transfer to a bowl and stir in the mayonnaise. Season.

To assemble, place an eggplant slice on each plate. Top with a slice of tomato, then a basil leaf and a slice of cheese. Repeat with the remaining ingredients to give two layers, then finish with a third piece of eggplant. Add a dollop of dressing and arrange the rocket around each stack. Serve immediately. Serves 4

370

371

372

373

370 TOMATO TARTE TATIN

12 roma (plum) tomatoes
80 ml (2$\frac{1}{2}$ fl oz/$\frac{1}{3}$ cup) olive oil
3 red onions, finely sliced
2 garlic cloves, finely sliced
1 tablespoon balsamic vinegar
1 teaspoon soft brown sugar
3 tablespoons finely shredded basil
60 g (2$\frac{1}{4}$ oz) goat's cheese, crumbled
1 sheet butter puff pastry

Preheat the oven to 150°C (300°F/Gas 2). Cut a cross in the base of the tomatoes. Cover with boiling water for 30 seconds, then plunge into cold water. Peel the skin away, then cut the tomatoes in half lengthways, and season well. Place the tomatoes, cut side up, on a rack on a baking tray. Cook in the oven for 3 hours.

Heat 2 tablespoons of oil in a heavy-based saucepan, add onions and cook over very low heat, stirring often, for 1 hour or until caramelised. When the tomatoes are ready, remove from the oven, and increase the oven temperature to 200°C (400°F/Gas 6).

In a 20 cm (8 inch) ovenproof frying pan, heat the remaining olive oil over medium heat. Add the garlic, vinegar, sugar and 1 tablespoon of water, and heat until the sugar dissolves. Remove from the heat. Arrange the tomatoes in concentric circles, cut side up, in one layer. Top with the onions, basil and goat's cheese. Cover with the pastry, trim the edges, and tuck the pastry down the side of the pan around the tomatoes. Bake for 25–30 minutes, or until the pastry is golden. Invert the tart onto a plate, cool to room temperature and serve. Serves 4

371 ITALIAN ZUCCHINI PIE

600 g (1 lb 5 oz) zucchini (courgettes), grated and mixed
    with $\frac{1}{4}$ teaspoon salt
150 g (5$\frac{1}{2}$ oz) provolone cheese, grated
120 g (4$\frac{1}{2}$ oz) ricotta cheese
3 eggs
2 garlic cloves, crushed
2 teaspoons finely chopped basil
pinch of ground nutmeg
2 sheets ready-rolled shortcrust pastry
1 egg, extra, lightly beaten

Preheat the oven to 200°C (400°F/Gas 6) and heat a baking tray. Grease a 23 cm (9 inch) pie dish. Drain the zucchini in a colander for 30 minutes, then squeeze out any excess liquid. Place in a bowl with the cheeses, eggs, garlic, basil and nutmeg. Season and mix well.

Using two-thirds of the pastry, line the base and sides of the dish. Spoon the filling into the pastry shell and level the surface. Brush the exposed rim of the pastry with egg. Use two-thirds of the remaining pastry to make a lid. Cover the filling with it, pressing the edges together firmly. Trim the edges and reserve the scraps. Crimp the rim. Prick the top all over with a skewer and brush with egg.

From the remaining pastry, cut a strip about 30 x 10 cm (12 x 4 inches). Cut this into nine lengths 1 cm ($\frac{1}{2}$ inch) wide. Press three ropes together at one end and press onto the workbench. Plait the ropes. Make two more plaits, trim the ends and space the plaits parallel across the centre of the pie. Brush with egg. Bake on the hot tray for 50 minutes, or until golden. Serves 6

372 VEGETABLE BAKE

400 g (14 oz) potatoes, thinly sliced lengthways
60 g (2$\frac{1}{4}$ oz) butter, melted
1$\frac{1}{2}$–2 teaspoons finely chopped thyme
400 g (14 oz) pumpkin (winter squash), thinly sliced
300 g (10$\frac{1}{2}$ oz) zucchini (courgettes), thinly sliced lengthways
250 ml (9 fl oz/1 cup) tomato pasta sauce
50 g (1$\frac{3}{4}$ oz/$\frac{1}{2}$ cup) grated parmesan cheese

Preheat the oven to 170°C (325°F/Gas 3). Grease a 1.5 litre (52 fl oz/ 6 cups) rectangular ovenproof dish. Combine the potato with one third each of the butter and thyme. Season, then place in the base of the prepared dish.

Combine the pumpkin and another third of the butter and thyme. Season and press onto the potato. Combine the zucchini with the remaining butter and thyme. Season and press onto the pumpkin.

Spread the pasta sauce evenly over the top and cover with greased foil. Bake for 45 minutes, remove the foil and sprinkle with the grated parmesan. Bake for another 15 minutes, or until the top is golden brown and the vegetables are cooked through. Can be served with a salad and crusty bread, if desired. Serves 4

373 BAKED RICOTTA WITH RATATOUILLE

1.5 kg (3 lb 5 oz) ricotta, well drained
4 eggs, lightly beaten
3 garlic cloves, finely chopped
2 tablespoons chopped thyme
80 ml (2$\frac{1}{2}$ fl oz/$\frac{1}{3}$ cup) olive oil
300 g (10$\frac{1}{2}$ oz) eggplant (aubergine), diced
3 capsicums (peppers), green, red and yellow, diced
425 g (15 oz) tin crushed tomatoes

Preheat the oven to 180°C (350°F/Gas 4). Place the ricotta, eggs, 1 finely chopped garlic clove and 1 tablespoon chopped thyme in a bowl. Season and mix well. Pour the mixture into a lightly greased 22 cm (8$\frac{1}{2}$ inch) spring-form pan and gently tap a couple of times on the bench to expel any air bubbles. Bake for 1 hour 30 minutes, or until firm and golden. Cool on a rack, pressing down from time to time to remove any air bubbles.

Meanwhile, heat 2 tablespoons oil in a frying pan, add the eggplant and cook for 4–5 minutes, or until golden. Add the capsicum and remaining garlic, and cook for 5 minutes, adding an extra tablespoon oil if necessary. Stir in the tomato and remaining thyme, and cook for 10–15 minutes, or until rich and pulpy. Season. Remove the ricotta from the spring-form pan and cut into wedges. Serve with a little ratatouille on the side, garnished with thyme sprigs. Serves 8

374

375

376

374 ASPARAGUS PIE

800 g (1 lb 12 oz) asparagus spears
20 g ($^3/_4$ oz) butter
$^1/_2$ teaspoon chopped thyme
1 French shallot, chopped
1 large sheet ready-rolled shortcrust pastry
80 ml (2$^1/_2$ fl oz/$^1/_3$ cup) cream
2 tablespoons grated parmesan cheese
1 egg
pinch of ground nutmeg
1 egg, extra, lightly beaten

Trim the asparagus spears to 10 cm (4 inches) and cut thick spears in half lengthways. Heat the butter in a large frying pan over medium heat and add the asparagus, thyme and shallot. Add a tablespoon of water and season with salt and pepper. Cook, stirring, for 3 minutes, or until the asparagus is tender.

Preheat the oven to 200°C (400°F/Gas 6) and grease a 21 cm (8$^1/_4$ inch) fluted, loose-based flan tin. Roll the pastry out to a 2 mm ($^1/_{16}$ inch) thick circle with a diameter of about 30 cm (12 inches). Line the flan tin and trim the pastry using kitchen scissors, leaving about 8 cm (3$^1/_4$ inches) above the top of the tin. Arrange half the asparagus in one direction across the bottom of the dish. Cover with the remaining asparagus, running in the opposite direction.

Combine the cream, parmesan, egg and nutmeg and season. Pour over the asparagus. Fold the pastry over the filling, forming loose pleats. Brush with beaten egg and bake in the centre of the oven for 25 minutes, or until golden. Serves 6

376 RUSTIC GREEK PIE

450 g (1 lb) packet frozen spinach, thawed
1 large sheet ready-rolled shortcrust pastry, thawed
3 garlic cloves, finely chopped
150 g (5$^1/_2$ oz) haloumi cheese, grated
120 g (4$^1/_4$ oz) feta cheese, crumbled
1 tablespoon oregano sprigs
2 eggs
3 tablespoons cream
lemon wedges, to serve

Preheat the oven to 210°C (415°F/Gas 6–7). Squeeze the excess liquid from the spinach. Place the pastry on a baking tray and spread the spinach in the middle, leaving a 3 cm (1$^1/_4$ inch) border around the edge. Sprinkle the garlic over the spinach and pile the haloumi and feta on top. Sprinkle with oregano and season well. Cut a short slit into each corner of the pastry, then tuck each side of pastry over to form a border around the filling.

Lightly beat the eggs with the cream and carefully pour the egg mixture over the spinach filling. Bake for 30–40 minutes, or until the pastry is golden and the filling is set. Serve with the lemon wedges. Serves 4

375 ZUCCHINI, THYME & BOCCONCINI PIZZA

PIZZA BASE
500 g (1 lb 2 oz/4 cups) plain (all-purpose) flour
7 g ($^1/_8$ oz) sachet instant dried yeast
1 teaspoon salt
1 teaspoon sugar
1 tablespoon olive oil

8 zucchini (courgettes), cut into fine rounds
2 teaspoons grated lemon zest
3 tablespoons finely chopped flat-leaf (Italian) parsley
2 teaspoons thyme sprigs
4 garlic cloves, crushed
4 tablespoons olive oil
500 g (1 lb 2 oz) bocconcini cheese, finely diced
50 g (1$^3/_4$ oz/$^1/_2$ cup) grated parmesan cheese
1 tablespoon extra virgin olive oil

Preheat the oven to 220°C (425°F/Gas 7). To make the pizza base, mix together the flour, yeast, salt and sugar in a large bowl, and make a well in the centre. Pour the oil and 310 ml (10$^3/_4$ fl oz/1$^1/_4$ cups) lukewarm water into the well and mix until the flour is incorporated and a soft dough forms.

Turn onto a floured bench and knead for 10 minutes, or until the dough is smooth and elastic. Put the dough in a lightly greased bowl, cover with plastic wrap and leave in a warm place for about 40 minutes, or until doubled in size. Punch the dough down, and knead for 1 minute. Divide in half and roll each half out to 5 mm ($^1/_4$ inch) thick. Transfer the bases to two pizza trays.

Place the zucchini rounds, lemon zest, parsley, thyme, garlic and olive oil in a bowl and mix together. Top each pizza base evenly with half the bocconcini and half the parmesan, then spoon on the zucchini mixture.

Evenly distribute the remaining bocconcini and parmesan over the top, season well with salt and pepper, and drizzle with the extra virgin olive oil. Cook for 15–20 minutes, or until the base is crisp, and the topping is warmed through and golden. Makes 2

377

378

379

377 BAKED POTATOES WITH ROCKET, BROAD BEANS & BLUE CHEESE

4 large potatoes
coarse salt
300 g (10½ oz) broad (fava) beans
80 ml (2½ fl oz/⅓ cup) cream
120 g (4¼ oz) blue cheese, crumbled
4 handfuls rocket (arugula), chopped

Put the oven on to 200°C (400°F/Gas 6). Wash the potatoes and, while they are still damp, rub them with a little of the coarse salt. Prick them several times and then put them in the oven, sitting directly on the oven shelf. This will help them get a good all-round heat. Bake for 1 hour, then squeeze them gently — they should be soft. If they are still hard, give them another 15 minutes or so.

Cook the broad beans in boiling water for 3 minutes, then drain them well. Peel off the outer grey skins. When the potatoes are cooked, cut a cross in one side of each and squeeze the potatoes around the middle until they open up. Put the cream in a small saucepan, add the broad beans, cook them gently for a minute or two, then add the blue cheese and rocket. Stir everything together and when the rocket has wilted, spoon the mixture into the potatoes. Season with black pepper. Serves 4

379 BAKED POTATO WITH AVOCADO, TOMATO & CORN SALSA

4 large potatoes
2 vine-ripened tomatoes, seeded and chopped
125 g (4½ oz) tin corn kernels, drained
2 spring onions (scallions), chopped
1 tablespoon lime juice
½ teaspoon sugar
1 avocado, diced
3 tablespoons chopped coriander (cilantro) leaves
1 tablespoon sour cream (optional)

Preheat the oven to 210°C (415°F/Gas 6–7). Pierce the potatoes all over with a fork. Bake directly on the oven rack for 1 hour, or until tender when tested with a skewer. Leave for about 2 minutes. Cut a cross in the top of each potato and squeeze gently from the base to open (if the potato is still too hot, hold the potato in a clean cloth).

While the potatoes are cooking, put the tomatoes, corn kernels, spring onions, lime juice and sugar in a bowl and mix well. Add the avocado and coriander leaves. Season. Spoon some mixture onto each potato and, if desired, dollop with the sour cream. Serves 4

378 VEGETARIAN PATTIES WITH CORIANDER GARLIC CREAM

250 g (9 oz/1 cup) red lentils
1 tablespoon oil
2 onions, sliced
1 tablespoon tandoori mix powder
425 g (15 oz) tin chickpeas, drained
1 tablespoon grated fresh ginger
1 egg
3 tablespoons chopped flat-leaf (Italian) parsley
2 tablespoons chopped coriander (cilantro) leaves
180 g (6¼ oz/2¼ cups) fresh breadcrumbs
plain (all-purpose) flour, for dusting

CORIANDER GARLIC CREAM
125 g (4½ oz/½ cup) sour cream
125 ml (4 fl oz/½ cup) cream
1 garlic clove, crushed
2 tablespoons chopped coriander (cilantro) leaves
2 tablespoons chopped flat-leaf (Italian) parsley

Simmer the lentils in a large pan of water for 8 minutes or until tender. Drain well. Heat the oil in a pan and cook the onion until tender. Add the tandoori mix and stir until fragrant.

Put the chickpeas, half the lentils, the ginger, egg and onion mixture in a food processor. Process for 20 seconds or until smooth. Transfer to a bowl. Stir in the remaining lentils, parsley, coriander and breadcrumbs.

Divide into 10 portions and shape into burgers (if the mixture is too soft, refrigerate for 15 minutes to firm). Toss the burgers in flour and place on a hot, lightly oiled barbecue grill or flat plate. Cook for 3–4 minutes each side or until browned.

For the coriander garlic cream, mix together the sour cream, cream, garlic and herbs. Serve with the burgers. Makes 10 burgers

380 TOFU, SNOW PEA & MUSHROOM STIR-FRY

250 g (9 oz/1¼ cups) jasmine rice
3 tablespoons peanut oil
600 g (1 lb 5 oz) firm tofu, drained, cut into 2 cm (¾ inch) cubes
2 teaspoons sambal oelek or chilli paste
2 garlic cloves, finely chopped
400 g (14 oz) fresh Asian mushrooms, such as shiitake, oyster or black fungus, sliced
300 g (10½ oz) snow peas (mangetout), trimmed
3 tablespoons kecap manis

Bring a large saucepan of water to the boil. Add the rice and cook for 12 minutes, stirring occasionally. Drain well. Meanwhile, heat a wok until very hot. Add 2 tablespoons of the peanut oil and swirl to coat. Add the tofu in two batches and stir-fry on all sides for 2–3 minutes, or until lightly browned. Transfer to a plate.

Heat the remaining oil in the wok, add the sambal oelek, garlic, mushrooms, snow peas and 1 tablespoon water and stir-fry for 1–2 minutes, or until the vegetables are almost cooked but still crunchy.

Return the tofu to the wok, add the kecap manis and stir-fry for 1 minute, or until heated through and well combined. Serve immediately with the jasmine rice. Serves 4

Notes: Firm tofu is suitable to stir-fry as it will hold its shape. As a variation, use 3 teaspoons grated fresh ginger instead of sambal oelek.

381 ORANGE SWEET POTATO, SPINACH & WATER CHESTNUT STIR-FRY

300 g (10½ oz/1½ cups) long-grain rice
500 g (1 lb 2 oz) orange sweet potato
1 tablespoon oil
2 garlic cloves, crushed
2 teaspoons sambal oelek
225 g (8 oz) tin water chestnuts, sliced
2 teaspoons grated palm sugar (jaggery)
400 g (14 oz) English spinach, stems removed
2 tablespoons soy sauce
2 tablespoons vegetable stock

Bring a large saucepan of water to the boil. Add the rice and cook for 12 minutes, stirring occasionally. Drain well. Meanwhile, cut the sweet potato into 1.5 cm (⅝ inch) cubes and cook in a large saucepan of boiling water for 15 minutes, or until tender. Drain well.

Heat a wok until very hot, add the oil and swirl to coat. Stir-fry the garlic and sambal oelek for 1 minute, or until fragrant. Add the sweet potato and water chestnuts and stir-fry over medium–high heat for 2 minutes. Reduce the heat to medium, add the palm sugar and cook for a further 2 minutes, or until the sugar has melted. Add the spinach, soy sauce and stock and toss until the spinach has just wilted. Serve on a bed of steamed rice. Serves 4

382 YELLOW CURRY OF PUMPKIN WITH GREEN BEANS & CASHEW NUTS

500 ml (17 fl oz/2 cups) tin coconut cream (do not shake the tin)
3 teaspoons yellow curry paste
125 ml (4 fl oz/½ cup) vegetable or chicken stock
500 g (1 lb 2 oz) Jap (kent) pumpkin, peeled and diced
300 g (10½ oz) green beans, trimmed and cut in half
2 tablespoons soy sauce
2 tablespoons lime juice
1 tablespoon grated palm sugar (jaggery)
3 tablespoons coriander (cilantro) leaves
3 tablespoons cashew nuts, toasted
steamed jasmine rice, to serve

Spoon the thick coconut cream from the top of the tin into the wok, and heat until boiling. Add the curry paste, then reduce the heat and simmer, stirring, for 5 minutes, until the oil begins to separate.

Add the remaining coconut cream, stock and pumpkin, and simmer for 10 minutes. Add the green beans and cook for a further 8 minutes, or until the vegetables are tender. Gently stir in the soy sauce, lime juice, and palm sugar. Garnish with the coriander leaves and cashew nuts and serve with steamed jasmine rice. Serves 4

383 GREEN CURRY WITH SWEET POTATO & EGGPLANT

1 tablespoon oil
1 onion, chopped
1–2 tablespoons green curry paste (see Note)
1 eggplant (aubergine), quartered and sliced
400 ml (14 fl oz) tin coconut milk
250 ml (9 fl oz/1 cup) vegetable stock
6 kaffir lime leaves
1 orange sweet potato, cut into cubes
2 teaspoons soft brown sugar
2 tablespoons lime juice
2 teaspoons lime zest
coriander (cilantro) leaves, to garnish

Heat the oil in a large wok or frying pan. Add the onion and curry paste and cook, stirring, over medium heat for 3 minutes. Add the eggplant and cook for a further 4–5 minutes, or until softened. Pour in the coconut milk and stock, bring to the boil, then reduce the heat and simmer for 5 minutes. Add the lime leaves and sweet potato and cook, stirring occasionally, for 10 minutes, or until the vegetables are very tender.

Mix in the sugar, lime juice and lime zest until well combined with the vegetables. Season to taste with salt. Garnish with coriander leaves and serve with steamed rice. Serves 4–6

Note: If this is to be a vegetarian meal, make sure you choose a green curry paste that does not contain shrimp paste.

384

385

386

384 NORI OMELETTE WITH STIR-FRIED VEGETABLES

18 x 10 cm (7 x 4 inch) sheet nori
8 eggs, lightly beaten
3 tablespoons oil
1 garlic clove, crushed
3 teaspoons finely grated fresh ginger
1 carrot, cut into thick matchsticks
2 zucchini (courgettes), halved lengthways, sliced on the diagonal
200 g (7 oz) mix of Swiss brown, enoki and oyster mushrooms, large ones sliced
1 tablespoon Japanese soy sauce
1 tablespoon mirin
2 teaspoons yellow miso paste

Roll the nori up tightly and snip with scissors into very fine strips. Add to the eggs and season to taste with salt and freshly ground black pepper. Heat a wok over high heat, add 2 teaspoons of the oil and swirl to coat the side of the wok. Add 80 ml (2^1/$_2$ fl oz/^{1}/$_3$ cup) of the egg mixture and swirl to coat the base of the wok. Cook for 2 minutes, or until set, then turn over and cook the other side for 1 minute. Remove and keep warm. Repeat with the remaining mixture, adding another 2 teaspoons of the oil each time, to make four omelettes.

Heat the remaining oil in the wok, add the garlic and ginger and stir-fry for 1 minute. Add the carrot, zucchini and mushrooms in two batches and stir-fry for 3 minutes, or until softened. Return all the vegetables to the wok. Add the soy sauce, mirin and miso paste, and simmer for 1 minute. Divide the vegetables evenly among the omelettes, roll them up and serve immediately with steamed rice. Serves 4

386 GOAT'S CHEESE, LEEK & TAPENADE PARCELS

110 g (3^3/$_4$ oz) butter
4 leeks, thinly sliced
8 sheets filo pastry
2 tablespoons tapenade
4 small thyme sprigs
4 small rounds of goat's cheese or 4 thick slices off a log

Turn the oven on to 180°C (350°F/Gas 4). Melt half of the butter in a saucepan, add the leeks and stir until they are coated in the butter. Cook them slowly over a low heat until they are completely tender.

Melt the rest of the butter in a small saucepan on the stove. Place one of the sheets of filo on the work surface with the short end facing you. Brush the pastry with butter. Lay another sheet right on top of it and cover it with a tea towel to stop the pastry drying out. Do the same with the other six sheets.

When the leeks are cooked, uncover the filo. Spread a quarter of the tapenade over the middle of each piece of pastry, leaving a wide border around the edges. Divide the leeks among the filo, putting them on the tapenade. Top each pile of leek with the goat's cheese and then a thyme sprig. Now fold the bottom bit of pastry up and the two sides in, to enclose the filling, then fold the top end of the pastry down and roll the whole parcel over. Repeat with the remaining parcels. Brush the pastry with the butter and bake the parcels for 20 minutes. The pastry should be browned and the filling melted. Serves 4

385 CHINESE OMELETTES WITH MUSHROOM SAUCE

6 whole dried Chinese mushrooms
6 eggs, lightly beaten
4 spring onions (scallions), thinly sliced
1 small red capsicum (pepper), thinly sliced
90 g (3^1/$_4$ oz/1 cup) bean sprouts
2 teaspoons sesame oil
1 teaspoon soy sauce
1 tablespoon oil
1^1/$_2$ tablespoons oil, extra
2 garlic cloves, crushed
250 ml (9 fl oz/1 cup) chicken stock
1 tablespoon oyster sauce
2 teaspoons soy sauce
1 teaspoon sugar
2 spring onions (scallions), sliced diagonally, extra
2 teaspoons cornflour (cornstarch)

Place the mushrooms in a heatproof bowl, cover with boiling water and soak for 15 minutes. Drain, discard the stems and thinly slice the caps. Meanwhile, mix the egg, spring onion, capsicum, bean sprouts, sesame oil and soy sauce in a bowl. Season.

Heat a wok over high heat, add 2 teaspoons oil and swirl to coat. Add a quarter of the egg mixture to the wok, swirl to coat evenly and cook for 1–2 minutes, or until almost set. Turn over and cook for 1 minute, or until brown. Remove and keep warm. Repeat with the remaining mixture, adding more oil if necessary.

Reheat the wok over high heat, add the extra oil and swirl. Add the garlic and mushrooms and cook for 1 minute. Add the stock, oyster sauce, soy sauce, sugar and extra spring onion. Bring to the boil, then reduce the heat and simmer for 1 minute. Combine the cornflour with 1 tablespoon water, add to the wok and simmer for 2 minutes, or until thickened slightly. Serve the omelettes topped with the sauce. Serves 2–4

387

388

389

390

387 VEGETABLE TAGINE WITH COUSCOUS

3 tablespoons olive oil
1 large red capsicum (pepper), seeded and cut into quarters
1 large eggplant (aubergine), sliced into 1 cm (1/2 inch) rounds,
   then in half again
400 g (14 oz) tin chopped tomatoes
1 tablespoon harissa paste
1 tablespoon Moroccan spice blend
250 ml (9 fl oz/1 cup) vegetable stock
2 large zucchini (courgettes), cut into 2 cm (3/4 inch) chunks
280 g (10 oz/1 1/2 cups) couscous
20 g (3/4 oz) butter

Heat 1 tablespoon of the oil in a saucepan over medium–high heat. Sauté the capsicum, skin side down, covered, for 3–4 minutes, or until well browned. Remove from the pan. Peel, then cut the flesh into 1 cm (1/2 inch) slices. Heat the remaining oil in the pan and cook the eggplant in batches over medium–high heat for 4–5 minutes, until well browned.

Return the capsicum to the pan, then stir in the tomato, harissa paste and Moroccan spice blend. Pour in the stock and bring to the boil. Reduce the heat to medium–low and simmer, uncovered, for 15 minutes. Add the zucchini and eggplant and cook for another 8 minutes, or until the vegetables are tender.

About 10 minutes before the vegetables are ready, place the couscous in a heatproof bowl, add 375 ml (13 fl oz/1 1/2 cups) boiling water, and leave for 3–5 minutes. Stir in the butter and fluff with a fork until the butter has melted and the grains separate. Serve the vegetable tagine with the couscous. Serves 4

388 SWEET & SOUR CHICKPEAS

500 g (1 lb 2 oz/2 1/4 cups) chickpeas
2 tablespoons oil or ghee
2 large red onions, thinly sliced
2 cm (3/4 inch) piece of ginger, finely chopped
2 teaspoons sugar
2 teaspoons ground coriander
2 teaspoons ground cumin
pinch of chilli powder (optional)
1 teaspoon garam masala
3 tablespoons tamarind purée
4 ripe tomatoes, chopped
4 tablespoons coriander (cilantro) or mint leaves, finely chopped

Soak the chickpeas overnight in water. Drain, then put the chickpeas in a large saucepan with 2 litres (70 fl oz/8 cups) water. Bring to the boil, spooning off any scum from the surface. Cover and simmer over low heat for 1–1 1/2 hours until soft. It is important they are soft at this stage as they won't soften any more once the sauce has been added. Drain well and set aside.

Heat the oil in a heavy-based frying pan. Fry the onion until soft and brown, then stir in the ginger. Add the chickpeas, sugar, coriander, cumin, chilli powder, garam masala and a pinch of salt. Stir, then add the tamarind and tomato and simmer for 2–3 minutes. Add 500 ml (17 fl oz/2 cups) water, bring to the boil and cook until the sauce has thickened. Stir in the coriander leaves. Serves 6

389 POTATO MASALA

2 tablespoons oil
1 teaspoon black mustard seeds
10 curry leaves
1/4 teaspoon ground turmeric
1 cm (1/2 inch) piece of ginger, grated
2 green chillies, finely chopped
2 onions, chopped
500 g (1 lb 2 oz) waxy potatoes, cut into 2 cm (3/4 inch) cubes
1 tablespoon tamarind purée

Heat the oil in a heavy-based frying pan, add the mustard seeds, cover, and when they start to pop add the curry leaves, turmeric, ginger, chilli and onion and cook, uncovered, until the onion is soft.

Add the potato cubes and 250 ml (9 fl oz/1 cup) water to the pan, bring to the boil, cover and cook until the potato is tender and almost breaking up. If there is any liquid left in the pan, let it simmer a little, uncovered, until it evaporates. If the potato isn't cooked and there is no liquid left, add a little more and continue to cook. Add the tamarind and season with salt. Serves 4

Note: This filling is traditionally rolled in dosas — large pancakes made with rice flour — and served for breakfast or as a snack in southern India. However, it also makes an excellent spicy potato side dish.

390 GREEN STIR-FRY WITH SESAME & SOY

2 tablespoons light soy sauce
1 tablespoon hoisin sauce
1 tablespoon vegetable or chicken stock
2 tablespoons vegetable oil
1 teaspoon sesame oil
4 garlic cloves, finely sliced
2 teaspoons julienned ginger
2 kg (4 lb 8 oz/4 bunches) baby bok choy (pak choy),
   cut into quarters
200 g (7 oz) snow peas (mangetout), trimmed
200 g (7 oz) sugar snap peas, trimmed
2 tablespoons bamboo shoots, julienned
jasmine rice, to serve

In a small jug mix together the light soy sauce, hoisin sauce and stock. Heat a wok over high heat and add the vegetable and sesame oils. Stir-fry the garlic, ginger and bok choy for 3 minutes. Add the snow peas, sugar snap peas and bamboo shoots and stir-fry for a further 5 minutes. Pour in the sauce, and gently toss until the sauce has reduced slightly to coat the just tender vegetables. Serve immediately with jasmine rice. Serves 4

391

392

393

391 POTATO & ZUCCHINI CASSEROLE

1 large red capsicum (pepper)
3 tablespoons olive oil
2 onions, sliced
2 garlic cloves, crushed
400 g (14 oz) zucchini (courgettes), thickly sliced
400 g (14 oz) small waxy potatoes (pontiac, kipfler, desiree), unpeeled, cut into 1 cm (1/2 inch) slices
1 kg (2 lb 4 oz) ripe tomatoes, peeled and roughly chopped
1 teaspoon dried oregano
2 tablespoons chopped flat-leaf (Italian) parsley
2 tablespoons chopped dill
1/2 teaspoon ground cinnamon

Preheat the oven to 180°C (350°F/ Gas 4). Remove the seeds and membrane from the capsicum and cut the flesh into squares. Heat 2 tablespoons of the olive oil in a heavy-based frying pan over medium heat. Cook the onion, stirring frequently, for 10 minutes. Add the garlic and cook for another 2 minutes. Place all the other ingredients in a large bowl and season generously with salt and pepper. Add the softened onion and garlic and toss everything together. Transfer to a large baking dish and drizzle the remaining oil over the vegetables.

Cover and bake for 1–1 1/2 hours, or until the vegetables are tender, stirring every 30 minutes. Check for doneness by inserting the point of a small knife into the potatoes. When the knife comes away easily, the potato is cooked. Serves 4–6

393 MUSHROOM POT PIES

100 ml (3 1/2 fl oz) olive oil
1 leek, sliced
1 garlic clove, crushed
1 kg (2 lb 4 oz) large field mushrooms, roughly chopped
1 teaspoon chopped thyme
300 ml (10 1/2 fl oz) cream
1 sheet ready-rolled puff pastry, thawed
1 egg yolk, beaten, to glaze

Preheat the oven to 180°C (350°F/Gas 4). Heat 1 tablespoon of the oil in a frying pan over medium heat. Cook the leek and garlic for 5 minutes, or until the leek is soft and translucent. Transfer to a large saucepan.

Heat the remaining oil in the frying pan over high heat and cook the mushrooms in two batches, stirring frequently, for 5–7 minutes per batch, or until the mushrooms have released their juices and are soft and slightly coloured. Transfer to the saucepan, then add the thyme.

Place the saucepan over high heat and stir in the cream. Cook, stirring occasionally, for 7–8 minutes, or until the cream has reduced to a thick sauce. Remove from the heat and season well with salt and pepper.

Divide the filling among four 310 ml (10 3/4 fl oz/1 1/4 cup) ramekins or ovenproof bowls. Cut the pastry into rounds slightly larger than each dish. Brush the rim of the ramekins with a little of the egg yolk, place the pastry on top and press down to seal. Brush the top with the remaining egg yolk. Place the ramekins on a metal tray. Bake for 20–25 minutes, or until the pastry has risen and is golden brown. Serves 4

392 COUSCOUS VEGETABLE LOAF

1 litre (35 fl oz/4 cups) vegetable stock
500 g (1 lb 2 oz) couscous
30 g (1 oz) butter
3 tablespoons olive oil
2 garlic cloves, crushed
1 onion, finely chopped
1 tablespoon ground coriander
1 teaspoon ground cinnamon
1 teaspoon garam masala
250 g (9 oz) cherry tomatoes, quartered
1 zucchini (courgette), diced
130 g (4 1/2 oz) tin corn kernels, drained
8 large basil leaves
150 g (5 1/2 oz) sun-dried capsicum (pepper) in oil
1 large handful chopped basil, extra
80 ml (2 1/2 fl oz/1/3 cup) orange juice
1 tablespoon lemon juice
3 tablespoons chopped flat-leaf (Italian) parsley
1 teaspoon honey
1 teaspoon ground cumin

Bring the vegetable stock to the boil in a saucepan. Place the couscous and butter in a bowl, cover with the stock and leave for 10 minutes.

Meanwhile, heat 1 tablespoon of the oil in a large frying pan and cook the garlic and onion over low heat for 5 minutes, or until the onion is soft. Add the spices and cook for 1 minute, or until fragrant. Remove from the pan. Add the remaining oil to the pan and cook the tomatoes, zucchini and corn over high heat until soft.

Line a 3 litre (100 fl oz/12 cup) loaf (bar) tin with plastic wrap, letting it overhang the sides. Form the basil into two flowers on the base. Drain the capsicums, reserving 2 tablespoons of oil, then roughly chop. Add the onion mixture, tomato mixture, capsicum and extra basil to the couscous and mix. Cool.

Press the mixture into the tin and fold the plastic wrap over to cover. Weigh down with food tins and chill overnight.

To make the dressing, place the remaining ingredients and reserved capsicum oil in a jar with a lid and shake. Turn out the loaf, cut into slices and serve with the dressing. Serves 6

394

395

396

397

394 BAKED SWORDFISH STEAKS WITH SALSA VERDE

4 x 200 g (7 oz) swordfish steaks

SALSA VERDE
2 tablespoons olive oil
1 large onion, finely chopped
1 garlic clove, finely chopped
1 large green capsicum (pepper)
40 g (1 1/2 oz) jalapeño chillies
2 tablespoons roughly chopped coriander (cilantro) leaves

Preheat the oven to 180°C (350°F/Gas 4). Put the swordfish steaks in a large rectangular ovenproof dish.

To make the salsa verde, heat 1 tablespoon of the oil in a small saucepan and, when hot, add the onion and garlic and cook for 10 minutes, or until the onion has softened. Allow to cool for a few minutes. Blanch the capsicum in boiling water for 8 minutes, then drain. Put the softened onion and garlic in a food processor with the capsicum, chillies, coriander and remaining oil. Blend to a purée and season with salt. Alternatively, finely chop the ingredients by hand and mix together well.

Spread the salsa verde on top of the swordfish steaks, dividing it equally. Bake in the preheated oven for 20–25 minutes, or until the fish is firm and opaque. Serve with crispy baked potato chunks. Serves 4

395 MARINATED & SEARED TUNA

80 ml (2 1/2 fl oz/1/3 cup) soy sauce
3 tablespoons mirin
1 tablespoon sake
1 teaspoon caster (superfine) sugar
1 teaspoon finely grated fresh ginger
2 teaspoons lemon juice
4 x 175 g (6 oz) tuna steaks
1 tablespoon oil
coriander (cilantro) leaves, for garnish

Mix the soy sauce, mirin, sake, sugar, ginger and lemon juice together in a jug. Put the tuna steaks in a shallow dish and spoon the marinade over the top. Turn the fish in the marinade, ensuring it is well coated. Cover and leave to marinate for 30 minutes in the fridge.

Preheat a chargrill pan or barbecue hotplate until hot. Lift the tuna out of the marinade and pour the marinade into a small saucepan. Bring the marinade to the boil and reduce for 1 minute.

Meanwhile, lightly oil the surface of the chargrill pan and add the tuna steaks. Cook for 2–3 minutes on each side so that the tuna is cooked on the outside but still pink in the middle. Serve with some of the marinade spooned over the top and garnished with coriander. Great with rice and steamed vegetables. Serves 4

396 MEXICAN BAKED FISH

3 tomatoes, chopped
1/2 teaspoon ground cumin
1/2 teaspoon ground allspice
1/2 teaspoon ground cinnamon
1 habanero chilli, seeded and finely chopped
4 tablespoons coriander (cilantro) leaves
4 x 175–200 g (6–7 oz) skinless red snapper fillets
1/2 small red onion, chopped
1/2 small green capsicum (pepper), chopped
1 tablespoon sour or seville orange juice, or 2 teaspoons orange juice and 2 teaspoons vinegar
juice of 1 lime

Preheat the oven to 190°C (375°F/Gas 5). Mix the tomatoes in a bowl with the cumin, allspice, cinnamon, chilli and coriander. Cut four squares of foil, each large enough to enclose a fish fillet. Put a piece of fish on each of the foil squares and divide the tomato mixture among the four fillets.

Mix the red onion and green capsicum together and divide among the parcels. Stir the orange and lime juice together and drizzle over the top of the fish and vegetables. Season with salt and pepper.

Wrap the fish in the foil and transfer the parcels to a baking dish. Bake for 15–20 minutes, or until the fish flakes easily when tested with a fork. Serves 4

397 CRUNCHY FISH FILLETS WITH CHIVE MAYO

160 g (5 3/4 oz/2/3 cup) good-quality mayonnaise
2 tablespoons chopped chives
1 tablespoon sweet chilli sauce
75 g (2 3/4 oz/1/2 cup) cornmeal
4 x 200 g (7 oz) skinless perch fillets
3 tablespoons oil

For the chive mayo, combine the mayonnaise, chives and chilli sauce in a small bowl. Keep refrigerated until needed.

Put the cornmeal on a plate. Score four diagonal slashes in the skin side of each fish fillet, to prevent the fish curling during cooking. Press both sides of the fillets into the cornmeal to coat thoroughly.

Heat the oil in a frying pan over medium heat. Add the fish and cook for 3 minutes. Turn and cook for another 3 minutes, or until tender and the fish flakes easily when tested with a fork. Remove and drain on crumpled paper towels. Serve with the chive mayo. Serves 4

398

399

400

398 TOMATO & BASIL BLACK MUSSELS

125 ml (4 fl oz/½ cup) dry white wine
2 bay leaves
1 kg (2 lb 4 oz) black mussels, scrubbed and beards removed
500 g (1 lb 2 oz/2 cups) tomato pasta sauce
1–2 teaspoons sugar, to taste
2 tablespoons extra virgin olive oil
4 tablespoons shredded basil
2 tablespoons snipped chives

Place the wine and bay leaves in a large wide saucepan and bring to the boil. Discard any broken mussels, add the rest to the saucepan and cook, covered with a tight-fitting lid, over high heat for 4 minutes, or until the mussels open. Place the pasta sauce, sugar, oil and basil in a bowl, and mix together well.

Discard any mussels which have not opened. Drain, reserving the cooking juices. Return the mussels to the saucepan, add the tomato mixture and 125 ml (4 fl oz/½ cup) of the reserved cooking juices, and stir over high heat for 3–4 minutes, or until warmed through. Sprinkle with chives and serve in warmed bowls with bread. Serves 4

400 INDIAN-STYLE BUTTER PRAWNS

1 kg (2 lb 4 oz) large raw prawns (shrimp)
100 g (3½ oz) butter
2 large garlic cloves, crushed
1 teaspoon ground cumin
1 teaspoon paprika
1½ teaspoons garam masala
2 tablespoons good-quality ready-made tandoori paste
2 tablespoons tomato paste (concentrated purée)
300 ml (10½ fl oz) thick (double/heavy) cream
1 teaspoon sugar
90 g (3¼ oz/⅓ cup) plain yoghurt
2 tablespoons chopped coriander (cilantro) leaves
1 tablespoon flaked almonds, toasted
lemon wedges, to serve

Peel and devein the prawns, leaving the tails intact. Melt the butter in a large saucepan over medium heat, then add the garlic, cumin, paprika and 1 teaspoon of the garam masala and cook for 1 minute, or until fragrant. Add the tandoori paste and tomato paste, and cook for a further 2 minutes. Stir in the cream and sugar, then reduce the heat and simmer for 10 minutes, or until the sauce thickens slightly.

Add the prawns to the pan and cook for 8–10 minutes, or until they are pink and cooked through. Remove the pan from the heat and stir in the yoghurt, the remaining garam masala and half the coriander. Season. Garnish with the flaked almonds and remaining coriander and serve with steamed rice and lemon wedges. Serves 4

399 FISH PIE

POTATO TOPPING
500 g (1 lb 2 oz) floury potatoes, diced
3 tablespoons milk or cream
1 egg, lightly beaten
30 g (1 oz) butter
60 g (2¼ oz/½ cup) finely grated cheddar cheese

800 g (1 lb 12 oz) skinless ling fillets, cut into large chunks
375 ml (13 fl oz/1½ cups) milk
30 g (1 oz) butter
1 onion, finely chopped
1 garlic clove, crushed
2 tablespoons plain (all-purpose) flour
2 tablespoons lemon juice
2 teaspoons lemon zest
1 tablespoon chopped dill

Preheat the oven to 180°C (350°F/Gas 4). To make the topping, steam the potatoes until tender. Mash, then push to one side of the pan, add the milk and heat gently. Beat the milk into the potato until it is fluffy, then season and stir in the egg and butter. Mix in half the cheddar, then set aside and keep warm.

Put the fish in a frying pan and cover with the milk. Bring to the boil, then reduce the heat and simmer for 2 minutes, or until the fish is opaque and flaky. Drain, reserving the milk, and put the fish in a 1.5 litre (52 fl oz/6 cup) ovenproof dish.

Melt the butter in a saucepan and cook the onion and garlic for 2 minutes. Stir in the flour and cook for 1 minute, or until pale and foaming. Remove from the heat and gradually stir in the reserved milk. Return to the heat and stir constantly until it boils and thickens. Reduce the heat and simmer for 2 minutes. Add the lemon juice, zest and dill, and season. Mix with the fish. Spoon the topping over the fish and top with the remaining cheddar. Bake for 35 minutes, or until golden. Serves 4

401

402

403

404

401 PRAWNS WITH SPICY TAMARIND SAUCE

80 g (2³/₄ oz/¹/₂ cup) raw cashew nuts
250 g (9 oz/1¹/₄ cups) jasmine rice
2 garlic cloves, finely chopped
1¹/₂ tablespoons fish sauce
1 tablespoon sambal oelek
1 tablespoon peanut oil
1 kg (2 lb 4 oz) raw prawns (shrimp), peeled and deveined,
    tails intact
2 teaspoons tamarind concentrate
1¹/₂ tablespoons grated palm sugar (jaggery)
350 g (12 oz) choy sum, cut into 10 cm (4 inch) lengths

Preheat the oven to 180°C (350°F/Gas 4). Spread the cashews on a baking tray and bake for 5–8 minutes, or until light golden — watch carefully, as they burn easily. Meanwhile, bring a large saucepan of water to the boil. Add the rice and cook for 12 minutes, stirring occasionally. Drain well. Place the garlic, fish sauce, sambal oelek and toasted cashews in a blender or food processor, adding 2–3 tablespoons of water, if needed, and blend to a rough paste.

Heat a wok until very hot, add the oil and swirl to coat. Add the prawns, toss for 1–2 minutes, or until starting to turn pink. Remove from the wok. Add the cashew paste and stir-fry for 1 minute, or until it starts to brown slightly. Add the tamarind, sugar and about 80 ml (2¹/₂ fl oz/ ¹/₃ cup) water, then bring to the boil, stirring well. Return the prawns to the wok and stir to coat. Cook for 2–3 minutes, or until the prawns are cooked through. Place the choy sum in a paper-lined bamboo steamer and steam over a wok or saucepan of simmering water for 3 minutes, or until tender. Serve with the prawns and rice. Serves 4

402 TANDOORI PRAWN PIZZA

1 tablespoon olive oil
2 teaspoons ground paprika
¹/₂ teaspoon ground cumin
¹/₄ teaspoon ground cardamom
¹/₄ teaspoon ground ginger
¹/₄ teaspoon cayenne pepper
90 g (3¹/₄ oz/¹/₃ cup) Greek-style yoghurt, plus extra, for serving
1 teaspoon lemon juice
2 garlic cloves, crushed
16 prawns (shrimp), peeled and deveined, tails intact
30 cm (12 inch) ready-made pizza base
1 onion, sliced
1 small red capsicum (pepper), sliced
3 tablespoons torn basil

Preheat the oven to 220°C (425°F/Gas 7). To make the tandoori sauce, heat the oil in a frying pan over medium heat, add the spices and cook until the oil starts to bubble, then cook for another minute. Stir in the yoghurt, lemon juice and garlic, then add the prawns. Cook for 5 minutes, or until the prawns are pink and cooked.

Remove the prawns from the tandoori sauce with a slotted spoon and spread the sauce over the pizza base, leaving a 1 cm (¹/₂ inch) border. Sprinkle with some of the onion and capsicum, then arrange all the prawns on top. Top with the remaining onion and capsicum and bake for about 20 minutes. Scatter with basil, then serve with the extra yoghurt. Serves 4

403 SESAME-COATED TUNA WITH CORIANDER SALSA

4 tuna steaks
115 g (4 oz/³/₄ cup) sesame seeds
100 g (3¹/₂ oz) baby rocket (arugula) leaves

CORIANDER SALSA
2 tomatoes, seeded and diced
1 large garlic clove, crushed
2 tablespoons finely chopped coriander (cilantro) leaves
2 tablespoons virgin olive oil, plus extra for shallow-frying
1 tablespoon lime juice

Cut each tuna steak into 3 pieces. Place the sesame seeds on a sheet of baking paper. Roll the tuna in the sesame seeds to coat. Refrigerate for 15 minutes. To make the salsa, place the tomato, garlic, coriander, oil and lime juice in a bowl, and mix together well. Cover and refrigerate until ready to use.

Fill a heavy-based frying pan to 1.5 cm (⁵/₈ inch) with the extra oil and place over high heat. Add the tuna in two batches and cook for 2 minutes each side (it should be pink in the centre). Remove and drain on paper towels. To serve, divide the rocket among four serving plates and arrange the tuna over the top. Spoon the salsa on the side and serve immediately. Top with a teaspoon of chilli jam, if desired, and season. Serves 4

404 FISH FILLETS WITH FENNEL & RED CAPSICUM SALSA

750 g (1 lb 10 oz) small new potatoes
1 teaspoon fennel seeds
125 ml (4 fl oz/¹/₂ cup) olive oil
2 tablespoons drained baby capers
1 small red capsicum (pepper), seeded and finely diced
250 g (9 oz) mixed salad leaves, washed and picked over
2 tablespoons balsamic vinegar
4 white fish fillets (blue eye cod or john dory), (about 200 g/
    7 oz each)

Cook the potatoes in a saucepan of boiling water for 15–20 minutes, or until tender. Drain and keep warm. Meanwhile, to make the salsa, dry-fry the fennel seeds in a frying pan over medium heat for 1 minute, or until fragrant. Remove the seeds and heat 1 tablespoon oil in the same pan over medium heat. When the oil is hot but not smoking, flash-fry the capers for 1–2 minutes, or until crisp. Remove from the pan. Heat 1 tablespoon oil and cook the capsicum, stirring, for 4–5 minutes, or until cooked through. Remove and combine with the fennel seeds and fried capers.

Place the salad leaves in a serving bowl. To make the dressing, combine the balsamic vinegar and 3 tablespoons of the olive oil in a bowl. Add 1 tablespoon to the salsa, then toss the rest through the salad leaves.

Wipe the frying pan, then heat the remaining oil over medium–high heat. Season the fish well. When the oil is hot, but not smoking, cook the fish for 2–3 minutes each side, or until cooked through. Serve immediately with the salsa, potatoes and salad. Serves 4

405

406

407

405 STIR-FRIED SCALLOPS WITH SUGAR SNAP PEAS

2 tablespoons oil
2 large garlic cloves, crushed
3 teaspoons finely chopped fresh ginger
300 g (10½ oz) sugar snap peas
500 g (1 lb 2 oz) scallops without roe, membrane removed
2 spring onions (scallions), cut into 2 cm (¾ inch) lengths
2½ tablespoons oyster sauce
2 teaspoons soy sauce
½ teaspoon sesame oil
2 teaspoons sugar

Heat a wok over medium heat, add the oil and swirl to coat the surface of the wok. Add the garlic and ginger, and stir-fry for 30 seconds, or until fragrant.

Add the peas to the wok and cook for 1 minute, then add the scallops and spring onion and cook for 1 minute, or until the spring onion is wilted. Stir in the oyster and soy sauces, sesame oil and sugar and heat for 1 minute, or until warmed through. Serve with rice. Serves 4

407 PIRI PIRI PRAWNS

125 ml (4 fl oz/½ cup) oil
2 teaspoons chilli flakes
4 large garlic cloves, crushed
1 kg (2 lb 4 oz) prawns (shrimp), peeled and deveined, tails intact
75 g (2¾ oz) butter
3 tablespoons lemon juice

Put the oil, chilli flakes, garlic and 1 teaspoon salt in a large non-metallic bowl and mix well. Add the prawns and coat them in the mixture. Refrigerate for 3 hours, stirring and turning occasionally.

Preheat the grill (broiler) to very hot. Put the prawns in a single layer on a baking tray and brush with the remaining oil and chilli mixture. Cook for about 5 minutes, turning once, or until cooked through.

Meanwhile, melt the butter with the lemon juice in a small saucepan. Serve the prawns hot, drizzled with the lemon juice and butter mixture and accompanied with rice. Serves 4

406 LIGHT RED SEAFOOD CURRY

CHU CHEE PASTE
10 large dried red chillies
1 tablespoon shrimp paste
1 tablespoon white peppercorns
1 teaspoon coriander seeds
2 teaspoons finely grated kaffir lime zest
10 kaffir lime leaves, finely shredded
1 tablespoon chopped coriander (cilantro) stem
1 lemongrass stem, white part only, finely chopped
3 tablespoons chopped fresh galangal
6 garlic cloves, chopped
10 red Asian shallots, chopped

2 x 270 ml (9½ fl oz) tins coconut cream
500 g (1 lb 2 oz) raw king prawns (shrimp), peeled, deveined, with tails intact
500 g (1 lb 2 oz) scallops, without roe
2–3 tablespoons fish sauce
2–3 tablespoons grated palm sugar (jaggery) or soft brown sugar
8 kaffir lime leaves, finely shredded
2 small red chillies, thinly sliced (optional)
1 large handful Thai basil

Soak the chillies in hot water for 15 minutes. Drain, remove the seeds and chop. Preheat the oven to 180°C (350°F/Gas 4). Put the shrimp paste, peppercorns and coriander seeds on a foil-lined baking tray and bake for 5 minutes. Blend the baked spices in a food processor with the remaining paste ingredients until smooth.

Remove 250 ml (9 fl oz/1 cup) thick coconut cream from the top of the tins (reserve the rest) and place in a wok. Heat until just boiling, then stir in 3 tablespoons of the curry paste. Reduce the heat. Simmer for 10 minutes, or until fragrant and the oil begins to separate.

Stir in the seafood and remaining coconut cream and cook for 5 minutes. Add the fish sauce, sugar, lime leaves and chilli and cook for 1 minute. Stir in half the basil and use the rest to garnish. Serves 4

408

409

410

411

408 BARBECUED SALMON CUTLETS WITH SWEET CUCUMBER DRESSING

2 small Lebanese (short) cucumbers, peeled, seeded
    and finely diced
1 red onion, finely chopped
1 red chilli, finely chopped
2 tablespoons pickled ginger, shredded
2 tablespoons rice vinegar
$^{1}/_{2}$ teaspoon sesame oil
4 salmon cutlets
1 sheet toasted nori (dried seaweed), cut into thin strips

Combine the cucumber, onion, chilli, ginger, rice vinegar and sesame oil in a bowl, cover and stand at room temperature while you cook the salmon cutlets.

Preheat a barbecue flatplate and lightly brush it with oil. Cook the salmon on the barbecue for about 2 minutes on each side, or until cooked as desired. Be careful you do not overcook the fish or it will be dry — it should be still just pink in the centre. Serve the salmon topped with the cucumber dressing, then sprinkle with strips of toasted nori. Serve with steamed rice. Serves 4

409 FRESH TUNA & GREEN BEAN STIR-FRY

300 g (10$^{1}/_{2}$ oz) small green beans, trimmed
2 tablespoons oil
600 g (1 lb 5 oz) piece of tuna, cut into small cubes
250 g (9 oz) small cherry tomatoes
16 small black olives
2–3 tablespoons lemon juice
2 garlic cloves, finely chopped
8 anchovy fillets, rinsed, dried and finely chopped
3 tablespoons small basil

Blanch the beans in a small saucepan of boiling water for 2 minutes. Drain and refresh under cold water, then set aside. Heat a wok until very hot, add the oil and swirl it around to coat the side. Stir-fry the tuna in batches for about 5 minutes each batch, or until cooked on the outside but still a little pink on the inside.

Add the cherry tomatoes, olives and beans to the wok, then gently toss until heated through. Add the lemon juice, garlic and anchovies and stir well. Season to taste with salt and freshly ground black pepper. Serve scattered with the basil. Serves 4

410 STIR-FRIED SQUID FLOWERS WITH CAPSICUM

400 g (14 oz) squid tubes
3 tablespoons oil
2 tablespoons salted, fermented black beans, mashed
1 small onion, cut into small cubes
1 small green capsicum (pepper), cut into small cubes
3–4 small slices of peeled fresh ginger
1 spring onion (scallion), cut into short lengths
1 small red chilli, chopped
1 tablespoon Chinese rice wine
$^{1}/_{2}$ teaspoon roasted sesame oil

Open up the squid tube and scrub off any soft jelly-like substance, then score the inside of the flesh with a fine crisscross pattern, making sure you do not cut all the way through. Cut the squid into pieces that are about 3 x 5 cm (1$^{1}/_{4}$ x 2 inches).

Blanch the squid in a saucepan of boiling water for 25–30 seconds — each piece will curl up and the crisscross pattern will open out, hence the name 'squid flower'. Remove and refresh in cold water, then drain and dry well.

Heat a wok over high heat, add the oil and heat until very hot. Stir-fry the black beans, onion, green capsicum, ginger, spring onion and chilli for 1 minute. Add the squid and rice wine, blend well and stir for 1 minute. Sprinkle with the sesame oil. Serves 4

411 CHARGRILLED JUMBO PRAWNS

8 large raw king prawns (shrimp) (about 800 g/1 lb 12 oz)
80 ml (2$^{1}/_{2}$ fl oz/$^{1}/_{3}$ cup) olive oil
3 garlic cloves, crushed
1 tablespoon sweet chilli sauce
2 tablespoons lime juice
3 tablespoons olive oil, extra
2 tablespoons lime juice, extra
mixed lettuce leaves, to serve

Remove the heads from the prawns and, using a sharp knife, cut through the centre of the prawns lengthways to form two halves, leaving the tails and shells intact. Place the olive oil, 2 crushed garlic cloves, sweet chilli sauce and lime juice in a bowl, and mix together well. Add the prawns, toss to coat and marinate for 30 minutes.

Meanwhile, combine the extra oil and lime juice and remaining garlic in a bowl. Heat a barbecue or chargrill plate until hot. Drain the prawns and cook, cut side down first, brushing with the marinade, for 1–2 minutes each side, or until cooked. Divide the lettuce among four serving plates, place the prawns on top and spoon over the dressing. Season and serve. Serves 4

412

413

414

412 LOBSTER THERMIDOR

1 cooked lobster
85 g (3 oz) butter
4 spring onions (scallions), finely chopped
1½ tablespoons plain (all-purpose) flour
½ teaspoon mustard powder
2 tablespoons white wine or sherry
250 ml (9 fl oz/1 cup) milk
3 tablespoons cream
1 tablespoon chopped flat-leaf (Italian) parsley
65 g (2¼ oz/½ cup) grated gruyère cheese
lemon wedges, for serving

Cut the lobster in half lengthways through the shell. Lift the meat from the tail and body. Remove the cream-coloured vein and soft body matter and discard. Cut the meat into 2 cm (³⁄₄ inch) pieces, cover and refrigerate. Wash the head and shell halves, then drain and pat dry.

Heat 60 g (2¼ oz) of the butter in a frying pan, add the spring onion and stir for 2 minutes. Stir in the flour and mustard and cook for 1 minute, or until pale and foaming. Remove from the heat and gradually stir in the wine and milk. Return to the heat and stir constantly until the mixture boils and thickens. Reduce the heat and simmer for 1 minute. Stir in the cream, parsley and lobster meat, then season. Stir over low heat until the lobster is heated through.

Spoon the mixture into the lobster shells, sprinkle with cheese and dot with the remaining butter. Place under a hot grill (broiler) and cook for 2 minutes, or until lightly browned. Serve with salad and some wedges of lemon. Serves 2

414 SALMON & DILL POTATO PATTIES WITH LIME MAYO

400 g (14 oz) new potatoes, cut in half
2 teaspoons grated lime zest
310 g (11 oz/1¼ cups) whole-egg mayonnaise
425 g (15 oz) tin salmon, drained, bones removed
1 tablespoon chopped dill
2 spring onions (scallions), thinly sliced
1 egg
80 g (2¾ oz/1 cup) fresh breadcrumbs
3 tablespoons oil
200 g (7 oz) rocket (arugula) leaves
lime wedges, to serve

Cook the potatoes in a large saucepan of boiling water for 12–15 minutes, or until tender. Drain well and cool. Meanwhile, combine the lime zest and 250 g (9 oz/1 cup) of the mayonnaise. Transfer the potato to a large bowl, then mash roughly with the back of a spoon, leaving some large chunks. Stir in the salmon, dill and spring onion and season. Mix in the egg and the remaining mayonnaise. Divide into eight portions, forming palm-size patties. Press lightly into the breadcrumbs to coat.

Heat the oil in a non-stick frying pan and cook the patties, turning, for 3–4 minutes, or until golden brown. Drain on paper towels. Serve with a dollop of lime mayonnaise, rocket leaves and lime wedges. Serves 4

413 PRAWN POT PIES

60 g (2¼ oz) butter
1 leek, white part only, thinly sliced
1 garlic clove, finely chopped
1 kg (2 lb 4 oz) prawns (shrimp), peeled and deveined, tails intact
1 tablespoon plain (all-purpose) flour
185 ml (6 fl oz/¾ cup) chicken or fish stock
125 ml (4 fl oz/½ cup) dry white wine
500 ml (17 fl oz/2 cups) cream
2 tablespoons lemon juice
1 tablespoon chopped dill
1 tablespoon chopped flat-leaf (Italian) parsley
1 teaspoon dijon mustard
1 sheet frozen puff pastry, just thawed
1 egg, lightly beaten

Preheat the oven to 220°C (425°F/Gas 7). Melt the butter in a saucepan over low heat. Cook the leek and garlic for 2 minutes, then add the prawns and cook for 1–2 minutes, or until just pink. Remove the prawns with a slotted spoon and set aside.

Stir the flour into the pan and cook for 1 minute. Add the stock and wine, bring to the boil and cook for 10 minutes, or until nearly all the liquid has evaporated. Stir in the cream, bring to the boil, then reduce the heat and simmer for 20 minutes, or until the liquid reduces by half. Stir in the lemon juice, herbs and mustard.

Using half the sauce, pour an even amount into four 250 ml (9 fl oz/ 1 cup) ramekins. Divide the prawns among the ramekins, then top with the remaining sauce.

Cut the pastry into four rounds, slightly larger than the rim of the ramekins. Place the pastry rounds over the prawn mixture and press around the edges. Prick the pastry and brush with beaten egg. Bake for 20 minutes, or until the pastry is crisp and golden. Serve with a salad and bread. Serves 4

415

416

417

418

415 AROMATIC SNAPPER PARCELS

1 large handful basil, chopped
2 large garlic cloves, chopped
1 tablespoon lemon juice
1 teaspoon grated lemon zest
3 tablespoons olive oil
4 skinless snapper fillets, trimmed and boned (about 200 g/
    7 oz each)
500 g (1 lb 2 oz) small new potatoes
20 asparagus spears
12 yellow baby squash

Preheat the oven to 200°C (400°F/Gas 6). Combine the basil, garlic, lemon juice, zest and 2 tablespoons of the olive oil. Season. Place a fish fillet in the centre of a sheet of foil large enough to fully enclose it. Season. Smear the fillet with 2 teaspoons of the basil mixture, then wrap into a secure parcel with the foil. Repeat with the remaining fillets. Place on a baking tray and refrigerate until required.

Cook the potatoes in a saucepan of boiling water for 15–20 minutes, or until tender. Drain and keep warm. While the potatoes are cooking, brush the asparagus and squash with the remaining oil. Place on a baking tray and season with freshly ground black pepper. Bake for 8–10 minutes, or until golden and tender.

About 10 minutes before the vegetables are ready, place the fish parcels in the oven and cook for 5–7 minutes, or until the flesh flakes easily when tested with a fork. Check one of the parcels after 5 minutes to see if the fish is cooked through. Place the opened parcels on plates with the vegetables, season to taste and serve. Serves 4

416 TUNA STEAKS WITH OLIVE MAYO & POTATO WEDGES

3 large pontiac potatoes, unpeeled and cut lengthways
    into 8 wedges
345 ml (11$\frac{1}{2}$ fl oz) olive oil
2 egg yolks, at room temperature
5 teaspoons lemon juice
40 g (1$\frac{1}{2}$ oz/$\frac{1}{3}$ cup) pitted black olives, finely chopped
200 g (7 oz) baby rocket (arugula) leaves
1 tablespoon finely chopped rosemary
4 tuna steaks (about 200 g/7 oz each)

Preheat the oven to 200°C (400°F/Gas 6). Toss the potatoes with 2 tablespoons oil in a baking tin. Bake for 45–50 minutes, or until crisp and golden. Meanwhile, process the egg yolks in a food processor, adding 3 tablespoons of the oil drop by drop. With the motor running, pour in 185 ml (6 fl oz/$\frac{3}{4}$ cup) of the oil in a thin stream until the mixture thickens and becomes creamy. With the motor still running, add 1 teaspoon of the lemon juice, season with salt and blend for 30 seconds. Stir in the olives, cover and refrigerate.

To make the salad, toss the rocket leaves, 2 tablespoons oil and 1 tablespoon lemon juice in a bowl. Press the rosemary into the tuna steaks. Heat the remaining tablespoon of oil in a large frying pan and sear the tuna steaks over medium–high heat for 2–3 minutes on each side, or until cooked to your liking. Serve with a dollop of olive mayonnaise, potato wedges and rocket salad. Serves 4

Note: To save time, use 250 g (9 oz/1 cup) of whole-egg mayonnaise.

417 SWORDFISH WITH TOMATO SALSA & GARLIC MASH

500 g (1 lb 2 oz) potatoes, cubed
2 large vine-ripened tomatoes
2 tablespoons finely shredded basil
1 tablespoon balsamic vinegar
3 garlic cloves, finely chopped
145 ml (4$\frac{3}{4}$ fl oz) olive oil
4 swordfish steaks (about 200 g/7 oz each)

Cook the potato in a large saucepan of boiling water for 12–15 minutes, or until tender. To make the salsa, score a cross in the base of each tomato. Place in a heatproof bowl and cover with boiling water. Leave for 30 seconds, then plunge into iced water and peel away from the cross. Cut the tomatoes in half, scoop out the seeds and discard. Finely dice the flesh, then combine with the basil, vinegar, 2 garlic cloves and 2 tablespoons oil. Season.

Heat 3 tablespoons of the olive oil in a large non-stick frying pan over medium–high heat. Season the swordfish well, then add to the frying pan and cook for 2–3 minutes on each side for medium-rare, or until cooked to your liking.

Just before the swordfish is ready, drain the potato. Add the remaining oil and garlic, and season to taste. Mash until smooth with a potato masher. To serve, put the swordfish steaks on four serving plates and top with the tomato salsa. Serve the garlic mash on the side. Serves 4

418 THAI GINGER FISH WITH CORIANDER BUTTER

60 g (2$\frac{1}{4}$ oz) butter, at room temperature
1 tablespoon finely chopped coriander (cilantro) leaves
2 tablespoons lime juice
1 tablespoon oil
1 tablespoon grated palm sugar (jaggery)
4 long red chillies, seeded and chopped
2 lemongrass stems, trimmed
4 firm white fish fillets (blue eye or john dory), (about 200 g/
    7 oz each)
1 lime, thinly sliced
1 tablespoon finely shredded fresh ginger

Thoroughly mix the butter and coriander and roll it into a log. Wrap the log in plastic wrap and chill in the refrigerator until required. Preheat the oven to 200°C (400°F/Gas 6). Combine the lime juice, oil, palm sugar and chilli in a small non-metallic bowl and stir until the sugar has dissolved. Cut the lemongrass into halves.

Place a piece of lemongrass in the centre of a sheet of foil large enough to fully enclose one fillet. Place a fish fillet on top and smear the surface with the lime juice mixture. Top with some lime slices and ginger shreds, then wrap into a secure parcel. Repeat with the remaining ingredients to make four parcels.

Place the parcels in an ovenproof dish and bake for 8–10 minutes, or until the fish flakes easily when tested with a fork. To serve, place the parcels on individual serving plates and serve open with slices of coriander butter, steamed rice and steamed greens. Serves 4

419

420

421

419 FISH BALL CURRY

1 large onion, chopped
1 teaspoon sambal oelek
1 tablespoon finely chopped fresh ginger
1 lemongrass stem, white part only, finely chopped
3 tablespoons chopped coriander (cilantro) roots
1/2 teaspoon ground cardamom
1 tablespoon tomato paste (concentrated purée)
1 tablespoon oil
1 tablespoon fish sauce
500 ml (17 fl oz/2 cups) coconut milk
750 g (1 lb 10 oz) fish balls (if frozen, thawed)
3 tablespoons chopped coriander (cilantro) leaves
coriander (cilantro) leaves, extra, to garnish

Place the onion, sambal oelek, ginger, lemongrass, coriander, cardamom and tomato paste in a food processor, and process to a smooth paste. Heat the oil in a large saucepan. Add the spice paste and cook, stirring, over medium heat for 4 minutes, or until fragrant.

Stir in the fish sauce, coconut milk and 500 ml (17 fl oz/2 cups) water. Bring to the boil, then reduce the heat and simmer for 15 minutes, or until the sauce has reduced and thickened slightly. Add the fish balls and cook for 2 minutes. Do not overcook or the fish balls will be tough and rubbery. Stir in the coriander and garnish with extra coriander. Serve with rice. Serves 6

421 YELLOW FISH CURRY

150 ml (5 fl oz) vegetable stock
1 tablespoon ready-made yellow curry paste (see Note)
1 tablespoon tamarind purée
1 tablespoon grated palm sugar (jaggery) or soft brown sugar
1 1/2 tablespoons fish sauce
150 g (5 1/2 oz) green beans, trimmed and cut into 4 cm (1 1/2 inch) lengths
140 g (5 oz/1 cup) sliced, tinned bamboo shoots, rinsed and drained
400 ml (14 fl oz) coconut cream
400 g (14 oz) perch fillet, cubed
1 tablespoon lime juice
lime wedges, to serve
coriander (cilantro) leaves, to garnish

Place the vegetable stock in a large saucepan and bring to the boil. Add the curry paste and cook, stirring, for 3–4 minutes, or until fragrant. Stir in the combined tamarind purée, palm sugar and 1 tablespoon of the fish sauce. Add the beans and bamboo shoots, and cook over medium heat for 3–5 minutes, or until the beans are almost tender.

Add the coconut cream and bring to the boil, then reduce the heat, add the fish and simmer for 3–5 minutes, or until the fish is just cooked. Stir in the lime juice and remaining fish sauce. Garnish with the lime wedges and coriander leaves. Serve with rice. Serves 4

Note: Yellow curry paste can be bought at supermarkets and Asian food stores.

420 GOAN FISH CURRY

4 cardamom pods
1 teaspoon coriander seeds
2 teaspoons mustard seeds
2 tablespoons shredded coconut
3 tablespoons oil
1 large onion, chopped
2 garlic cloves, finely chopped
3 small green chillies, seeded and finely chopped
1 tablespoon grated fresh ginger
1/2 teaspoon ground turmeric
pinch of freshly grated nutmeg
4 cloves
2 tablespoons tamarind purée
6 curry leaves
2 cinnamon sticks
800 ml (28 fl oz) coconut milk
600 g (1 lb 5 oz) skinless pomfret fillets, cut into strips
12 small prawns (shrimp), peeled and deveined
coriander (cilantro) leaves, for garnish

Lightly crush the cardamom pods until the pods split, then remove the seeds from the pods and put in a small frying pan with the coriander seeds. Dry-fry until fragrant and the seeds begin to jump. Remove from the heat and tip into a mortar and pestle or spice grinder. Grind the seeds to a powder.

Tip the mustard seeds into the frying pan with the coconut and toast together until the seeds begin to pop and the coconut turns light golden. Remove from the heat and set aside.

Heat the oil in a saucepan and add the onion. Cook for 4–5 minutes, or until it is starting to soften. Add the garlic, chilli, ginger, turmeric and nutmeg and cook for a further minute. Tip in the ground spices, the toasted coconut and mustard seeds, the cloves, tamarind, curry leaves, cinnamon sticks and coconut milk. Stir well and heat to just below boiling point, then reduce the heat and simmer, uncovered, for 10 minutes, or until slightly thickened.

Add the strips of fish and the prawns and poach for 5 minutes, or until the fish is opaque and the prawns are pale pink. Garnish with coriander leaves. Serves 4

422

423

424

425

422 PAN-FRIED RAINBOW TROUT WITH ALMONDS

2 rainbow trout, scaled and gutted
plain (all-purpose) flour, for coating
60 g (2¼ oz) butter
1 tablespoon oil
3 tablespoons flaked almonds
2 tablespoons lemon juice
1 tablespoon finely chopped flat-leaf (Italian) parsley, plus some extra leaves, for garnish
lemon wedges, for serving

Wash the fish and pat dry with paper towels. Coat the fish with flour and season well on each side as well as inside. Heat half the butter and all of the oil in a large frying pan until it is very hot, then add the fish. Cook for 4 minutes on each side, or until golden brown and cooked through. Lift up one side of the fish to check if the flesh on the inside is opaque and cooked through. If cooked, the dorsal fin should pull out easily. Remove the fish and place on heated serving plates. Cover very loosely with foil and place in a warm oven.

Heat the remaining butter in a frying pan, add the flaked almonds and stir until the almonds turn light golden. Add the lemon juice and parsley, and season with salt and pepper. Stir until the sauce is heated through. Pour over the fish, garnish with parsley, then serve with lemon wedges. Serves 2

423 SOLE MEUNIÈRE

4 dover sole, gutted and dark skin removed
3 tablespoons plain (all-purpose) flour
200 g (7 oz) clarified butter (see Note)
2 tablespoons lemon juice
4 tablespoons chopped flat-leaf (Italian) parsley
lemon wedges, for serving

Pat the fish dry with paper towels, cut the fine bones and frill of skin away from around the edge of the fish, remove the heads if you prefer, and then dust lightly with the flour and season. Heat 150 g (5½ oz) of the butter in a frying pan large enough to fit all four fish, or use half the butter and cook the fish in two batches.

Put the fish in the pan, skin side up, and cook for 4 minutes, or until golden (this will be the service side), turn over carefully and cook on the other side for another 4 minutes, or until the fish is cooked through (the flesh will feel firm). Lift the fish out onto warm plates and drizzle with the lemon juice and sprinkle with the parsley. Add the remaining butter to the pan and heat until it browns, but be careful not to overbrown it or the sauce will taste burnt. Pour over the fish (it will foam as it mixes with the lemon juice) and serve with lemon wedges and steamed greens. Serves 4

Note: Clarified butter has a higher burning point than other butters. To clarify butter, heat a pack of butter until liquid. Leave until the white milk solids settle to the bottom. Use a spoon to skim off any foam, then strain off the golden liquid, leaving the white solids behind.

424 STEAMED WHOLE SNAPPER WITH ASIAN FLAVOURS

800 g (1 lb 12 oz) whole snapper, scaled and gutted
3 lemongrass stems
1 handful coriander (cilantro) leaves
small knob of fresh ginger, peeled and cut into thin matchsticks
1 large garlic clove, peeled and cut into thin slivers
2 tablespoons soy sauce
3 tablespoons oil
1 tablespoon fish sauce
1 small red chilli, seeded and finely chopped

Score the fish with diagonal cuts on both sides. Cut each stem of lemongrass into three and lightly squash each piece with the end of the handle of a large knife. Put half of the lemongrass in the middle of a large piece of foil and lay the fish on top. Put the remaining lemongrass and half of the coriander leaves inside the cavity of the fish.

Mix the ginger, garlic, soy sauce, oil, fish sauce and chilli together. Drizzle the mixture over the fish and scatter with the remaining coriander leaves.

Enclose the fish in the foil and sit in a large bamboo or metal steamer over a pan of simmering water. Steam for 25 minutes, or until the flesh of the fish is opaque and white. Serve with stir-fried Asian greens and rice. Serves 2

425 BAKED ATLANTIC SALMON

16 cherry tomatoes, cut in half
150 g (5½ oz) ripe pineapple flesh, diced
4 x 200 g (7 oz) Atlantic salmon fillets, skin on
2 tablespoons balsamic vinegar
2 tablespoons olive oil
100 g (3½ oz) rocket (arugula) or baby English spinach
4 tablespoons shredded basil leaves

Preheat the oven to 180°C (350°F/Gas 4). Mix the tomatoes and pineapple together. Line a baking tray with a piece of foil, bearing in mind that the foil needs to be large enough to enclose the four salmon fillets. Place the salmon fillets on the foil and season with salt and pepper. Spoon the tomato and pineapple mixture on top of the fillets, dividing it equally. Whisk the balsamic vinegar and olive oil together in a small bowl and drizzle over the top. Wrap the parcel to enclose the fish and put in the preheated oven for 20–25 minutes, or until the salmon is opaque but still moist and succulent.

Make a small bed of rocket or spinach leaves in the centre of each plate. Lift the salmon fillets out of the foil and sit on top of the leaves. Spoon on the pineapple and tomato mixture, drizzle with the cooking juices and sprinkle with basil. Serves 4

426

427

428

426 SCALLOPS IN BLACK BEAN SAUCE

24 scallops, cleaned
2 tablespoons oil
1 tablespoon soy sauce
2 tablespoons Chinese rice wine
1 teaspoon sugar
1 garlic clove, finely chopped
1 spring onion (scallion), finely chopped
$1/2$ teaspoon finely grated fresh ginger
1 tablespoon salted fermented black beans, rinsed and drained (see Note)
1 teaspoon roasted sesame oil

Begin by preparing the scallops. Heat 1 tablespoon of the oil in a wok and, when hot, add the scallops. Cook for 2 minutes, or until firm. Remove to a plate. Mix together the soy sauce, rice wine and sugar in a cup with a tablespoon of water and set aside.

Add the remaining tablespoon of oil to the wok and heat until it is beginning to smoke. Add the garlic, spring onion and ginger. Cook for 30 seconds. Add the beans and the soy sauce mixture and bring to the boil. Return the scallops to the sauce with the sesame oil and allow to simmer for about 30 seconds. Serve immediately with rice and steamed Asian greens. Serves 4

Note: Salted fermented black beans are fermented soy beans that have a distinct, salty flavour. They are used in the cooking of southern China.

428 PRAWN & SNOW PEA STIR-FRY

$1\frac{1}{2}$ tablespoons peanut oil
3 garlic cloves, thinly sliced
1 lemongrass stem, white part only, finely chopped
$1\frac{1}{2}$ tablespoons thinly sliced fresh ginger
1 kg (2 lb 4 oz) raw prawns (shrimp), peeled and deveined, tails intact
200 g (7 oz) snow peas (mangetout), trimmed and cut into 3–4 strips lengthways
6 spring onions (scallions), cut into thin slices on the diagonal
75 g ($2\frac{3}{4}$ oz) snow pea (mangetout) sprouts
1 tablespoon Chinese rice wine or dry sherry
1 tablespoon oyster sauce
1 tablespoon soy sauce

Heat a wok to very hot, add the oil and swirl to coat the side. Add the garlic, lemongrass and ginger and stir-fry for 1–2 minutes, or until fragrant. Add the prawns and cook for 2–3 minutes, or until pink and cooked through.

Add the snow peas, spring onion, sprouts, rice wine, oyster and soy sauces and toss until heated through and the vegetables start to wilt. Serves 4–6

427 GREEK-STYLE CALAMARI

STUFFING
1 tablespoon olive oil
2 spring onions (scallions), chopped
280 g (10 oz/$1\frac{1}{2}$ cups) cold, cooked rice (see Note)
60 g ($2\frac{1}{4}$ oz) pine nuts
75 g ($2\frac{3}{4}$ oz/$\frac{1}{2}$ cup) currants
2 tablespoons chopped flat-leaf (Italian) parsley
2 teaspoons finely grated lemon zest
1 egg, lightly beaten
1 kg (2 lb 4 oz) squid (calamari) tubes, washed and patted dry

SAUCE
4 large ripe tomatoes
1 tablespoon olive oil
1 onion, finely chopped
1 garlic clove, crushed
3 tablespoons good-quality red wine
1 tablespoon chopped oregano

Preheat the oven to 160°C (315°F/Gas 2–3). For the stuffing, mix the oil, spring onion, rice, pine nuts, currants, parsley and lemon zest in a bowl. Season well with salt and freshly ground black pepper. Add enough egg to moisten all the ingredients. Three-quarters fill each squid tube with the stuffing. Secure the ends with toothpicks. Put in a single layer in a casserole dish.

For the sauce, score a cross in the base of each tomato, put in a bowl of boiling water for 30 seconds, then plunge into cold water and peel the skin away from the cross. Chop the flesh. Heat the oil in a pan. Add the onion and garlic and cook over low heat for 2 minutes, or until the onion is soft. Add the tomato, wine and oregano and bring to the boil. Reduce the heat, cover and cook over low heat for 10 minutes.

Pour the hot sauce over the squid, cover and bake for 20 minutes, or until the squid is tender. Remove the toothpicks before cutting into thick slices for serving. Spoon the sauce over the calamari just before serving. Serves 4–6

Note: You will need to cook 100 g ($3\frac{1}{2}$ oz/$\frac{1}{2}$ cup) rice for this recipe.

429

430

431

432

429 SAGE & RICOTTA STUFFED CHICKEN

250 g (9 oz/1 cup) fresh ricotta cheese, well drained
1 tablespoon shredded sage leaves
2 garlic cloves, crushed
1½ teaspoons grated lemon zest
40 g (1½ oz) finely grated parmesan cheese
4 chicken breast fillets, tenderloin removed
8 thin slices prosciutto
olive oil, for brushing

Mix together the ricotta, sage, garlic, zest and parmesan until they are well combined. Use a sharp knife to cut a large pocket into the side of each chicken breast and fill each pocket with a quarter of the ricotta mixture. Pin the pockets closed with toothpicks and wrap each breast in two slices of prosciutto, securing it with a toothpick.

Heat a barbecue flat plate to medium direct heat, brush the chicken parcels with olive oil and season them with freshly ground black pepper. Cook them for 8 minutes on each side, or until they are cooked through. Serves 4

430 MARGARITA CHICKEN

4 chicken breasts, skin on, tenderloin and any excess fat removed
3 tablespoons tequila
3 tablespoons lime juice
2 small chillies, finely chopped
3 garlic cloves, crushed
3 tablespoons finely chopped coriander (cilantro) leaves
1 tablespoon olive oil
lime wedges

Put the chicken, tequila, lime juice, chilli, garlic, coriander and olive oil in a non-metallic bowl and mix it all together so that the chicken is coated in the marinade. Cover the bowl and refrigerate for at least 2 hours, or preferably overnight.

Preheat a barbecue chargrill to medium–high direct heat. Remove the chicken breasts from the marinade, season them with salt and pepper, and grill for 7–8 minutes on each side or until they are cooked through. Slice the chicken breasts on the diagonal and serve with lime wedges. Serves 4

431 MIRIN & SAKE CHICKEN

4 large chicken breast fillets
2 tablespoons mirin
2 tablespoons sake
1 tablespoon oil
5 cm (2 inch) piece of fresh ginger, very finely sliced
3 teaspoons soy sauce
salad leaves, to serve

Put the chicken in a non-metallic dish. Combine the mirin, sake and oil and pour over the chicken. Marinate for 15 minutes, then drain the chicken, reserving the marinade.

Cook the chicken on a hot, lightly oiled barbecue grill or flat plate for 4 minutes each side, or until tender. Put the ginger in a pan and add the reserved marinade. Boil for about 7 minutes, or until thickened. Drizzle the soy sauce over the chicken and top with the ginger. Serve immediately on a bed of salad leaves. Serves 4

432 SPICED DUCK BREAST WITH PEACH & CHILLI SALAD

6 ripe peaches
1 lime plus 1 tablespoon lime juice, extra
1 tablespoon extra virgin olive oil
1 small red chilli, seeded and finely sliced
2 tablespoons chopped mint
4 duck breasts
2 teaspoons ground coriander
lime wedges

Dip the peaches into a saucepan of boiling water for 5 seconds then plunge them into iced water. Remove the skins, which should slip off easily. Cut each peach in half, remove the stone, then cut each half into eight wedges. Peel the lime, removing all the pith, and separate the lime sections by carefully cutting each piece away from the membrane. Toss the peach slices with the lime segments, extra lime juice, olive oil, chilli and mint, and season with a little pepper.

Trim the duck breasts of fat and sinew, and sprinkle each breast with the ground coriander. Preheat a barbecue flat plate to medium direct heat and cook the duck on the flat plate for 4 minutes or until the skin is golden, then turn it and cook for another 4 minutes. Turn the breasts over again and cook them for 1 minute longer to make the skin crispy, then leave to rest in a warm place for 10 minutes.

Slice each breast into four pieces on the diagonal and serve them with the peach salad and lime wedges. Serves 4

433

434

435

433 BACON-WRAPPED CHICKEN

2 tablespoons olive oil
2 tablespoons lime juice
1/4 teaspoon ground coriander
6 chicken breast fillets
4 tablespoons fruit chutney
3 tablespoons chopped pecan nuts
6 bacon slices

Mix together the olive oil, lime juice, coriander and salt and pepper. Using a sharp knife, cut a pocket in the thickest section of each fillet. Mix together the chutney and nuts. Spoon 1 tablespoon of the chutney mixture into each chicken breast pocket.

Turn the tapered ends of the fillets to the underside. Wrap a slice of bacon around each fillet to enclose the filling and secure with a toothpick. Put the chicken parcels on a hot, lightly oiled barbecue grill or flat plate and cook for 5 minutes on each side, or until cooked through, turning once. Brush with the lime juice mixture several times during cooking and drizzle with any leftover lime juice mixture to serve. Serves 6

435 THAI-SPICED CHICKEN WITH POTATO RÖSTI

600 g (1 lb 5 oz) chicken breast fillet, cut into strips
1 tablespoon chopped lemongrass
2 tablespoons lime juice
1 1/2 tablespoons oil
2 garlic cloves, crushed
1 tablespoon grated fresh ginger
2 teaspoons sweet chilli sauce
2 spring onions (scallions), chopped
1 lime, cut into 6 wedges

POTATO RÖSTI
600 g (1 lb 5 oz) potatoes
3 tablespoons plain (all-purpose) flour
1 egg, lightly beaten

Put the chicken in a shallow, non-metallic dish. Mix together the lemongrass, lime juice, oil, garlic, ginger, sweet chilli sauce and spring onion. Pour over the chicken, cover and refrigerate for at least 2 hours.

To make the potato rösti, peel and grate the potatoes. Squeeze the excess moisture from the potato with your hands until it feels quite dry. Mix the potato with the flour and egg and season well. Divide into six portions. Cook on a hot, lightly oiled barbecue flat plate for 10 minutes, or until golden brown on both sides.

Drain the chicken and reserve the marinade. Cook on a barbecue grill or flat plate for 3 minutes each side, or until tender and golden brown. Brush with the reserved marinade while cooking. Serve with the rösti and a squeeze of lime juice. Serves 6

434 SPICY BUFFALO WINGS WITH RANCH DRESSING

12 large chicken wings
2 teaspoons garlic salt
2 teaspoons onion powder
oil, for deep-frying
125 ml (4 fl oz/1/2 cup) tomato sauce (ketchup)
2 tablespoons worcestershire sauce
50 g (1 3/4 oz) butter, melted
Tabasco sauce, to taste

RANCH DRESSING
1 small garlic clove, crushed
185 g (6 1/2 oz/3/4 cup) mayonnaise
125 ml (4 fl oz/1/2 cup) buttermilk
2 tablespoons finely chopped flat-leaf (Italian) parsley
1 tablespoon finely chopped chives
1 1/2 teaspoons lemon juice
1 1/2 teaspoons dijon mustard
1 teaspoon onion powder

Pat the wings dry with paper towels, remove and discard the tip of each wing, then cut them in half at the joint. Combine the garlic salt, onion powder and 2 teaspoons of ground black pepper, and rub the spice mixture into each chicken piece.

Deep-fry the chicken in batches for 2–3 minutes without letting it brown, then remove from the oil and drain on crumpled paper towels. When the chicken has cooled a little, put it in a non-metallic bowl with the combined tomato sauce, worcestershire sauce, butter and Tabasco, and toss so that all of the pieces are well coated in the marinade. Cover and refrigerate for at least 2 hours, or overnight.

To make the ranch dressing, mash the garlic and 1/4 teaspoon salt to a paste then add the mayonnaise, buttermilk, parsley, chives, lemon juice, mustard and onion powder, and whisk it all together. Season well, cover and chill for at least 1 hour before serving.

Preheat a barbecue to medium direct heat. Cook the chicken for 6–8 minutes on each side, or until it is caramelised and sticky, turning and basting with the marinade as it cooks. Serve hot with the ranch dressing. Serves 4

436

437

438

439

436 MALAYSIAN NONYA CHICKEN CURRY

CURRY PASTE
2 red onions, chopped
4 small red chillies, seeded and sliced
4 garlic cloves, sliced
2 lemongrass stems, white part only, sliced
3 x 2 cm (1¼ x ¾ inch) piece galangal, sliced
8 kaffir lime leaves, roughly chopped
1 teaspoon ground turmeric
½ teaspoon shrimp paste, dry-roasted

2 tablespoons oil
750 g (1 lb 10 oz) chicken thigh fillets, cut into bite-size pieces
400 ml (14 fl oz) coconut milk
3 tablespoons tamarind purée
1 tablespoon fish sauce
3 kaffir lime leaves, shredded

To make the curry paste, place all of the ingredients in a food processor or blender and process to a thick paste. Heat a wok or large saucepan over high heat, add the oil and swirl to coat the side. Add the curry paste and cook, stirring occasionally, over low heat for 8–10 minutes, or until fragrant. Add the chicken and stir-fry with the paste for 2–3 minutes.

Add the coconut milk, tamarind purée and fish sauce to the wok, and simmer, stirring occasionally, for 15–20 minutes, or until the chicken is tender. Garnish with the lime leaves. Serve with rice and steamed bok choy (pak choy). Serves 4

437 HOT & SWEET CHICKEN

125 ml (4 fl oz/½ cup) rice vinegar
145 g (5¼ oz/⅔ cup) caster (superfine) sugar
6 garlic cloves, crushed
large pinch of chilli flakes
1 teaspoon ground coriander
1 teaspoon ground white pepper
2 large handfuls coriander (cilantro), finely chopped, including roots and stems
3 tablespoons olive oil
2 tablespoons lemon juice
8 boneless and skinless chicken thighs, cut in half
2 tablespoons caster (superfine) sugar, extra
2 tablespoons fish sauce
1 small cucumber, peeled and sliced

Put the vinegar and sugar in a small saucepan, bring to the boil, then turn down the heat and simmer for a minute. Take the mixture off the heat and add two crushed garlic cloves, the chilli flakes and a pinch of salt. Leave the dressing to cool. Heat a frying pan for a minute, add the ground coriander and white pepper and stir it around for a minute. This will make the spices more fragrant. Add the rest of the garlic, the coriander and a pinch of salt. Add 2 tablespoons of the oil and all the lemon juice and mix to a paste. Rub this all over the chicken pieces.

Heat the rest of the oil in a wok, add the chicken and fry it on both sides for 8 minutes, or until it is cooked through. Sprinkle in the extra sugar and the fish sauce and cook for another minute or two until any excess liquid has evaporated and the chicken pieces are sticky. Serve with the sliced cucumber and some rice. Dress with the sauce. Serves 4

438 GREEN CHICKEN CURRY

250 ml (9 fl oz/1 cup) coconut cream
4 tablespoons green curry paste
8 skinless chicken thighs or 4 chicken breasts, cut into pieces
250 ml (9 fl oz/1 cup) coconut milk
4 Thai eggplants (aubergines) or ½ purple eggplant (aubergine), cut into chunks
2 tablespoons shaved palm sugar (jaggery) or soft brown sugar
2 tablespoons fish sauce
4 kaffir lime leaves, torn
1 handful Thai basil
1–2 large red chillies, sliced
coconut milk or cream, for drizzling

Put a wok over a low heat, add the coconut cream and let it come to the boil. Stir it for a while until the oil separates out. Don't let it burn. Add the green curry paste, stir for a minute, then add the chicken. Cook the chicken until it turns opaque, then add the coconut milk and eggplant. Cook for a minute or two until the eggplant is tender.

Add the sugar, fish sauce, lime leaves and half of the basil, then mix together. Garnish with the rest of the basil, the chilli and a drizzle of coconut milk or cream. Serve with rice. Serves 4

439 SPANISH-STYLE CHICKEN CASSEROLE

2 tablespoons light olive oil
750 g (1 lb 10 oz) chicken thighs
750 g (1 lb 10 oz) chicken drumsticks
1 large onion, chopped
2 garlic cloves, crushed
2 teaspoons sweet paprika
1 large red capsicum (pepper), sliced
200 ml (7 fl oz) dry sherry
415 g (14¾ oz) tin peeled tomatoes
2 tablespoons tomato paste (concentrated purée)
165 g (5¾ oz/¾ cup) green olives, pitted, halved
1 teaspoon sweet paprika, extra

Preheat the oven to 180°C (350°F/Gas 4). Heat the oil in a large frying pan, add the chicken in batches and cook over medium heat for 3–4 minutes, or until browned. Transfer to a 4 litre (140 fl oz/16 cup) flameproof casserole dish. Add the onion, garlic, paprika and capsicum to the frying pan, and cook for 5–8 minutes, or until softened.

Add the sherry and cook for 2 minutes, or until slightly reduced. Add the tomatoes and tomato paste, stir well and cook for 2 minutes. Pour the tomato mixture over the chicken and add 250 ml (9 fl oz/ 1 cup) water. Bake, covered, for 1 hour 15 minutes, then uncovered for 15 minutes. Add the olives and leave for 10 minutes. Garnish with the extra paprika and serve with rice. Serves 4

440

441

442

440 CHICKEN WITH THAI BASIL

3 tablespoons peanut oil
500 g (1 lb 2 oz) chicken breast fillets, trimmed
   and cut into thin strips
1 garlic clove, crushed
4 spring onions (scallions), thinly sliced
150 g (5$\frac{1}{2}$ oz) snake beans, trimmed and cut into 5 cm
   (2 inch) lengths
2 small red chillies, thinly sliced
1 handful Thai basil
2 tablespoons chopped mint
1 tablespoon fish sauce
1 tablespoon oyster sauce
2 teaspoons lime juice
1 tablespoon grated palm sugar (jaggery)
Thai basil, extra, to garnish

Heat a wok over high heat, add 1 tablespoon of the oil and swirl to coat. Cook the chicken in batches for 3–5 minutes, or until lightly browned and almost cooked — add more oil if needed. Remove and keep warm.

Heat the remaining oil. Add the garlic, onion, snake beans and chilli, and stir-fry for 1 minute, or until the onion is tender. Add the chicken to the wok. Toss in the basil and mint, then add the combined fish sauce, oyster sauce, lime juice, palm sugar and 2 tablespoons water and cook for 1 minute. Garnish with the extra basil and serve with jasmine rice. Serves 4

442 CHICKEN, ARTICHOKE & BROAD BEAN STEW

8 chicken thighs on the bone (skin removed, optional)
60 g (2$\frac{1}{4}$ oz/$\frac{1}{2}$ cup) seasoned plain (all-purpose) flour
2 tablespoons oil
1 large red onion, cut into small wedges
125 ml (4 fl oz/$\frac{1}{2}$ cup) dry white wine
310 ml (10$\frac{3}{4}$ fl oz/1$\frac{1}{4}$ cups) chicken stock
2 teaspoons finely chopped rosemary
340 g (12 oz) marinated artichokes, well drained and quartered
155 g (5$\frac{1}{2}$ oz/1 cup) frozen broad beans, skins removed
800 g (1 lb 12 oz) potatoes, cut into large pieces
60 g (2$\frac{1}{4}$ oz) butter

Coat the chicken in the flour, shaking off the excess. Heat the oil in a saucepan, then brown the chicken in two batches on all sides over medium heat. Remove and drain on crumpled paper towels.

Add the onion to the pan and cook for 3–4 minutes, or until soft but not brown. Increase the heat to high, pour in the wine and boil for 2 minutes, or until reduced to a syrup. Stir in 250 ml (9 fl oz/1 cup) stock and bring just to the boil, then return the chicken to the saucepan with the rosemary. Reduce the heat to low and simmer, covered, for 45 minutes. Add the artichokes, increase the heat to high and return to the boil. Reduce to a simmer and cook, uncovered, for 10–15 minutes. Add the beans and cook for 5 minutes.

Meanwhile, cook the potato in a saucepan of boiling water for 15–20 minutes, or until tender. Drain, then return to the pan. Add the butter and the remaining stock and mash with a potato masher. Serve on the side of the stew. Serves 4

441 BLACKENED CHICKEN WITH CRISPY TORTILLAS

4 vine-ripened tomatoes, cut into 1 cm ($\frac{1}{2}$ inch) slices
1 teaspoon caster (superfine) sugar
1 red onion, sliced
150 ml (5 fl oz) olive oil
1 ripe avocado
3 tablespoons sour cream
100 ml (3$\frac{1}{2}$ fl oz) milk
2 tablespoons lime juice
2 x 16 cm (6$\frac{1}{4}$ inch) corn tortillas
1 teaspoon dried oregano
2$\frac{1}{2}$ teaspoons ground cumin
1$\frac{1}{4}$ teaspoons garlic salt
$\frac{1}{2}$ teaspoon cayenne pepper
4 small skinless chicken breast fillets (about 600 g/1 lb 5 oz)
1 small handful coriander (cilantro) leaves

Place the tomato slices in a wide dish, sprinkle with sugar and season well. Layer the onion over the top and drizzle with 3 tablespoons of oil. Chill for 20 minutes. Blend the avocado, sour cream, milk, lime juice and 80 ml (2$\frac{1}{2}$ fl oz/$\frac{1}{3}$ cup) water in a food processor for 1 minute, or until smooth. Season.

Cut each of the corn tortillas into eight 2 cm ($\frac{3}{4}$ inch) strips. Combine the oregano, cumin, garlic salt and cayenne pepper, and coat the chicken breasts in the spice mixture, pressing down firmly with your fingers. Heat 1$\frac{1}{2}$ tablespoons of oil over medium–high heat in a large, non-stick frying pan until hot. Cook the chicken breasts for 4–5 minutes on each side, or until cooked through. Cool, then refrigerate. In the same pan add 3 tablespoons of oil. Fry the tortilla strips until golden, turning once during cooking.

On each plate arrange the tomato and onion slices in a small circle. Slice each chicken breast on the diagonal into 2 cm ($\frac{3}{4}$ inch) pieces and arrange over the tomato. Spoon the dressing over the chicken and arrange four tortilla strips over the top. Sprinkle with coriander leaves and serve immediately. Serves 4

443

444

445 446

443 QUICK DUCK CURRY

1 kg (2 lb 4 oz) Chinese roast duck (see Note)
1 tablespoon oil
1 red onion, finely chopped
2 garlic cloves, crushed
1 red chilli, seeded, chopped
1 tablespoon red curry paste
1 tablespoon smooth peanut butter
400 ml (14 fl oz) coconut milk
310 ml (10³/₄ fl oz/1¹/₄ cups) chicken stock
1 tablespoon lime juice
1 tablespoon fish sauce
2 tablespoons chopped coriander (cilantro) leaves

Remove the skin and bones from the Peking duck and cut the meat into bite-size pieces. Heat the oil in a saucepan over medium heat, add the onion and cook for 5 minutes. Add the garlic and chilli, and cook for 2 minutes. Stir in the curry paste and cook for 1–2 minutes, or until fragrant, then stir in the peanut butter.

Gradually whisk in the coconut milk and cook for 2 minutes, or until well combined. Add the stock, bring to the boil, then reduce the heat and simmer for 10 minutes. Add the duck and simmer for 10 minutes. Stir in the lime juice and fish sauce. Scatter the coriander over the top and serve with rice or noodles. Serves 4

Note: Chinese roast duck is available from Chinese barbecue and roast meat outlets. Leave the skin on the duck, if preferred.

444 BUTTER CHICKEN

2 tablespoons peanut oil
1 kg (2 lb 4 oz) chicken thigh fillets, quartered
60 g (2¹/₄ oz) butter or ghee
2 teaspoons garam masala
2 teaspoons sweet paprika
2 teaspoons ground coriander
1 tablespoon finely chopped fresh ginger
¹/₄ teaspoon chilli powder
1 cinnamon stick
6 cardamom pods, bruised
350 g (12 oz) puréed tomatoes
1 tablespoon sugar
3 tablespoons plain yoghurt
125 ml (4 fl oz/¹/₂ cup) cream
1 tablespoon lemon juice

Heat a wok until very hot, add 1 tablespoon oil and swirl to coat. Add half the chicken thigh fillets and stir-fry for 4 minutes, or until browned. Remove. Add extra oil, as needed, and cook the remaining chicken. Remove. Reduce the heat, add the butter to the wok and melt. Add the garam masala, sweet paprika, coriander, ginger, chilli powder, cinnamon stick and cardamom pods, and stir-fry for 1 minute, or until fragrant. Return the chicken to the wok and mix to coat in the spices.

Add the tomato and sugar, and simmer, stirring, for 15 minutes, or until the chicken is tender and the sauce has thickened. Add the yoghurt, cream and juice and simmer for 5 minutes, or until the sauce has thickened slightly. Serve with rice and pappadums. Serves 4–6

445 CHICKEN CASSEROLE WITH MUSTARD & TARRAGON

3 tablespoons olive oil
1 kg (2 lb 4 oz) chicken thigh fillets, halved, then quartered
1 onion, finely chopped
1 leek, sliced
1 garlic clove, finely chopped
350 g (12 oz) button mushrooms, sliced
¹/₂ teaspoon dried tarragon
375 ml (13 fl oz/1¹/₂ cups) chicken stock
185 ml (6 fl oz/³/₄ cup) cream
2 teaspoons lemon juice
2 teaspoons dijon mustard

Preheat the oven to 180°C (350°F/ Gas 4). Heat 1 tablespoon of the oil in a flameproof casserole dish over medium heat, and cook the chicken in batches for 6–7 minutes each, or until golden. Remove from the dish.

Add the remaining oil to the casserole dish and cook the onion, leek and garlic over medium heat for 5 minutes, or until soft. Add the mushrooms and cook for 5–7 minutes, or until they are soft and browned, and most of the liquid has evaporated. Add the tarragon, chicken stock, cream, lemon juice and mustard, bring to the boil and cook for 2 minutes. Return the chicken pieces to the dish and season well. Cover.

Place the casserole in the oven and cook for 1 hour, or until the sauce has reduced and thickened. Season to taste with salt and pepper, and serve with potatoes and a green salad. Serves 4–6

446 CHICKEN BRAISED WITH GINGER & STAR ANISE

1 teaspoon sichuan peppercorns
2 tablespoons peanut oil
3 x 2 cm (1¹/₄ x ³/₄ inch) fresh ginger, julienned
2 garlic cloves, chopped
1 kg (2 lb 4 oz) chicken thigh fillets, cut in half
80 ml (2¹/₂ fl oz/¹/₃ cup) Chinese rice wine
1 tablespoon honey
3 tablespoons light soy sauce
1 star anise

Heat a wok over medium heat, add the peppercorns and cook, stirring to prevent burning, for 2–4 minutes, or until fragrant. Remove and lightly crush with the back of a knife.

Reheat the wok, add the oil and swirl to coat. Add the ginger and garlic, and cook over low heat for 1–2 minutes, or until slightly golden. Add the chicken, increase the heat to medium and cook for 3 minutes, or until browned all over.

Add the peppercorns, wine, honey, soy sauce and star anise to the wok, reduce the heat to low and simmer, covered, for 20 minutes, or until the chicken is tender. Divide among four plates and serve with steamed rice. Serves 4

447

448

449

447 PERSIAN CHICKEN SKEWERS

2 teaspoons ground cardamom
$\frac{1}{2}$ teaspoon ground turmeric
1 teaspoon ground allspice
4 garlic cloves, crushed
3 tablespoons lemon juice
3 tablespoons olive oil
4 large chicken thigh fillets, excess fat removed
lemon wedges, to serve
plain yoghurt, to serve

To make the marinade, whisk together the cardamom, turmeric, allspice, garlic, lemon juice and oil. Season with salt and ground black pepper. Cut each chicken thigh fillet into 3–4 cm ($1\frac{1}{4}$–$1\frac{1}{2}$ inch) cubes. Toss the cubes in the spice marinade. Cover and refrigerate overnight.

Thread the chicken onto metal skewers and cook on a hot, lightly oiled barbecue grill or flat plate for 4 minutes on each side, or until the chicken is cooked through. Serve with lemon wedges and plain yoghurt. Serves 4

449 MEDITERRANEAN CHICKEN SKEWERS

2 large chicken breast fillets, cut into 32 cubes
24 cherry tomatoes
6 cap mushrooms, cut into quarters
2 garlic cloves, crushed
zest of 1 lemon, grated
2 tablespoons lemon juice
2 tablespoons olive oil
1 tablespoon oregano, chopped

Soak eight wooden skewers in water to prevent scorching. Thread a piece of chicken onto each skewer, followed by a tomato, then a piece of mushroom. Repeat twice for each skewer and finish with a piece of chicken. Put the skewers in a shallow, non-metallic dish.

Combine the garlic, lemon zest, lemon juice, olive oil and chopped oregano, pour over the skewers and toss well. Marinate for at least 2 hours, or overnight if time permits.

Cook the skewers on a hot, lightly oiled barbecue grill or flat plate for 4 minutes on each side, basting occasionally, until the chicken is cooked and the tomatoes have shrivelled slightly. Makes 8 skewers

448 CHICKEN TIKKA WITH GARLIC NAAN & APPLE RAITA

100 g ($3\frac{1}{2}$ oz/$\frac{1}{3}$ cup) tikka paste
3 tablespoons Greek-style yoghurt
600 g (1 lb 5 oz) chicken breast fillet, cut into 3 cm ($1\frac{1}{4}$ inch) cubes
2 small red onions, quartered
oil, for brushing
2 tablespoons chopped coriander (cilantro) leaves

APPLE RAITA
1 green apple, grated
2 teaspoons lemon juice
3 tablespoons sour cream
3 tablespoons chopped mint

GARLIC NAAN
1 garlic clove, crushed
2 tablespoons butter, softened
4 plain naan bread

Stir the tikka paste and yoghurt together, add the chicken and turn it until it is evenly coated in the tikka mixture. Cover the chicken with plastic wrap and refrigerate it for 4 hours or overnight.

To make the raita, put the grated apple, lemon juice, sour cream and mint in a small bowl and stir it all together. Cover the bowl and refrigerate it until you are ready to dish up. Mash the crushed garlic and butter together and brush one side of each piece of naan with about 2 teaspoons of garlic butter.

Soak four wooden skewers in cold water for 1 hour and preheat the barbecue to low–medium direct heat. Thread the chicken and onion pieces onto the skewers and cook them on the flat plate for 5–6 minutes on each side, turning once. A little before the chicken is ready, lightly brush the chargrill plate with some oil. Grill the naan, buttered side down, for 1–2 minutes, or until the bread is golden and marked. Turn it and grill for another minute on the other side.

Sprinkle the skewers with the chopped coriander and serve them with the garlic naan and apple raita. Serves 4

450

451

452

453

450 FIVE-SPICE ROAST CHICKEN

1.8 kg (4 lb) chicken
1 tablespoon soy sauce
2 garlic cloves, crushed
1 teaspoon finely grated fresh ginger
1 tablespoon honey
1 tablespoon rice wine
1 teaspoon Chinese five-spice
1 tablespoon peanut oil

Wash the chicken and pat it thoroughly dry inside and out with paper towels. Whisk the soy sauce, garlic, ginger, honey, rice wine and five-spice together in a small bowl and brush it all over the chicken, ensuring every bit of skin is well coated. Put the chicken on a wire rack over a baking tray and refrigerate it, uncovered, for at least 8 hours, or overnight.

Preheat a kettle or covered barbecue to medium indirect heat and put a drip tray under the rack. Brush the chicken liberally with the peanut oil and put it, breast side up, in the middle of the barbecue over the drip tray. Cover the barbecue and roast the chicken for 1 hour 10 minutes, or until the juices run clear when you pierce it with a skewer between the thigh and body. Check the chicken every so often, and if it appears to be over-browning, cover it loosely with foil. Leave it to rest, covered, for 10 minutes before carving and serving. The flavours in this style of chicken go well with steamed Asian greens and fried rice. Serves 4

451 DRUMSTICKS IN TOMATO & MANGO CHUTNEY

8 chicken drumsticks, scored
1 tablespoon mustard powder
2 tablespoons tomato sauce (ketchup)
1 tablespoon sweet mango chutney
1 teaspoon worcestershire sauce
1 tablespoon dijon mustard
3 tablespoons raisins
1 tablespoon oil

Toss the chicken in the mustard powder and season with salt and ground black pepper. Combine the tomato sauce, mango chutney, worcestershire sauce, mustard, raisins and oil. Spoon over the chicken and toss well. Marinate for at least 2 hours, turning once.

Cook the chicken on a hot, lightly oiled barbecue flat plate for about 20 minutes, or until cooked through. Serves 4

452 BARBECUED CRISPY CHICKEN WINGS

12 chicken wings
3 tablespoons soy sauce
3 tablespoons hoisin sauce
125 g (4$\frac{1}{2}$ oz/$\frac{1}{2}$ cup) tomato sauce (ketchup)
2 tablespoons honey
1 tablespoon soft brown sugar
1 tablespoon cider vinegar
2 garlic cloves, crushed
$\frac{1}{4}$ teaspoon Chinese five-spice
2 teaspoons sesame oil

Tuck the chicken wing tips to the underside and place in a non-metallic bowl. Mix together all the remaining ingredients and pour over the wings, tossing to coat. Cover and leave in the fridge for at least 2 hours, turning occasionally. Drain, reserving the marinade.

Cook the wings on a hot, lightly oiled barbecue grill or flat plate for 5 minutes, or until cooked through, brushing with the reserved marinade several times. Serves 6

453 BLACKENED CAJUN SPICED CHICKEN

1$\frac{1}{2}$ tablespoons onion powder
1$\frac{1}{2}$ tablespoons garlic powder
2 teaspoons paprika
1 teaspoon white pepper
2 teaspoons dried thyme
$\frac{1}{2}$–1 teaspoon chilli powder
8 chicken drumsticks, scored

Combine the onion powder, garlic powder, paprika, white pepper, thyme, chilli powder and 1 teaspoon salt in a plastic bag. Place the drumsticks in the bag and shake until all the pieces are coated. Leave the chicken in the fridge for at least 30 minutes to allow the flavours to develop, or overnight if time permits.

Cook the chicken on a lightly oiled barbecue grill for 55–60 minutes, or until slightly blackened and cooked through. Brush lightly with some oil to prevent drying out during cooking. Serves 4

454

455

456

454 CHICKEN & LEEK PIES

60 g (2¼ oz) butter
1 leek, thinly sliced
4 chicken breasts (about 200 g/7 oz each)
50 g (1¾ oz) plain (all-purpose) flour
250 ml (9 fl oz/1 cup) chicken and herb stock
300 ml (10½ fl oz) cream
155 g (5½ oz/1 cup) fresh or frozen peas, blanched
1 sheet ready-rolled puff pastry, thawed

Melt the butter in a saucepan over medium heat and cook the leek for 2–3 minutes, or until soft. Add the chicken and cook for 45 minutes, or until cooked. Add the flour and cook, stirring, until it starts to bubble. Add the stock and cook until the mixture starts to thicken. Add the cream, reserving 1 tablespoon to glaze the pastry. Cook until the mixture just starts to boil. Stir in the peas. Season. Remove from the heat. Preheat the oven to 200°C (400°F/Gas 6).

Divide the filling among four individual pie dishes or ramekins. Top with a circle of pastry, cut just bigger than the top of the dish, then press around the edges to seal. Brush the surface with the reserved cream. Make a small slit in the top to allow steam to escape. Place the dishes on a metal tray and bake for 20–25 minutes, or until the pastry is golden. Serve with a green salad. Serves 4

456 STUFFED CHICKEN BREAST WITH TOMATO, GOAT'S CHEESE & ASPARAGUS

4 large chicken breast fillets
100 g (3½ oz) semi-dried tomatoes
100 g (3½ oz) goat's cheese, sliced
200 g (7 oz) asparagus spears, trimmed, halved and blanched
50 g (1¾ oz) butter
375 ml (13 fl oz/1½ cups) chicken stock
2 zucchini (courgettes), cut into 5 cm (2 inch) batons
250 ml (9 fl oz/1 cup) cream
8 spring onions (scallions), thinly sliced

Pound each chicken breast between two sheets of plastic wrap with a mallet or rolling pin until 1 cm (½ inch) thick. Divide the tomato, goat's cheese and 155 g (5½ oz) of the asparagus pieces among the breasts. Roll up tightly lengthways, securing along the seam with toothpicks.

Heat the butter in a large frying pan over medium heat. Add the chicken, then brown on all sides. Pour in the stock, then reduce the heat to low. Cook, covered, for 10 minutes, or until the chicken is cooked through. Remove the chicken and keep warm.

Meanwhile, bring a saucepan of lightly salted water to the boil. Add the zucchini and remaining asparagus and cook for 2 minutes, or until just tender. Remove from the pan. Whisk the cream into the frying pan. Add the spring onion and simmer over medium–low heat for 4 minutes, or until reduced and thickened. To serve, cut each chicken roll in half on the diagonal and place on serving plates. Spoon on the sauce and serve with the greens. Serves 4

455 LEMON & THYME ROASTED CHICKEN WITH ZUCCHINI

1.8 kg (4 lb) whole chicken
12 garlic cloves, unpeeled
10 sprigs lemon thyme
1 lemon, halved
1 tablespoon olive oil
8 small zucchini (courgettes), halved lengthways
2 tablespoons chopped flat-leaf (Italian) parsley
1 tablespoon plain (all-purpose) flour
250 ml (9 fl oz/1 cup) chicken stock

Remove the giblets and any large fat deposits from inside the chicken, then pat it dry inside and out with paper towels. Season the cavity with salt and pepper and stuff it with the unpeeled garlic cloves and the sprigs of thyme. Rub the skin with the cut lemon, making sure that it is evenly coated all over, then brush it with 2 teaspoons of the oil and season with salt and black pepper. Tie the legs together.

Preheat a kettle or covered barbecue to medium indirect heat, with a drip tray underneath the grill. Position the chicken on the barbecue directly over the drip tray, close the hood and roast the chicken for 1 hour, or until the juices run clear when it is pierced with a skewer between the thigh and the body.

When the chicken has been cooking for about 40 minutes, toss the zucchini with the remaining olive oil and season it with salt and black pepper. Arrange the zucchini on the grill around the chicken, re-cover the kettle and cook the chicken and the zucchini for 20–25 minutes, or until the zucchini is tender, but not soggy. Put the zucchini in a serving dish and sprinkle it with the parsley. When the chicken is ready, remove it from the barbecue, cover it loosely with foil and leave it to rest for 10 minutes. Remove the garlic from the chicken cavity but do not peel the cloves.

If you would like gravy to go with the chicken, pour the contents of the drip tray into a container and skim off as much fat as possible. Tip the remaining juices into a saucepan, add the flour and stir well to combine. Cook the gravy over medium heat for 3–4 minutes, or until it has thickened, then add the chicken stock and any juices that have been released from the chicken while it was resting. Bring the gravy to the boil, then reduce the heat and simmer it for 3–4 minutes. Season the gravy to taste, strain it into a jug and serve with the chicken, garlic and zucchini. Serves 4

457

458

459

460

457 ROASTED CHICKEN PIECES WITH HERBED CHEESE

150 g (5½ oz) herbed cream cheese
1 teaspoon grated lemon zest
4 whole chicken leg quarters or breasts, skin on
2 leeks, cut into chunks
2 parsnips, cut into chunks
2 teaspoons olive oil

Preheat the oven to 200°C (400°F/Gas 6). Mix the cream cheese with the lemon zest. Loosen the skin from the leg quarters or chicken breasts and spread 2 tablespoons of the cream cheese between the skin and flesh on each. Press the skin back down and season it.

Bring a saucepan of water to the boil and cook the leek and parsnip for 4 minutes. Drain them well and put them in a single layer in a baking dish. Drizzle with the oil and season well. Put the chicken on top and put the dish in the oven.

Roast for 40 minutes, by which time the skin should be browned and the cream cheese should have mostly melted out to form a sauce over the vegetables. Check that the vegetables are cooked and tender by prodding them with a knife. If they need a little longer, cover the dish with foil and cook for another 5 minutes. Keep the chicken warm under foil in the meantime. Serves 4

458 GRILLED CHICKEN WITH CAPSICUM COUSCOUS

200 g (7 oz/1 cup) couscous
1 tablespoon olive oil
1 onion, finely chopped
2 zucchini (courgettes), sliced
½ red or yellow chargrilled capsicum (pepper), chopped
12 semi-dried (sun-blushed) tomatoes, chopped
½ tablespoon grated orange zest
250 ml (9 fl oz/1 cup) orange juice
1 large handful chopped mint
8 chicken thighs or 4 chicken breasts, skin on
2 tablespoons butter, softened

Heat the grill (broiler). Bring 500 ml (17 fl oz/2 cups) water to the boil in a saucepan, throw in the couscous, then take the pan off the heat and leave it to stand for 10 minutes.

Heat the oil in a frying pan and fry the onion and zucchini until lightly browned. Add the capsicum and semi-dried tomatoes, then stir in the couscous. Stir in the orange zest, one-third of the orange juice and the mint.

Put the chicken in a large shallow baking dish in a single layer and dot it with the butter. Sprinkle with the remaining orange juice and season well with salt and pepper. Grill the chicken for 8–10 minutes, turning it over halfway through. The skin should be browned and crisp. Serve the chicken on the couscous with any juices poured over it. Serves 4

459 TANDOORI CHICKEN WITH CARDAMOM RICE

250 g (9 oz/1 cup) plain yoghurt, plus extra for serving
3 tablespoons tandoori paste
2 tablespoons lemon juice
1 kg (2 lb 4 oz) chicken breast fillets, cut into 4 cm (1½ inch) cubes
1 tablespoon oil
1 onion, finely diced
300 g (10½ oz/1½ cups) long-grain rice
2 cardamom pods, bruised
750 ml (26 fl oz/3 cups) hot chicken stock
400 g (14 oz) English spinach leaves

Soak eight wooden skewers in water for 30 minutes. Combine the yoghurt, tandoori paste and lemon juice in a non-metallic dish. Add the chicken and coat well, then cover and marinate for at least 10 minutes. Meanwhile, heat the oil in a saucepan. Add the onion and cook for 3 minutes, then add the rice and cardamom pods. Cook, stirring often, for 3–5 minutes, or until the rice is slightly opaque. Add the hot chicken stock and bring to the boil. Reduce the heat to low, cover, and cook the rice, without removing the lid, for 15 minutes.

Heat a barbecue plate or oven grill (broiler) to very hot. Thread the chicken cubes onto the skewers, leaving the bottom quarter of the skewers empty. Cook on each side for 5 minutes, or until cooked through. Wash the spinach and put in a large saucepan with just the water clinging to the leaves. Cook, covered, over medium heat for 1–2 minutes, or until the spinach has wilted. Uncover the rice, fluff up with a fork and serve with the spinach, chicken and extra yoghurt. Serves 4

460 RED ROAST DUCK CURRY

1 tablespoon peanut oil
2 garlic cloves, crushed
8 spring onions (scallions), cut into 3 cm (1¼ inch) lengths
1 tablespoon red curry paste, or to taste
400 ml (14 fl oz) coconut milk
750 g (1 lb 10 oz) Chinese roast duck, chopped (see Note)
450 g (1 lb) tin pineapple pieces in syrup, drained
3 kaffir lime leaves
3 tablespoons chopped coriander (cilantro) leaves
2 tablespoons chopped mint

Heat a wok until very hot, add the oil and swirl to coat. Add the garlic, spring onion and paste and stir-fry for 1 minute, or until fragrant.

Stir in the coconut milk, duck, pineapple, lime leaves, coriander leaves and mint. Bring to the boil, then reduce the heat and simmer for 10 minutes, or until the duck is heated through. Serve with steamed jasmine rice. Serves 4–6

Note: Chinese roast duck is available from Chinese barbecue and roast meat outlets.

461

462

463

461 EASY CHICKEN STIR-FRY

1 tablespoon cornflour (cornstarch)
2 teaspoons finely chopped ginger
2 garlic cloves, crushed
1 small red chilli, finely chopped
1 teaspoon sesame oil
3 tablespoons light soy sauce
500 g (1 lb 2 oz) chicken breast fillet, thinly sliced
1 tablespoon peanut oil
1 onion, halved and thinly sliced
115 g (4 oz) baby corn, halved on the diagonal
425 g (15 oz) baby bok choy (pak choy), trimmed
    and quartered lengthwise
2 tablespoons oyster sauce
3 tablespoons chicken stock

Combine half the cornflour with the ginger, crushed garlic, chilli, sesame oil and 2 tablespoons soy sauce in a large bowl. Add the chicken, toss until well coated and marinate for 10 minutes.

Heat a wok over high heat, add the peanut oil and swirl to coat. Stir-fry the onion for 2 minutes, or until soft and golden. Add the chicken in two batches and stir-fry for 5 minutes, or until almost cooked through. Add the baby corn and stir-fry for a further 2 minutes, then add the bok choy and cook for 2 minutes, or until wilted.

Mix the remaining soy sauce and cornflour with the oyster sauce and chicken stock in a bowl, add to the wok and stir-fry for 1–2 minutes, or until the sauce has thickened to coating consistency and the chicken is cooked. Serve immediately with steamed rice or noodles. Serves 4

463 CHICKEN FRICASSEE

25 g (1 oz) butter
1 tablespoon olive oil
200 g (7 oz) button mushrooms, sliced
1.5 kg (3 lb 5 oz) chicken pieces
1 onion, chopped
2 celery stalks, sliced
250 ml (9 fl oz/1 cup) dry white wine
250 ml (9 fl oz/1 cup) chicken stock
1 bay leaf
250 ml (9 fl oz/1 cup) cream
1 kg (2 lb 4 oz) king edward or russet potatoes, peeled and chopped
170 ml (5$\frac{1}{2}$ fl oz/$\frac{2}{3}$ cup) milk, heated
70 g (2$\frac{1}{2}$ oz) butter, extra
2 tablespoons chopped flat-leaf (Italian) parsley

Heat half the butter and oil in a large saucepan. Add the mushrooms and cook over medium heat for 5 minutes, or until golden. Remove from the pan. Heat the remaining oil and butter, add the chicken in batches and cook for 4 minutes, or until browned. Remove from the pan. Add the onion and celery to the pan, and cook for 8 minutes, or until soft. Pour in the wine and stir well. Add the stock, chicken, mushrooms, bay leaf and cream. Bring to the boil, then reduce the heat and simmer, covered, for 30–45 minutes, or until the chicken is cooked through.

Meanwhile, bring a large saucepan of water to the boil, add the potato and cook for 10 minutes, or until tender. Drain, add the milk and extra butter, and mash with a potato masher until smooth. Season with salt and freshly ground black pepper. Add the chopped parsley to the chicken and season. Serve with mashed potato. Serves 4

462 MEDITERRANEAN CHICKEN STEW

1 teaspoon ground cumin
1 teaspoon ground coriander
1 teaspoon paprika
$\frac{1}{4}$ teaspoon ground ginger
1.5 kg (3 lb 5 oz) chicken thigh fillets, quartered
2 tablespoons olive oil
1 large onion, sliced
3 garlic cloves, finely chopped
2 teaspoons oregano, chopped
250 ml (9 fl oz/1 cup) dry white wine
425 g (15 oz) tin crushed tomatoes
300 ml (10$\frac{1}{2}$ fl oz) chicken stock
2 bay leaves, crushed
$\frac{1}{4}$ teaspoon saffron threads, soaked in 2 tablespoons warm water
3 tablespoons good-quality pitted green olives
3 tablespoons good-quality pitted black olives
$\frac{1}{2}$ preserved lemon, flesh removed and rind cut into fine slivers
3 tablespoons finely chopped flat-leaf (Italian) parsley
basil sprigs, to garnish

Combine the cumin, coriander, paprika and ginger, and rub over the chicken pieces. Heat the oil in a large saucepan. Add the chicken in batches and cook over medium heat for 5 minutes, or until browned. Remove from the pan.

Reduce the heat, add the onion and cook, stirring constantly, for 5 minutes, or until golden. Add the garlic and oregano, and cook for 2 minutes, then add the wine and cook for 6 minutes, or until nearly evaporated. Add the tomato, stock, bay leaves and saffron and soaking liquid, and bring to the boil. Return the chicken to the pan and season well. Reduce the heat and simmer, covered, for 30 minutes, or until the chicken is cooked through.

Stir in the olives and preserved lemon, and cook, uncovered, for 10 minutes. Stir in the parsley, garnish with the sprigs of basil and serve. Serves 4–6

Note: This stew is delicious served with mashed potato. For extra flavour, stir some shredded basil through the potato before serving.

464

465

466

467

464 HONEY MUSTARD CHICKEN

175 g (6 oz/$\frac{1}{2}$ cup) honey
3 tablespoons dijon mustard
2 tablespoons oil
2 tablespoons white wine vinegar
3 garlic cloves, crushed
2 tablespoons chopped flat-leaf (Italian) parsley
1.8 kg (4 lb) chicken, cut into 10 serving pieces

Put the honey, mustard, oil, white wine vinegar, garlic, parsley and $\frac{1}{4}$ teaspoon freshly ground black pepper in a large, non-metallic bowl. Mix it all together well, and put aside 3 tablespoons of the marinade to baste the chicken during cooking. Add the chicken pieces to the rest of the marinade and turn them so that they are thoroughly coated. Cover the bowl and refrigerate it for at least 4 hours, or overnight.

Preheat a covered or kettle barbecue to medium indirect heat and cook the chicken pieces for 20–30 minutes, or until they are cooked through. The breast pieces may take as little as 15 minutes, while dark meat will take longer. Baste the chicken with the reserved marinade during the last 5–8 minutes of cooking, but no earlier or it is likely to burn. Serves 4–6

465 CHICKEN WITH SALSA VERDE

1 garlic clove
2 large handfuls flat-leaf (Italian) parsley
80 ml (2$\frac{1}{2}$ fl oz/$\frac{1}{3}$ cup) extra virgin olive oil
3 tablespoons chopped dill
1$\frac{1}{2}$ tablespoons dijon mustard
1 tablespoon sherry vinegar
1 tablespoon baby capers, drained
6 large chicken breast fillets

Place the garlic, parsley, olive oil, dill, mustard, vinegar and capers in a food processor or blender and process until almost smooth.

Cook the chicken fillets on a very hot, lightly oiled barbecue grill or flat plate for 4–5 minutes each side, or until cooked through. Cut each chicken fillet into three on the diagonal and arrange on serving plates. Top with a spoonful of salsa verde and season to taste. Serves 6

466 CAJUN CHICKEN WITH FRESH TOMATO & CORN SALSA

2 corn cobs
2 vine-ripened tomatoes, diced
1 Lebanese (short) cucumber, diced
2 tablespoons roughly chopped coriander (cilantro) leaves
4 chicken breast fillets (about 200 g/7 oz each)
3 tablespoons Cajun seasoning
2 tablespoons lime juice
lime wedges, to serve

Cook the corn cobs in a saucepan of boiling water for 5 minutes, or until tender. Remove the kernels using a sharp knife and place in a bowl with the tomato, cucumber and coriander. Season and mix well.

Heat a chargrill pan or barbecue plate to medium heat and brush lightly with oil. Pound each chicken breast between two sheets of plastic wrap with a mallet or rolling pin until 2 cm ($\frac{3}{4}$ inch) thick. Lightly coat the chicken with the Cajun seasoning and shake off any excess. Cook for 5 minutes on each side, or until just cooked through.

Just before serving, stir the lime juice into the salsa. Place a chicken breast on each plate and spoon the salsa on the side. Serve with the lime wedges, a green salad and crusty bread. Serves 4

467 PORTUGUESE SPATCHCOCK

1 red onion, chopped
6 garlic cloves, chopped
3 teaspoons grated lemon zest
2 teaspoons chilli flakes
1$\frac{1}{2}$ teaspoons paprika
3 tablespoons oil
3 tablespoons red wine vinegar
4 x 500 g (1 lb 2 oz) spatchcocks (poussin)
4 tablespoons chopped flat-leaf (Italian) parsley
lemon halves

Put the onion, garlic, lemon zest, chilli flakes, paprika, oil and vinegar in a food processor and blend them to a smooth paste. Cut each of the spatchcocks down the backbone with sharp kitchen scissors and press down on the breastbone to flatten it out. Score the flesh and brush it with the spice mixture, then put the spatchcocks in a non-metallic dish, cover and refrigerate overnight.

Preheat the chargrill plate to low–medium direct heat. Grill the spatchcocks for 10 minutes on each side, or until they are cooked through (test by piercing the thigh with a skewer — if the juices run clear, they are ready), then sprinkle with parsley and serve with the lemon halves. Serves 4

Note: Try grilling the lemon halves for a bit of extra flavour.

468

469

470

468 CHICKEN CASSEROLE WITH OLIVES & TOMATOES

1 tablespoon olive oil
1 large onion, chopped
2 garlic cloves, crushed
8 pieces chicken, skin on
1 tablespoon tomato paste (concentrated purée)
375 ml (13 fl oz/1^1/$_2$ cups) white wine
pinch of sugar
8 large ripe tomatoes, chopped
4 tablespoons flat-leaf (Italian) parsley, chopped
180 g (6^1/$_4$ oz) green beans, topped, tailed and halved
130 g (4^1/$_2$ oz) olives

Heat the oil in a large flameproof casserole and fry the onion for a minute or two. Add the garlic and the chicken and fry for as long as it takes to brown the chicken all over. Add the tomato paste and white wine, along with the sugar, and stir everything together. Add the tomato and any juices, the parsley and the beans and bring to the boil. Turn down the heat, season well and simmer for 40 minutes.

Add the olives and simmer for another 5 minutes. The sauce should be thick by now and the chicken fully cooked. Add more salt and pepper, if necessary. Serve with potatoes, pasta or rice. Serves 4

470 MOROCCAN CHICKEN

1 tablespoon Moroccan spice blend
800 g (1 lb 12 oz) chicken thigh fillets, trimmed and halved
1 tablespoon oil
60 g (2^1/$_4$ oz) butter
1 large onion, cut into wedges
1 cinnamon stick
2 garlic cloves, crushed
2 tablespoons lemon juice
250 ml (9 fl oz/1 cup) chicken stock
75 g (2^3/$_4$ oz/^{1}/$_3$ cup) pitted prunes, halved
225 g (8 oz/1^1/$_2$ cups) couscous
lemon wedges, for serving

Sprinkle half the spice blend over the chicken. Heat the oil and 20 g (^{3}/$_4$ oz) of the butter in a large saucepan or deep-sided frying pan over medium heat. Cook the chicken in two batches for 5 minutes, or until evenly browned. Remove from the pan, then add the onion and cinnamon stick and cook for 2–3 minutes before adding the garlic. Return the chicken to the pan and add the lemon juice and the remaining spice blend. Season, then cook, covered, for 5 minutes.

Add the stock and prunes to the pan and bring to the boil. Reduce the heat to medium–low and cook, uncovered, for 15 minutes, or until the chicken is cooked and the liquid has reduced to a sauce. Before serving, stir 20 g (^{3}/$_4$ oz) of the butter into the sauce. About 10 minutes before the chicken is ready, place the couscous in a heatproof bowl, add 375 ml (13 fl oz/1^1/$_2$ cups) boiling water, and stand for 3–5 minutes. Stir in the remaining butter and fluff with a fork until the butter has melted and the grains separate. Serve with the chicken. Serves 4

469 COQ AU VIN

1 tablespoon olive oil
12 white baby onions, peeled
3 rindless bacon slices, chopped
40 g (1^1/$_2$ oz) butter
1.5 kg (3 lb 5 oz) chicken pieces
2 garlic cloves, crushed
375 ml (13 fl oz/1^1/$_2$ cups) dry red wine
2 tablespoons brandy
1 tablespoon chopped thyme
1 bay leaf
4 flat-leaf (Italian) parsley stalks
250 g (9 oz) button mushrooms, halved
20 g (^{3}/$_4$ oz) butter, extra, softened
20 g (^{3}/$_4$ oz) plain (all-purpose) flour
chopped flat-leaf (Italian) parsley, to serve

Preheat the oven to 170°C (325°F/Gas 3). Heat the oil in a large heavy-based frying pan and add the onions. Cook until browned, then add the bacon and cook until browned. Remove the bacon and onions and add the butter to the pan. When the butter is foaming add the chicken in a single layer and cook in batches until well browned. Transfer the chicken to an ovenproof dish, draining it of any fat, then add the onions and bacon.

Tip any excess fat out of the frying pan and add the garlic, wine, brandy, thyme, bay leaf and parsley stalks. Bring to the boil and pour over the chicken. Cook, covered, in the oven for 1 hour and 25 minutes, then add the mushrooms and cook for 30 minutes. Drain through a colander and reserve the liquid in a pan. Keep the chicken warm in the oven.

Mix the softened butter and flour together, bring the liquid in the pan to the boil and whisk in the flour and butter paste in two batches, then reduce the heat and simmer until the liquid thickens slightly. Remove the parsley stalks and bay leaf from the chicken and return it to the ovenproof dish. Pour in the sauce, scatter on the chopped parsley and serve. Serves 4

471

472

473

474

471 CHICKEN BREASTS WITH MUSTARD CREAM SAUCE

4 chicken breasts (about 200 g/7 oz each)
2 tablespoons oil
1 garlic clove, crushed
3 tablespoons dry white wine
2 tablespoons wholegrain mustard
2 teaspoons chopped thyme
300 ml (10$^1/_2$ fl oz) cream
240 g (8$^1/_2$ oz) green beans, topped and tailed
320 g (11$^1/_4$ oz) baby yellow squash, halved

Pound each chicken breast between sheets of plastic wrap with a mallet or rolling pin until about 1 cm ($^1/_2$ inch) thick. Heat the oil in a frying pan over high heat. Brown the chicken breasts for 4–5 minutes on each side, or until brown. Remove and cover with foil.

Add the garlic to the frying pan and cook for 1 minute over medium heat, then stir in the wine, mustard and thyme. Increase the heat to medium–high and pour in the cream. Simmer for about 5 minutes, or until the sauce has reduced and thickened slightly, then season to taste.

Meanwhile, bring a saucepan of lightly salted water to the boil, add the beans and squash and cook for 2–4 minutes, or until just tender. Season to taste. To serve, pour a little of the sauce over the chicken and serve with the vegetables on the side. Serves 4

472 LEBANESE CHICKEN

250 g (9 oz/1 cup) Greek-style yoghurt
2 teaspoons soft brown sugar
4 garlic cloves, crushed
3 teaspoons ground cumin
1$^1/_2$ teaspoons ground coriander
3 tablespoons chopped flat-leaf (Italian) parsley
3 tablespoons lemon juice
1.8 kg (4 lb) whole chicken, cut into 10 serving pieces
cooking oil spray

Put the yoghurt, sugar, garlic, cumin, coriander, parsley and lemon juice in a large non-metallic bowl and mix them together. Add the chicken pieces to the marinade and turn them so that they are completely coated, then cover and refrigerate for at least 2 hours, or overnight.

Lightly spray the barbecue plates with oil, then preheat the barbecue to medium direct heat. Take the chicken pieces out of the marinade and season them with salt and pepper. Cook the chicken pieces on the flat plate, turning them frequently, for 20–30 minutes, or until they are cooked through. If you have a barbecue with a lid, cover the barbecue while the chicken is cooking. This way, the breast pieces will take only 15 minutes to cook, while the pieces on the bone will take about 10 minutes longer. Serves 4–6

473 SALT & PEPPER CHICKEN WITH ASIAN GREENS & OYSTER SAUCE

250 g (9 oz/1$^1/_4$ cups) jasmine rice
40 g (1$^1/_2$ oz/$^1/_3$ cup) plain (all-purpose) flour
$^3/_4$ teaspoon Chinese five-spice
1$^1/_2$ teaspoons sea salt
1 teaspoon ground white pepper
750 g (1 lb 10 oz) chicken breast fillets, cut into 1 x 5 cm
  ($^1/_2$ x 2 inch) thin strips
145 ml (4$^3/_4$ fl oz) peanut oil
1.25 kg (2 lb 12 oz) mixed Asian greens, such as bok choy
  (pak choy), choy sum or gai larn (Chinese broccoli)
125 ml (4 fl oz/$^1/_2$ cup) oyster sauce

Bring a large saucepan of water to the boil. Add the rice and cook for 12 minutes, stirring occasionally. Drain well. Meanwhile, combine the flour, five-spice, salt and pepper in a large bowl. Toss the chicken strips in the flour until well coated. Heat 3 tablespoons of the oil in a large frying pan over medium–high heat. Add the chicken in three batches and cook, turning, for about 3 minutes, or until browned. Drain on crumpled paper towels and keep warm.

Heat the remaining oil and cook the mixed Asian greens over medium–high heat for 1–2 minutes. Add the oyster sauce and toss through. Serve on a bed of jasmine rice topped with the chicken strips. Serves 4

474 PARMESAN CHICKEN WITH SALSA VERDE

3 eggs
1 large handful basil
2 tablespoons capers, rinsed
1 tablespoon dijon mustard
2 tablespoons freshly grated parmesan cheese
185 ml (6 fl oz/$^3/_4$ cup) olive oil
100 g (3$^1/_2$ oz/1 cup) dry breadcrumbs
4 chicken breast fillets (about 120 g/4$^1/_4$ oz each)
150 g (5$^1/_2$ oz) rocket (arugula) leaves
lemon wedges, to serve

Place 1 egg in a saucepan of cold water, bring to the boil and cook for 1 minute. Remove from the heat and refresh under cold water. Peel, then place in a food processor with the basil, capers, mustard and 1 tablespoon of the parmesan, until combined. Gradually add 3 tablespoons of the olive oil and process until you have a coarse sauce, taking care not to overprocess.

Beat the remaining eggs together with 1 tablespoon water. Combine the breadcrumbs with the remaining parmesan on a plate. Pound each chicken breast between two sheets of plastic wrap with a mallet or rolling pin until 5 mm ($^1/_4$ inch) thick. Dip the chicken in the egg mixture, then coat in the breadcrumb mixture. Place on a paper-lined baking tray and refrigerate for 10 minutes, or until needed.

Heat the remaining oil in a large frying pan over high heat. Cook the chicken breasts in batches for 2–3 minutes each batch, or until golden on both sides and cooked through — keep each batch warm. Serve with the salsa verde, rocket leaves and lemon wedges. Serves 4

475

476

477

475 SICHUAN CHICKEN

1/4 teaspoon Chinese five-spice
750 g (1 lb 10 oz) chicken thigh fillets, halved
2 tablespoons peanut oil
1 tablespoon julienned fresh ginger
1 teaspoon sichuan peppercorns, crushed
1 teaspoon chilli bean paste (toban jian)
2 tablespoons light soy sauce
1 tablespoon Chinese rice wine
250 g (9 oz/1 1/4 cups) jasmine rice
600 g (1 lb 5 oz) baby bok choy (pak choy), leaves separated

Sprinkle the five-spice over the chicken. Heat a saucepan or wok until very hot, add half the oil and swirl to coat. Add the chicken and cook for 2 minutes each side, or until browned. Remove from the pan or wok.

Reduce the heat to medium and cook the ginger for 30 seconds. Add the peppercorns and chilli bean paste. Return the chicken to the pan or wok, add the soy sauce, wine and 125 ml (4 fl oz/1/2 cup) water, then simmer for 15–20 minutes, or until cooked.

Meanwhile, add the rice to a large saucepan of rapidly boiling water and cook for 12 minutes, stirring occasionally. Drain well.

Heat the remaining oil in a saucepan. Add the bok choy and toss for 1 minute, or until the leaves wilt and the stems are tender. Serve with the chicken and rice. Serves 4

477 STIR-FRIED CHICKEN WITH GINGER & CASHEWS

1 1/2 tablespoons oil
8 spring onions (scallions), cut into pieces
3 garlic cloves, crushed
8 cm (3 1/4 inch) piece of ginger, finely shredded
2 chicken breast fillets, cut into strips
2 red capsicums (peppers), cut into strips
150 g (5 1/2 oz) snow peas (mangetout)
100 g (3 1/2 oz) cashews
2 tablespoons soy sauce
1 1/2 teaspoons sesame oil

Heat the oil in a wok until it is smoking — this will only take a few seconds. Add the spring onion, garlic and ginger and stir them around for a few seconds. Next, add the chicken and stir it around until it has all turned white. Add the red capsicum and keep stirring, then throw in the snow peas and cashews and stir-fry for another minute or so.

Once the red capsicum has started to soften a little, add the soy sauce and sesame oil, toss everything together and then tip the stir-fry out into a serving dish. Serve with rice or noodles and more soy sauce if you like. Serves 4

476 CHICKEN WITH CHILLI JAM & CASHEWS

CHILLI JAM
10 dried long red chillies
80 ml (2 1/2 fl oz/1/3 cup) peanut oil
1 red capsicum (pepper), chopped
1 head garlic, peeled and roughly chopped
200 g (7 oz) red Asian shallots, chopped
100 g (3 1/2 oz) palm sugar (jaggery), grated, or soft brown sugar
2 tablespoons tamarind purée (see Note)

1 tablespoon peanut oil
6 spring onions (scallions), cut into 3 cm (1 1/4 inch) lengths
500 g (1 lb 2 oz) chicken breast fillet, cut into slices
50 g (1 3/4 oz/1/3 cup) roasted unsalted cashews
1 tablespoon fish sauce
1 small handful Thai basil

To make the chilli jam, soak the chillies in a bowl of boiling water for 15 minutes. Drain, remove the seeds and chop. Put in a food processor, then add the oil, capsicum, garlic and shallots and blend until smooth.

Heat a wok over medium heat and add the chilli mixture. Cook, stirring occasionally, for 15 minutes. Add the sugar and tamarind and simmer for 10 minutes, or until it darkens and reaches a jam-like consistency. Remove from the wok.

Clean and reheat the wok over high heat, add the oil and swirl to coat. Stir-fry the spring onion for 1 minute, then add the chicken and stir-fry for 3–5 minutes, or until golden brown and tender. Stir in the cashews, fish sauce and 4 tablespoons of the chilli jam. Stir-fry for a further 2 minutes, then stir in the basil and serve. Serves 4

Note: Use a non-stick or stainless steel wok to cook this recipe because the tamarind purée will react with the metal in a regular wok and will taint the dish.

478

479

480

481

478 LIME & CORIANDER CHARGRILLED CHICKEN

3 teaspoons finely grated fresh ginger
1 small handful chopped coriander (cilantro) leaves
1¹/₂ teaspoons grated lime zest
80 ml (2¹/₂ fl oz/¹/₃ cup) lime juice
4 chicken breast fillets (about 750 g/1 lb 10 oz), trimmed
250 g (9 oz/1¹/₄ cups) jasmine rice
2 tablespoons oil
3 zucchini (courgettes), cut into wedges
4 large flat mushrooms, stalks trimmed

Combine the ginger, coriander, lime zest and 2 tablespoons of the lime juice. Spread 2 teaspoons of the herb mixture over each fillet and season well. Marinate for 1 hour. Combine the remaining herb mixture with the remaining lime juice in a screwtop jar. Set aside until needed. Bring a large saucepan of water to the boil. Add the rice and cook for 12 minutes, stirring occasionally. Drain well.

Meanwhile, heat a chargrill pan or barbecue plate to medium — this will take about 5 minutes and lightly brush with oil. Brush the zucchini and mushrooms with the remaining oil. Place the chicken on the chargrill and cook on each side for 4–5 minutes, or until cooked through. Add the vegetables during the last 5 minutes of cooking, and turn frequently until browned on the outside and just softened. Cover with foil until ready to serve.

Divide the rice among four serving bowls. Cut the chicken fillets into long thick strips, then arrange on top of the rice. Shake the dressing well and drizzle over the chicken and serve with the chargrilled vegetables. Serves 4

479 SATAY CHICKEN STIR-FRY

300 g (10¹/₂ oz/1¹/₂ cups) jasmine rice
1¹/₂ tablespoons peanut oil
6 spring onions (scallions), cut into 3 cm (1¹/₄ inch) lengths
800 g (1 lb 12 oz) chicken breast fillets, thinly sliced on the diagonal
1–1¹/₂ tablespoons Thai red curry paste
90 g (3¹/₄ oz/¹/₃ cup) crunchy peanut butter
270 ml (9¹/₂ fl oz) coconut milk
2 teaspoons soft brown sugar
1¹/₂ tablespoons lime juice

Bring a large saucepan of water to the boil. Add the rice and cook for 12 minutes, stirring occasionally. Drain well. Meanwhile, heat a wok until very hot, add 1 teaspoon of the peanut oil and swirl to coat. When hot, add the spring onion and stir-fry for 30 seconds, or until softened slightly. Remove from the wok. Add a little extra peanut oil to the wok as needed and stir-fry the chicken in three batches for about 1 minute per batch, or until the meat just changes colour. Remove from the wok.

Add a little more oil to the wok, add the curry paste and stir-fry for 1 minute, or until fragrant. Add the peanut butter, coconut milk, sugar and 250 ml (9 fl oz/1 cup) water and stir well. Bring to the boil and boil for 3–4 minutes, or until thickened and the oil starts to separate — reduce the heat slightly if the sauce spits at you. Return the chicken and the spring onion to the wok, stir well and cook for 2 minutes, or until heated through. Stir in the lime juice and season. Serve at once with the rice and a crisp green salad. Serves 4

480 TERIYAKI CHICKEN WITH GINGER CHIVE RICE

4 small chicken breast fillets, skin on (about 170 g/6 oz each)
3 tablespoons Japanese soy sauce
2 tablespoons sake
1¹/₂ tablespoons mirin
1¹/₂ tablespoons soft brown sugar
3 teaspoons finely grated fresh ginger
300 g (10¹/₂ oz/1¹/₂ cups) long-grain rice
2 tablespoons finely chopped chives
2 tablespoons oil

Pound each breast between sheets of plastic wrap with a mallet until 1 cm (¹/₂ inch) thick. Put the soy sauce, sake, mirin, sugar and 1 teaspoon ginger in a flat non-metallic dish and stir until the sugar has dissolved. Add the chicken and turn to coat. Cover and refrigerate for 1 hour, turning once halfway through.

Bring a large saucepan of water to the boil. Add the rice and cook for 12 minutes, stirring occasionally. Drain. Stir in the chives and remaining ginger, then cover until ready to serve.

Drain the chicken, reserving the marinade. Heat the oil in a deep frying pan and cook the chicken, skin side down, over medium heat for 5 minutes, until the skin is crisp. Turn and cook for 4 minutes (not quite cooked). Add the marinade and 3 tablespoons water to the pan and scrape up any sediment. Bring to the boil over high heat, then add the chicken, skin side up, and juices. Cook for 5–6 minutes, until cooked through, turning once. (If the sauce is runny, remove the chicken and boil the sauce until syrupy.) Serve the chicken whole or sliced, drizzled with the sauce. Serves 4

481 MEXICAN CHICKEN BAKE

165 g (5³/₄ oz/³/₄ cup) short-grain rice
300 g (10¹/₂ oz) tin red kidney beans, drained and thoroughly rinsed
3¹/₂ tablespoons chopped coriander (cilantro) leaves
1 tablespoon oil
600 g (1 lb 5 oz) skinless chicken thigh fillets, unrolled
2 x 200 g (7 oz) jars spicy taco sauce
250 g (9 oz/2 cups) grated cheddar cheese
125 g (4¹/₂ oz/¹/₂ cup) sour cream

Preheat the oven to 180°C (350°F/Gas 4). Lightly grease a 21 cm (8¹/₄ inches) round x 7 cm (2³/₄ inches) deep ceramic casserole dish. Bring a large saucepan of water to the boil, add the rice and cook for 10–12 minutes, stirring occasionally. Drain. In the prepared dish, combine the beans and 1¹/₂ tablespoons of the coriander, then add the rice and toss together. Lightly press the mixture so the beans are mixed into the rice and the mixture is flat.

Heat the oil in a large frying pan over medium–high heat. Sauté the chicken thighs for 3 minutes, then turn over. Add the spicy taco sauce, and cook for another 3 minutes. To assemble, spread half the cheese over the rice. Arrange the thighs and sauce on top in a star shape, sprinkle with 1¹/₂ tablespoons coriander, then sprinkle with cheese. Cover with foil. Bake for 35–40 minutes, or until the mixture is bubbling and the cheese is melted and slightly browned — remove the foil for the last 5 minutes. Cut into four servings with a knife and scoop out carefully, keeping the layers intact. Serve sprinkled with the remaining coriander and a dollop of sour cream. Serves 4

482

483

484 485

482 BEEF MASALA WITH COCONUT RICE

1 tablespoon oil
1 kg (2 lb 4 oz) chuck steak, trimmed and cut into 2 cm
     (³/₄ inch) cubes
1 large onion, thinly sliced
3 garlic cloves, chopped
60 g (2³/₄ oz/¹/₃ cup) tikka masala curry paste
2 teaspoons tamarind concentrate
2 x 400 ml (14 fl oz) tins coconut milk
4 fresh curry leaves
300 g (10¹/₂ oz/1¹/₂ cups) jasmine rice

Heat the oil in a large saucepan over high heat. Add the meat and
cook in three batches for 4 minutes per batch, or until evenly browned.
Reduce the heat to medium, add the onion to the pan, cook for
5 minutes, then add the garlic and cook for 1 minute. Stir in the curry
paste and tamarind for 30–60 seconds, until fragrant. Return the beef
to the pan, add 550 ml (19 fl oz) coconut milk and the curry leaves and
bring to the boil. Reduce the heat and simmer gently for 1¹/₂ hours, or
until the meat is tender and the sauce has reduced. Add some water
if the sauce starts to stick to the base of the pan.

Meanwhile, to make the coconut rice, wash and thoroughly drain the
rice. Put the rice, the remaining coconut milk and 250 ml (9 fl oz/
1 cup) water in a saucepan and bring slowly to the boil, stirring
constantly. Boil for 1 minute, then reduce the heat to low and cook,
covered tightly, for 20 minutes. Remove from the heat and leave,
covered, for 10 minutes. Fluff the rice with a fork before serving.
To serve, season to taste and remove the curry leaves if you wish.
Serve with the rice. Serves 4

483 PORK LOIN ROAST WITH APPLE WALNUT STUFFING & ROAST VEGETABLES

50 g (1³/₄ oz/¹/₂ cup) walnuts, chopped
1 green apple, peeled and cored
¹/₂ teaspoon ground cinnamon
2 tablespoons port
1.5 kg (3 lb 5 oz) rindless, boned pork loin
100 ml (3¹/₂ fl oz) maple syrup
8 parsnips, sliced thinly lengthways
500 g (1 lb 2 oz) baby carrots
2 tablespoons oil

Preheat the oven to 200°C (400°F/Gas 6). Grease a large roasting tin.
Spread the walnuts on a baking tray and place under a medium–high
grill (broiler) for 2–3 minutes, or until lightly toasted.

Coarsely grate the apple and squeeze out the excess juice. Combine
the apple, cinnamon, walnuts and port and season to taste. Unroll the
pork loin, then spread the stuffing evenly over one third of the loin
lengthways. Re-roll the loin, tie securely and place, seam side down,
in the prepared tin. Roast for 20 minutes. Reduce the heat to 180°C
(350°F/Gas 4), baste the pork with some maple syrup and roast for a
further 30 minutes.

Toss together the parsnip, carrots and oil in a large bowl and season.
Add to the roasting tin and roast for a further 30–35 minutes, or
until the vegetables are golden and tender. In the last 10 minutes of
cooking, baste the pork again with the syrup. Remove the roast pork
from the tin, cover with foil and allow to rest for 10 minutes before
slicing. Serve with the vegetables and any pan juices. Serves 4

484 PAN-FRIED LAMB FILLETS WITH RED WINE

600 g (1 lb 5 oz) small new potatoes
160 g (5³/₄ oz) snow peas (mangetout), trimmed
2 tablespoons olive oil
4 lamb backstraps or eye of loin fillets (about 200 g/
     7 oz each), trimmed
170 ml (5¹/₂ fl oz/²/₃ cup) red wine
1 tablespoon redcurrant jelly
2 teaspoons chopped thyme
30 g (1 oz) butter, chilled and cut into cubes

Cook the potatoes in a large saucepan of lightly salted boiling water
for 15–20 minutes, or until tender. Add the snow peas and cook for
another minute. Drain the vegetables, return to the pan and toss
gently with 1 tablespoon of the oil.

Meanwhile, heat the remaining oil in a large frying pan and cook
the lamb fillets over medium–high heat for 4–5 minutes each side,
or until cooked, but still pink inside. Remove from the pan, cover
and keep warm.

Add the wine, redcurrant jelly and thyme to the pan and bring to the
boil. Boil rapidly for 5 minutes, or until reduced and syrupy. Stir in the
butter. To serve, slice the lamb on the diagonal, divide among plates
and spoon some sauce on top. Serve with the vegetables. Serves 4

485 VEAL SCHNITZEL WITH DILL POTATO SALAD

750 g (1 lb 10 oz) desiree potatoes, unpeeled
500 g (1 lb 2 oz) veal leg steaks
60 g (2¹/₄ oz/¹/₂ cup) seasoned plain (all-purpose) flour
2 eggs, lightly beaten
100 g (3¹/₂ oz/1 cup) dry breadcrumbs
125 ml (4 fl oz/¹/₂ cup) virgin olive oil
2 tablespoons lemon juice
1¹/₂ tablespoons finely chopped dill
200 g (7 oz) mixed salad leaves

Cook the potatoes in a saucepan of boiling water for 15–20 minutes,
or until tender. Drain, then cut into quarters lengthways and cover to
keep warm. Meanwhile, beat the veal between two sheets of plastic
wrap to 5 mm (¹/₄ inch) thickness. Coat the veal in the flour and shake
off the excess. Dip the veal in the egg, then coat in breadcrumbs. Place
the schnitzel on a flat tray, cover and freeze for 5 minutes.

Heat 3 tablespoons of the oil in a large frying pan and cook the veal in
two batches, over medium–high heat for 2–3 minutes on each side, or
until golden and cooked through. Drain on crumpled paper towels and
keep warm.

Whisk the lemon juice, dill and remaining oil together in a small bowl
and pour over the potatoes. Season with salt and freshly ground black
pepper and toss gently. Serve the schnitzel with the potatoes and a
mixed salad. Serves 4

486

487

488

486 LAMB CHOPS WITH CITRUS POCKETS

4 lamb chump chops, about 250 g (9 oz) each
2 tablespoons lemon juice

CITRUS FILLING
3 spring onions (scallions), finely chopped
1 celery stalk, finely chopped
2 teaspoons grated fresh ginger
60 g (2^1/$_4$ oz/^{3}/$_4$ cup) fresh breadcrumbs
2 tablespoons orange juice
2 teaspoons finely grated orange zest
1 teaspoon chopped rosemary

Cut a deep, long pocket in the side of each lamb chop. Mix together the spring onion, celery, ginger, breadcrumbs, orange juice, zest and rosemary and spoon into the pockets in the lamb.

Cook on a hot, lightly oiled barbecue flat plate or grill, turning once, for 15 minutes, or until the lamb is cooked through but still pink in the centre. Drizzle with the lemon juice before serving. Serves 4

488 FILLET STEAK WITH FLAVOURED BUTTERS

4 fillet steaks

CAPSICUM BUTTER
1 small red capsicum (pepper)
125 g (4^1/$_2$ oz) butter
2 teaspoons chopped oregano
2 teaspoons chopped chives

GARLIC BUTTER
125 g (4^1/$_2$ oz) butter
3 garlic cloves, crushed
2 spring onions (scallions), finely chopped

Cut a pocket in each steak. For the capsicum butter, cut the capsicum into large pieces and place, skin side up, under a hot grill (broiler) until the skin blisters and blackens. Put in a plastic bag until cool, then peel away the skin and dice the flesh. Beat the butter until creamy. Add the capsicum, oregano and chives, season and beat until smooth.

For the garlic butter, beat the butter until creamy, add the garlic and spring onion and beat until smooth.

Push capsicum butter into the pockets in two of the steaks and garlic butter into the other two. Cook on a hot, lightly oiled barbecue grill or flat plate for 4–5 minutes each side, turning once. Brush frequently with any remaining flavoured butter while cooking. These steaks are delicious served with a simple green salad. Serves 4

487 STUFFED PORK CHOPS WITH CHARGRILLED SPRING ONIONS

2 tablespoons dry sherry
4 dried dessert figs
1 tablespoon butter
3 tablespoons olive oil
1 small onion, finely diced
2 garlic cloves, crushed
1 large granny smith apple, peeled, cored and grated
2 tablespoons slivered almonds, lightly toasted
1 tablespoon finely chopped sage leaves
6 large pork loin chops (250 g/9 oz each), on the bone
16 large bulb spring onions (scallions), green parts
    removed, halved

Bring the sherry and 1 tablespoon of water to the boil in a small saucepan. Soak the figs in the hot sherry mixture for about 20 minutes, then slice them finely and keep the soaking liquid to use later.

Heat the butter and 1 tablespoon of olive oil in a frying pan, add the onion and garlic, and cook over low heat for 5 minutes, or until they are softened. Add the grated apple, figs and sherry liquid, and simmer for a further 5 minutes, or until the apple has softened and most of the liquid has evaporated. Remove the pan from the heat and stir in the almonds and sage, then season well and allow the mixture to cool.

Trim the pork chops of any excess fat and make an incision into the middle of the chop from the side. Be careful — you only want to make a pocket in the flesh and not cut right through.

Fill the pocket with the apple and fig stuffing, pushing it well into the cavity so that none is spilling out — you should fit about 1^1/$_2$ tablespoons of filling in each chop. Brush the chops all over with 1 tablespoon of the olive oil, and season with salt and freshly ground black pepper. Toss the spring onion with the remaining oil, and season it well.

Heat a barbecue chargrill plate to medium direct heat. Cook the chops for 8 minutes on each side, or until the outside is slightly charred and the meat is cooked through. While the chops are cooking, add the spring onions to the chargrill plate and cook them for 10 minutes, or until they are softened. Serve the chops and spring onions as soon as they come off the barbecue. Serves 6

489

490

491

492

489 ROAST PEPPERED BEEF WITH ONIONS & POTATOES

1 kg (2 lb 4 oz) piece beef sirloin
2 tablespoons freshly ground black peppercorns
1 large red onion
4 large potatoes
50 g (1³⁄₄ oz) butter
3 tablespoons beef stock
3 tablespoons red wine
500 g (1 lb 2 oz) mixed yellow and green beans

Preheat the oven to 180°C (350°F/Gas 4). Trim the excess fat from the beef, leaving a thin layer. Press the pepper all over the beef. Cut the onion and potatoes into 5 mm (¹⁄₄ inch) thick slices and place in a roasting tin. Sit the beef on top, fat side up. Cut 40 g (1¹⁄₂ oz) of the butter into small pieces and dot all over the beef and potatoes. Pour in the stock and wine and bake for 35–40 minutes, for medium–rare, or until cooked to your liking. Remove the beef from the oven and rest for at least 5 minutes before carving.

Meanwhile, bring a saucepan of lightly salted water to the boil. Add the mixed beans and cook for 2–4 minutes, or until just tender. Drain well, then add the remaining butter and toss. Keep warm until ready to serve. To serve, divide the onion and potato mixture among four serving plates and top with slices of beef. Spoon on any pan juices and serve with the beans. Serves 4

490 LAMB, MINT & CHILLI STIR-FRY

250 g (9 oz/1¹⁄₄ cups) jasmine rice
2 tablespoons oil
750 g (1 lb 10 oz) lamb backstrap or eye of loin fillets, sliced thinly
2 garlic cloves, finely chopped
1 small red onion, cut into wedges
1 bird's eye chilli, finely chopped
3 tablespoons lime juice
2 tablespoons sweet chilli sauce
2 tablespoons fish sauce
1 handful mint

Bring a large saucepan of water to the boil. Add the rice and cook for 12 minutes, stirring occasionally. Drain well. Meanwhile, heat a wok until very hot, add 1 tablespoon oil and swirl to coat. Add the lamb in batches and cook for 2 minutes, or until browned. Remove from the wok.

Heat the remaining oil in the wok, add the garlic and onion and stir-fry for 1 minute, then add the chilli and cook for 30 seconds. Return the lamb to the wok, then add the lime juice, sweet chilli sauce and fish sauce and stir-fry for 2 minutes over high heat. Stir in the mint and serve with the rice. Serves 4

Note: You can use chicken breasts or pork loin, adding 80 g (2³⁄₄ oz/¹⁄₂ cup) cashews and using basil instead of mint.

491 SAUSAGE & BEAN HOTPOT WITH ROASTED ORANGE SWEET POTATO

1 kg (2 lb 4 oz) spicy Italian-style sausages
2 garlic cloves, roughly chopped
2 x 400 g (14 oz) tins cannellini beans
2 x 425 g (15 oz) tins crushed tomatoes
2 teaspoons dijon mustard
750 g (1 lb 10 oz) orange sweet potato, cut into 3 cm (1¹⁄₄ inch) cubes
2 tablespoons olive oil
2 tablespoons coarsely chopped flat-leaf (Italian) parsley

Preheat the oven to 200°C (400°F/Gas 6). Cook the sausages in a large frying pan over medium heat for 5–7 minutes, or until golden. Cut into 5 cm (2 inch) pieces and place in a 4 litre (140 fl oz/16 cup) casserole dish. Add the garlic, beans, tomato, mustard and 2 tablespoons water to the dish and season with freshly ground black pepper. Stir well and cover with a lid. Place in the oven.

Meanwhile, toss the sweet potato with the oil and place snugly in a baking dish. Sprinkle with salt. Place in the oven with the casserole dish and bake for 25 minutes. Uncover the casserole dish and bake for another 10–15 minutes, or until the hotpot is golden and bubbling and the sweet potato is soft and lightly golden brown. Serve the hotpot garnished with the parsley and the sweet potato on the side. Serves 4

492 LAMB KOFTA CURRY

250 g (9 oz/1¹⁄₄ cups) jasmine rice
1 kg (2 lb 4 oz) lean minced (ground) lamb
1 egg, lightly beaten
2 onions, finely chopped
120 g (4¹⁄₄ oz) korma curry paste
4 tablespoons chopped coriander (cilantro) leaves
2 garlic cloves, crushed
2 tablespoons oil
400 g (14 oz) tin diced tomatoes

Preheat the oven to 220°C (425°F/Gas 7) and lightly grease two baking trays. Bring a large saucepan of water to the boil. Add the rice and cook for 12 minutes, stirring occasionally. Drain. Meanwhile, combine the minced lamb, egg, 1 onion, 2 tablespoons curry paste, 3 tablespoons coriander, 1 garlic clove and salt and form tablespoons of the mixture into balls. Place on one of the baking trays.

Heat 1 tablespoon oil in a large non-stick frying pan over medium heat. Cook the balls in batches for 1 minute on each side, or until evenly golden, but not cooked through. Place on the second tray and bake for 5–7 minutes, or until cooked through. Wipe the pan clean.

Heat the remaining oil over medium heat. Add the remaining onion and garlic and cook for 3 minutes, or until the onion is soft. Add the remaining curry paste, cook for 1 minute, then add the tomato and 250 ml (9 fl oz/1 cup) water. Bring to the boil, then reduce the heat and simmer for 10 minutes, or until the sauce thickens slightly. Season. Stir the meatballs and their juices into the sauce. Simmer for 5 minutes to warm the meatballs. Serve with rice and coriander. Serves 4

493

494

495

493 PORK LOIN WITH APPLE GLAZE & WEDGES

1 teaspoon aniseed
135 g (4³/₄ oz/¹/₂ cup) apple sauce
2 tablespoons soft brown sugar
1.5 kg (3 lb 5 oz) boned pork loin with the skin on
2 teaspoons oil
4 large potatoes, each cut into 8 wedges
2 tablespoons olive oil
2 teaspoons garlic salt

Dry-fry the aniseed over medium heat for 30 seconds, or until it becomes fragrant. Add the apple sauce and brown sugar, reduce the heat to low and cook, stirring, for 1 minute.

Use a sharp knife to remove the skin from the pork loin. Score the skin in a diamond pattern and rub the oil and 1 tablespoon salt over the skin, working into the cuts. Put the potato wedges in a bowl with the olive oil and garlic salt, season with pepper and toss until well coated.

Preheat a kettle or covered barbecue to medium indirect heat. Tie the pork loin with string to help keep its shape, then put the pork and the skin in the barbecue and arrange the wedges around them. After 30 minutes, baste the pork with the apple glaze, and repeat every 10 minutes for another 30 minutes (for 1 hour cooking time in all). Turn the skin and the wedges as you go so that they cook evenly.

When the pork is ready, remove it from the barbecue and leave to rest, covered, for 10 minutes before carving. Cut the crackling with a sharp knife, arrange it on a platter with the pork and serve with the wedges. Serves 6–8

495 LAMB CUTLETS WITH MINT GREMOLATA

1 handful mint
1 tablespoon flat-leaf (Italian) parsley
2 garlic cloves
1¹/₂ tablespoons lemon zest (white pith removed), cut into thin strips
2 tablespoons extra virgin olive oil
8 French-trimmed lamb cutlets
2 carrots
2 zucchini (courgettes)
1 tablespoon lemon juice

To make the gremolata, finely chop the mint, parsley, garlic and lemon strips, then combine well. Heat a chargrill pan or barbecue plate to very hot. Lightly brush with 1 tablespoon of the oil. Season the cutlets and cook over medium heat for 2 minutes on each side, or until cooked to your liking. Remove the cutlets and cover to keep warm.

Trim the ends from the carrots and zucchini and, using a vegetable peeler, peel the vegetables lengthways into ribbons. Heat the remaining oil in a large saucepan, add the vegetables and toss over medium heat for 3–5 minutes, or until sautéed but tender. Season lightly. Divide the lamb cutlets among the serving plates, sprinkle the cutlets with the gremolata and drizzle with the lemon juice. Serve with the vegetable ribbons. Serves 4

494 ROAST SIRLOIN WITH MUSTARD PEPPER CRUST & HASSELBACK POTATOES

90 g (3¹/₄ oz/¹/₃ cup) dijon mustard
2 tablespoons light soy sauce
2 tablespoons plain (all-purpose) flour
3 tablespoons olive oil
3 teaspoons chopped thyme
4 garlic cloves, crushed
2.5 kg (5 lb 8 oz) piece of sirloin, trimmed but with the fat still on top
6 potatoes
2 tablespoons butter, melted
1 onion, roughly diced
1 large carrot, roughly diced
2 celery stalks, roughly chopped
250 ml (9 fl oz/1 cup) red wine
500 ml (17 fl oz/2 cups) beef stock
2 bay leaves
2 teaspoons cornflour (cornstarch)

Mix the mustard, soy sauce, flour, 2 tablespoons of oil, 2 teaspoons of thyme, two of the crushed garlic cloves and 1 tablespoon of freshly ground black pepper in a small bowl. Coat the sirloin with the mustard mixture, put it on a wire rack over a tray and refrigerate it for 1 hour so the crust sets.

To make the hasselback potatoes, boil the potatoes in their skins for 10–12 minutes, or until they are just cooked. Once they are cool enough to handle, peel and cut them in half lengthways. Make small even slices across the top of the potato, cutting only two-thirds of the way down, brush each one liberally with butter and season them well with salt and ground pepper.

Heat the remaining olive oil in a large saucepan, add the onion, carrot, celery and remaining garlic, and cook them for 5 minutes. Pour in the red wine, cook for another 5 minutes, then add the beef stock, the bay leaves and the remaining thyme. Mix the cornflour with 1 tablespoon water until it is smooth and add it to the pan. Simmer the sauce over low heat for 20 minutes, or until it is slightly thickened, then strain and season to taste with salt and pepper.

Preheat a kettle or covered barbecue to medium indirect heat, put the sirloin in the middle of the barbecue and arrange the potatoes around it. Replace the cover and cook for 45 minutes.

Remove the sirloin from the barbecue, and leave it to rest, covered, for about 10 minutes before carving. Serve the steak with the hasselback potatoes and red wine sauce. Serves 6–8

496

497

498

499

496 BEEF IN BLACK BEAN SAUCE

4 tablespoons tinned salted black beans in soy sauce
750 g (1 lb 10 oz) rump steak
1 tablespoon peanut oil
1 tablespoon sesame oil
1 large onion, thinly sliced
1 garlic clove, finely chopped
4 x 1 cm (1 1/2 x 1/2 inch) piece of fresh ginger, peeled
    and finely chopped
1 small red chilli, finely chopped
2 teaspoons cornflour (cornstarch)
2 tablespoons dark soy sauce
1 teaspoon sugar
3 tablespoons beef stock
1 spring onion (scallion), thinly sliced on the diagonal, to garnish

Rinse and then soak the black beans in cold water for 5 minutes. Drain and roughly mash the beans with a fork. Trim the steak of all fat and sinew, then cut the meat in thin slices across the grain.

Heat a saucepan over medium heat, add half each of the peanut and sesame oils. Add the beef in two batches, and stir each for 2 minutes, or until well browned. Transfer the beef and any liquid to a bowl. Heat the remaining oils, add the onion and stir for 2 minutes. Add the garlic, ginger and chilli, and stir for 1 minute.

Mix the cornflour with 1 teaspoon water, then return the beef and any cooking liquid to the pan with the black beans, soy sauce, sugar, stock and cornflour paste. Stir for 1–2 minutes, or until the sauce boils and thickens. Garnish with the spring onions and serve with steamed rice. Serves 4

497 CHINESE BEEF & BROCCOLI STIR-FRY

3 tablespoons peanut oil
1 kg (2 lb 4 oz) fresh rice noodle rolls, cut into 2 cm
    (3/4 inch) strips, separated
500 g (1 lb 2 oz) rump steak, trimmed and thinly sliced
1 onion, cut into wedges
4 garlic cloves, chopped
400 g (14 oz) Chinese broccoli, cut into 3 cm (1 1/4 inch) lengths
1 tablespoon soy sauce
3 tablespoons kecap manis
1 small red chilli, chopped
125 ml (4 fl oz/1/2 cup) beef stock

Heat a wok over medium heat, add 2 tablespoons of the peanut oil and swirl to coat the side of the wok. Add the noodles and stir-fry gently for 2 minutes. Remove from the wok.

Reheat the wok over high heat, add the remaining oil and swirl to coat. Add the beef in batches and cook for 3 minutes, or until it is browned. Remove from the wok. Add the onion and stir-fry for 1–2 minutes, then add the garlic and cook for a further 30 seconds.

Return all the beef to the wok and add the Chinese broccoli, soy sauce, kecap manis, chilli and beef stock, and cook over medium heat for 2–3 minutes. Divide the rice noodles among four large serving bowls and top with the beef mixture. Serve immediately. Serves 4

498 CHILLI BEEF

3 tablespoons kecap manis
2 1/2 teaspoons sambal oelek
2 garlic cloves, crushed
1/2 teaspoon ground coriander
1 tablespoon grated palm sugar (jaggery) or soft brown sugar
1 teaspoon sesame oil
400 g (14 oz) beef fillet, partially frozen, thinly sliced
1 tablespoon peanut oil
2 tablespoons chopped roasted peanuts
3 tablespoons chopped coriander (cilantro) leaves

Combine the kecap manis, sambal oelek, crushed garlic, ground coriander, palm sugar, sesame oil and 2 tablespoons water in a large bowl. Add the beef slices and coat well. Cover with plastic wrap and refrigerate for 20 minutes.

Heat a wok over high heat, add the peanut oil and swirl to coat. Add the meat in batches, cooking each batch for 2–3 minutes, or until browned. Arrange the beef on a serving platter, sprinkle with the chopped peanuts and coriander, and serve with steamed rice. Serves 4

499 PORK WITH PLUM SAUCE & CHOY SUM

600 g (1 lb 5 oz) choy sum, cut into 6 cm (2 1/2 inch) lengths
125 ml (4 fl oz/1/2 cup) peanut oil
1 large onion, sliced
3 garlic cloves, finely chopped
2 teaspoons finely chopped fresh ginger
500 g (1 lb 2 oz) pork loin, thinly sliced
2 tablespoons cornflour (cornstarch), seasoned with
    salt and pepper
3 tablespoons plum sauce
1 1/2 tablespoons soy sauce
1 teaspoon sesame oil
2 tablespoons dry sherry or Chinese rice wine

Bring a large saucepan of lightly salted water to the boil, add the choy sum and cook for 2–3 minutes, or until the stems are crisp but still tender. Plunge into iced water to chill completely, then drain.

Heat a wok over high heat, add 1 tablespoon oil and swirl to coat. Add the onion, garlic and ginger and cook over medium heat for 3 minutes, or until softened. Remove from the wok. Toss the pork in the seasoned cornflour to coat, shaking off any excess. Reheat the wok over high heat, add the remaining oil and swirl to coat. Add the pork in batches and cook for 3 minutes, or until golden on both sides. Remove.

Drain the oil from the wok and return the meat and any juices. Combine the plum sauce, soy sauce, sesame oil and sherry, and add to the wok. Cook over high heat for 2–3 minutes, then add the choy sum and return the onion mixture. Cook, stirring, for a further 2 minutes. Serve immediately with rice. Serves 4

500

501

502

500 BEEF, STOUT & POTATO PIE

2 tablespoons olive oil
1.25 kg (2 lb 12 oz) chuck steak, cut into 3 cm (1¼ inch) cubes,
    fat trimmed
2 onions, sliced
2 bacon slices, roughly chopped
4 garlic cloves, crushed
2 tablespoons plain (all-purpose) flour
435 ml (15¼ fl oz/1¾ cups) stout
375 ml (13 fl oz/1½ cups) beef stock
1½ tablespoons chopped thyme
2 large potatoes, thinly sliced
olive oil, for brushing

Heat 1 tablespoon of the oil over high heat in a flameproof casserole dish, add the beef in batches and cook, turning occasionally, for 5 minutes, or until browned. Remove from the dish. Reduce the heat to low, add the remaining oil to the dish, then cook the onion and bacon for 10 minutes, stirring occasionally. Add the garlic and cook for another minute. Return the beef to the dish. Sprinkle the flour over the beef, cook for a minute, stirring, then gradually add the stout, stirring constantly. Add the stock, increase the heat to medium–high and bring to the boil. Stir in the thyme, season, then reduce the heat and simmer for 2 hours, or until the beef is tender and the mixture has thickened.

Preheat the oven to 200°C (400°F/Gas 6). Lightly grease a 1.25 litre (44 fl oz/5 cup) ovenproof dish and pour in the beef mixture. Arrange potato slices in a single overlapping layer over the top to cover the meat. Brush over the top with olive oil and sprinkle with salt. Bake for 30–40 minutes, or until the potato is golden. Serves 6

502 SHEPHERD'S PIE

1 tablespoon oil
1 onion, finely chopped
1 carrot, finely chopped
1 kg (2 lb 4 oz) minced (ground) lamb, raw or cooked
plain (all-purpose) flour, for thickening
2 tablespoons tomato sauce (ketchup)
2 beef stock (bouillon) cubes
worcestershire sauce
6 potatoes, cut into chunks
80 ml (2½ fl oz/⅓ cup) milk
butter

Preheat the oven to 200°C (400°F/Gas 6). Heat the oil in a frying pan, add the onion and carrot and cook until they begin to brown around the edges. Add the meat and cook, turning over every now and then, mashing out any large lumps with the back of a fork. When the meat is browned, add about a teaspoon of flour and stir it in. Add the tomato sauce and sprinkle on the stock cube. Add about 500 ml (17 fl oz/ 2 cups) water and mix everything together. Bring the mixture to the boil, then turn down the heat and simmer gently for about 30 minutes, or until thick. Season with salt, pepper and worcestershire sauce.

While the meat is cooking, cook the potato chunks in simmering water until they are tender (this will take about 12 minutes). When they are soft, drain and mash them with the milk and plenty of seasoning. Pour the meat into a large ovenproof dish or four individual dishes and dollop the potato on top. Dot some butter over the potato and bake for about 20 minutes, by which time the top of the potato should be lightly browned. Serve with peas. Serves 4

501 STEAK & KIDNEY PIE

60 g (2¼ oz/½ cup) plain (all-purpose) flour, seasoned
1.5 kg (3 lb 5 oz) chuck steak, cut into 2 cm (¾ inch) cubes
1 ox kidney (500 g/1 lb 2 oz), cut into 2 cm (¾ inch) cubes
2 tablespoons olive oil
2 onions, chopped
125 g (4½ oz) button mushrooms, quartered
40 g (1½ oz) butter
250 ml (9 fl oz/1 cup) beef or veal stock
185 ml (6 fl oz/¾ cup) stout
2 tablespoons worcestershire sauce
1 tablespoon anchovy essence
1 tablespoon chopped flat-leaf (Italian) parsley
600 g (1 lb 5 oz) puff pastry
1 egg, lightly beaten

Place the flour in a bowl. Toss the steak and kidney pieces through the flour and shake off any excess. Heat the oil in a large pan over medium heat, add the onion and cook for 5 minutes. Add the mushrooms and cook for 5 minutes. Remove from the pan.

Melt a third of the butter in the pan, add a third of the beef and kidney and cook over medium heat, turning occasionally, for 5 minutes, or until brown. Remove and repeat twice with the remaining butter, beef and kidney. Return all the meat to the saucepan, add the stock and stout, stir and bring slowly to boil. Reduce the heat and simmer for 2 hours. Remove from the heat, leave to cool, then add the onion and mushrooms, worcestershire sauce, anchovy essence and parsley.

Preheat the oven to 180°C (350°F/Gas 4). Place the filling into a ceramic pie dish measuring 20 cm (8 inches) on the base and 4 cm (1½ inches) deep. Roll out the pastry between two sheets of baking paper to fit the top of the pie dish. Moisten the rim of the dish with milk and place the pastry over the filling. Press firmly into place and brush with egg. Decorate with pastry scraps, brush with egg and bake for 40–45 minutes until golden. Serves 6

503

504

505

506

503 PORK & VEAL TERRINE

8–10 thin slices rindless streaky bacon
1 tablespoon olive oil
1 onion, chopped
2 garlic cloves, crushed
1 kg (2 lb 4 oz) minced (ground) pork and veal
80 g (2¾ oz/1 cup) fresh breadcrumbs
1 egg, beaten
3 tablespoons brandy
3 teaspoons chopped thyme
3 tablespoons chopped flat-leaf (Italian) parsley

Preheat the oven to 180°C (350°F/Gas 4). Lightly grease a 25 x 11 cm (10 x 4¼ inch) terrine. Line the terrine with the bacon so that it hangs over the sides. Heat the oil in a frying pan, add the onion and garlic and cook for 2–3 minutes, or until the onion is soft. Mix the onion with the minced pork and veal, breadcrumbs, egg, brandy, thyme and parsley in a large bowl. Season. Fry a piece of the mixture to check the seasoning, and adjust if necessary.

Spoon the mixture into the lined terrine, pressing down firmly. Fold the bacon over the top, cover with foil and place in a baking dish.

Place enough cold water in the baking dish to come half-way up the side of the terrine. Bake for 1–1¼ hours, or until the juices run clear when the terrine is pierced with a skewer. Remove the terrine from the water-filled baking dish and pour off the excess juices. Cover with foil, then put a piece of heavy cardboard, cut to fit, on top of the terrine. Put weights or food tins on top of the cardboard to compress the terrine. Refrigerate overnight, then cut into slices to serve. Serves 6

504 BEEF WELLINGTON

1.25 kg (2 lb 12 oz) piece of beef fillet or rib eye, trimmed
1 tablespoon oil
125 g (4½ oz) pâté
60 g (2¼ oz) button mushrooms, sliced
375 g (13 oz) block of puff pastry, thawed
1 egg, lightly beaten
1 sheet puff pastry, thawed
green beans and rosemary, to serve

To help the beef keep its shape, tie it four or five times along its length, then rub with pepper. Heat the oil over high heat in a large, heavy-based pan, then cook the meat until it is browned all over. Take the beef out of the pan and let it cool, then cut off the string. Smear the pâté over the top and sides of the beef, then use this as glue to stick the mushrooms on.

The idea is to enclose the beef in puff pastry. Start by rolling the block of pastry out on a lightly floured surface until it is big enough. Then sit the beef on the pastry, brush the edges with egg and bring the edges up until you have a parcel of beef. Use some more of the beaten egg to seal the parcel, then neatly fold in the ends. Lift the beef onto a greased baking tray so the seam is underneath.

Cut shapes from the sheet of pastry. Use the egg to stick the shapes on, then brush all over the Wellington with more of the egg. Cut a few slits in the top to allow the steam to escape. Cook in a 210°C (415°F/Gas 6–7) oven for 45 minutes for rare, 1 hour for medium or 1½ hours for well done. Rest for 10 minutes, then slice and serve. Serve with green beans and rosemary. Serves 6–8

505 FILLET STEAK WITH MUSHROOMS & SHERRY

250 g (9 oz) broccoli, cut into large florets
250 g (9 oz) green beans, trimmed
1 tablespoon oil
60 g (2¼ oz) butter
4 rib eye steaks (scotch fillet) (160 g/5¾ oz each), 2.5 cm (1 inch) thick
3 garlic cloves, finely chopped
250 g (9 oz) mixed mushrooms, such as Swiss brown, shiitake or button
2 teaspoons chopped thyme
125 ml (4 fl oz/½ cup) dry sherry

Bring a saucepan of salted water to the boil. Add the broccoli and beans and cook for 3–4 minutes, or until tender but still crisp. Drain.

Melt the oil and 20 g (¾ oz) of the butter in a large frying pan. Cook the steaks for 3–4 minutes on each side for medium-rare, or until cooked to your liking. Remove from the pan, cover with foil and rest.

Melt another 20 g (¾ oz) of the butter in the pan over medium heat. Add the garlic and mushrooms and season to taste. Cook for 3–4 minutes, or until the mushrooms have softened. Stir in the thyme. Remove from the pan.

Add the sherry and any juices from the rested meat to the pan and stir to scrape up any sediment from the base. Bring to the boil, then reduce the heat and simmer for 2–3 minutes, or until reduced to 80 ml (2½ fl oz/⅓ cup) and thickened slightly. Whisk in the remaining butter in small amounts, until glossy. To serve, put the steaks on four serving plates, top with the mushrooms and spoon the sauce over the top. Serve with the broccoli and green beans. Serves 4

506 TORTILLA PIE

1 tablespoon oil
500 g (1 lb 2 oz) lean minced (ground) beef
35 g (1¼ oz) packet taco seasoning mix
425 g (15 oz) tin Mexican chilli beans, drained
8 flour tortillas
250 g (9 oz/2 cups) grated cheddar cheese
300 g (10½ oz) Mexican tomato salsa
150 g (5½ oz) sour cream
1 avocado, diced

Preheat the oven to 180°C (350°F/Gas 4). Grease a 23 cm (9 inch) pie dish. Heat the oil in a large non-stick frying pan. Add the mince and cook for 5 minutes, or until brown, breaking up the lumps with the back of a spoon. Drain off the excess oil. Add the seasoning mix and cook for 5 minutes. Stir in the beans until heated through.

Lay a tortilla in the base of the pie dish, then spread 125 g (4½ oz/½ cup) of the beef mixture on top. Sprinkle with 3 tablespoons cheese and 1 tablespoon salsa. Continue layering with the remaining tortillas, beef mixture, cheese and salsa, ending with a tortilla sprinkled with a little cheese — it should end up looking like a dome shape.

Bake for 15 minutes, or until all the cheese has melted and browned. Cool slightly, cut into wedges and top with a dollop of sour cream and the diced avocado. Serve with a tomato salad, if desired. Serves 4

507

508

509

507 MARINATED LAMB

4 tablespoons finely chopped flat-leaf (Italian) parsley
4 tablespoons finely chopped coriander (cilantro) leaves
4 garlic cloves, crushed
1 tablespoon paprika
1 teaspoon dried thyme
125 ml (4 fl oz/$\frac{1}{2}$ cup) olive oil
3 tablespoons lemon juice
2 teaspoons ground cumin
4 x 250 g (9 oz) lamb rumps or pieces of tenderloin, trimmed

Mix the parsley, coriander, garlic, paprika, thyme, oil, lemon juice and 1$\frac{1}{2}$ teaspoons cumin together in a non-metallic dish. Score diagonal lines in the fat on the lamb pieces with a sharp knife, then put them in the marinade, turning so they are evenly coated. Cover and refrigerate for at least 2 hours or overnight.

Heat a barbecue flat plate to medium direct heat. Season the lamb to taste with white pepper, the remaining cumin and some salt. Cook the rumps, fat side up, for 3 minutes and then cook the other side for 2–3 minutes, making sure the fat is well cooked. Take the lamb off the barbecue as soon as it is done, cover it with foil and put it aside to rest for about 5 minutes before carving. Serves 4

509 PEPPER STEAK

4 x 200 g (7 oz) fillet steaks
2 tablespoons oil
6 tablespoons black peppercorns, crushed
40 g (1$\frac{1}{2}$ oz) butter
3 tablespoons Cognac or brandy
125 ml (4 fl oz/$\frac{1}{2}$ cup) thick (double/heavy) cream
green salad, to serve

Rub the steaks on both sides with the oil and press the crushed peppercorns into the meat so they don't come off while you're frying. Melt the butter in a large frying pan and cook the steaks for 2–4 minutes on each side, depending on how you like your steak.

Now for the fun part: add the Cognac or brandy and flambé by lighting the pan with your gas flame or a match (stand well back when you do this and keep a pan lid handy for emergencies). Lift the steaks out onto a warm plate. Add the wine to the pan and boil, stirring, for 1 minute to deglaze the pan. Add the cream and stir for a couple of minutes. Season with salt and pepper and pour over the steaks. Serve with green salad. Serves 4

508 VEAL PARMIGIANA

3 tablespoons olive oil
1 garlic clove, crushed
pinch of cayenne pepper
pinch of caster (superfine) sugar
400 g (14 oz) tin crushed tomatoes
3 teaspoons chopped oregano
40 g (1$\frac{1}{2}$ oz/$\frac{1}{3}$ cup) plain (all-purpose) flour
2 eggs
65 g (2$\frac{1}{4}$ oz/$\frac{2}{3}$ cup) dry breadcrumbs
4 large veal cutlets, well trimmed
100 g (3$\frac{1}{2}$ oz) mozzarella cheese, thinly sliced
35 g (1$\frac{1}{4}$ oz/$\frac{1}{3}$ cup) grated parmesan cheese

Preheat the oven to 190°C (375°F/Gas 5). Heat 1 tablespoon of the oil in a pan over medium heat, add the garlic and cook for 30 seconds. Add the cayenne, sugar, tomato and half the oregano and cook, stirring occasionally, for 20 minutes, or until thickened. Season well. Place the flour in a wide shallow bowl and season well. Beat the eggs with 2 tablespoons of water in another bowl. Mix the breadcrumbs with the remaining oregano, season and place in a third bowl.

Pound the cutlets between two sheets of plastic wrap until flattened to 5 mm ($\frac{1}{4}$ inch) thick, taking care not to tear the flesh from the bone. Coat in the seasoned flour, shaking off the excess, then dip both sides in the egg mixture and then coat in the breadcrumbs. Heat the remaining oil in a large frying pan. Add the cutlets in two batches and brown over medium–high heat for 2 minutes on each side. Transfer to a shallow baking dish large enough to fit them side by side.

Spread the sauce over each cutlet. Cover with the mozzarella and sprinkle with the parmesan. Bake for 20 minutes, or until the cheeses have melted and browned. Serve. Serves 4

510

511

512

513

510 BARBECUED CHILLI PORK RIBS

1 kg (2 lb 4 oz) pork spareribs
125 g (4¹/₂ oz) tin puréed tomatoes
2 tablespoons honey
2 tablespoons chilli sauce
2 tablespoons hoisin sauce
2 tablespoons lime juice
2 garlic cloves, crushed
1 tablespoon oil

Cut each rib into thirds, then lay them in a single layer in a shallow non-metallic dish. Mix together all the other ingredients except the oil and pour over the meat, turning to coat well. Cover with plastic wrap and refrigerate overnight, turning occasionally.

Drain the ribs, reserving the marinade, and cook them over medium heat on a lightly oiled barbecue grill or flat plate. Baste often with the marinade and cook for 15–20 minutes, or until the ribs are tender and well browned, turning occasionally. Season to taste and serve immediately. Serves 4–6

511 GINGER-ORANGE PORK

6 pork butterfly steaks
250 ml (9 fl oz/1 cup) ginger wine
150 g (5¹/₂ oz/¹/₂ cup) orange marmalade
2 tablespoons oil
1 tablespoon grated fresh ginger

Trim the pork steak of excess fat and sinew. Mix together the wine, marmalade, oil and ginger. Place the steaks in a shallow non-metallic dish and add the marinade. Store, covered with plastic wrap, in the refrigerator for at least 3 hours, turning occasionally. Drain well, reserving the marinade.

Cook the pork on a hot, lightly oiled barbecue flat plate or grill for 5 minutes each side or until tender, turning once. While the meat is cooking, place the reserved marinade in a small pan. Bring to the boil, reduce the heat and simmer for 5 minutes, or until the marinade has reduced and thickened slightly. Pour over the pork. Serves 6

Note: Steaks of uneven thickness may curl when cooked. Prevent this by leaving a layer of fat on the outside and making a few deep cuts in it prior to cooking. Remove before serving.

512 LAMB CUTLETS WITH ONION MARMALADE

2 tablespoons butter
80 ml (2¹/₂ fl oz/¹/₃ cup) olive oil
4 onions, finely sliced
2 teaspoons soft brown sugar
2 teaspoons thyme leaves
2 tablespoons finely chopped flat-leaf (Italian) parsley
12 French-trimmed lamb cutlets
2 tablespoons lemon juice

Heat the butter and half the olive oil together in a saucepan. Add the onion, sugar and thyme and stir well. Turn the heat to low, cover the saucepan and cook the onion, stirring it occasionally for 30–35 minutes, or until it is very soft and golden. Season well, stir the parsley through and keep it warm over a very low heat.

Heat the remaining oil in a frying pan or brush a chargrill pan with oil and, when it is hot, add the cutlets in a single layer. Fry for 2 minutes on each side, or until the lamb is browned on the outside but still feels springy when you press it. Add the lemon juice and season well. Put a small pile of the onion and herb marmalade on each plate and place the cutlets around it. Serves 4

513 CHILLI LAMB CUTLETS

4 garlic cloves, crushed
1 tablespoon grated ginger
1 teaspoon oil
1 teaspoon sambal oelek
2 teaspoons ground coriander
2 teaspoons ground cumin
2 tablespoons soy sauce
2 teaspoons sesame oil
2 tablespoons sweet chilli sauce
2 tablespoons lemon juice
12 lamb cutlets

Combine the garlic, ginger, oil, sambal oelek, coriander, cumin, soy sauce, sesame oil, sweet chilli sauce and lemon juice in a bowl. Season with salt and freshly ground black pepper. Place the cutlets in a non-metallic dish and pour on the marinade, coating all sides. Leave to marinate for 20 minutes.

Cook the cutlets on a very hot chargrill pan or barbecue for 3 minutes each side, or until cooked to your liking. Serve with rice. Serves 4

514

515

516

517

514 BRAISED LAMB SHANKS IN RICH TOMATO SAUCE

2 tablespoons olive oil
1 large red onion, sliced
4 French-trimmed lamb shanks (about 250 g/9 oz each)
2 garlic cloves, crushed
400 g (14 oz) tin peeled chopped tomatoes
125 ml (4 fl oz/½ cup) red wine
2 teaspoons chopped rosemary
150 g (5½ oz/1 cup) instant polenta (cornmeal)
50 g (1¾ oz) butter
50 g (1¾ oz/½ cup) grated parmesan cheese

Preheat the oven to 160°C (315°F/Gas 2-3). Heat the oil in a 4 litre (140 fl oz/16 cup) flameproof casserole dish over medium heat and cook the onion for 3-4 minutes, or until soft. Add the lamb shanks and cook for 2-3 minutes, or until lightly browned. Add the garlic, tomato and wine, then bring to the boil and cook for 3-4 minutes. Stir in the rosemary. Season. Cover, transfer to the oven and cook for 2 hours. Remove the lid, return to the oven and simmer for a further 15 minutes, or until the lamb just starts to fall off the bone. Check periodically that the sauce is not too dry, adding water if needed.

About 20 minutes before serving, bring 1 litre (35 fl oz/4 cups) water to the boil in a saucepan. Add the polenta in a thin stream, whisking continuously, then reduce the heat to very low. Simmer for 8-10 minutes, or until thick and coming away from the side of the saucepan. Stir in the butter and parmesan. To serve, spoon the polenta onto serving plates, top with the shanks and a little sauce from the casserole over the shanks. Serves 4

516 ROAST LAMB

2 rosemary sprigs
3 garlic cloves
75 g (2¾ oz) pancetta
2 kg (4 lb 8 oz) leg of lamb, shank bone cut off just above the joint, trimmed of excess fat and tied
1 large onion
125 ml (4 fl oz/½ cup) olive oil
375 ml (13 fl oz/1½ cups) dry white wine

Preheat the oven to 230°C (450°F/Gas 8). Strip the leaves off the rosemary sprigs and chop them with the garlic and pancetta until paste-like. Season. With the point of a sharp knife, make incisions about 1 cm (½ inch) deep all over the lamb. Rub the rosemary filling over the surface of the lamb, pushing it into the incisions.

Cut the onion into four thick slices and put them in the centre of a roasting tin. Place the lamb on top and gently pour the olive oil over it. Roast for 15 minutes. Reduce the temperature to 180°C (350°F/Gas 4) and pour in 250 ml (9 fl oz/1 cup) of the wine. Roast for 1½ hours for medium-rare, or longer if you prefer. Baste a couple of times and add a little water if the juices start to burn in the tin. Transfer the lamb to a carving platter and leave to rest for 10 minutes.

Remove the onion and spoon off the excess fat from the tin. Place over high heat on the stovetop, pour in the remaining wine and cook for 3-4 minutes, or until the sauce reduces and thickens. Taste for seasoning. Slice the lamb and serve with the sauce spooned over the top. Serves 4

515 HONEY ROASTED PORK FILLET

1 tablespoon finely grated fresh ginger
6 garlic cloves
80 ml (2½ fl oz/⅓ cup) soy sauce
2 tablespoons oil
2 kg (4 lb 8 oz) piece pork neck or blade roast
2 tablespoons honey

Mix the ginger, garlic, soy sauce and oil in a large, non-metallic bowl. Put the pork in the marinade and turn it so that it is well coated, then cover the bowl and refrigerate it overnight. Remove the pork from the marinade, pour the marinade into a small saucepan and simmer it over low heat for 5 minutes or until it is slightly reduced. Stir the honey into the warm marinade and remove it from the heat.

Preheat a kettle or covered barbecue to low-medium indirect heat, then put the pork in the middle of the barbecue and roast it, covered, for 45 minutes or until it is cooked through. In the last 10 minutes of cooking, baste the roast all over with the reduced marinade. Be careful not to let any of the marinade splash onto the grill, as it may burn and stick. Remove the roast from the barbecue and put it on a tray, covered, to rest for 10 minutes. Carve the roast and serve it with any pan juices left in the tray. Serves 6-8

517 BARBECUED ROAST LAMB

2.5 kg (5 lb 8 oz) leg of lamb
6 garlic cloves, peeled
2 tablespoons rosemary leaves
1 tablespoon olive oil

Make 12 small incisions in the fleshy parts of the lamb. Cut the garlic cloves in half lengthways, and push them into the incisions with the rosemary leaves. Rub the lamb with the oil and season it liberally with salt and pepper. Preheat a kettle or covered barbecue to medium indirect heat, put the lamb in the middle of the barbecue, replace the lid, and let it roast for 1 hour 30 minutes.

When the lamb is ready, remove it from the barbecue and let it rest, covered, for 10 minutes before carving and serving it with any juices that have been released while it rested. Serves 6

518

519

520

518 SAUSAGES COOKED WITH LENTILS

3 tablespoons olive oil
8 Italian sausages
1 onion, chopped
3 garlic cloves, thinly sliced
2 tablespoons finely chopped rosemary
800 g (1 lb 12 oz) tin tomatoes
16 juniper berries, lightly crushed
1 teaspoon freshly grated nutmeg
1 bay leaf
1 dried chilli
200 ml (7 fl oz) red wine
100 g (3½ oz) green lentils
extra rosemary, to garnish

Heat the oil in a saucepan and cook the sausages for 5–10 minutes, browning well all over. Remove the sausages and set aside.

Reduce the heat to low, add the onion and garlic to the pan and cook until the onion is soft and translucent, but not browned. Stir in the rosemary, then add the tomatoes and cook gently until the sauce has thickened.

Add the juniper berries, nutmeg, bay leaf, chilli, red wine and 400 ml (14 fl oz) water. Bring to the boil, then add the lentils and the cooked sausages. Stir well, cover the saucepan and simmer gently for about 40 minutes, or until the lentils are soft. Stir the lentils a few times to prevent them sticking to the base of the pan and add a little more water if you need to cook them for a bit longer. Remove the bay leaf and chilli before serving. Garnish with rosemary. Serves 4

520 BEEF STROGANOFF

500 g (1 lb 2 oz) rump steak
2 tablespoons plain (all-purpose) flour
2 tablespoons olive oil
1 onion, finely chopped
1 garlic clove, crushed
400 g (14 oz) button mushrooms, sliced
1 tablespoon tomato paste (concentrated purée)
300 g (10½ oz) sour cream
finely chopped flat-leaf (Italian) parsley, to serve

Trim excess fat off the meat and slice it across the grain into thin pieces. Put the flour in a plastic bag and season well with salt and freshly ground black pepper. Add the steak and shake to coat the meat. Shake off any excess flour.

Heat 1 tablespoon oil in a large heavy-based frying pan over high heat. Add the meat and cook in batches until well browned. Remove from the pan and set aside.

Heat the remaining oil and add the onion. Cook for 2–3 minutes, or until soft and translucent, then add the garlic and stir briefly. Add the mushrooms and cook for about 3 minutes, or until soft. Stir in the tomato paste and sour cream, then add the beef strips. Stir until well combined and heated through. Sprinkle with chopped parsley before serving with rice. Serves 4

519 SWEET & SOUR PORK

600 g (1 lb 5 oz) pork loin, cubed
2 eggs
60 g (2¼ oz/½ cup) cornflour (cornstarch)
1 tablespoon oil
1 onion, cubed
1 red capsicum (pepper), cubed
2 spring onions (scallions), cut into lengths
250 ml (9 fl oz/1 cup) clear rice vinegar
    or white vinegar
80 ml (2½ fl oz/⅓ cup) tomato sauce (ketchup)
220 g (7¾ oz/1 cup) sugar
2 tablespoons oil, extra

Put the pork cubes and egg in a bowl with 4 tablespoons of the cornflour. Stir everything around to coat the pork well, then tip into a sieve and shake off any excess cornflour.

Heat a wok over a high heat, add a tablespoon of oil and heat it until it just starts to smoke. Add the onion and cook it for a minute. Add the red capsicum and spring onion and cook for another minute. Add the rice vinegar, tomato ketchup and sugar, turn down the heat and stir everything together until the sugar dissolves. Bring to the boil and simmer it for about 3 minutes.

Mix 2 tablespoons of cornflour with 2 tablespoons of water, add it to the sweet-and-sour mixture, then simmer for a minute until the sauce thickens a bit. Pour the sauce into a bowl.

Heat half the remaining oil in a non-stick frying pan over a medium heat. As soon as the oil is hot, slide in half the pork cubes into the pan and cook them until they are browned and crisp. Remove from pan. Repeat with remaining oil and pork. Return all the pork to the pan and add the sauce. Reheat everything until the sauce is bubbling. Serves 4

521

522

523

524

521 VEAL SCALOPPINE WITH WHITE WINE & PARSLEY

4 x 170 g (6 oz) veal escalopes
30 g (1 oz) butter
3 tablespoons dry white wine or dry Marsala
100 ml (3½ fl oz) thick (double/heavy) cream
1 tablespoon wholegrain mustard
2 tablespoons chopped flat-leaf (Italian) parsley

Place the veal escalopes between two sheets of plastic wrap and either press down hard with the heel of your hand until flattened, or flatten with a rolling pin or mallet. Heat the butter in a frying pan and cook the escalopes in batches for 1 minute each side, or until just cooked. Remove and cover.

Add the wine to the pan, bring to the boil and cook for 1–2 minutes, or until reduced by half. Then add the cream, bring to the boil and reduce by half again. Stir in the mustard and 1 tablespoon parsley until just combined. Return the veal to the pan to warm through and coat in the sauce. Serve the veal with a little sauce and sprinkle with the remaining parsley. Serve with potatoes and a green salad. Serves 4

522 ROSEMARY & RED WINE STEAKS WITH BARBECUED VEGETABLES

12 small new potatoes
3 tablespoons olive oil
1 tablespoon finely chopped rosemary
6 garlic cloves, sliced
sea salt flakes, to season
4 large, thick field mushrooms
12 asparagus spears
250 ml (9 fl oz/1 cup) red wine
4 scotch fillet steaks (about 260 g/9¼ oz each)

Heat a barbecue plate or chargrill pan to hot. Toss the potatoes with 1 tablespoon of the oil, half the rosemary and half the garlic and season with the sea salt flakes. Divide the potatoes among four large sheets of foil and wrap into neat packages, sealing firmly around the edges. Cook on the barbecue, turning frequently for 30–40 minutes, or until tender.

Meanwhile, brush the mushrooms and asparagus with a little of the remaining oil and set aside. Combine the red wine with the remaining oil, rosemary and garlic in a non-metallic dish. Season with lots of freshly ground black pepper. Add the steaks and coat in the marinade. Allow to marinate for 25 minutes, then drain.

Cook the steaks and mushrooms on the barbecue for 4 minutes each side, or until cooked to your liking. Transfer the steaks and mushrooms to a plate, cover and allow to rest. Add the asparagus to the barbecue, turning regularly for about 2 minutes, or until tender. Pierce the potatoes with a skewer to check for doneness. Season. Serve the steaks with the vegetables. Serves 4

523 MOROCCAN ROAST LAMB WITH MINT COUSCOUS

2 tablespoons olive oil
3 teaspoons ground cumin
3 teaspoons ground coriander
3 teaspoons sweet paprika
3 garlic cloves, crushed
1.5 kg (3 lb 5 oz) easy-carve leg of lamb
245 g (8½ oz/1⅓ cups) couscous
2 tablespoons chopped mint

Preheat the oven to 180°C (350°F/Gas 4). Combine the oil, spices and 2 cloves crushed garlic to form a smooth paste. Season with salt and pepper. Rub a thick coating of the paste all over the lamb. Place on a rack in a roasting tin and roast for 1 hour 15 minutes, basting two or three times. Allow to rest in a warm place for 10 minutes.

Meanwhile, place the couscous in a heatproof bowl with 500 ml (17 fl oz/2 cups) boiling water. Stir in the mint, the remaining garlic and ½ teaspoon salt. Cover and leave for 5 minutes, or until all the water has been absorbed, then gently fluff with a fork.

To serve, carve the lamb into thick slices and place on a bed of couscous. Pour the pan juices into a small jug and serve with the lamb. Garnish with mint leaves, if desired. Serves 4

524 MUSTARD-CRUSTED SCOTCH FILLET WITH ROAST VEGETABLES

16 French shallots
125 g (4½ oz/½ cup) wholegrain mustard
3 garlic cloves, crushed
1.2–1.5 kg (2 lb 10 oz–3 lb 5 oz) scotch fillet
200 g (7 oz) parsnips, cut into 2 cm (¾ inch) chunks
400 g (14 oz) potatoes, cut lengthways into wedges
200 g (7 oz) orange sweet potato, cut into wedges
80 ml (2½ fl oz/⅓ cup) olive oil

Preheat the oven to 200°C (400°F/Gas 6). Peel four of the French shallots, slice into thick rings and arrange them in the centre of a large roasting tin. Combine the mustard and garlic, and season well with salt and pepper. Rub the mixture over the surface of the beef, then place the beef on top of the sliced shallots.

Toss the parsnip, potato, sweet potato, the remaining shallots, and 3 tablespoons of the oil together, then arrange around the beef. Drizzle the remaining oil over the beef and roast for 30 minutes. Season and turn the vegetables — don't worry if some of the mustard mixes through. Roast for a further 30 minutes for a medium–rare result, or until cooked to your liking. Rest in a warm place for 10 minutes. To serve, carve the beef and spoon the pan juices on the top. Serve with the roasted vegetables, whole shallots, and some steamed greens, if desired. Serves 4

525

526

527

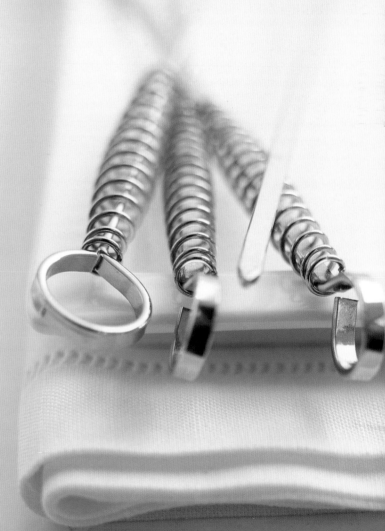

525 PAPRIKA LAMB KEBABS WITH SKORDALIA

1 kg (2 lb 4 oz) lamb backstraps, cut into 2 cm ($^3/_4$ inch) cubes
1 tablespoon sweet paprika
1 tablespoon hot paprika
125 ml (4 fl oz/$^1/_2$ cup) lemon juice
125 ml (4 fl oz/$^1/_2$ cup) olive oil
3 large (750 g/1 lb 10 oz) floury potatoes, cut into large cubes
3–4 garlic cloves, crushed with a pinch of salt
300 g (10$^1/_2$ oz) English spinach leaves
lemon wedges, to serve

Soak 12 wooden skewers in water for 30 minutes. Thread six lamb cubes onto each, then place in a non-metallic rectangular dish large enough to hold all the skewers in one layer. Combine the paprikas, 80 ml (2$^1/_2$ fl oz/$^1/_3$ cup) lemon juice and 3 tablespoons oil in a small non-metallic jug. Pour over the skewers. Season. Cover and refrigerate.

For the skordalia, boil the potatoes for 20 minutes, or until tender. Drain and put in a food processor with the garlic and 1 tablespoon of the lemon juice. With the motor running, slowly add the remaining oil in a thin stream and continue blending for 30–60 seconds, or until all the oil is incorporated — avoid overprocessing as it will become gluey. Season. Set aside to serve at room temperature.

Heat a chargrill pan or barbecue plate and brush with oil. Cook the skewers for 3–4 minutes each side for medium–rare, or 5–6 minutes for well done. Wash the spinach and add to a pan with just the water clinging to the leaves. Cook, covered, over medium heat for 1–2 minutes, or until wilted. Remove and stir in the remaining lemon juice. Serve the kebabs with skordalia, spinach and lemon wedges. Serves 4

527 BAKED MEDITERRANEAN PORK CUTLETS

4 large pork loin cutlets, trimmed
2 tablespoons olive oil
2 garlic cloves, finely chopped
1 tablespoon finely chopped rosemary
2 tablespoons thyme leaves
2 tablespoons balsamic vinegar
4 roma (plum) tomatoes, halved lengthways
1 large red capsicum (pepper), cut into 2 cm ($^3/_4$ inch) slices
4 small zucchini (courgettes), trimmed and halved lengthways

Preheat the oven to 220°C (425°F/Gas 7) and lightly grease a baking tin. Arrange the pork cutlets in a single layer in the tin. Combine the olive oil, garlic, rosemary, thyme and 1 tablespoon of the balsamic vinegar, then spoon half the mixture over the pork cutlets. Season to taste with salt and black pepper. Cover with plastic wrap and marinate for 20 minutes.

Place 2 tomato halves, cut side down, on each pork cutlet and sprinkle the tomatoes with the remaining balsamic vinegar. Toss the capsicum and zucchini with the remaining herb mixture, then add to the dish around the cutlets. Bake for 45 minutes, or until cooked through and well browned. Season, to taste. Serve the cutlets with the roast vegetables, a green salad and crusty bread. Serves 4

526 THAI BEEF SKEWERS WITH PEANUT SAUCE

1 onion, chopped
2 garlic cloves, crushed
2 teaspoons sambal oelek
1 lemongrass stem, white part only, chopped
2 teaspoons chopped fresh ginger
1$^1/_2$ tablespoons oil
270 ml (9$^1/_2$ fl oz) coconut cream
125 g (4$^1/_2$ oz/$^1/_2$ cup) crunchy peanut butter
1$^1/_2$ tablespoons fish sauce
2 teaspoons soy sauce
1 tablespoon grated palm sugar (jaggery) or soft brown sugar
2 tablespoons lime juice
2 tablespoons chopped coriander (cilantro) leaves
750 g (1 lb 10 oz) round or rump steak, cut into 2 x 10 cm ($^3/_4$ x 4 inch) pieces
2 teaspoons oil, extra
red chilli, chopped, to garnish (optional)
chopped roasted peanuts, to garnish (optional)

Put the onion, garlic, sambal oelek, lemongrass and ginger in a food processor and process to a smooth paste.

Heat the oil in a saucepan over medium heat, add the paste and cook, stirring, for 2–3 minutes, or until fragrant. Add the coconut cream, peanut butter, fish sauce, soy sauce, sugar and lime juice and bring to the boil. Reduce the heat and simmer for 5 minutes, then stir in the chopped coriander.

Meanwhile, thread the meat onto 12 metal skewers, and cook on a hot chargrill or in a non-stick frying pan with the extra oil for 2 minutes each side, or until cooked to your liking. Serve the skewers on a bed of rice with the sauce and a salad on the side. Garnish with chopped chilli and peanuts, if desired. Serves 4

Note: If using wooden skewers, soak them for 30 minutes before grilling to prevent them from burning.

528

529

530

531

528 CURRIED SAUSAGES

9 thick beef or pork sausages
1 tablespoon vegetable oil
20 g ($^3/_4$ oz) butter
2 teaspoons grated ginger
3 garlic cloves, crushed
2 large onions, sliced
3 teaspoons curry powder
1 teaspoon garam masala
2 teaspoons tomato paste (concentrated purée)
1 tablespoon plain (all-purpose) flour
625 ml ($21^1/_2$ fl oz/$2^1/_2$ cups) hot chicken stock
2 bay leaves

Place the sausages in a saucepan, cover with cold water and bring to the boil. Lower the heat and simmer for 3 minutes. Remove from the heat and allow the sausages to cool in the water, then drain, pat dry, and cut into 2 cm ($^3/_4$ inch) pieces.

Heat the oil in a large frying pan over high heat and cook the sausages for 2–3 minutes, or until golden all over. Drain on paper towels.

Using the same pan, melt the butter, then add the ginger, garlic and onion. Cook over medium heat for about 5 minutes, or until the onion is soft and golden. Add the curry powder and garam masala and cook for 1 minute, or until fragrant. Stir in the tomato paste and cook for 1 minute, then add the flour. Stir to combine, then gradually pour in the stock, taking care that no lumps form. Bring to a simmer, add the bay leaves and the sausages and cook over low heat for 15 minutes, or until thickened. Season and serve with mashed potato. Serves 6

530 ITALIAN BEEF CASSEROLE WITH POLENTA DUMPLINGS

2 tablespoons olive oil
1 onion, sliced
2 garlic cloves, crushed
1 tablespoon plain (all-purpose) flour
1 kg (2 lb 4 oz) blade or chuck steak, cut into 3 cm ($1^1/_4$ inch) cubes
375 ml (13 fl oz/$1^1/_2$ cups) beef stock
1 tablespoon chopped oregano
2 x 425 g (15 oz) tins tomatoes
2 red capsicums (peppers), roasted, peeled and cut into strips
100 g ($3^1/_2$ oz/$^2/_3$ cup) instant polenta
90 g ($3^1/_4$ oz/$^1/_3$ cup) ready-made pesto

Preheat the oven to 150°C (300°F/Gas 2). Heat the oil in a 4 litre (140 fl oz/16 cup) flameproof casserole dish, add the onion and garlic, and cook over medium heat for 8 minutes, or until soft but not brown. Sprinkle the flour over the top and stir well. Add the beef, stock, oregano, tomato and capsicum, season and simmer for 15 minutes, then bake, covered, for 1 hour 30 minutes.

Place 300 ml ($10^1/_2$ fl oz) water in a saucepan, bring to the boil, then reduce the heat and simmer. Pour in the polenta in a thin stream, season and cook, stirring, for 2 minutes, or until it thickens and comes away from the side of the pan. Remove and cool.

Shape the cooled polenta into 12 round dumplings, place on top of the casserole and bake, covered for 1 hour, and then uncovered for 20–30 minutes. Garnish with the pesto and serve. Serves 4–6

529 OSSO BUCO WITH GREMOLATA

2 tablespoons olive oil
1 onion, finely chopped
1 garlic clove, crushed
1 kg (2 lb 4 oz) veal shin slices (osso buco)
2 tablespoons plain (all-purpose) flour
400 g (14 oz) tin tomatoes, roughly chopped
250 ml (9 fl oz/1 cup) white wine
250 ml (9 fl oz/1 cup) chicken stock

GREMOLATA
2 tablespoons finely chopped flat-leaf (Italian) parsley
2 teaspoons grated lemon zest
1 teaspoon finely chopped garlic

Heat 1 tablespoon oil in a large shallow flameproof casserole dish. Add the onion and cook over low heat until soft and golden. Add the garlic. Cook for 1 minute, then remove from the dish.

Heat the remaining oil and brown the veal in batches, then remove. Return the onion to the casserole and stir in the flour. Cook for 30 seconds and remove from the heat. Slowly stir in the tomatoes, wine and stock, combining well with the flour. Return the veal to the casserole. Return to the heat and bring to the boil, stirring. Cover and reduce the heat to low so that the casserole is just simmering. Cook for $2^1/_2$ hours, or until the meat is very tender and almost falling off the bones.

To make the gremolata, combine the parsley, lemon zest and garlic in a bowl. When the osso buco is ready, sprinkle the gremolata over the top and serve with risotto or plain rice. Serves 4

531 CYPRIOT PORK & CORIANDER STEW

$1^1/_2$ tablespoons coriander seeds
800 g (1 lb 12 oz) pork fillet, cut into 2 cm ($^3/_4$ inch) dice
1 tablespoon plain (all-purpose) flour
3 tablespoons olive oil
1 large onion, thinly sliced
375 ml (13 fl oz/$1^1/_2$ cups) red wine
250 ml (9 fl oz/1 cup) chicken stock
1 teaspoon sugar
coriander (cilantro) sprigs, to garnish

Crush the coriander seeds in a mortar and pestle. Combine the pork, crushed seeds and $^1/_2$ teaspoon freshly ground pepper in a bowl. Cover and marinate overnight in the fridge.

Combine the flour and pork and toss. Heat 2 tablespoons oil in a frying pan and cook the pork in batches over high heat for 1–2 minutes, or until brown. Remove. Heat the remaining oil, add the onion and cook over medium heat for 2–3 minutes, or until just golden. Return the meat to the pan, add the wine, stock and sugar, and season. Bring to the boil, then reduce the heat and simmer, covered, for 1 hour.

Remove the meat. Return the pan to the heat and boil over high heat for 3–5 minutes, or until reduced and slightly thickened. Pour over the meat and top with the coriander. Serves 4–6

532

533

534

532 HOISIN LAMB WITH CHARRED SPRING ONION

800 g (1 lb 12 oz) lamb loin
3 tablespoons hoisin sauce
2 tablespoons soy sauce
2 garlic cloves, bruised
1 tablespoon grated fresh ginger
2 teaspoons olive oil
16 spring onions (scallions), trimmed to 18 cm (7 inches) long
3 tablespoons chopped toasted peanuts

Trim the lamb of any excess fat and sinew. Combine the hoisin sauce, soy sauce, garlic, ginger and 1 teaspoon of the oil in a shallow dish, add the lamb and turn it so that it is well coated in the marinade. Cover the dish and refrigerate for 4 hours or overnight.

Toss the trimmed spring onions with the remaining oil and season them well. Remove the lamb from the marinade, season the meat and pour the marinade into a small saucepan. Simmer the marinade for 5 minutes, or until it is slightly reduced. Preheat a chargrill plate to medium direct heat. Cook the lamb for 5–6 minutes on each side, or until it is cooked to your liking, brushing it frequently with the reduced marinade, then let it rest, covered, for 3 minutes. Grill the spring onions for 1–2 minutes, or until they are tender, but still firm.

Cut the lamb across the grain into 2 cm ($^3/_4$ inch) thick slices, and arrange it on a serving plate. Drizzle any juices that have been released during resting over the lamb and sprinkle it with the toasted peanuts. Serve with the spring onions. Serves 4

534 RACK OF LAMB WITH MUSTARD CRUST & PARSLEY POTATOES

2 racks of lamb (6 chops per rack), trimmed, fat side scored
3 tablespoons oil
160 g (5$^3/_4$ oz/2 cups) fresh breadcrumbs
3 garlic cloves, chopped
1 teaspoon grated lemon zest
1 handful finely chopped flat-leaf (Italian) parsley
2 tablespoons tarragon dijon mustard
150 g (5$^1/_2$ oz) unsalted butter, softened
400 g (14 oz) baby new potatoes

Preheat the oven to 220°C (425°F/Gas 7). Rub 1 tablespoon of the oil over the racks and season well. Heat the remaining oil in a frying pan over medium heat and cook the racks for 5–8 minutes, or until the surface is completely brown. Remove from the pan.

Combine the breadcrumbs, garlic, lemon rind and three quarters of the parsley. Add the mustard and 100 g (3$^1/_2$ oz) of the butter to form a paste. Firmly press a layer of breadcrumb mixture over the fat side of the racks, then place in a roasting tin. Bake for 25 minutes, or until the breadcrumbs appear brown and crisp and the meat is cooked to medium. For well-done, continue to bake for 10 minutes. Cover the breadcrumb crust with foil to prevent it burning, if necessary.

About 25 minutes before the lamb is ready, toss the potatoes with the remaining butter until well coated. Season, then put in a roasting tin. Bake for 20 minutes, or until brown, then remove, sprinkle with the remaining parsley and season. To serve, cut the racks in half. Serve with the pan juices, potatoes and a tossed salad. Serves 4

533 KOREAN BARBECUE BEEF IN LETTUCE LEAVES

600 g (1 lb 5 oz) sirloin steak
1 onion, grated
5 garlic cloves, crushed
125 ml (4 fl oz/$^1/_2$ cup) Japanese soy sauce
1 teaspoon sesame oil
1 tablespoon oil
2 teaspoons finely grated fresh ginger
2 tablespoons soft brown sugar
1 tablespoon toasted sesame seeds, ground
1 butter lettuce
375 g (13 oz/2 cups) cooked white rice
2 spring onions (scallions), finely sliced on the diagonal
2 small red chillies, sliced, or chilli sauce (optional)

Trim any excess fat from the steak then put it in the freezer for about 45 minutes, or until it is almost frozen through. Put the onion, garlic, soy sauce, oils, ginger, sugar, ground sesame seeds and 1 teaspoon of freshly ground black pepper in a large, non-metallic bowl and stir it all together well.

Using a very sharp, heavy knife cut the steak across the grain into 2–3 mm ($^1/_{16}$–$^1/_8$ inch) thick slices. Use a meat mallet or rolling pin to pound the meat until it is as thin as possible. Add the meat to the marinade and stir it to make sure that all of the meat is well coated in the marinade. Cover and refrigerate overnight.

Separate the lettuce leaves and put them in a large bowl with enough cold water to cover them and refrigerate until ready to serve.

When you are ready to start cooking, remove the meat and the lettuce from the refrigerator and drain the lettuce well or dry it in a salad spinner. Put the lettuce leaves, hot rice, spring onion and chilli in separate bowls and put them on the table ready for each person to serve themselves. Preheat the flat plate to high indirect heat and, working quickly, put the beef strips on a barbecue flat plate, spacing them out in a single layer, and cook them for about 10 seconds on each side. Do this in two batches if your barbecue isn't large enough to fit them all at once.

To make a wrap, put some rice in the bottom of a lettuce leaf, top it with a little meat, some spring onion and chilli if you like it, then wrap the leaf around the filling. Serves 4–6

535

536

537

538

535 LAMB WITH SPICED LENTILS & MINT RAITA

125 g (4¹/₂ oz/¹/₂ cup) plain yoghurt
2 tablespoons finely chopped mint
1 tablespoon garam masala
3 teaspoons ground cumin
¹/₂ teaspoon chilli powder
80 ml (2¹/₂ fl oz/¹/₃ cup) oil
4 lamb backstraps or eye of loin fillets (about 150 g/5¹/₂ oz each)
2 teaspoons grated fresh ginger
1 teaspoon ground turmeric
2 x 425 g (15 oz) tins lentils, drained and rinsed

Combine the yoghurt and half the mint in a bowl. Cover and set aside. Dry-fry the garam masala then the cumin in a frying pan over medium heat for 1 minute, or until fragrant. Combine 2 teaspoons each of garam masala and cumin, the chilli and 2 tablespoons oil. Put the lamb in a non-metallic dish. Brush with the spiced oil, cover and marinate for 10 minutes, or overnight, if possible.

Meanwhile, heat 1 tablespoon of the remaining oil in a saucepan. Add the ginger, turmeric and remaining cumin and cook for 30 seconds, or until fragrant. Add the lentils and stir until heated through. Reduce the heat to low, add the remaining garam masala and season with salt. Cover and cook for 5 minutes, adding 3 tablespoons water if the lentils start to stick. Before serving, stir in the remaining mint.

Heat a frying pan over medium–high heat and add the remaining oil. Cook the lamb for 3–4 minutes each side for medium–rare, or until cooked to your liking. Rest for 5 minutes, then cut into 1 cm (¹/₂ inch) slices. Serve the lamb with the lentils and mint raita. Serves 4

536 LAMB TAGINE

1.5 kg (3 lb 5 oz) leg or shoulder lamb, cut into 2.5 cm (1 inch) pieces
3 garlic cloves, chopped
80 ml (2¹/₂ fl oz/¹/₃ cup) olive oil
2 teaspoons ground cumin
1 teaspoon ground ginger
1 teaspoon ground turmeric
1 teaspoon paprika
¹/₂ teaspoon ground cinnamon
2 onions, thinly sliced
580 ml (20¹/₄ fl oz/2¹/₃ cups) beef stock
zest of ¹/₄ preserved lemon, rinsed, and cut into thin strips
425 g (15 oz) tin chickpeas, drained
35 g (1¹/₄ oz) pitted green olives
3 tablespoons chopped coriander (cilantro) leaves

Place the lamb in a non-metallic bowl, add the garlic, 2 tablespoons of the oil and the cumin, ginger, turmeric, paprika, cinnamon, ¹/₂ teaspoon ground black pepper and 1 teaspoon salt. Mix well to coat and leave to marinate for 1 hour.

Heat the remaining oil in a large saucepan, add the lamb in batches and brown the meat over high heat for 2–3 minutes. Remove from the pan. Add the onion and cook for 2 minutes, return the meat to the pan and add the beef stock. Reduce the heat and simmer, covered, for 1 hour. Add the lemon zest, chickpeas and olives and cook, uncovered, for a further 30 minutes, or until the meat is tender and the sauce reduced and thickened. Stir in the coriander. Serve in bowls with couscous. Serves 6–8

537 BEEF WITH BLUE CHEESE BUTTER

100 g (3¹/₂ oz) butter, softened
2 garlic cloves, crushed
100 g (3¹/₂ oz) Blue Castello or other creamy blue cheese
2 teaspoons finely shredded sage leaves
1 kg (2 lb 4 oz) beef eye fillet (thick end), trimmed
1 tablespoon olive oil

To make the blue cheese butter, mash together the softened butter, garlic, cheese and sage until they are well combined. Form the mixture into a log and wrap it in baking paper, twisting the ends to seal them. Refrigerate the butter until firm, then cut it into 5 mm (¹/₄ inch) slices and leave it at room temperature until needed.

Cut the beef into four thick, equal pieces and tie a piece of string around the edge of each so it will keep its shape during cooking. Brush both sides of each steak with the oil and season with freshly ground pepper. Heat a barbecue to medium–high direct heat and cook the beef on the chargrill plate for 6–7 minutes each side for medium, or to your liking.

Put two slices of blue cheese butter on top of each steak as soon as you remove it from the barbecue and remove the string. Serves 4

Note: Any leftover butter can be wrapped in baking paper and foil, and frozen for up to 2 months. It is also delicious with chicken and pork.

538 PORK LOIN WITH PICKED EGGPLANT

2 x 500 g (1 lb 2 oz) pieces pork loin fillet (about 10 cm/ 4 inches long)
2 tablespoons hoisin sauce
large pinch of Chinese five-spice
80 ml (2¹/₂ fl oz/¹/₃ cup) oil
1 eggplant (aubergine), cut into wedges
2 tablespoons soy sauce
2 teaspoons sesame oil
2 tablespoons balsamic vinegar
¹/₄ teaspoon caster (superfine) sugar
2 bok choy (pak choy), cut into quarters

Put the pork in a dish and add the hoisin sauce, five-spice and a tablespoon of oil. Rub the mixture over the pork and set it to one side. Heat another 2 tablespoons of oil in a non-stick frying pan and add the eggplant. Fry it until it softens and starts to brown, then add the soy sauce, sesame oil, vinegar and sugar and toss everything together for a minute. Tip the eggplant out onto a plate and wipe out the frying pan.

Put the last tablespoon of oil in the frying pan and put it over a medium heat. Add the pork and fry it on all sides until it is browned and cooked through. The time this takes will depend on how thick your piece of pork is — when it is cooked, it will feel firm when pressed. Put the eggplant back in the pan to heat through.

Take out the pork and leave it to sit for a minute or two. Cook the bok choy in a saucepan with a little bit of boiling water for 1 minute, then drain well. Slice the pork into medallions and serve it with the pickled eggplant and bok choy. Serves 4

539 MUSAMAN BEEF CURRY

1 tablespoon tamarind pulp
2 tablespoons oil
750 g (1 lb 10 oz) lean stewing beef, cubed
500 ml (17 fl oz/2 cups) coconut milk
4 cardamom pods, bruised
500 ml (17 fl oz/2 cups) coconut cream
2–3 tablespoons prepared musaman curry paste
2 tablespoons fish sauce
8 baby onions, peeled
8 baby potatoes, peeled
2 tablespoons grated palm sugar (jaggery) or soft brown sugar
80 g (2^3/$_4$ oz/^{1}/$_2$ cup) unsalted peanuts, roasted and ground

Combine the tamarind pulp and 125 ml (4 fl oz/^{1}/$_2$ cup) boiling water, and set aside to cool. Mash the pulp with your fingertips to dissolve, then strain, reserving the liquid.

Heat the oil in a wok. Add the beef in batches and cook over high heat for 5 minutes per batch, or until browned. Reduce the heat, add the coconut milk and cardamom, and simmer for 1 hour, or until the beef is tender. Remove the beef, then strain and reserve the cooking liquid.

Heat the coconut cream in the wok and stir in 2–3 tablespoons of the curry paste. Cook for 10 minutes, or until it 'cracks', or the oil separates from the cream. Add the fish sauce, onions, potatoes, beef mixture, palm sugar, peanuts, tamarind water and the reserved liquid. Simmer for 25–30 minutes. Serves 4

541 MADRAS BEEF CURRY

1 tablespoon oil or ghee
1 onion, chopped
3–4 tablespoons madras curry paste
1 kg (2 lb 4 oz) skirt or chuck steak, trimmed and cut into
    2.5 cm (1 inch) cubes
3 tablespoons tomato paste (concentrated purée)
250 ml (9 fl oz/1 cup) beef stock

Heat the oil in a large frying pan, add the onion and cook over medium heat for 10 minutes, or until browned. Add the curry paste and stir for 1 minute, or until fragrant.

Add the meat and cook, stirring, until coated with the curry paste. Stir in the tomato paste and beef stock. Reduce the heat and simmer, covered, for 1 hour 15 minutes, and then uncovered for 15 minutes, or until the meat is tender. Serves 4

540 LAMB KORMA

2 tablespoons blanched almonds
2 teaspoons grated fresh ginger
4 garlic cloves, crushed
^{1}/$_2$ teaspoon ground cinnamon
^{1}/$_2$ teaspoon ground cardamom
^{1}/$_4$ teaspoon ground cloves
^{1}/$_2$ teaspoon chilli powder
^{1}/$_2$ teaspoon ground mace
1^1/$_2$ teaspoons paprika
1 teaspoon ground coriander
80 g (2^3/$_4$ oz/^{1}/$_3$ cup) ghee
2 onions, thinly sliced
1 kg (2 lb 4 oz) boned leg of lamb, cubed
^{1}/$_4$ teaspoon saffron threads, soaked in 1 tablespoon warm water
250 g (9 oz/1 cup) plain yoghurt
125 g (4^1/$_2$ oz/^{1}/$_2$ cup) sour cream
coriander (cilantro) sprigs, to garnish

Place the almonds, ginger and garlic in a blender with 3 tablespoons water. Blend until smooth. Add the ground spices, and blend for 10 seconds, or until combined.

Heat the ghee in a casserole dish, add the onion and cook over medium heat for 10–15 minutes, or until caramelised. Add the spice paste and cook, stirring to prevent sticking, for 5 minutes, or until fragrant.

Add the meat and toss to coat in the spices. Cook, stirring, for 5 minutes, or until browned. Add the saffron and soaking liquid, half the yoghurt and half the sour cream. Season with salt and bring to the boil, then reduce the heat and simmer, covered, for 2 hours, or until the meat is tender. Stir frequently to prevent sticking, as the curry is quite dry when cooked. Skim any fat from the surface. Stir in the remaining yoghurt and sour cream, and garnish with the coriander. Serve with rice. Serves 4–6

542

543

544

545

542 SALTIMBOCCA

8 small veal escalopes
8 slices prosciutto
8 sage leaves
2 tablespoons olive oil
60 g (2¼ oz) butter
185 ml (6 fl oz/¾ cup) dry Marsala or dry white wine

Place the veal between two sheets of baking paper and pound with a meat mallet or rolling pin until they are 5 mm (¼ inch) thick. Make sure you pound them evenly. Peel off the paper and season lightly. Cut the prosciutto slices to the same size as the veal. Cover each piece of veal with a slice of prosciutto and place a sage leaf in the centre. Secure the sage leaf with a cocktail stick.

Heat the olive oil and half the butter in a large frying pan. Add the veal in batches and fry, prosciutto side up, over medium heat for 3–4 minutes, or until the veal is just cooked through. Briefly flip the saltimbocca over and fry the prosciutto side. Transfer each batch to a warm plate as it is done.

Pour off the oil from the pan and add the Marsala or wine. Bring to the boil and cook over high heat until reduced by half, scraping up the bits from the bottom of the pan. Add the remaining butter and, when it has melted, season the sauce. Remove the cocktail sticks and spoon the sauce over the veal to serve. Serves 4

543 PORK CHOPS PIZZAIOLA

4 pork chops
80 ml (2½ fl oz/⅓ cup) olive oil
600 g (1 lb 5 oz) ripe tomatoes
3 garlic cloves, crushed
3 basil leaves, torn into pieces
1 teaspoon finely chopped flat-leaf (Italian) parsley, to serve

Using scissors or a knife, cut the pork fat at 5 mm (¼ inch) intervals around the rind. Brush the chops with 1 tablespoon of the olive oil and season well.

Remove the stems from the tomatoes and score a cross in the bottom of each one. Blanch in boiling water for 30 seconds. Transfer to cold water, peel the skin away from the cross and chop the tomatoes.

Heat 2 tablespoons of the oil in a saucepan over low heat and add the garlic. Soften without browning for 1–2 minutes, then add the tomato and season. Increase the heat, bring to the boil and cook for 5 minutes until thick. Stir in the basil.

Heat the remaining oil in a large frying pan with a tight-fitting lid. Brown the chops in batches over medium–high heat for 2 minutes on each side. Place in a slightly overlapping row down the centre of the pan and spoon the sauce over the top, covering the chops completely. Cover the pan and cook over low heat for about 5 minutes. Sprinkle with parsley to serve. Serves 4

544 CORNISH PASTIES

310 g (2½ cups) plain (all-purpose) flour
125 g (4½ oz) butter, chilled and chopped
150 g (5½ oz) round steak, finely chopped
1 small potato, finely chopped
1 small onion, finely chopped
1 small carrot, finely chopped
1–2 teaspoons worcestershire sauce
2 tablespoons beef stock
1 egg, lightly beaten

Grease a baking tray. Place the flour, butter and a pinch of salt in a food processor and process for 15 seconds, or until crumbly. Add 4–5 tablespoons water and process in short bursts until the mixture comes together (add more water if needed). Turn out onto a floured surface and form into a ball. Cover with plastic wrap and chill for 30 minutes. Preheat the oven to 210°C (415°F/Gas 6–7). Mix together the steak, potato, onion, carrot, worcestershire sauce and stock. Season.

Divide the dough into six portions and roll out each to 3 mm (⅛ inch) thick. Using a 16 cm (6¼ inch) diameter plate as a guide, cut out six circles. Divide the filling evenly and put in the centre of each pastry circle.

Brush the edges of each pastry round with beaten egg and form into a semi-circle. Pinch the edges to form a frill and place on the tray. Brush with the remaining beaten egg and bake for 10 minutes. Lower the heat to 180°C (350°F/Gas 4). Cook for 20–25 minutes, or until golden. Makes 6

545 BEEF & BAMBOO SHOOTS

3 tablespoons oil
400 g (14 oz) rump steak, thinly sliced across the grain
225 g (8 oz) tin sliced bamboo shoots, drained and rinsed
3 garlic cloves, crushed with ¼ teaspoon salt
2 tablespoons fish sauce
8 spring onions (scallions), cut into 4 cm (1½ inch) lengths on the diagonal
3 tablespoons sesame seeds, toasted

Heat a wok over high heat, add 2 tablespoons of the oil and swirl. When the oil is hot, add the beef in two batches and stir-fry for 1 minute, or until it starts to turn pink. Remove and set aside.

Add an extra tablespoon of oil if necessary, then stir-fry the bamboo shoots for 3 minutes, or until starting to brown. Add the garlic, fish sauce and ¼ teaspoon salt and stir-fry for 2–3 minutes. Add the spring onion and stir-fry for 1 minute, or until starting to wilt. Return the beef to the wok, stir quickly and cook for 1 minute until heated through. Remove from the heat, toss with the sesame seeds and serve with rice. Serves 4

546 STIR-FRIED HOISIN PORK & GREENS WITH GINGERED RICE

250 g (9 oz/1$\frac{1}{4}$ cups) jasmine rice
500 g (1 lb 2 oz) pork fillet, thinly sliced
1 tablespoon caster (superfine) sugar
2 tablespoons oil
125 ml (4 fl oz/$\frac{1}{2}$ cup) white wine vinegar
250 ml (9 fl oz/1 cup) hoisin sauce
2 tablespoons stem ginger in syrup (or glacé ginger), chopped
1.25 kg (2 lb 12 oz) mixed Asian greens

Rinse the rice and place in a large saucepan. Add 435 ml (15$\frac{1}{4}$ fl oz/ 1$\frac{3}{4}$ cups) water and bring to the boil. Cover, reduce the heat to very low and cook for 10 minutes. Remove from the heat and leave to stand, covered, for 10 minutes.

Meanwhile, place the pork in a bowl and sprinkle with the sugar. Toss to coat. Heat a wok over high heat, add 1 tablespoon oil and swirl to coat. Add the pork in batches and stir-fry for 3 minutes, or until brown. Remove. Add the vinegar to the wok and boil for 3–5 minutes, or until reduced by two-thirds. Reduce the heat, add the hoisin sauce and 1 tablespoon ginger, and simmer for 5 minutes. Season to taste. Remove from the wok.

Reheat the cleaned wok over high heat, add the remaining oil and swirl to coat. Add the greens and stir-fry for 3 minutes, or until crisp and cooked. Stir the remaining ginger through the rice, then press into four round teacups or small bowls, smoothing the surface. Unmould the rice onto four serving plates, arrange the pork and greens on the side and drizzle the sauce over the top. Serves 4

548 PORK, ASPARAGUS & BABY CORN STIR-FRY

1 garlic clove, chopped
1 teaspoon grated fresh ginger
2 tablespoons soy sauce
$\frac{1}{4}$ teaspoon ground white pepper
1 tablespoon Chinese rice wine
600 g (1 lb 5 oz) pork fillet, thinly sliced
1 tablespoon peanut oil
1 teaspoon sesame oil
6 fresh shiitake mushrooms, thinly sliced
150 g (5$\frac{1}{2}$ oz) baby corn
100 g (3$\frac{1}{2}$ oz) asparagus, cut into 4 cm (1$\frac{1}{2}$ inch) lengths on the diagonal
2 tablespoons oyster sauce

Place the garlic, ginger, soy sauce, pepper and wine in a bowl and mix together well. Add all the pork and stir until it is well coated in the marinade. Heat a wok over high heat, add half the oils and swirl to coat the side of the wok. Add half the pork mixture and stir-fry for about 2 minutes, or until the pork changes colour. Remove the pork from the wok. Repeat with the remaining oils and pork mixture.

Add the mushrooms, corn and asparagus to the wok and stir-fry for 2 minutes. Return the pork and any juices to the wok and stir in the oyster sauce. Cook, stirring, for another 2 minutes, or until it is evenly heated through. Divide among four plates and serve with rice. Serves 4

547 BARBECUED ASIAN PORK RIBS WITH SPRING ONION RICE

1 kg (2 lb 4 oz) American-style pork ribs, cut into sections of 4–5 ribs
3 tablespoons hoisin sauce
1 tablespoon Chinese rice wine or dry sherry
3 tablespoons soy sauce
2 garlic cloves, chopped
2 tablespoons oil
3 spring onions (scallions), finely chopped
1 tablespoon grated fresh ginger
250 g (9 oz/1$\frac{1}{4}$ cups) jasmine rice
600 g (1 lb 5 oz) baby bok choy (pak choy), leaves separated

Place the ribs in a non-metallic bowl. Combine the hoisin sauce, rice wine, soy sauce, garlic, 1 tablespoon oil, 2 tablespoons spring onion and half the ginger. Pour over the ribs and marinate for at least 10 minutes, or overnight in the refrigerator.

Bring a large saucepan of water to the boil. Add the rice and cook for 12 minutes, stirring occasionally. Drain. Heat the remaining oil in a small pan over medium–low heat. When the oil is warm but not smoking, remove the pan from the heat and add the rest of the spring onion and ginger. Stir in $\frac{1}{4}$ teaspoon salt. Stir through the rice.

Heat a chargrill pan or barbecue plate and brush with oil. Remove the ribs from the marinade, reserving the marinade. Cook the ribs in batches, if necessary, 8–10 minutes on each side, or until cooked through, basting with the marinade during cooking.

Before the ribs are cooked, bring the reserved marinade to the boil in a pan — add 80 ml (2$\frac{1}{2}$ fl oz/$\frac{1}{3}$ cup) water if necessary. Boil for 2 minutes, then add the bok choy. Cover and cook for 1–2 minutes, or until just wilted. Serve the ribs with the rice and bok choy, and drizzle with the marinade. Serves 4

549

550

549 PORK & WHITE BEAN CHILLI

1.3 kg (3 lb) pork shoulder, boned, trimmed and cut into 2 cm
   (³/₄ inch) cubes (700–800 g/1 lb 9 oz–1 lb 12 oz meat)
2–3 tablespoons oil
1 large onion, diced
3 garlic cloves, finely chopped
1 tablespoon sweet paprika
¹/₂ teaspoon chilli powder
2 tinned chipotle peppers or jalapeño chillies, chopped
1 tablespoon ground cumin
425 g (15 oz) tin diced tomatoes
2 x 400 g (14 oz) tins cannellini beans, rinsed and drained
1 large handful coarsely chopped coriander (cilantro) leaves
sour cream, to serve
lime wedges, to serve

Season the pork. Heat 2 tablespoons oil in a large casserole dish over high heat. Add half the pork and cook for 5 minutes, or until brown. Remove. Repeat with the remaining pork, using more oil if necessary.

Lower the heat to medium, add the onion and garlic and cook for 3–5 minutes, or until soft. Add the paprika, chilli powder, chipotle peppers and cumin, and cook for 1 minute.

Return the pork to the pan. Add the tomato and 750 ml (26 fl oz/ 3 cups) water and simmer, partially covered, for 1–1¹/₂ hours, or until the pork is very tender. Add the beans and heat through. Boil a little longer to reduce the liquid if necessary. Stir in the coriander and season. Serve with sour cream and lime wedges. Serves 4

550 CHILLI CON CARNE

2 teaspoons ground cumin
¹/₂ teaspoon ground allspice
1–2 teaspoons chilli powder
1 teaspoon paprika
1 tablespoon vegetable oil
1 large onion, finely chopped
2 garlic cloves, crushed
2 small red chillies, seeded and finely chopped
500 g (1 lb 2 oz) minced (ground) beef
400 g (14 oz) tin whole tomatoes
2 tablespoons tomato paste (concentrated purée)
425 g (15 oz) tin red kidney beans, drained and rinsed
250 ml (9 fl oz/1 cup) beef stock
1 tablespoon chopped oregano
1 teaspoon sugar

Heat a frying pan over medium heat and dry-fry the cumin, allspice, chilli and paprika for 1 minute, or until fragrant. Remove from the pan.

Heat the oil in a large saucepan over medium heat and cook the onion for 2–3 minutes, or until soft. Add the garlic and chilli and cook for 1 minute. Add the beef and cook over high heat for 4–5 minutes, or until the meat is browned, breaking up any lumps with a fork.

Add the tomatoes, tomato paste, kidney beans, stock, oregano, sugar and spices. Reduce the heat and simmer, stirring occasionally and gently breaking up the tomatoes, for 1 hour, or until reduced and thickened. Season with salt and black pepper. Serves 4

551 PORK CHOPS WITH APPLES & CIDER

1 tablespoon oil
2 onions, sliced
2 golden delicious apples, cored and cut into wedges
2 teaspoons caster (superfine) sugar
10 g (¹/₄ oz) butter
4 thick pork chops, snipped around the edges
80 ml (2¹/₂ fl oz/¹/₃ cup) cider
80 ml (2¹/₂ fl oz/¹/₃ cup) cream

Heat the oil in a large non-stick frying pan, add the onion and fry for about 5 minutes, or until soft and just beginning to brown. Tip the onion out onto a plate. Add the apple wedges to the pan and fry them for a minute or two — they should not break up, but should start to soften and brown. Add the sugar and butter and shake everything around in the pan until the apples start to caramelise. Transfer the apples to the plate with the onion.

Put the pork chops in the frying pan, add a bit of seasoning and fry them for 4 minutes on each side, or until they are cooked through. Put the onion and apple back in the pan and heat them up, then add the cider and bring to a simmer. Once the liquid is bubbling, add the cream and shake the pan so everything mixes together. Let it bubble for a minute, then season well and serve with potatoes and a green salad — watercress goes particularly well. Serves 4

552 IRISH STEW

20 g (³/₄ oz) butter
1 tablespoon vegetable oil
8 lamb neck chops, trimmed
4 bacon slices, cut into strips
1 teaspoon plain (all-purpose) flour
600 g (1 lb 5 oz) potatoes, peeled and cut into thick slices
3 carrots, cut into thick slices
1 onion, cut into 16 wedges
1 small leek, cut into thick slices
150 g (5¹/₂ oz) savoy cabbage, thinly sliced
500 ml (17 fl oz/2 cups) beef stock
2 tablespoons finely chopped flat-leaf (Italian) parsley

Heat the butter and oil in a flameproof casserole dish or a large heavy-based saucepan over high heat. Add the chops and cook for 1–2 minutes on each side, or until browned, then remove from the dish. Add the bacon and cook for 2–3 minutes, or until crisp. Remove with a slotted spoon, leaving the drippings in the dish.

Sprinkle the flour into the dish and stir to combine. Remove from the heat and layer half the potato, carrot, onion, leek, cabbage and bacon in the base of the dish. Arrange the chops in a single layer over the bacon and cover with layers of the remaining vegetables and bacon.

Pour in enough of the stock to cover, then bring to the boil over high heat. Reduce the heat, cover, and simmer for 1¹/₂ hours, or until the meat is very tender and the sauce is slightly reduced. Season well with salt and freshly ground black pepper and serve sprinkled with the parsley. Serves 4

553

554

555

556

553 BARBECUED CORN IN THE HUSK

8 young corn cobs
125 ml (4 fl oz/½ cup) olive oil
6 garlic cloves, chopped
4 tablespoons chopped flat-leaf (Italian) parsley
butter, to serve

Peel back the corn husks, leaving them intact. Pull off the white silks, then wash the corn and pat dry with paper towels. Combine the olive oil, garlic, parsley and some salt and black pepper and brush over each cob. Pull up the husks and tie together at the top with string. Steam over boiling water for 5 minutes, then pat dry.

Cook on a hot, lightly oiled barbecue grill or flat plate for 20 minutes, turning regularly. Spray with water during the cooking to keep the corn moist. Serve hot with knobs of butter. Serves 8

554 DEEP-FRIED PARMESAN CARROTS

500 g (1 lb 2 oz) baby carrots
60 g (2¼ oz/½ cup) plain (all-purpose) flour
2 teaspoons ground cumin
2 eggs
250 g (9 oz/3 cups) fine fresh white breadcrumbs
1 tablespoon chopped flat-leaf (Italian) parsley
65 g (2¼ oz/⅔ cup) finely grated parmesan cheese
oil, for deep-frying

Trim the leafy carrot tops, leaving about 2 cm (³/₄ inch), and wash the carrots. Bring a large saucepan of water to the boil, add 1 teaspoon of salt and cook the carrots for 5 minutes, or until tender (test with a metal skewer). Drain, dry well with paper towels and leave to cool.

Sift the flour and cumin onto a sheet of baking paper, then beat the eggs together in a wide, shallow bowl. Combine the breadcrumbs, parsley and parmesan, and season with salt and pepper. Roll the carrots in the flour, then the eggs and finally the breadcrumbs. For an extra crispy coating repeat this process.

Fill a deep, heavy-based saucepan one-third full of oil and heat until a cube of bread dropped into the oil browns in 20 seconds. Deep-fry the carrots in batches until golden and crisp. Serve immediately. Serves 6

555 CHARGRILLED EGGPLANT WITH FRESH LEMON PESTO

2 large eggplants (aubergines), cut into 1.5 cm (⅝ inch) slices
    or 8 small eggplants (aubergines), halved lengthways
170 ml (5½ fl oz/⅔ cup) extra virgin olive oil
3 large handfuls basil
1 large handful flat-leaf (Italian) parsley
50 g (1¾ oz/⅓ cup) pine nuts, toasted
1½ garlic cloves
60 g (2¼ oz) grated parmesan cheese
grated zest of 1 lemon
3 tablespoons lemon juice

Brush both sides of the eggplant slices with 2 tablespoons of extra virgin olive oil. Heat a chargrill pan until hot, and cook the eggplant slices for 3 minutes, or until golden and cooked through on both sides. If you are using baby eggplant, grill only on the cut side, and finish off in a 200°C (400°F/Gas 6) oven for 5–8 minutes, or until soft. Cover the eggplant to keep warm.

Place the basil, parsley, pine nuts, garlic, parmesan, lemon zest and lemon juice in a food processor, and blend together. Slowly add the remaining olive oil and process until the mixture forms a smooth paste. Season with salt and freshly ground black pepper. Stack the eggplant on a platter, drizzling some pesto between each layer. Serve immediately. Serves 4–6

556 PARSLEY CARROTS

600 g (1 lb 5 oz) baby carrots
2 teaspoons olive oil
30 g (1 oz) butter
2 tablespoons finely chopped flat-leaf (Italian) parsley

Bring a saucepan of salted water to the boil, and blanch the carrots for 3 minutes, or until they start to soften. Drain and refresh them under cold water and pat them dry with paper towels. Toss the carrots in olive oil and season with salt and pepper.

When you are nearly ready to serve the main meal, preheat a barbecue chargrill plate to medium heat and cook the carrots for 5 minutes, or until they are charred and golden all over. Toss the carrots with the butter and parsley until they are well coated, season to taste with salt and freshly ground black pepper and serve. Serves 6–8

557

558

559

560

557 BARBECUED BABY POTATOES

750 g (1 lb 10 oz) baby potatoes, unpeeled
2 tablespoons olive oil
2 tablespoons thyme leaves
2 teaspoons crushed sea salt

Cut any large potatoes in half so that they are all the same size for even cooking. Boil, steam or microwave the potatoes until just tender. Drain and lightly dry with paper towels. Put the potatoes in a large bowl and add the oil and thyme. Toss gently and leave for 1 hour.

Lightly oil a barbecue flat plate and preheat it to high direct heat. Cook the potatoes for 15 minutes, turning frequently and brushing with the remaining oil and thyme mixture, until golden brown. Sprinkle with sea salt to serve. Serves 6

Note: The potatoes can be left in the marinade for up to 2 hours before barbecuing, but should be served as soon as they are cooked.

558 BAKED SWEET POTATO WITH SAFFRON & PINE NUT BUTTER

1 kg (2 lb 4 oz) white sweet potatoes
2 tablespoons vegetable oil
1 tablespoon milk
pinch of saffron threads
100 g (3 1/2 oz) unsalted butter, softened
3 tablespoons pine nuts, toasted
2 tablespoons finely chopped flat-leaf (Italian) parsley
2 garlic cloves, crushed

Preheat the oven to 180°C (350°F/ Gas 4). Peel the sweet potatoes and chop into large chunks. Toss to coat with oil. Place them on a baking tray, cover with foil and roast for 20 minutes. Warm the milk, add the saffron and leave to infuse for 5 minutes. Put the butter, milk mixture, pine nuts, parsley and garlic in a food processor and pulse to combine. Take care not to overprocess, the nuts should still have some texture. Place a sheet of plastic wrap on the workbench, put the butter in the centre and roll up to form a neat log, about 4 cm (1 1/2 inches) in diameter. Refrigerate the butter for half an hour.

Remove the foil from the potatoes and roast, uncovered, for another 30 minutes, or until they are cooked through (test this by piercing with a skewer). Bring the butter to room temperature, unwrap, cut into 1 cm (1/2 inch) slices and return to the refrigerator to keep cool. Arrange the butter slices over the sweet potato, season with salt and ground black pepper and serve. Serves 4–6

559 SWEET CORN WITH LIME & CHILLI BUTTER

4 corn cobs
50 g (1 3/4 oz) butter
2 tablespoons olive oil
1 lemongrass stem, bruised and cut in half
3 small bird's eye chillies, seeded and finely chopped
2 tablespoons lime zest, finely grated
2 tablespoons lime juice
2 tablespoons finely chopped coriander (cilantro) leaves

Remove the skins and silky threads from the corn cobs. Wash well, then using a long sharp knife cut each cob into 2 cm (3/4 inch) chunks. Heat the butter and oil in a large saucepan over low heat. Add the lemongrass and braise gently for 5 minutes, then remove from the pan. Add the chilli and cook for 2 minutes. Stir in the grated lime zest, lime juice, 3 tablespoons of water and the corn. Cover and cook, shaking the pan frequently, for 5–8 minutes, or until the corn is tender. Season well, then stir in the coriander and serve hot. Serves 4

560 BRUSSELS SPROUTS WITH CHESTNUT & SAGE BUTTER

25 g (1 oz) butter, softened
25 g (1 oz) peeled, cooked chestnuts, finely chopped (see Note)
1 teaspoon chopped sage
700 g (1 lb 9 oz) brussels sprouts, trimmed

Put the butter, chopped chestnuts and sage in a bowl and mix together well. Scrape onto a large piece of baking paper and shape into a log, using the paper to help shape the butter. Wrap in the paper and refrigerate until firm.

Cook the brussels sprouts in salted, boiling water for 10–12 minutes, or until tender. Drain well. Take care not to overcook the sprouts or they will become soggy. Cut the chilled chestnut butter into thin slices. Toss four of the slices with the sprouts until they are evenly coated in butter, and season well. Arrange the remaining slices on top of the sprouts and serve immediately. Serves 4

Note: If chestnuts are unavailable, use toasted walnuts.

561

562

563 • 564

561 CARROTS WITH COCONUT, GINGER & CHILLI

1 kg (2 lb 4 oz) carrots, peeled and cut into thick batons
60 g (2¼ oz) creamed coconut (in a block)
1 garlic clove, crushed
2 teaspoons grated fresh ginger
2 green chillies, seeded and chopped
1 teaspoon ground coriander
1 teaspoon ground cumin
1 teaspoon soy sauce
1 teaspoon chopped lime zest
1 tablespoon lime juice
1 teaspoon palm sugar (jaggery)
3 tablespoons peanut oil
2 tablespoons chopped coriander (cilantro) leaves
lime wedges, to serve

Preheat the oven to 200°C (400°F/Gas 6). Bring a saucepan of water to the boil, blanch the carrots for 5 minutes, then drain well. Grate the creamed coconut and mix with 2–3 tablespoons of hot water to form a paste. Stir in the garlic, ginger, chilli, coriander, cumin, soy sauce, lime zest, lime juice and palm sugar. Add the carrots and toss to combine.

Pour the peanut oil into a large, shallow-sided roasting tin and heat in the oven for 5 minutes. Toss the carrots in the hot oil, then roast in the oven for 5 minutes. Reduce the heat to 180°C (350°F/Gas 4) and roast for another 20 minutes, or until crisp and golden. Sprinkle with the coriander leaves and serve with lime wedges. Serves 6

562 ROSEMARY & GARLIC ROASTED POTATOES

1.5 kg (3 lb 5 oz) potatoes, peeled and cut into large chunks
80 ml (2½ fl oz/⅓ cup) olive oil
12 garlic cloves in the skin, root end trimmed
2 tablespoons rosemary leaves

Preheat the oven to 200°C (400°F/Gas 6). Cook the potatoes in a large saucepan of boiling salted water for 10 minutes, or until just tender. Drain in a colander, and sit for 5 minutes so they dry slightly.

Meanwhile, pour the olive oil into a large roasting tray, and heat in the oven for 5 minutes. Add the potatoes to the tray (they should sizzle in the hot oil), add the garlic and rosemary and season liberally with salt and pepper. Roast, stirring occasionally, so they cook evenly, for about 1 hour, or until golden and crisp. Serve with the roasted garlic cloves popped from their skin and the rosemary leaves. Serves 4–6

563 FENNEL WITH WALNUT PARSLEY CRUST

2 tablespoons lemon juice
9 small fennel bulbs, halved lengthways
1 teaspoon fennel seeds
100 g (3½ oz/1 cup) grated parmesan cheese
160 g (5¾ oz/2 cups) fresh breadcrumbs
100 g (3½ oz) chopped walnuts
1 tablespoon chopped flat-leaf (Italian) parsley
2 teaspoons lemon zest
2 garlic cloves, chopped
250 ml (9 fl oz/1 cup) vegetable or chicken stock
45 g (1½ oz) butter

Bring a large saucepan of water to the boil and add the lemon juice and 1 teaspoon of salt. Cook the fennel in the acidulated water for 5–10 minutes, or until tender, then drain and cool.

Heat a dry frying pan and roast the fennel seeds over medium heat for 1 minute to release their flavour. Tip the seeds into a food processor, add the parmesan, breadcrumbs, walnuts, parsley, lemon zest and garlic, and pulse gently to combine. Stir in 2 tablespoons of stock to moisten the mixture.

Place the fennel, flat side up, in an ovenproof dish and spoon on the stuffing, spreading to completely cover each piece. Pour the remaining stock around the fennel and top each piece with ½ teaspoon of butter. Bake for 25 minutes, basting from time to time, until the top is golden and the fennel is cooked through. Serve drizzled with the braising juices. Serves 4

564 GAI LARN WITH GINGER, LIME & PEANUTS

600 g (1 lb 5 oz) gai larn (Chinese broccoli)
40 g (1½ oz) tamarind pulp
1 small red chilli
1 tablespoon peanut oil
2 garlic cloves, finely chopped
3 teaspoons finely grated fresh ginger
1 tablespoon sugar
1 tablespoon lime juice
1 teaspoon sesame oil
1 tablespoon roasted unsalted peanuts, finely chopped

Trim the ends from the gai larn and slice in half. Place the tamarind in a bowl and pour in 3 tablespoons boiling water. Allow to steep for 5 minutes, then strain, discarding the solids.

Slice the chilli in half, remove the seeds and membrane and chop finely. Heat a wok until very hot, add the peanut oil and swirl it around to coat the wok. Add the gai larn and stir-fry for 2–3 minutes, or until wilted. Add the chilli, garlic and ginger, and cook for another minute. Add the sugar, lime juice and 1 tablespoon of tamarind liquid and simmer for 1 minute.

Remove the gai larn to a serving plate and drizzle with the sesame oil. Scatter with peanuts and season to taste with salt and pepper. Serves 4

565

566

567

568

565 PEPPERONATA

3 red capsicums (peppers)
3 yellow capsicums (peppers)
2 tablespoons olive oil
1 large red onion, thinly sliced
3 large tomatoes, finely chopped
1 tablespoon sugar
2 tablespoons balsamic vinegar
2 garlic cloves, finely chopped
3 tablespoons flat-leaf (Italian) parsley, chopped

Slice the red and yellow capsicums into 2 cm ($^3/_4$ inch) wide strips. Heat the oil in a large heavy-based frying pan and cook the onion over low heat for 5 minutes, or until softened. Add the capsicum strips and cook for another 5 minutes. Add the tomatoes and cook, covered, over low–medium heat for 10 minutes, or until the vegetables are soft. Remove the lid and simmer for an extra 2 minutes.

Stir in the sugar and vinegar. Place in a serving bowl and scatter with the garlic and parsley. Season with salt and freshly ground black pepper. Serves 4

566 INDIAN-STYLE SPINACH

2 tablespoons ghee or vegetable oil
1 onion, thinly sliced
2 garlic cloves, finely chopped
2 teaspoons finely grated ginger
1 teaspoon brown mustard seeds
$^1/_2$ teaspoon ground cumin
$^1/_4$ teaspoon ground coriander
1 teaspoon ground turmeric
$^1/_2$ teaspoon garam masala
350 g (12 oz) English spinach, trimmed
3 tablespoons cream
1 tablespoon lemon juice

Heat a wok until very hot. Add the ghee and swirl it around to coat the wok. Stir-fry the onion over medium heat for 2 minutes to soften. Add the garlic, ginger, brown mustard seeds, cumin, coriander, turmeric and garam masala, and cook for 1 minute, or until fragrant.

Roughly tear the spinach leaves in half and add to the spice mixture. Cook for 1–2 minutes, or until wilted. Add the cream, simmer for 2 minutes, then add the lemon juice and season with salt and freshly ground black pepper. Serve hot. Serves 4

567 MUSHROOMS WITH STICKY BALSAMIC SYRUP

80 ml (2$^1/_2$ fl oz/$^1/_3$ cup) olive oil
750 g (1 lb 10 oz) baby button mushrooms
2 large garlic cloves, finely chopped
3 tablespoons soft brown sugar
3 tablespoons balsamic vinegar
3 teaspoons thyme leaves

Heat the oil in a large, heavy-based, non-stick frying pan. Add the button mushrooms and cook over high heat for 5 minutes, or until slightly softened and golden. Season the mushrooms with salt while they are cooking.

Add the garlic and cook for 1 minute. Stir in the brown sugar, vinegar and 1 tablespoon of water, and boil for 5 minutes, or until reduced by one-third. Season to taste with pepper. Arrange the mushrooms on a serving plate. Reduce the remaining liquid for 1 minute, or until thick and syrupy. Pour over the mushrooms and garnish with the thyme. Serves 4

568 CREAMED SPINACH

1.5 kg (3 lb 5 oz) English spinach
10 g ($^1/_4$ oz) butter
1 garlic clove, crushed
$^1/_4$ teaspoon freshly grated nutmeg
80 ml (2$^1/_2$ fl oz/$^1/_3$ cup) thick (double/heavy) cream
1 tablespoon grated parmesan cheese

Remove the tough ends from the spinach stalks and wash the leaves well. Shake to remove any excess water from the leaves, but do not dry completely. Melt the butter in a large frying pan. Add the crushed garlic and the spinach, season with nutmeg, salt and pepper, and cook over medium heat until the spinach is just wilted. Remove from the heat and place the spinach in a sieve. Press down well to squeeze out all of the excess moisture. Transfer to a chopping board and, using a mezzaluna or a sharp knife, chop the spinach finely.

Pour the cream into the frying pan and heat gently. Add the spinach to the pan and stir until warmed through. Arrange the spinach on a serving dish and sprinkle with the parmesan. Serves 4–6

569

570

571

569 JERUSALEM ARTICHOKES ROASTED WITH RED WINE & GARLIC

800 g (1 lb 12 oz) Jerusalem artichokes
1 tablespoon lemon juice
2 tablespoons red wine
2 tablespoons olive oil
1 tablespoon tamari
2 garlic cloves, crushed
dash of Tabasco sauce
2 tablespoons vegetable stock
2 tablespoons chopped flat-leaf (Italian) parsley

Preheat the oven to 200°C (400°F/ Gas 6). Scrub the artichokes well, then cut them in half lengthways, and place in a bowl of water mixed with the lemon juice.

Combine the red wine, olive oil, tamari, garlic, Tabasco sauce and stock in a baking tray. Drain and quickly dry the artichoke halves with paper towels. Place in the baking tray, and toss all the ingredients together. Season with salt and freshly ground black pepper.

Bake, covered, for 40 minutes, or until tender, then uncover and bake for another 5 minutes, or until the juices have formed a reduced glaze. Remove from the oven, and toss with the parsley before serving. Serves 4

571 FRIED GREEN TOMATOES WITH A CORNMEAL CRUST

750 g (1 lb 10 oz) unripe, green tomatoes
60 g (2^1/$_4$ oz/^{1}/$_2$ cup) plain (all-purpose) flour
225 g (8 oz/1^1/$_2$ cups) yellow cornmeal
2 teaspoons finely chopped thyme
2 teaspoons finely chopped marjoram
50 g (1^3/$_4$ oz/^{1}/$_2$ cup) grated parmesan cheese
2 eggs, beaten with 1 tablespoon water
olive oil, for pan-frying

Preheat the oven to 180°C (350°F/ Gas 4). Cut the tomatoes into 1 cm (^{1}/$_2$ inch) slices and season with salt. Season the flour well with salt and freshly ground black pepper and place in a shallow bowl. Combine the cornmeal, thyme, marjoram and parmesan. Dip the tomato slices in the flour, coating all surfaces. Next dip in the beaten egg, followed by the cornmeal mixture. Set the tomatoes aside in a single layer.

Fill a large, heavy-based frying pan with olive oil to 5 mm (^{1}/$_4$ inch) deep. Heat over medium heat, or until a cube of bread dropped in the oil browns in 20 seconds. Reduce the heat a little, then cook the tomato slices in batches for 2–3 minutes each side, or until golden. Remove with tongs and drain on paper towels. Transfer the tomato slices to a plate and keep them warm in the oven while the rest are being cooked. Add more oil to the pan as necessary to maintain the level. Serve hot. Serves 4–6

570 BAKED ONIONS STUFFED WITH GOAT'S CHEESE & SUN-DRIED TOMATOES

6 large onions
3 tablespoons extra virgin olive oil
1 garlic clove, crushed
100 g (3^1/$_2$ oz) sun-dried tomatoes, finely chopped
25 g (1 oz/^{1}/$_3$ cup) fresh white breadcrumbs
1 tablespoon chopped flat-leaf (Italian) parsley
2 teaspoons chopped thyme
100 g (3^1/$_2$ oz) mild soft goat's cheese, crumbled
80 g (2^3/$_4$ oz) parmesan cheese, grated
1 egg
250 ml (9 fl oz/1 cup) vegetable or chicken stock
20 g (^{3}/$_4$ oz) butter

Preheat the oven to 180°C (350°F/ Gas 4). Peel the onions, cut a slice off the top and reserve. Using a teaspoon scrape out a cavity almost to the base of the onion, leaving a hole to stuff. Blanch the onions in a large saucepan of boiling water for 5 minutes, then drain. Heat 2 tablespoons of oil in a small frying pan and cook the garlic for 3 minutes, or until soft. Add the tomato, breadcrumbs and herbs and cook for 1 minute. Remove from the heat and add the goat's cheese and parmesan. Season and stir in the egg.

Stuff the mixture into each onion cavity. Arrange the onions in a large ovenproof ceramic dish. Pour the stock around the onions and drizzle with the remaining oil. Cover with foil and bake for 45 minutes, basting from time to time. Remove the foil for the last 10 minutes of cooking.

Remove the onions to a serving plate and, over medium heat, simmer the remaining stock for 5–8 minutes, or until reduced by half and syrupy. Reduce the heat and whisk in the butter. The sauce should be smooth and glossy. Season to taste and spoon over the onions. Serves 6

572

573

574

575

572 GREEN BEANS WITH FETA & TOMATO

1 tablespoon olive oil
1 onion, chopped
2 garlic cloves, crushed
1 1/2 tablespoons chopped oregano
125 ml (4 fl oz/1/2 cup) white wine
425 g (15 oz) tin diced tomatoes
250 g (9 oz) green beans, trimmed
1 tablespoon balsamic vinegar
200 g (7 oz) feta cheese, cut into 1.5 cm (5/8 inch) cubes

Heat the oil in a saucepan, add the onion and cook over medium heat for 3–5 minutes, or until soft. Add the garlic and half the oregano, and cook for another minute. Pour in the white wine and cook for 3 minutes, or until reduced by one-third.

Stir in the diced tomato and cook, uncovered, for 10 minutes. Add the beans and cook, covered, for another 10 minutes. Stir in the balsamic vinegar, feta and remaining oregano. Season with salt and pepper, and serve. Serves 4

573 ROASTED BEETROOT WITH HORSERADISH CREAM

8 beetroot
2 tablespoons olive oil
2 teaspoons honey
1 1/2 tablespoons creamed horseradish
100 g (3 1/2 oz) sour cream
chopped flat-leaf (Italian) parsley, to garnish

Preheat the oven to 200°C (400°F/ Gas 6). Scrub and peel the beetroot, trim the ends and cut into quarters. Place the oil and honey in a small bowl and mix well. Season with salt and freshly ground black pepper.

Place the beetroot on a large square of foil and drizzle with the honey mixture, coating them well. Enclose the beetroot loosely in the foil. Bake for 1 hour, or until the beetroot are tender when pierced with a skewer.

Meanwhile, combine the horseradish and sour cream, and season lightly. Once the beetroot are cooked, remove from the oven and leave in the foil for 5 minutes. Remove from the foil and serve with a generous dollop of the horseradish cream and the parsley garnish. Serves 4

574 PUMPKIN WITH CHILLI

800 g (1 lb 12 oz) butternut pumpkin (squash)
2 tablespoons oil
2 garlic cloves, crushed
1 teaspoon grated ginger
2 bird's eye chillies, finely chopped
1 teaspoon finely grated lime zest
1 tablespoon lime juice
1 1/2 tablespoons light soy sauce
185 ml (6 fl oz/3/4 cup) vegetable or chicken stock
1 tablespoon soy sauce
1 teaspoon shaved palm sugar (jaggery)
1 handful chopped coriander (cilantro) leaves

Peel the pumpkin, and scoop out the seeds to give about 600 g (1 lb 5 oz) of flesh. Cut the flesh into 1.5 cm (5/8 inch) cubes. Heat the oil in a large frying pan or wok over medium heat, add the garlic, ginger and chilli, and stir-fry for 1 minute. Keep moving the garlic and chilli around the pan to ensure they don't burn, as this will make them taste bitter.

Add the pumpkin, lime zest, lime juice, light soy sauce, stock, soy sauce and palm sugar, then cover and cook for 10 minutes or until the pumpkin is tender. Remove the lid and gently stir for 5 minutes, or until any remaining liquid has reduced. Gently stir in the chopped coriander and serve immediately. Serves 4

575 SNAKE BEANS STIR-FRIED WITH THAI BASIL, GARLIC & CHILLI

3 tablespoons soy sauce
3 tablespoons vegetable or chicken stock
2 tablespoons vegetable oil
1 teaspoon red curry paste
1 red Asian shallot, finely chopped
3 garlic cloves, finely sliced
1 small red chilli, seeds removed and sliced
500 g (1 lb 2 oz) snake beans, cut into 8 cm (3 inch) lengths on the diagonal
1 small handful Thai basil

Combine the soy sauce, stock and 3 tablespoons water and set aside. Heat a wok over high heat, add the vegetable oil, red curry paste, shallot, garlic and chilli and stir-fry until fragrant. Add the snake beans and cook for 5 minutes. Stir in the sauce and cook, tossing gently, until the beans are tender. Remove from the heat and season well. Stir in half the basil and scatter the rest on top as a garnish. Serve immediately. Serves 4

576

577

578

579

576 CAULIFLOWER WITH MUSTARD

2 teaspoons each yellow and black mustard seeds
1 teaspoon ground turmeric
1 teaspoon tamarind purée
2–3 tablespoons mustard oil or oil
2 garlic cloves, finely chopped
$1/2$ onion, finely chopped
600 g (1 lb 5 oz) cauliflower, broken into small florets
3 mild green chillies, seeded and finely chopped
2 teaspoons kalonji (nigella) seeds

Grind the mustard seeds together to a fine powder in a spice grinder or mortar and pestle. Mix with the turmeric, tamarind purée and 100 ml ($3^1/2$ fl oz) water to form a smooth, quite liquid paste.

Heat 2 tablespoons of the oil in a large heavy-based saucepan over medium heat until almost smoking. Reduce the heat to low, add the garlic and onion and fry until golden. Cook the cauliflower in batches, adding more oil if necessary, and fry until lightly browned, then remove. Add the chilli and fry for 1 minute, or until brown around the edges.

Return all the cauliflower to the pan, sprinkle it with the mustard mixture and kalonji and stir well. Increase the heat to medium and bring to the boil, even though there's not much sauce. Reduce the heat to low, cover and cook until the cauliflower is nearly tender and the seasoning is dry. Sprinkle a little water on the cauliflower as it cooks to stop it sticking to the pan. If there is still excess liquid when the cauliflower is cooked, simmer with the lid off until it dries out. Season with salt, and remove from the heat. Serve with rice or Indian bread, or as an accompaniment to meat dishes. Serves 4

577 MASHED CARROTS WITH CUMIN SEEDS

6 carrots
1 tablespoon olive oil
2 garlic cloves, finely chopped
1 teaspoon ground turmeric
2 teaspoons finely grated fresh ginger
3 tablespoons Greek-style yoghurt
2 teaspoons prepared harissa
2 tablespoons chopped coriander (cilantro) leaves
2 teaspoons lime juice
1 teaspoon cumin seeds

Peel the carrots and cut into 2.5 cm (1 inch) chunks. Place them in a large saucepan and cover with cold water. Bring to the boil, then reduce the heat and simmer for 3 minutes. Drain and allow to dry.

Heat the olive oil in a heavy-based, non-stick saucepan. Cook the garlic, ground turmeric and ginger over medium heat for 1 minute, or until fragrant. Add the carrots, and cook for 3 minutes. Stir in 1 tablespoon water and cook, covered, over low heat for 10–15 minutes, or until the carrots are soft. Transfer the mixture to a bowl and roughly mash.

Add the yoghurt, harissa, coriander and lime juice to the carrots and stir to combine. Season to taste with salt and freshly ground black pepper. Heat a heavy-based frying pan, add the cumin seeds, and dry-fry for 1–2 minutes, or until fragrant. Scatter over the mashed carrots and serve. Serves 4

578 CABBAGE WITH LEEK & MUSTARD SEEDS

1 tablespoon oil
40 g ($1^1/2$ oz) unsalted butter
2 teaspoons black mustard seeds
2 leeks, thinly sliced
500 g (1 lb 2 oz) thinly shredded cabbage
1 tablespoon lemon juice
100 g ($3^1/2$ oz) crème fraîche
2 tablespoons chopped flat-leaf (Italian) parsley

Heat the oil and butter together, add the mustard seeds, and cook until they start to pop. Add the leeks and cook gently for 5–8 minutes, or until softened. Stir in the cabbage and cook over low heat for 4 minutes, or until it wilts and softens.

Season the cabbage well with salt and pepper. Add the lemon juice and crème fraîche, and cook for 1 minute longer. Stir in the chopped parsley and serve immediately. Serves 4-6

579 ZUCCHINI WITH MINT & FETA

6 zucchini (courgettes)
1 tablespoon olive oil
70 g ($2^1/2$ oz) feta cheese, crumbled
1 teaspoon finely grated lemon zest
$1/2$ teaspoon chopped garlic
1 tablespoon lemon juice
1 tablespoon extra virgin olive oil
2 tablespoons shredded mint
2 tablespoons shredded flat-leaf (Italian) parsley

Slice each zucchini lengthways into four thick batons. Heat the olive oil in a heavy-based, non-stick frying pan and cook the zucchini over medium heat for 3–4 minutes, or until just tender and lightly golden. Arrange on a serving plate.

Crumble the feta over the zucchini. Mix the lemon zest, garlic and lemon juice in a jug. Whisk in the extra virgin olive oil with a fork until well combined, then pour the dressing over the zucchini. Top with the mint and parsley, and season with salt and pepper. Serve warm. Serves 4

580

581

582

583

580 CHARGRILLED POTATOES WITH PISTACHIO SALSA

PISTACHIO SALSA
150 g (5½ oz) pistachio nuts, toasted
2 ripe tomatoes, chopped
2 garlic cloves, finely chopped
1 small red chilli, finely chopped
2 tablespoons chopped flat-leaf (Italian) parsley
1 tablespoon chopped mint
1 teaspoon finely grated lemon zest

750 g (1 lb 10 oz) potatoes
3 tablespoons plain (all-purpose) flour
2 tablespoons olive oil
sour cream, to serve

To make the pistachio salsa, roughly chop the nuts and combine with the tomato, garlic, chilli, herbs and lemon zest. Season with salt and pepper. Peel the potatoes and cut into large wedges. Place in a pan and cover with water, bring to the boil and cook for 5 minutes. Transfer to a colander and rinse under running water to stop the cooking. Pat the wedges dry with paper towels.

Sprinkle the flour over the potatoes in a bowl and toss to lightly coat. Cook the potato wedges in a single layer on a hot, lightly oiled barbecue flat plate or grill for 5–10 minutes, or until golden brown and tender. Drizzle with the olive oil and turn the potatoes regularly during cooking. Serve with the salsa and a bowl of sour cream. Serves 4

581 HONEY ROASTED ROOT VEGETABLES

60 g (2¼ oz) butter
2 tablespoons honey
4 thyme sprigs
3 carrots, cut into chunks
2 parsnips, cut into chunks
1 orange sweet potato, cut into chunks
1 white sweet potato, cut into chunks
8 baby onions
8 Jerusalem artichokes
1 garlic head

Preheat the oven to 200°C (400°F/ Gas 6). Melt the butter in a large ovenproof baking dish over medium heat. Add the honey and thyme and stir. Remove from the heat and add the carrot, parsnip, orange and white sweet potato, onions and Jerusalem artichokes. Season well with salt and freshly ground black pepper and toss gently so they are evenly coated with the honey butter.

Trim the base of the garlic and wrap in foil. Add to the baking dish and place in the oven for 1 hour, turning the vegetables occasionally so they caramelise evenly. When cooked, remove the foil from the garlic and pop the cloves from their skin. Add to the other vegetables and serve. Serves 4

582 POTATOES IN PARCHMENT

700 g (1 lb 9 oz) baby potatoes, halved
30 g (1 oz) butter, cut into small cubes
1 tablespoon thyme sprigs
6 garlic cloves, unpeeled
2 tablespoons olive oil
sea salt, to serve

Preheat the oven to 200°C (400°F/ Gas 6). Cut two pieces of baking paper, each 50 cm (20 inches) long. Place half of the potatoes in a single layer on one piece of paper, scatter with half of the butter, half of the thyme and 3 cloves of garlic. Drizzle with 1 tablespoon of olive oil. Bring the long edges of the paper together and fold over twice. Fold over the short edges so that the potatoes are sealed within the paper, and place the parcels on a baking tray with the fold side facing down.

Repeat with the remaining ingredients to form a second potato parcel. Bake for 1 hour and 10 minutes, or until the potatoes are tender (test by piercing with a skewer). Serve sprinkled with sea salt. Serves 4

583 SPRING ONION MASH

1 kg (2 lb 4 oz) floury (starchy) potatoes
2 tablespoons butter
90 ml (3 fl oz) milk
60 ml (2 fl oz/¼ cup) cream
3 spring onions (scallions), finely sliced

Peel the potatoes and cut them into large chunks. Steam or boil the pieces for 12 minutes, or until they are tender, then drain the water away and briefly return the potato to the heat, shaking the pan, to dry any excess moisture.

Add the butter, milk and cream, and mash the potato until it is smooth and lump-free. Stir in the spring onion, season to taste and serve warm. Serves 4-6

584

585

586

587

584 ROASTED RED ONION & ROMA TOMATOES WITH BALSAMIC VINAIGRETTE

oil, to brush
8 roma (plum) tomatoes
2 red onions
2 garlic cloves
1¹/₂ tablespoons balsamic vinegar
1 teaspoon French mustard
3 tablespoons extra virgin olive oil

Preheat the oven to 150°C (300°F/Gas 2) and lightly brush a baking tray with oil. Cut the tomatoes into quarters and arrange on the tray. Remove the tops of the onion and peel. Cut each onion into 8 wedges and place on the tray with the tomatoes. Place the garlic in the middle of the tray, spaced 5 cm (2 inches) apart and season all of the vegetables well. Roast for 1 hour.

Arrange the tomatoes and onions on a serving plate. Peel the garlic and crush in a small bowl. Add the balsamic vinegar and mustard to the garlic and, using a small wire whisk, beat in the olive oil, adding it slowly in a thin stream. Season the dressing well and drizzle over the onions and tomatoes. Serve immediately. Serves 4

585 BARBECUE SAUCE

2 teaspoons oil
1 small onion, finely chopped
1 tablespoon malt vinegar
1 tablespoon soft brown sugar
80 ml (2¹/₂ fl oz/¹/₃ cup) tomato sauce (ketchup)
1 tablespoon worcestershire sauce

Heat the oil in a small pan and cook the onion over low heat for 3 minutes, or until soft, stirring occasionally. Add the remaining ingredients and bring to the boil. Reduce the heat and simmer for 3 minutes, stirring occasionally. Serve warm or at room temperature. Can be kept, covered and refrigerated, for up to a week. Serves 4

586 PINEAPPLE MINT SALSA

1 small ripe pineapple
1 tablespoon grated palm sugar (jaggery) or soft brown sugar
1 small red chilli, seeded and finely diced
¹/₂ teaspoon rice vinegar
2 tablespoons lime juice
4 spring onions (scallions), finely chopped
3 tablespoons chopped mint

Peel the pineapple, remove all of the eyes and slice it lengthways into quarters. Remove the central core and cut the flesh into 1 cm (¹/₂ inch) dice. Put the pineapple in a non-metallic mixing bowl with the sugar, chilli, rice vinegar, lime juice, spring onion and mint and stir them together. Cover the bowl and refrigerate for 1 hour to let the flavours develop. Serves 4

587 BRAISED RED CABBAGE

60 g (2¹/₄ oz) butter
1 onion, chopped
2 garlic cloves, crushed
900 g (2 lb) red cabbage, sliced
2 green apples, peeled, cored and diced
4 cloves
¹/₄ teaspoon nutmeg
1 bay leaf
2 juniper berries
1 cinnamon stick
80 ml (2¹/₂ fl oz/¹/₃ cup) red wine
2¹/₂ tablespoons red wine vinegar
2 tablespoons soft brown sugar
1 tablespoon redcurrant jelly
500 ml (17 fl oz/2 cups) vegetable or chicken stock

Preheat the oven to 150°C (300°F/Gas 2). Heat 40 g (1¹/₂ oz) of butter in a large casserole dish, add the onion and garlic and cook over medium heat for 5 minutes. Add the cabbage and cook for another 10 minutes, stirring frequently.

Add the apples, cloves, nutmeg, bay leaf, juniper berries and cinnamon stick to the dish. Pour in the red wine and cook for 5 minutes, then add the red wine vinegar, brown sugar, redcurrant jelly and stock. Bring to the boil, then cover and cook in the oven for 2 hours.

After 2 hours of cooking check the liquid level — there should be only about 125 ml (4 fl oz/¹/₂ cup) left. Stir in the remaining butter, season well with salt and pepper, and serve. Serves 4–6

588

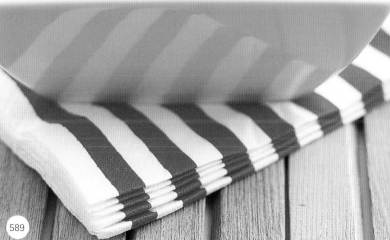

589

590

588 TOMATO SALSA

4 ripe tomatoes, finely diced
3 tablespoons finely chopped red onion
1 handful chopped coriander (cilantro) leaves
1 tablespoon lime juice

Combine the tomato, onion, coriander and lime juice, season to taste, then cover the salsa with plastic wrap and refrigerate. Remove the salsa from the refrigerator 15 minutes before you are ready to use it so the ingredients have time to return to room temperature and their full flavour. Serves 4

590 RED CAPSICUM RELISH

1 kg (2 lb 4 oz) red capsicums (peppers)
1 teaspoon black peppercorns
2 teaspoons black mustard seeds
2 red onions, thinly sliced
4 garlic cloves, chopped
375 ml (13 fl oz/1$\frac{1}{2}$ cups) red wine vinegar
2 apples, peeled, cored and grated
1 teaspoon grated ginger
185 g (6$\frac{1}{2}$ oz/1 cup) soft brown sugar

Remove the capsicum seeds and membrane and thinly slice. Tie the peppercorns in a piece of muslin and secure with string. Combine the capsicum, peppercorns, mustard seeds, onion, garlic, vinegar, apple and ginger in a large saucepan. Simmer, covered, for 30 minutes, or until the capsicum is soft.

Add the sugar and stir over low heat until completely dissolved. Cover and simmer, stirring occasionally, for 1$\frac{1}{4}$ hours, or until the relish has reduced and thickened. Remove the muslin bag.

Rinse the jars with boiling water then dry in a warm oven. Spoon the relish into the hot jars and seal. Turn the jars upside down for 2 minutes, then turn them the other way up and leave to cool. Label and date. Leave for a few weeks before using. Will keep in a cool dark place for 1 year. Refrigerate after opening. Fills three 250 ml (9 fl oz/1 cup) jars

589 SMOKY TOMATO SAUCE

SMOKING MIX
2 tablespoons Chinese or ceylon tea leaves
2 star anise, crushed
1 strip orange zest
$\frac{1}{2}$ teaspoon Chinese five-spice
6 juniper berries, crushed

2 onions, quartered
2 red capsicums (peppers), cut into large pieces
2 red chillies, cut in half
3 tablespoons oil
3 garlic cloves, chopped
500 g (1 lb 2 oz) tomatoes, chopped
2 tablespoons worcestershire sauce
125 ml (4 fl oz/$\frac{1}{2}$ cup) barbecue sauce
2 tablespoons tamarind concentrate
1 tablespoon white vinegar
1 tablespoon soft brown sugar

Combine all the ingredients for the smoking mix in a bowl. Pour the mix into the centre of a sheet of foil and fold the edges to prevent spreading. (This will form an open container to allow the mix to smoke.) Place the foil container on the bottom of a dry wok or wide frying pan. Put an open rack or steamer in the wok or frying pan, making sure it is elevated over the mix.

Place the onion, capsicum and chilli on the rack and cover with a lid, or alternatively cover the entire wok or frying pan tightly with foil to prevent the smoke from escaping.

Smoke over medium heat for about 10–15 minutes, or until the vegetables are tender. For a very smoky sauce cook the vegetables for longer; if you prefer it less so, reduce the time. Remove the smoking mix container.

Dice the onion, capsicum and chilli quite finely. Heat the oil in the wok and add the garlic and cooked vegetables. Fry over medium heat for 3 minutes, then add the tomato and cook until pulpy. Add the sauces, tamarind, vinegar and sugar. Simmer, stirring occasionally, for about 20–25 minutes, or until the sauce is quite thick. Store in the refrigerator. Makes about 1 litre (35 fl oz/4 cups)

591

592

593

594

591 STRAWBERRIES WITH BALSAMIC VINEGAR

750 g (1 lb 10 oz) ripe small strawberries
3 tablespoons caster (superfine) sugar
2 tablespoons balsamic vinegar
125 g (4 1/2 oz/1/2 cup) mascarpone

Wipe the strawberries with a clean damp cloth and carefully remove the green stalks. If the strawberries are large, cut each one in half. Place all the strawberries in a large glass bowl, sprinkle the caster sugar evenly over the top and toss gently to coat. Set aside for 2 hours to macerate, then sprinkle the balsamic vinegar over the strawberries. Toss them again, then refrigerate for about 30 minutes.

Spoon the strawberries into four glasses, drizzle with the syrup and top with a dollop of mascarpone. Serves 4

Note: If you leave the strawberries for more than 2 hours, it is best to refrigerate them.

592 CHOCOLATE RUM MOUSSE

250 g (9 oz) good-quality dark chocolate, chopped
3 eggs
3 tablespoons caster (superfine) sugar
2 teaspoons dark rum
250 ml (9 fl oz/1 cup) cream, lightly whipped
whipped cream, extra, to serve
dark chocolate, extra, grated, to garnish

Put the chocolate in a heatproof bowl. Half fill a saucepan with water and bring to the boil. Remove from the heat and place the bowl over the pan, making sure it is not touching the water. Stir occasionally until the chocolate has melted. Leave to cool.

Using electric beaters, beat the eggs and sugar in a bowl for 5 minutes, or until the mixture is thick, pale and increased in volume. Transfer to a large bowl. Using a metal spoon, fold in the melted chocolate with the rum, leave the mixture to cool, then gently fold in the lightly whipped cream until just combined.

Spoon into four 250 ml (9 fl oz/1 cup) ramekins or dessert glasses. Refrigerate for 2 hours, or until set. Serve with extra whipped cream and garnish with grated chocolate. Serves 4

593 PISTACHIO CRÈME BRÛLEE

500 ml (17 fl oz/2 cups) cream
3 tablespoons finely chopped pistachios
1/2 vanilla bean, halved lengthways
1/2 teaspoon grated orange zest
115 g (4 oz/1/2 cup) caster (superfine) sugar
5 egg yolks
1–3 tablespoons caster (superfine) sugar, extra
pistachio biscotti, to serve

Preheat the oven to 140°C (275°F/Gas 1). Put the cream, pistachios, vanilla bean, zest and half the sugar in a saucepan over medium heat and stir to dissolve the sugar, then slowly bring to the boil. Remove from the heat and infuse for 10 minutes.

Whisk the egg yolks and remaining sugar in a bowl. Strain the cream mixture into a jug, then add to the egg mixture, stirring continuously. Ladle the custard into six 125 ml (4 fl oz/1/2 cup) ramekins and place in a roasting tin. Pour in cold water to come halfway up the sides of the ramekins, then place in the oven and cook for 1 hour, or until the custard has set and is only just wobbly. Cool the ramekins on a wire rack, then refrigerate for 4 hours.

Preheat the grill (broiler) to very hot. Sprinkle 1–2 teaspoons of the extra sugar over the top of each brûlée. Put the brûlées in a roasting tin full of ice, then put the tin under the grill for 4 minutes, or until the tops of the brûlées have melted and caramelised. Remove the ramekins from the roasting tin and dry around the outside edges. Refrigerate for 1–2 hours but not more than 3 hours (or the toffee will start to go sticky and lose its crunch). Serve with pistachio biscotti. Serves 6

594 PEACHES CARDINAL

4 large ripe peaches
300 g (10 1/2 oz/2 1/2 cups) raspberries
1 tablespoon icing (confectioners') sugar, plus extra, to dust

If the peaches are very ripe, put them in a bowl and pour boiling water over them. Leave for a minute, then drain and carefully peel away the skin. If the fruit you have is not so ripe, dissolve 2 tablespoons sugar in a saucepan of water, add the peaches and cover the pan. Gently poach the peaches for 5–10 minutes, or until they are tender. Drain and peel.

Let the peaches cool and then halve each one and remove the stone. Put two halves in each serving glass. Put the raspberries in a food processor or blender and mix until puréed (or mix by hand). Pass through a fine nylon sieve to get rid of the seeds.

Sift the icing sugar over the raspberry purée and stir in. Drizzle the purée over the peaches, cover and chill thoroughly. Dust a little icing sugar over the top to serve. Serves 4

595

596

597

595 SUMMER PUDDING

150 g (5$\frac{1}{2}$ oz) blackcurrants
150 g (5$\frac{1}{2}$ oz) redcurrants
150 g (5$\frac{1}{2}$ oz) raspberries
150 g (5$\frac{1}{2}$ oz) blackberries
200 g (7 oz) strawberries, hulled and quartered or halved
115 g (4 oz/1/2 cup) caster (superfine) sugar, or to taste
6–8 slices good-quality sliced white bread, crusts removed

Put all the berries except the strawberries in a saucepan with 125 ml (4 fl oz/$\frac{1}{2}$ cup) water and heat for 5 minutes, or until the berries begin to soften. Add the strawberries and remove from the heat. Add sugar, to taste (how much you need will depend on how ripe the fruit is). Cool.

Line six 170 ml (5$\frac{1}{2}$ fl oz/$\frac{2}{3}$ cup) moulds or a 1 litre (35 fl oz/4 cups) pudding basin with the bread. For the small moulds cut a circle to fit the bottom and strips to fit around the sides. For the basin, cut a large circle out of one slice for the bottom and cut the rest of the bread into strips to fit the side. Drain a little of the juice off the fruit. Dip one side of each piece of bread in the juice before fitting it, juice side down, into the basin, leaving no gaps. Do not squeeze the bread or it will not absorb the juice.

Fill each mould with fruit and add some juice. Cover the top with the remaining dipped bread, juice side up. Cover with plastic wrap. For the small moulds, sit a small tin on top of each. For the basin, sit a small plate onto the plastic wrap, then weigh it down with a large tin. Place on a tray to catch any juice which may overflow, and chill overnight. Carefully turn out the pudding and serve with leftover fruit mixture and cream if desired. Serves 6

597 PRALINE SEMIFREDDO

195 g (6$\frac{3}{4}$ oz/1$\frac{1}{4}$ cups) blanched almonds
230 g (8$\frac{1}{4}$ oz/1 cup) caster (superfine) sugar
625 ml (21$\frac{1}{2}$ fl oz/2$\frac{1}{2}$ cups) thick (double/heavy) cream
2 eggs, separated
90 g (3$\frac{1}{4}$ oz/$\frac{3}{4}$ cup) icing (confectioners') sugar, sifted
2 tablespoons Mandorla (almond-flavoured Marsala) or brandy

To make the praline, put the blanched almonds in a hot frying pan and dry-fry until well browned all over, then set aside. Melt the sugar in a saucepan over medium heat until golden, tipping the pan from side to side so the sugar melts evenly. Remove from the heat and stir in the almonds. Carefully pour into a greased baking tray and smooth out with the back of a spoon. Leave to cool completely, then finely crush the praline in a food processor. Pour the cream into a large bowl and whisk until soft peaks form.

Beat the egg yolks with a quarter of the icing sugar until pale. Whisk the egg whites in a clean, dry glass bowl until firm peaks form, then gradually add the rest of the icing sugar and whisk until glossy firm peaks form. Gently fold the egg yolks into the cream, then fold in the egg whites. Fold in the praline and Mandorla.

Line six 250 ml (9 fl oz/1 cup) metal dariole moulds with two long strips of foil each, leaving the ends to overhang the edge. Spoon in the mixture, level the surface and tap each mould on the bench. Cover with foil and freeze for 24 hours. To unmould, leave at room temperature for 5 minutes, then lift out with the foil 'handles'. Serves 6

596 STICKY DATE PUDDINGS

180 g (6$\frac{1}{4}$ oz/1 cup) dates, pitted and roughly chopped
1 teaspoon bicarbonate of soda (baking soda)
75 g (2$\frac{3}{4}$ oz) unsalted butter, softened
155 g (5$\frac{1}{2}$ oz/$\frac{2}{3}$ cup) soft brown sugar
1 teaspoon natural vanilla extract
2 eggs
185 g (6$\frac{1}{2}$ oz/1$\frac{1}{2}$ cups) self-raising flour, sifted
100 g (3$\frac{1}{2}$ oz/1 cup) walnut halves, roughly chopped

CARAMEL SAUCE
155 g (5$\frac{1}{2}$ oz/$\frac{2}{3}$ cup) soft brown sugar
60 g (2$\frac{1}{4}$ oz) unsalted butter
250 ml (9 fl oz/1 cup) cream

Preheat the oven to 180°C (350°F/Gas 4). Lightly brush six 250 ml (9 fl oz/1 cup) moulds with melted butter and line the bases with circles of baking paper. Put the dates and bicarbonate of soda in a pan and pour in 250 ml (9 fl oz/1 cup) water. Bring to the boil, remove from the heat and set aside to cool (the mixture will become foamy).

Beat the butter, sugar and vanilla with electric beaters until light and creamy. Add 1 egg, beat well and fold through 1 tablespoon of the flour. Add the other egg and repeat the process.

Fold through the remaining flour, walnuts and date mixture, and mix well. Divide the mixture among the moulds, filling them three-quarters full. Bake for 30–35 minutes, or until slightly risen and firm to the touch.

To make the caramel sauce, put the brown sugar, butter and cream in a pan and simmer for 5 minutes. When the puddings are cooked, remove from the oven and prick a few holes in each one. Drizzle with some of the caramel sauce and return to the oven for 5 minutes. Loosen the side of each pudding with a small knife, turn out, remove the baking paper and serve with the remaining sauce. Serves 6

598

599

600

601

598 WATERMELON GRANITA

450 g (1 lb) watermelon, skin and seeds removed
1 tablespoon liquid glucose or caster (superfine) sugar
$\frac{1}{2}$ teaspoon lemon juice

Purée the watermelon in a blender or food processor, or chop it finely and push it through a metal sieve. Heat the glucose, lemon juice and 75 ml (2$\frac{1}{2}$ fl oz) water in a small saucepan for 4 minutes, or until dissolved. Add the watermelon and stir well.

Pour into a plastic freezer box, cover and freeze. Stir every 30 minutes with a fork during freezing to break up the ice crystals and give a better texture. Keep in the freezer until ready to serve, then roughly fork to break up the ice crystals. Serves 4

599 MANDARIN ICE

10 mandarins
115 g (4 oz/$\frac{1}{2}$ cup) caster (superfine) sugar

Squeeze the mandarins to make 500 ml (17 fl oz/2 cups) juice and strain. Place the sugar and 250 ml (9 fl oz/1 cup) water in a small saucepan. Stir over low heat until the sugar has dissolved, then simmer for 5 minutes. Remove from the heat and cool slightly.

Stir the mandarin juice into the sugar syrup, then pour into a shallow metal tray. Freeze for 2 hours, or until frozen. Transfer to a food processor and blend until slushy. Return to the freezer and repeat the process three more times. Serves 4–6

600 CINNAMON GELATO

1 vanilla bean
560 ml (19$\frac{1}{4}$ fl oz/2$\frac{1}{4}$ cups) thick (double/heavy) cream
560 ml (19$\frac{1}{4}$ fl oz/2$\frac{1}{4}$ cups) milk
2 cinnamon sticks
6 egg yolks
115 g (4 oz/$\frac{1}{2}$ cup) caster (superfine) sugar

Split the vanilla bean down the middle, leaving it joined at one end, and put it in a saucepan with the cream, milk and cinnamon. Bring just to the boil, then remove from the heat and leave to infuse for 1 hour.

Whisk the egg yolks and sugar in a bowl until pale and creamy. Pour the milk over the egg yolk mixture and whisk quickly to combine. Pour the custard back into the saucepan and cook over very low heat to just thicken it, stirring continuously with a wooden spoon. Remove from the heat and dip the spoon into the custard. Draw a line on the back of the spoon — if the line stays and the custard does not run through it, then it is ready; if not, cook a little longer. Do not allow the custard to boil.

Scrape out the vanilla seeds and mix them into the custard. Strain into a bowl, removing the vanilla bean and cinnamon sticks, and leave to cool. Churn in an ice-cream maker following the manufacturer's instructions. Or, pour into a metal or plastic freezer box and freeze, whisking every 30 minutes to break up the ice crystals and give a creamy texture. Once set, keep in the freezer until ready to serve. Serves 8

601 COFFEE GRANITA

230 g (8$\frac{1}{4}$ oz/1 cup) caster (superfine) sugar
1.25 litres (44 fl oz/5 cups) very strong espresso coffee

Heat the caster sugar with 5 teaspoons hot water in a saucepan until the sugar dissolves. Simmer for 3 minutes to make a sugar syrup. Add the coffee and stir well.

Pour the mixture into a plastic or metal freezer box. The mixture should be no deeper than 3 cm (1$\frac{1}{4}$ inches) so that the granita freezes quickly and breaks up easily. Stir every 2 hours with a fork to break up the ice crystals as they form. Repeat this two or three times. The granita is ready when almost set but still grainy. Stir a fork through it just before serving. Serves 6

602

603

604

602 KEY LIME PIE

375 g (13 oz) sweet shortcrust pastry
4 egg yolks
400 g (14 oz) tin condensed milk
125 ml (4 fl oz/$^{1}/_{2}$ cup) lime juice
2 teaspoons grated lime zest
lime slices, to garnish
icing (confectioners') sugar, to dust
whipped cream, to serve

Preheat the oven to 180°C (350°F/Gas 4). Grease a 23 cm (9 inch) loose-based flan tin. Roll the dough out between two sheets of baking paper until it is large enough to fit into the pie tin. Remove the top sheet of paper and invert the pastry into the tin. Use a small ball of pastry to help press the pastry into the tin, allowing any excess to hang over the sides. Use a small sharp knife to trim away any extra pastry.

Line the pastry shell with a piece of crumpled baking paper that is large enough to cover the base and side of the tin and pour in some baking beads or rice. Bake for 10 minutes, remove the paper and beads and return the pastry to the oven for another 4–5 minutes, or until the base is dry. Leave to cool.

Using electric beaters, beat the egg yolks, condensed milk, lime juice and zest in a large bowl for 2 minutes, or until well combined. Pour into the pie shell and smooth the surface. Bake for 20–25 minutes, or until set. Allow the pie to cool, then refrigerate for 2 hours, or until well chilled. Garnish with lime slices, dust with sifted icing sugar and serve with whipped cream. Serves 6–8

604 APPLE TARTE TATIN

100 g (3$^{1}/_{2}$ oz) unsalted butter, chopped
165 g (5$^{3}/_{4}$ oz/$^{3}/_{4}$ cup) sugar
6 large pink lady, fuji or golden delicious apples, peeled,
    cored and quartered
1 sheet ready-made puff pastry
thick (double/heavy) cream or ice cream, to serve

Preheat the oven to 220°C (425°F/Gas 7). Lightly grease a 23 cm (9 inch) shallow cake tin. Melt the unsalted butter in a frying pan, add the sugar and cook, stirring, over medium heat for 4–5 minutes, or until the sugar starts to caramelise and turn brown. Continue to cook, stirring, until the caramel turns golden brown.

Add the apple to the pan and cook over low heat for 20–25 minutes, or until it starts to turn golden brown. Carefully turn the apple over and cook the other side until evenly coloured. Cook off any liquid that comes out of the apple over a higher heat. The caramel should be sticky rather than runny. Remove from the heat. Using tongs, arrange the hot apple in circles in the tin and pour the sauce over it.

Place the pastry over the apple to cover it, tucking the pastry down firmly at the edges using the end of a spoon. Bake for 30–35 minutes, or until the pastry is cooked. Leave the tarte tatin to stand for 15 minutes before inverting onto a serving plate. Remove the paper and serve warm or cold with thick cream or ice cream. Serves 6

603 TARTE AU CITRON

PASTRY
340 g (12 oz/2$^{3}/_{4}$ cups) plain (all-purpose) flour
small pinch of salt
150 g (5$^{1}/_{2}$ oz) unsalted butter
90 g (3$^{1}/_{4}$ oz/$^{3}/_{4}$ cup) icing (confectioners') sugar
2 eggs, beaten

FILLING
4 eggs
2 egg yolks
285 g (10 oz/1$^{1}/_{4}$ cups) caster (superfine) sugar
185 ml (6 fl oz/$^{3}/_{4}$ cup) thick (double/heavy) cream
250 ml (9 fl oz/1 cup) lemon juice
finely grated zest of 3 lemons

To make the pastry, sift the flour and salt onto a work surface and make a well. Put the butter into the well and work, using a pecking action with your fingertips and thumb, until it is very soft. Add the sugar to the butter and mix. Add the eggs to the butter and mix. Gradually incorporate the flour, flicking it onto the mixture, then chop through it until you have a rough dough. Bring together, knead a few times to make a smooth dough, then roll into a ball. Cover in plastic wrap and refrigerate for at least 1 hour.

Preheat the oven to 190°C (375°F/Gas 5). Roll out the pastry to line a 23 cm (9 inch) round loose-based fluted tart tin. Chill for 20 minutes. To make the filling, whisk together the eggs, egg yolks and sugar. Add the cream, whisking all the time, then the lemon juice and zest.

Line the pastry with baking paper and baking beads or rice and blind bake the pastry for 10 minutes, then remove the paper and beads and bake for 3–5 minutes, or until the pastry is dry. Remove from the oven and reduce the oven to 150°C (300°F/Gas 2). Put the tin on a baking tray and carefully pour the filling into the pastry case. Return to the oven for 35–40 minutes, or until set. Cool before serving. Serves 8

605

606

607

608

605 VENETIAN RICE PUDDING

750 ml (26 fl oz/3 cups) milk
250 ml (9 fl oz/1 cup) thick (double/heavy) cream
1 vanilla bean, split
3 tablespoons caster (superfine) sugar
1/4 teaspoon ground cinnamon
pinch of grated nutmeg
1 tablespoon grated orange zest
85 g (3 oz) sultanas
2 tablespoons brandy or sweet Marsala
110 g (3 3/4 oz/1/2 cup) risotto or pudding rice

Put the milk, double cream and vanilla bean in a heavy-based saucepan, and bring just to the boil, then remove from the heat. Add the sugar, cinnamon, nutmeg and orange zest, and set aside.

Put the sultanas and brandy in a small bowl and leave to soak. Add the rice to the infused milk and return to the heat. Bring to a simmer and stir slowly for 35 minutes, or until the rice is creamy. Stir in the sultanas and remove the vanilla bean at the end of cooking. Serve warm or cold. Serves 4

606 TIRAMISU

5 eggs, separated
170 g (6 oz/3/4 cup) caster (superfine) sugar
250 g (9 oz) mascarpone cheese
250 ml (9 fl oz/1 cup) cold very strong coffee
3 tablespoons brandy or sweet Marsala
44 small sponge finger biscuits (savoiardi)
80 g (2 3/4 oz) dark chocolate, finely grated

Beat the egg yolks with the sugar until the sugar has dissolved and the mixture is light and fluffy and leaves a ribbon trail when dropped from the whisk. Add the mascarpone and beat until the mixture is smooth. Whisk the egg whites in a clean dry glass bowl until soft peaks form. Fold into the mascarpone mixture.

Pour the coffee into a shallow dish and add the brandy. Dip some of the sponge finger biscuits into the coffee mixture, using enough biscuits to cover the base of a 25 cm (10 inch) square dish. The biscuits should be fairly well soaked on both sides but not so much so that they break up. Arrange the biscuits in one tightly packed layer in the base of the dish.

Spread half the mascarpone mixture over the layer of biscuits. Add another layer of soaked biscuits and then another layer of mascarpone, smoothing the top layer neatly. Leave to rest in the fridge for at least 2 hours or overnight. Dust with the grated chocolate to serve. Serves 4

607 ETON MESS

4–6 ready-made meringues
250 g (9 oz) strawberries
1 teaspoon caster (superfine) sugar
250 ml (9 fl oz/1 cup) thick (double/heavy) cream

Break the meringues into pieces. Cut the strawberries into quarters and put them in a bowl with the sugar. Using a potato masher or the back of a spoon, squash them slightly so they start to become juicy. Whip the cream with a balloon or electric whisk until it is quite thick but not solid. Mix everything together gently and spoon it into glasses. Serves 4

608 TIPSY STRAWBERRY TRIFLE

2 x 85 g (3 oz) packets red jelly (gelatin dessert) crystals
250 ml (9 fl oz/1 cup) brandy or rum
250 ml (9 fl oz/1 cup) milk
2 x 250 g (9 oz) packets thin sponge finger biscuits (savoiardi)
500 g (1 lb 2 oz) strawberries, hulled and sliced
750 ml (26 fl oz/3 cups) ready-made custard
310 ml (10 3/4 fl oz/1 1/4 cups) cream

Mix the jelly crystals with 435 ml (15 1/4 fl oz/1 3/4 cups) boiling water and stir to dissolve. Pour into a shallow tin and refrigerate until the jelly has just set but is not firm. Combine the brandy and milk in a dish. Dip half the biscuits in the brandy mixture, then place in a single layer in a 3 litre (100 fl oz/12 cup) glass or ceramic dish. Spoon half the jelly over the biscuits. Scatter with half the strawberries and then pour on half of the custard.

Dip the remaining sponge fingers in the brandy mixture and place evenly over the custard, followed by most of the remaining jelly and custard. Whip the cream and spread it evenly over the custard and top with the remaining strawberries and jelly. Cover and refrigerate for 4 hours before serving. Serves 8

609

610

611

609 CHERRY CLAFOUTIS

500 g (1 lb 2 oz) fresh cherries (see Note)
90 g (3¼ oz/¾ cup) plain (all-purpose) flour
2 eggs, lightly beaten
80 g (2¾ oz/⅓ cup) caster (superfine) sugar
250 ml (9 fl oz/1 cup) milk
3 tablespoons thick (double/heavy) cream
50 g (1¾ oz) unsalted butter, melted
icing (confectioners') sugar, to dust

Preheat the oven to 180°C (350°F/Gas 4). Lightly brush a 1.5 litre (52 fl oz/6 cup) ovenproof dish with melted butter. Carefully pit the cherries, then spread into the dish in a single layer. Sift the flour into a bowl, add the egg and whisk until smooth. Add the caster sugar, milk, cream and butter, whisking until just combined, but being careful not to overbeat.

Pour the batter over the cherries and bake for 30–40 minutes, or until a skewer comes out clean when inserted into the centre. Remove from the oven and dust with icing sugar. Serve immediately. Serves 6–8

Note: You can use a 720 g jar (1 lb 9 oz) of cherries. Make sure you thoroughly drain the juice away.

611 RHUBARB & BERRY CRUMBLE

850 g (1 lb 14 oz) rhubarb, cut into 2.5 cm (1 inch) lengths
150 g (5½ oz/1¼ cups) blackberries
1 teaspoon grated orange zest
230 g (8¼ oz/1 cup) caster (superfine) sugar
125 g (4½ oz/1 cup) plain (all-purpose) flour
115 g (4 oz/1 cup) ground almonds
½ teaspoon ground ginger
150 g (5½ oz) chilled unsalted butter, cubed

Preheat the oven to 180°C (350°F/Gas 4), and grease a deep 1.5 litre (52 fl oz/6 cup) ovenproof dish. Bring a saucepan of water to the boil over high heat, add the rhubarb, and cook for 2 minutes, or until just tender. Drain well and combine with the berries, orange zest and 80 g (2¾ oz/⅓ cup) of the caster sugar. Taste and add a little more sugar if needed. Spoon the fruit mixture into the prepared dish.

To make the topping, combine the flour, ground almonds, ginger and the remaining sugar. Rub the butter into the flour mixture with your fingertips until it resembles coarse breadcrumbs. Sprinkle the crumble mix over the fruit, pressing lightly. Don't press it down too firmly, or it will become flat and dense.

Put the dish on a baking tray and bake for 25–30 minutes, or until the topping is golden and the fruit is bubbling underneath. Leave for 5 minutes, then serve with cream or ice cream. Serves 4

Note: Substitute raspberries, loganberries or blueberries for the blackberries. Strawberries do not work well as they become too soft when cooked.

610 RHUBARB PIE

PASTRY
250 g (9 oz/2 cups) plain (all-purpose) flour
30 g (1 oz) unsalted butter, chilled and cubed
70 g (2½ oz) copha (white vegetable shortening)
2 tablespoons icing (confectioners') sugar
170 ml (5½ fl oz/⅔ cup) iced water

1.5 kg (3 lb 5 oz) rhubarb, trimmed and cut into 2 cm (¾ inch) pieces
230 g (8¼ oz/1 cup) caster (superfine) sugar
½ teaspoon ground cinnamon
2½ tablespoons cornflour (cornstarch), mixed with 3 tablespoons water
30 g (1 oz) unsalted butter, cubed
1 egg, lightly beaten
icing (confectioners') sugar, to dust

Grease a 25 x 20 x 4 cm (10 x 8 x 1½ inch) ceramic pie dish. Sift the flour and ½ teaspoon salt into a bowl and rub in the butter and copha until the mixture looks like breadcrumbs. Stir in the icing sugar. Make a well, add most of the water and mix with a flat-bladed knife, using a cutting action, until it comes together in beads. Add more water if needed. Gather the dough together and put on a floured surface. Press into a ball, flatten a little and cover in plastic wrap. Refrigerate for 30 minutes.

Put the rhubarb, sugar, cinnamon and 2 tablespoons water in a saucepan and stir over low heat until the sugar dissolves. Simmer, covered, for 5–8 minutes, or until the rhubarb is tender. Add the cornflour and water mixture. Bring to the boil, stirring until thickened. Cool. Preheat the oven to 180°C (350°F/Gas 4) and heat a baking tray.

Roll out two-thirds of the dough to a 30 cm (12 inch) circle and put into the pie dish. Spoon in the rhubarb and dot with butter. Roll out the remaining pastry for a lid. Brush the pie rim with egg and press the top in place. Trim the edges and make a slit in the top. Decorate with pastry scraps and brush with egg. Bake on the hot tray for 35 minutes, or until golden. Dust with icing sugar. Serves 6

612

613

614

615

612 GRILLED PANETTONE WITH PEACHES

115 g (4 oz/$\frac{1}{2}$ cup) caster (superfine) sugar
$\frac{1}{2}$ vanilla bean, halved and scraped
1 tablespoon Grand Marnier
4 ripe peaches
oil, for brushing
4 large slices panettone
80 g (2$\frac{3}{4}$ oz/$\frac{1}{3}$ cup) crème fraîche

Put the sugar, vanilla bean and 3 tablespoons water in a saucepan and stir over low heat until the sugar has dissolved. Simmer the mixture, without stirring it, for 10 minutes, then remove it from the heat, stir in the Grand Marnier and keep it warm.

Dip the peaches into a saucepan of boiling water for 5 seconds then refresh them under cold water and remove the skins, which should slip off easily. Cut the peaches in half, remove the stone and lightly brush the cut side with oil. Preheat a barbecue chargrill plate to medium direct heat and grill the peaches, cut side down, for 5 minutes, or until golden and warmed through.

Grill the panettone for 30 seconds to 1 minute on each side, or until it is marked and lightly toasted. The panettone will brown very quickly, so be careful to not burn it. Arrange the grilled peaches over the panettone, drizzle with the vanilla syrup and serve with a scoop of crème fraîche. Serves 4

613 FRUIT SKEWERS WITH RUM BUTTER

1 peach, peeled, stoned and cut into 8 pieces
1 mango, peeled, stoned and cut into 8 pieces
8 strawberries, hulled and halved
160 g (5$\frac{3}{4}$ oz) papaya, cut into 8 pieces
160 g (5$\frac{3}{4}$ oz) pineapple, cut into 8 pieces
2 bananas, cut into 2 cm ($\frac{3}{4}$ inch) pieces
185 ml (6 fl oz/$\frac{3}{4}$ cup) dark rum
60 g (2$\frac{1}{4}$ oz/$\frac{1}{3}$ cup) dark brown sugar
20 g ($\frac{3}{4}$ oz) butter
ice cream, to serve

Put the peach, mango, strawberries, papaya, pineapple and banana in a bowl with the rum and sugar, and stir gently until all of the fruit is coated in the marinade. Cover and refrigerate the bowl for 1 hour.

Soak eight wooden skewers in cold water for 1 hour. Drain the marinade into a heavy-based saucepan and thread the fruit onto the skewers. Bring the marinade to the boil over medium heat, then reduce the heat and simmer for 5 minutes, or until it is reduced and syrupy. Remove the pan from the heat and whisk in the butter until it becomes smooth and glossy.

Preheat a flat barbecue grill plate to medium direct heat and cook the skewers for 5–8 minutes on each side, or until they are golden, basting them all over with the rum glaze during the last minute of cooking. Arrange the skewers on a serving plate, drizzle them with the rum glaze and serve warm with ice cream. Serves 4

614 GRILLED FIGS WITH AMARETTO MASCARPONE

3 tablespoons caster (superfine) sugar
3 tablespoons cream
$\frac{1}{2}$ teaspoon natural vanilla extract
110 g (3$\frac{3}{4}$ oz/$\frac{1}{2}$ cup) mascarpone
2$\frac{1}{2}$ tablespoons amaretto
1$\frac{1}{2}$ tablespoons caster (superfine) sugar, extra
3 tablespoons blanched almonds, finely chopped
$\frac{1}{2}$ teaspoon ground cinnamon
6 fresh figs, halved

Line a baking tray with foil. Place the caster sugar and 3 tablespoons water in a small saucepan and stir over low heat until the sugar has dissolved, brushing down the side of the pan with a clean brush dipped in water if any crystals appear. Bring to the boil and cook, without stirring, for about 8 minutes, swirling occasionally until the mixture is golden. Quickly remove the pan from the heat and carefully pour in the cream, stirring constantly until smooth, then stir in the vanilla.

To make the amaretto mascarpone, mix together the mascarpone, amaretto and 2 teaspoons of the extra caster sugar in a bowl.

Combine the chopped almonds, cinnamon and remaining caster sugar on a plate. Press the cut side of each fig half into the almond mixture, then place, cut side up, onto the baking tray. Cook under a hot grill (broiler) for 4–5 minutes, or until the sugar has caramelised and the almonds are nicely toasted — watch carefully to prevent burning.

Arrange three fig halves on each plate, place a dollop of the amaretto mascarpone to the side and drizzle with the sauce. Serves 4

615 BANANA FRITTERS IN COCONUT BATTER

100 g (3$\frac{1}{2}$ oz/$\frac{1}{2}$ cup) glutinous rice flour
100 g (3$\frac{1}{2}$ oz) freshly grated coconut or 60 g (2$\frac{1}{4}$ oz) desiccated coconut
3 tablespoons sugar
1 tablespoon sesame seeds
3 tablespoons coconut milk
6 sugar bananas
oil, for deep-frying
ice cream, to serve

Place the flour, coconut, sugar, sesame seeds, coconut milk and 3 tablespoons water in a bowl and whisk to a smooth batter — add more water if the batter is too thick. Set aside to rest for 1 hour. Peel the bananas and cut in half lengthways (cut each portion in half crossways if the bananas are large).

Fill a wok or deep heavy-based saucepan one-third full of oil and heat to 180°C (350°F), or until a cube of bread dropped in the oil browns in 15 seconds. Dip each piece of banana into the batter, then drop gently into the hot oil. Cook in batches for 4–6 minutes, or until golden brown all over. Remove with a slotted spoon and drain on paper towels. Serve hot with ice cream. Serves 6

616

617

618

616 APPLE CRUMBLE

8 apples
80 g (2¾ oz/⅓ cup) caster (superfine) sugar
zest of 1 lemon
120 g (4¼ oz) butter
125 g (4½ oz/1 cup) plain (all-purpose) flour
1 teaspoon ground cinnamon
cream, to serve

Turn the oven to 180°C (350°/Gas 4). Peel and core the apples, then cut them into chunks. Put the apple, 2 tablespoons of the sugar and the lemon zest in a small baking dish and mix them together. Dot 40 g (¾ oz) of butter over the top.

Rub the remaining butter into the flour until you have a texture that resembles coarse breadcrumbs. Stir in the rest of the sugar and the cinnamon. Add 1–2 tablespoons of water and stir the crumbs together so they form bigger clumps.

Sprinkle the crumble mixture over the apple and bake the crumble for 1 hour 15 minutes, by which time the top should be browned and the juice bubbling up through the crumble. Serve with cream. Serves 4

618 BREAD & BUTTER PUDDING

2 tablespoons sultanas
1 tablespoon Grand Marnier
10 slices day-old white bread, crusts removed
2½ tablespoons marmalade
2 eggs
2 tablespoons caster (superfine) sugar
500 ml (17 fl oz/2 cups) milk
1 teaspoon natural vanilla extract

Place the sultanas in a bowl, add the Grand Marnier, toss to coat and leave for 30 minutes. Preheat the oven to 160°C (315°F/Gas 2–3). Spread the slices of bread with 1½ tablespoons of the marmalade. Cut each slice into four triangles. Lightly grease a 1.5 litre (52 fl oz/ 6 cup) ovenproof dish with oil. Layer the bread in the dish, sprinkling the sultanas between the layers.

Whisk the eggs, sugar, milk and vanilla extract together in a bowl. Pour over the bread and leave to soak for at least 30 minutes. Place the pudding dish in a large roasting tin and pour in boiling water to come halfway up the side of the pudding dish, then bake in the oven for 35–40 minutes. Remove the pudding dish from the roasting tin and brush with the remaining marmalade. Leave for 10 minutes, then serve. Serves 6

617 OLD-FASHIONED APPLE PIE

PASTRY
250 g (9 oz/2 cups) self-raising flour
85 g (3 oz/⅔ cup) cornflour (cornstarch)
180 g (6¼ oz) unsalted butter, chilled and cubed
80 g (2¾ oz/⅓ cup) caster (superfine) sugar
1 egg, lightly beaten

40 g (1½ oz) unsalted butter
6 green apples, peeled, cored and thinly sliced
1 tablespoon lemon juice
140 g (5 oz/¾ cup) soft brown sugar
1 teaspoon ground nutmeg
2 tablespoons plain (all-purpose) flour mixed with
    3 tablespoons water
3 tablespoons ground almonds
milk, to brush
sugar, to sprinkle

Lightly grease a 1 litre (35 fl oz/4 cup), 20 cm (8 inch) metal pie dish. Sift the flours into a large bowl and rub in the butter with your fingers until the mixture resembles fine breadcrumbs. Stir in the sugar and a pinch of salt. Make a well, add the egg and mix with a knife, using a cutting action, until the mixture comes together in beads. Put the dough on a floured surface and press into a smooth disc, cover with plastic wrap and refrigerate for 20 minutes.

Remove the dough from the refrigerator. Roll out two-thirds of the dough between two sheets of baking paper. Remove the top sheet and carefully invert the pastry over the tin to line the base and side of the dish. Roll out the remaining dough to make a lid. Cover and refrigerate for 20 minutes. Preheat the oven to 200°C (400°F/Gas 6) and heat a baking tray.

Melt the butter in a large frying pan, add the apple and toss. Stir in the lemon juice, sugar and nutmeg and cook for 10 minutes, or until tender. Add the flour and water mixture, then the almonds. Bring to the boil and cook, stirring, for 2–3 minutes. Pour into a bowl and cool. Put the apple in the pastry case. Cover with the pastry lid and press lightly onto the rim. Trim the edges and pinch together to seal. Prick over the top, brush with milk and sprinkle with sugar. Bake on the hot tray for 40 minutes, or until golden. Serves 8

619

620

621

622

619 CHOC-DIPPED ICE CREAM BALLS

500 ml (17 fl oz/2 cups) good-quality ice cream (use vanilla
    or a mixture of vanilla, pistachio and chocolate)
150 g (5½ oz) dark chocolate
150 g (5½ oz) white chocolate
150 g (5½ oz) milk chocolate
2 tablespoons toasted shelled walnuts, roughly chopped
2 tablespoons shelled pistachios, roughly chopped
2 tablespoons toasted shredded coconut

Line two large baking trays with baking paper and place in the freezer to chill. Working quickly, use a melon baller to form 36 balls of ice cream and place on the chilled baking trays. Place a cocktail stick in each ice cream ball. Return to the freezer for 1 hour to freeze hard.

Place the chocolate in three separate heatproof bowls. Bring a saucepan of water to the boil, then remove the pan from the heat. Sit one bowl at a time over the pan, making sure the base of the bowl does not sit in the water. Stir occasionally until the chocolate has melted. Remove the bowl from the heat and set aside to cool; the chocolate should remain liquid; if it hardens, repeat.

Put the walnuts, pistachios and coconut in three separate small bowls. Working with 12 of the ice cream balls, dip one at a time quickly in the dark chocolate, then into the bowl with the walnuts. Return to the freezer. Repeat the process with another 12 balls, dipping them in the melted white chocolate and the pistachios. Dip the last 12 balls in the milk chocolate, then the toasted coconut. Freeze all the ice cream balls for 1 hour. Makes 36

621 GRAPE FRITTERS WITH CINNAMON SUGAR

CINNAMON SUGAR
2 tablespoons caster (superfine) sugar
1 teaspoon ground cinnamon

2 eggs, separated
½ teaspoon natural vanilla extract
3 tablespoons caster (superfine) sugar
150 g (5½ oz) seedless red or black grapes
40 g (1½ oz/⅓ cup) self-raising flour
40 g (1½ oz) unsalted butter

To make the cinnamon sugar, combine the sugar and cinnamon in a bowl. Whisk the egg yolks with the vanilla and sugar until combined and just creamy. Slice each grape into four slices, then stir the grape slices into the egg yolk mixture. Sift the flour into the egg mixture. Beat the egg whites in a clean bowl until soft peaks form. Lightly fold half of the egg whites into the egg yolk mixture with a metal spoon until just combined, then repeat with the rest of the egg whites.

Melt 10 g (¼ oz) of the butter in a frying pan over low heat. Place 6 heaped teaspoons of the batter into the pan to make six fritters. Cook over low–medium heat for 2–3 minutes, turning very carefully when the base becomes firm and bubbles appear around the edges. Cook for a further 1–2 minutes, or until golden. Remove to a plate and keep warm. Repeat to make 24 fritters. Dust the fritters with cinnamon sugar and serve warm. Makes 24

620 CREPES WITH WARM FRUIT COMPOTE

CREPES
60 g (2¼ oz/½ cup) plain (all-purpose) flour
2 eggs
250 ml (9 fl oz/1 cup) milk
2 teaspoons caster (superfine) sugar

COMPOTE
100 g (3½ oz/½ cup) whole dried apricots
3 tablespoons port or muscat
1 vanilla bean, split, seeds scraped
2 firm pears, peeled, cored and quartered
2 cinnamon sticks
425 g (15 oz) tin pitted prunes in syrup, drained, syrup reserved

Place the flour in a bowl and gradually add the combined eggs and milk, whisking to remove any lumps. Cover the batter with plastic wrap and leave for 30 minutes. Meanwhile, to make the compote, put the apricots and port in a pan and cook, covered, over low heat for 2–3 minutes, or until softened. Add the vanilla seeds and bean to the pan along with the pear, cinnamon and prune syrup. Simmer, covered, stirring occasionally, for 4 minutes, or until the pear has softened. Add the prunes and simmer for 1 minute.

Heat a 20 cm (8 inch) non-stick crepe pan over medium heat. Lightly grease with oil. Pour 3 tablespoons of batter into the pan and swirl evenly over the base. Cook each crepe for 1 minute, or until the underside is golden. Turn it over and cook the other side for 30 seconds, then remove. Keep warm and repeat to make eight crepes. Fold the crepes into triangles and scatter with sugar. Serve with the compote. Serves 4

622 AMARETTI-STUFFED PEACHES

6 ripe peaches
60 g (2¼ oz) amaretti biscuits, crushed
1 egg yolk
2 tablespoons caster (superfine) sugar
3 tablespoons ground almonds
1 tablespoon amaretto
3 tablespoons white wine
1 teaspoon caster (superfine) sugar, extra
20 g (¾ oz) unsalted butter

Preheat the oven to 180°C (350°F/Gas 4) and lightly grease a 30 x 25 cm (12 x 10 inch) ovenproof dish with butter. Cut each peach in half and carefully remove the stones. Scoop a little of the pulp out from each and combine in a small bowl with the crushed biscuits, egg yolk, caster sugar, ground almonds and amaretto.

Spoon some of the mixture into each peach and place them, cut side up, in the dish. Sprinkle with the white wine and the extra sugar. Put a dot of butter on the top of each and bake for 20–25 minutes, or until golden. Serves 6

Note: When they are in season, you can also use ripe apricots or nectarines for this recipe.

623

624

625

626

623 SPICED FRUIT SALAD

115 g (4 oz/$\frac{1}{2}$ cup) caster (superfine) sugar
4 slices ginger
1 bird's eye chilli, cut in half
juice and zest of 2 limes
4 portions of fruit — a mixture of watermelon, melon,
    mango, banana, cherries, lychees, kiwi fruit, or anything
    else you fancy

Put the sugar in a saucepan with 125 ml (4 fl oz/$\frac{1}{2}$ cup) water and
the ginger and chilli. Heat it until the sugar melts, then leave it to cool
before adding the lime juice and zest. Take out the ginger and chilli.

Put your selection of fruit into a bowl and pour the syrup over it.
Leave it to marinate in the fridge for 30 minutes. Serve with coconut
ice cream or any other kind of ice cream or sorbet. Serves 4

624 FRUIT POACHED IN RED WINE

3 pears, peeled, quartered and cored
3 apples, peeled, quartered and cored
3 tablespoons sugar
1 vanilla bean, cut in half lengthways
2 small cinnamon sticks
400 ml (14 fl oz) red wine
200 ml (7 fl oz) dessert wine or port
700 g (1 lb 9 oz) red-skinned plums, halved

Put the pears and apples in a large saucepan. Add the sugar, vanilla
bean, cinnamon sticks, red wine and dessert wine and bring to the boil.
Reduce the heat and gently simmer for 5–10 minutes, or until just soft.

Add the plums, stirring them through the pears and apples, and bring
the liquid back to a simmer. Cook for another 5 minutes, or until the
plums are soft. Remove the saucepan from the heat, cover with a lid
and leave the fruit to marinate in the syrup for at least 6 hours. Reheat
gently to serve warm, or serve at room temperature with cream or ice
cream and a biscuit. Serves 6

625 RED FRUIT SALAD WITH BERRIES

SYRUP
3 tablespoons caster (superfine) sugar
125 ml (4 fl oz/$\frac{1}{2}$ cup) dry red wine
1 star anise
1 teaspoon finely chopped lemon zest

250 g (9 oz/1$\frac{2}{3}$ cups) strawberries, hulled and halved
150 g (5$\frac{1}{2}$ oz/1 cup) blueberries
150 g (5$\frac{1}{2}$ oz/1$\frac{1}{4}$ cups) raspberries, mulberries or other
    red berries
250 g (9 oz) cherries
5 small red plums (about 250 g/9 oz), stones removed
    and quartered
plain yoghurt, to serve

To make the syrup, place the sugar, wine, star anise, lemon zest and
125 ml (4 fl oz/$\frac{1}{2}$ cup) water in a saucepan. Bring to the boil over
medium heat, stirring to dissolve the sugar. Boil the syrup for 3 minutes,
then set aside to cool for 30 minutes. When cool, strain the syrup.

Mix the fruit together in a bowl and pour on the red wine syrup. Mix
well to coat the fruit in the syrup and refrigerate for 1 hour 30 minutes.
Serve the fruit dressed with a little syrup and the yoghurt. Serves 6

626 WINTER FRUIT IN ORANGE GINGER SYRUP

3 tablespoons caster (superfine) sugar
3 tablespoons orange juice
2 strips orange zest
1 cinnamon stick
250 g (9 oz) dried fruit salad, large pieces cut in half
100 g (3$\frac{1}{2}$ oz) pitted dried dates
1 teaspoon grated fresh ginger
200 g (7 oz) low-fat plain yoghurt

Place the caster sugar, orange juice, orange zest, cinnamon stick
and 375 ml (13 fl oz/1$\frac{1}{2}$ cups) water in a large saucepan. Stir over
low heat until the caster sugar dissolves, then increase the heat and
simmer, without stirring, for 5 minutes, or until the syrup mixture
has thickened slightly.

Add the dried fruit salad, dates and ginger, and toss well. Cover and
simmer over low heat for 5 minutes, or until the fruit has softened.
Remove from the heat and set aside, covered, for 5 minutes. Discard
the orange zest and cinnamon stick. If serving cold, remove from the
saucepan and allow to cool.

Place the fruits in individual serving dishes, top with the yoghurt and
drizzle a little of the syrup over the top. Serve immediately. Serves 4

627

628

629

627 SELF-SAUCING CHOCOLATE PUDDING

10 g ($^1/_4$ oz) unsalted butter, melted
50 g ($1^3/_4$ oz) unsalted butter, chopped, extra
75 g ($2^3/_4$ oz) good-quality dark chocolate, chopped
125 ml (4 fl oz/$^1/_2$ cup) milk
125 g ($4^1/_2$ oz/1 cup) self-raising flour
4 tablespoons unsweetened cocoa powder
170 g (6 oz/$^3/_4$ cup) caster (superfine) sugar
1 egg, lightly beaten
115 g (4 oz/$^1/_2$ cup) soft brown sugar
icing (confectioners') sugar, to dust
thick (double/heavy) cream or ice cream, to serve

Preheat the oven to 180°C (350°F/Gas 4) and lightly grease a 2 litre (70 fl oz/8 cup) ovenproof dish with the melted butter. Place the chopped butter, chocolate and milk in a small saucepan, and stir over medium heat for 3–4 minutes, or until the butter and chocolate have melted. Remove the pan from the heat and allow to cool slightly.

Sift the flour and 2 tablespoons of cocoa, and add to the chocolate mixture with the caster sugar and the egg, stirring until just combined. Spoon into the prepared dish.

Sift the remaining cocoa evenly over the top of the pudding and sprinkle with the brown sugar. Pour 560 ml ($19^1/_4$ fl oz/$2^1/_4$ cups) boiling water over the back of a spoon (this stops the water making holes in the cake mixture) over the top of the pudding. Bake for 40 minutes, or until the pudding is firm to the touch. Leave for 2 minutes before dusting with icing sugar. Serve with cream or ice cream. Serves 6

629 WHITE CHOCOLATE CHEESECAKES WITH MIXED BERRIES

4 butternut biscuits
75 g ($2^3/_4$ oz/$^1/_2$ cup) good-quality white chocolate bits (chocolate chips)
250 g (9 oz/1 cup) cream cheese, at room temperature
3 tablespoons cream
115 g (4 oz/$^1/_2$ cup) caster (superfine) sugar
1 egg
250 g (9 oz) mixed berries, such as raspberries, blueberries and sliced strawberries
Framboise or Cointreau (optional)

Preheat the oven to 160°C (315°F/Gas 2–3). Grease four 250 ml (9 fl oz/1 cup) muffin holes and line with 2 strips of baking paper to make a cross pattern. Put a biscuit in the base of each hole. Put the chocolate bits in a heatproof bowl. Bring a saucepan of water to the boil, then remove from the heat. Sit the bowl over the pan, making sure the base of the bowl does not sit in the water. Stir occasionally until the chocolate has melted.

Using electric beaters, beat the cream cheese, cream and half the sugar until thick and smooth. Beat in the egg and then the melted chocolate. Pour evenly into the muffin holes and bake for 25 minutes, or until set. Cool completely in the tin, then carefully run a small spatula or flat-bladed knife around the edge and lift out of the holes using the paper strips as handles. Refrigerate for 1 hour, or until ready to serve.

Place the berries in a bowl and fold in the remaining sugar. Leave for 10–15 minutes, or until juices form. Flavour with a little liqueur, if desired. Serve on plates topped with the berries. Serves 4

628 BAKED CHEESECAKE

250 g (9 oz) butternut cookies
1 teaspoon mixed spice
100 g ($3^1/_2$ oz) butter, melted
500 g (1 lb 2 oz/2 cups) cream cheese, softened
170 g (6 oz/$^3/_4$ cup) caster (superfine) sugar
4 eggs
1 teaspoon natural vanilla extract
1 tablespoon orange juice
1 tablespoon grated orange zest

TOPPING
250 g (9 oz/1 cup) sour cream
$^1/_2$ teaspoon natural vanilla extract
3 teaspoons orange juice
1 tablespoon caster (superfine) sugar
freshly grated nutmeg

Lightly grease the base of a 20 cm (8 inch) spring-form tin. Finely crush the biscuits in a food processor for 30 seconds, or put them in a plastic bag and roll with a rolling pin. Transfer to a bowl and add the mixed spice and butter. Stir until all the crumbs are moistened, then spoon the mixture into the tin and press it firmly into the base and side. Refrigerate for 20 minutes, or until firm.

Preheat the oven to 180°C (350°F/Gas 4). Beat the cream cheese until smooth. Add the sugar and beat until smooth. Add the eggs, one at a time, beating well after each addition. Mix in the vanilla extract, orange juice and zest.

Pour the mixture into the crumb case and bake for 45 minutes, or until just firm. To make the topping, combine the sour cream, vanilla, orange juice and sugar in a bowl. Spread over the hot cheesecake, sprinkle with nutmeg and return to the oven for 7 minutes. Cool, then refrigerate until firm. Serves 8

630

631

632

633

630 APRICOT HONEY SOUFFLÉ

180 g (6¼ oz/1 cup) dried whole apricots, chopped
2 tablespoons caster (superfine) sugar
2 egg yolks
1½ tablespoons honey, warmed
1 teaspoon finely grated lemon zest
4 egg whites
icing (confectioners') sugar, to dust

Place the apricots in a saucepan with 125 ml (4 fl oz/½ cup) cold water, or enough to cover. Bring to the boil, then reduce the heat and simmer for 20 minutes, or until the apricots are soft and pulpy. Drain, then process in a food processor to a purée.

Preheat the oven to 200°C (400°F/Gas 6). Lightly grease a 1.25 litre (44 fl oz/5 cup) soufflé dish and sprinkle the base and side with 1 tablespoon of caster sugar. Put the egg yolks, honey, zest and apricot purée in a bowl and beat until smooth.

Whisk the egg whites in a clean, dry bowl until soft peaks form, then whisk in the remaining sugar. Fold 1 tablespoon into the apricot mixture and mix well. Lightly fold in the remaining egg white, being careful to keep the mixture light and aerated. Spoon into the soufflé dish and level the surface. Run your thumb around the inside rim to create a gap between the mixture and the wall of the dish (this will encourage even rising).

Bake on the upper shelf in the oven for 25–30 minutes, or until risen and just set. Cover loosely with foil if the surface starts to overbrown. Dust with icing sugar and serve. Serves 4

631 GRANDMOTHER'S PAVLOVA

4 egg whites
230 g (8¼ oz/1 cup) caster (superfine) sugar
2 teaspoons cornflour (cornstarch)
1 teaspoon white vinegar
500 ml (17 fl oz/2 cups) cream
3 passionfruit, to decorate
strawberries, to decorate

Preheat the oven to 160°C (315°F/Gas 2–3). Line a 32 x 28 cm (12½ x 11¼ inch) baking tray with baking paper. Place the egg whites and a pinch of salt in a small, dry bowl. Using electric beaters, beat until stiff peaks form. Add the sugar gradually, beating constantly after each addition, until the mixture is thick and glossy and all the sugar has dissolved.

Using a metal spoon, fold in the cornflour and vinegar. Spoon the mixture into a mound on the prepared tray. Lightly flatten the top of the pavlova and smooth the sides. (This pavlova should have a cake shape and be about 2.5 cm/1 inch high.) Bake for 1 hour, or until pale cream and crisp. Remove from the oven while warm and carefully turn upside down onto a plate. Allow to cool.

Lightly whip the cream until soft peaks form and spread over the soft centre. Decorate with pulp from the passionfruit and halved strawberries. Cut into wedges to serve. Serves 6

632 BERRY & MARSHMALLOW GRATIN

600 g (1 lb 5 oz) mixed seasonal berries, such as strawberries, raspberries, blueberries or blackberries
2 tablespoons raspberry liqueur
150 g (5½ oz) pink and white marshmallows
vanilla ice cream

Put the berries and raspberry liqueur in a bowl, stir them gently to coat the berries and transfer them to a 1.5 litre (52 fl oz/6 cup) ceramic ovenproof dish. Top the berries with the marshmallows, making sure they are evenly distributed over the surface.

Preheat a covered or kettle barbecue to medium–high indirect heat and put the dish in the middle of the barbecue. Cook for 8–10 minutes or until the berries are bubbling and the marshmallow has puffed up and is starting to melt. Serve the gratin immediately with a big scoop of ice cream, but take care to not burn your mouth on the berries, which will be very hot. Serves 6

633 PASSIONFRUIT SOUFFLÉ

caster (superfine) sugar, for lining
40 g (1½ oz) unsalted butter
2 tablespoons plain (all-purpose) flour
185 ml (6 fl oz/¾ cup) milk
115 g (4 oz/½ cup) caster (superfine) sugar
250 ml (9 fl oz/1 cup) passionfruit pulp (about 7 large passionfruit)
6 egg whites
icing (confectioners') sugar, to dust

Preheat the oven to 180°C (350°F/Gas 4). Put an oven tray in the oven to heat. Lightly grease four 300 ml (10½ fl oz) ramekins with oil and sprinkle the base and side with caster sugar, shaking out any excess.

Melt the butter in a saucepan over medium heat, add the flour and stir for 1 minute, or until foaming. Remove from the heat and gradually add the milk. Return to the heat and stir constantly for 5–6 minutes, or until the sauce boils and thickens. Reduce the heat and simmer, stirring, for 2 minutes. Transfer to a bowl and stir in the sugar and passionfruit pulp. Do not worry if the mixture looks curdled.

Using electric beaters, beat the egg whites in a clean, dry bowl until firm peaks form. Using a metal spoon, fold a large dollop of the beaten egg white into the passionfruit mixture, then gently fold in the remaining egg white. Make sure you fold the mixture quickly and lightly to incorporate all of the egg white, without losing volume.

Spoon the mixture into the ramekins. Place on the oven tray and bake for 18–20 minutes, or until golden and well risen but still a bit wobbly. Dust with icing sugar and serve immediately. Serves 4

634

635

636

634 CHOCOLATE CROISSANT PUDDING

4 croissants, torn into pieces
125 g (4$\frac{1}{2}$ oz) good-quality dark chocolate, chopped into pieces
4 eggs
5 tablespoons caster (superfine) sugar
250 ml (9 fl oz/1 cup) milk
250 ml (9 fl oz/1 cup) cream
3 teaspoons orange liqueur
3 teaspoons grated orange zest
80 ml (2$\frac{1}{2}$ fl oz/$\frac{1}{3}$ cup) orange juice
2 tablespoons roughly chopped hazelnuts
cream, to serve

Preheat the oven to 180°C (350°F/Gas 4). Grease the base and side of a 20 cm (8 inch) deep-sided cake tin and line the bottom of the tin with baking paper. Put the croissant pieces into the tin, then scatter over 100 g (3$\frac{1}{2}$ oz) chocolate pieces.

Beat the eggs and sugar together until pale and creamy. Heat the milk, cream and liqueur and remaining chocolate pieces in a saucepan until almost boiling. Stir to melt the chocolate, then remove the pan from the heat. Gradually add to the egg mixture, stirring constantly. Next, stir in the orange zest and juice. Slowly pour the mixture over the croissants, allowing the liquid to be fully absorbed before adding more.

Sprinkle the hazelnuts over the top and bake for 50 minutes, or until a skewer comes out clean when inserted into the centre. Cool for 10 minutes. Turn the pudding out and invert onto a serving plate. Slice and serve warm with a dollop of cream. Serves 6–8

636 BLUEBERRY SOY CHEESECAKE

250 g (9 oz) wholemeal (whole-wheat) biscuits
3 teaspoons ground cinnamon
150 g (5$\frac{1}{2}$ oz) unsalted butter, melted
1$\frac{1}{2}$ tablespoons powdered gelatine
250 g (9 oz) silken tofu
3 tablespoons caster (superfine) sugar
250 g (9 oz/1 cup) cream cheese
300 g (10$\frac{1}{2}$ oz) vanilla yoghurt
300 g (10$\frac{1}{2}$ oz) blueberries, or 400 g (14 oz) tinned well-drained
    blueberries, or 300 g (10$\frac{1}{2}$ oz) frozen blueberries, thawed

Preheat the oven to 180°C (350°F/Gas 4). Grease a 23 cm (9 inch) spring-form tin. Place the biscuits and 1 teaspoon of the ground cinnamon in a food processor and blend together until it forms fine crumbs. Transfer to a bowl, add the melted butter and mix well. Press the crumb mixture onto the base of the prepared tin. Bake for 10 minutes, then cool.

Pour 170 ml (5$\frac{1}{2}$ fl oz/$\frac{2}{3}$ cup) water into a heatproof bowl, evenly sprinkle on the gelatine and leave until spongy – do not stir. Bring a saucepan of water to the boil and remove from the heat. Place the bowl of gelatine in the pan and stir until the gelatine is smooth.

Mix the tofu, sugar, cream cheese and yoghurt in a food processor until smooth. Add the gelatine and process in short bursts for 1–2 seconds. Place the blueberries on the biscuit base and pour the tofu mixture over the top, spreading evenly. Chill for at least 2 hours. Remove the side of the tin and dust the cheesecake with the remaining ground cinnamon just before serving. Serves 6–8

635 APRICOT & ALMOND TART

375 g (13 oz) sweet shortcrust pastry
200 g (7 oz/1$\frac{1}{4}$ cups) dried apricots
100 ml (3$\frac{1}{2}$ fl oz) brandy or grappa
icing (confectioners') sugar, to dust
crème fraîche or cream, to serve

ALMOND FILLING
180 g (6$\frac{1}{4}$ oz) unsalted butter, softened
170 g (6 oz/$\frac{3}{4}$ cup) caster (superfine) sugar
180 g (6$\frac{1}{4}$ oz/2 cups) flaked blanched almonds
2 eggs
1 teaspoon vanilla extract
1 heaped teaspoon plain (all-purpose) flour

Grease a 25 cm (10 inch) loose-based metal tart tin. Dust the work surface with flour and roll out the pastry to fit the tin. Line the tin and trim the edges. Refrigerate for 15 minutes. Preheat the oven to 200°C (400°F/Gas 6).

Line the pastry shell with crumpled baking paper and baking beads and bake for 12 minutes, then remove the paper and beads – if the pastry still looks wet, dry it out in the oven for 5 minutes. Cool for a few minutes. Reduce the oven to 180°C (350°F/Gas 4).

Put the dried apricots and brandy in a saucepan and cook over low heat for about 5 minutes, or until most of the liquid has evaporated. Leave to cool.

To make the almond filling, use a food processor to cream the butter and sugar until light and pale. Add the almonds, eggs, vanilla and flour and briefly blend. If you overbeat it, the mixture may separate. Spoon the filling into the pastry shell, then place the apricots in the shell, arranging them in two circles, one inside the other. Bake for 30–40 minutes, or until the filling is set. Cool and sprinkle with icing sugar just before serving. Serve with crème fraîche or cream. Serves 8

637

638

639

640

637 CINNAMON ORANGE MINI PAVLOVAS WITH BERRIES

2 egg whites
115 g (4 oz/$\frac{1}{2}$ cup) caster (superfine) sugar
2 teaspoons ground cinnamon
1 teaspoon finely grated orange zest
3 teaspoons cornflour (cornstarch)
1 teaspoon white vinegar
125 ml (4 fl oz/$\frac{1}{2}$ cup) cream
fresh berries, to serve

Preheat the oven to 140°C (275°F/Gas 1). Line a baking tray with baking paper and mark four 10 cm (4 inch) circles. Turn the baking paper upside down so the marks don't stain the meringue. Beat the egg whites with electric beaters until soft peaks form. Gradually add the sugar, beating well after each addition. Continue to beat for 4–5 minutes, or until the sugar has dissolved and the meringue is thick and glossy. Gently fold in the cinnamon, orange zest, cornflour and vinegar. Place 2 tablespoons of the mixture into each circle, gently spreading it out to the edges with the back of a spoon. Hollow out each centre to make nest shapes.

Bake for 10 minutes, then turn the tray around and bake for a further 30–35 minutes, or until the pavlovas are pale and crisp. Turn the oven off and leave them to cool completely with the door slightly ajar. The pavlovas may crack slightly on cooling. Whip the cream and spoon a little into each pavlova, top with the berries and serve. Serves 4

638 MANGO FOOL

2 very ripe mangoes
250 g (9 oz/1 cup) Greek-style yoghurt
80 ml (2$\frac{1}{2}$ fl oz/$\frac{1}{3}$ cup) cream

Take the flesh off the mangoes. The easiest way to do this is to slice down either side of the stone so you have two 'cheeks'. Make crisscross cuts through the mango flesh on each cheek, almost through to the skin, then turn each cheek inside out and slice the flesh from the skin into a bowl. Cut the rest of the flesh from the stone.

Purée the flesh either by using a food processor or blender, or if you don't have any of these, just mash the flesh thoroughly. Put a spoonful of mango purée in the bottom of four small glasses, bowls or cups, put a spoonful of yoghurt on top and then repeat. Spoon half the cream over each serving when you have used up all the mango and yoghurt. Swirl the layers together just before you eat them. Serves 4

639 CARAMEL ICE CREAM

75 g (2$\frac{3}{4}$ oz/$\frac{1}{3}$ cup) sugar
80 ml (2$\frac{1}{2}$ fl oz/$\frac{1}{3}$ cup) cream
3 egg yolks
375 ml (13 fl oz/1$\frac{1}{2}$ cups) milk
1 vanilla bean

To make the caramel, put 45 g (1$\frac{1}{2}$ oz) of the sugar in a heavy-based saucepan and heat until it dissolves and starts to caramelise — tip the saucepan from side to side as the sugar cooks to keep the colouring even. Remove from the heat and carefully add the cream (it will splutter). Stir over low heat until the caramel remelts.

Whisk the egg yolks and remaining sugar until light and fluffy. Put the milk and vanilla bean in a saucepan and bring just to the boil, then strain over the caramel. Bring back to the boil and pour over the egg yolk mixture, whisking continuously.

Pour the custard back into the pan and cook, stirring, until it is thick enough to coat the back of a wooden spoon. Do not let it boil or it will split. Pass through a sieve into a bowl and leave over ice to cool quickly.

Churn in an ice-cream maker following the manufacturer's instructions. Or, pour into a plastic freezer box, cover and freeze. Stir every 30 minutes with a whisk during freezing to break up the ice crystals. Freeze overnight with a layer of plastic wrap over the surface and the lid on the container. Keep in the freezer until ready to serve. Serves 4

640 STRAWBERRY ICE CREAM WITH STRAWBERRY SAUCE

500 g (1 lb 2 oz) strawberries, hulled and sliced
2 tablespoons caster (superfine) sugar
2 tablespoons Cointreau or fresh orange juice
500 ml (17 fl oz/2 cups) good-quality vanilla ice cream, slightly softened
125 g (4$\frac{1}{2}$ oz) blueberries (optional)

Place the strawberries in a saucepan, add the sugar and Cointreau and cook over low heat for 5 minutes, or until softened and the juices are released. Remove from the heat and refrigerate.

Place half the strawberry mixture in a food processor or blender and process for 20–30 seconds, or until smooth. Spoon the ice cream into the food processor and process for 10 seconds, or until well combined with the strawberry mixture. Pour into a rectangular tin and return to the freezer for 2–3 hours, or until firm. Serve the ice cream with the reserved strawberry sauce and blueberries. Serves 4

641

642

643

641 CHOCOLATE & RASPBERRY ICE CREAM SANDWICH

300 g (10½ oz) frozen chocolate pound cake
2 tablespoons raspberry liqueur (optional)
250 g (9 oz/2 cups) fresh or thawed raspberries
220 g (7¾ oz/1 cup) sugar
1 teaspoon lemon juice
1 litre (35 fl oz/4 cups) vanilla ice cream, softened
icing (confectioners') sugar, to dust

Cut the pound cake lengthwise into four thin slices. Using a 6.5 cm (2½ inch) plain cutter, cut eight rounds from the slices of cake. You will need two rounds of cake per person. Brush each round with half of the raspberry liqueur if using, then cover and set aside.

Line a 20 x 20 cm (8 x 8 inch) tin or dish with baking paper, leaving a generous overhang of paper on two opposite sides. Place the raspberries, sugar, lemon juice and remaining liqueur in a blender and blend to a smooth purée. Reserving 125 ml (4 fl oz/½ cup) of the purée, fold the remainder through the ice cream and pour into the tin. Freeze for 2 hours, or until firm. Remove the ice cream from the freezer and use the overhanging baking paper to lift from the tin. Using a 6.5 cm (2½ inch) cutter, cut four rounds from the ice cream.

To assemble, place four slices of cake on a tray, top each with a round of ice cream and then the remaining slices of cake. Smooth the sides of the ice cream to neaten, if necessary. Return the sandwiches to the freezer for 5 minutes to firm. Dust with icing sugar and serve with the remaining raspberry sauce. Serves 4

643 CRÈME CARAMEL

250 ml (9 fl oz/1 cup) milk
250 ml (9 fl oz/1 cup) cream
345 g (12 oz/1½ cups) caster (superfine) sugar
1 teaspoon natural vanilla extract
4 eggs, lightly beaten
80 g (2¾ oz/⅓ cup) caster (superfine) sugar, extra

Preheat the oven to 200°C (400°F/Gas 6). Place the milk and cream in a saucepan and gradually bring to boiling point. Put the sugar in a frying pan and cook over medium heat for 8–10 minutes. Stir occasionally as the sugar melts to form a golden toffee. The sugar may clump together – break up any lumps with a wooden spoon. Pour the toffee into the base of six 125 ml (4 fl oz/½ cup) ramekins or ovenproof dishes.

Combine the vanilla, eggs and extra sugar in a bowl. Remove the milk and cream from the heat and gradually add to the egg mixture, whisking well. Pour the custard mixture evenly over the toffee. Place the ramekins in a baking dish and pour in boiling water until it comes halfway up the sides of the dishes. Bake for 20 minutes, or until set. Use a flat-bladed knife to run around the edges of the dishes and carefully turn out the crème caramel onto a serving plate, toffee side up. Serves 6

Note: When making toffee, watch it carefully as it will take a little while to start melting, but once it starts it will happen very quickly. Stir occasionally to make sure it melts evenly and doesn't stick to the base of the saucepan.

642 CHOCOLATE FUDGE PUDDINGS

150 g (5½ oz) unsalted butter
170 g (6 oz/¾ cup) caster (superfine) sugar
100 g (3½ oz) dark chocolate, melted and cooled
2 eggs
60 g (2¼ oz/½ cup) plain (all-purpose) flour
125 g (4½ oz/1 cup) self-raising flour
3 tablespoons unsweetened cocoa powder
1 teaspoon bicarbonate of soda (baking soda)
125 ml (4 fl oz/½ cup) milk

SAUCE
50 g (1¾ oz) unsalted butter, chopped
125 g (4½ oz) dark chocolate, chopped
125 ml (4 fl oz/½ cup) cream
1 teaspoon natural vanilla extract

Preheat the oven to 180°C (350°F/Gas 4). Lightly grease eight 250 ml (9 fl oz/1 cup) metal moulds with melted butter and line each base with a round of baking paper. Beat the butter and caster sugar until light and creamy. Add the melted chocolate, beating well. Add the eggs one at a time, beating well after each addition.

Sift together the plain and self-raising flours, cocoa powder and bicarbonate of soda, then fold into the chocolate mixture. Add the milk and fold through. Half fill the moulds. Cover the moulds with pieces of greased foil and place in a large, deep baking dish. Pour in enough boiling water to come halfway up the sides of the moulds. Bake for 35–40 minutes, or until a skewer inserted into the centre of each pudding comes out clean.

To make the sauce, combine the butter, chocolate, cream and vanilla in a pan. Stir over low heat until the butter and chocolate have completely melted. Pour over the pudding and serve with whipped cream. Serves 8

644

645

646

647

644 GINGER & LYCHEE JELLY

565 g (1 lb 4 oz) tin lychees
500 ml (17 fl oz/2 cups) clear apple juice (no added sugar)
80 ml (2 1/2 fl oz/1/3 cup) strained lime juice
2 tablespoons caster (superfine) sugar
3 x 3 cm (1 1/4 x 1 1/4 inch) piece ginger, peeled and thinly sliced
4 sheets gelatine (about 5 g/1/8 oz)
mint leaves, to garnish

Drain the syrup from the lychees and reserve 250 ml (9 fl oz/1 cup) of the syrup. Discard the remaining syrup. Place the reserved syrup, apple juice, lime juice, sugar and ginger in a saucepan. Bring to the boil, then reduce the heat and simmer for 5 minutes. Strain into a heatproof bowl.

Place the gelatine sheets in a bowl of cold water and soak for 2 minutes, or until they soften. Squeeze out the excess water, then add to the syrup. Stir until the gelatine has completely dissolved. Leave to cool.

Pour 2 tablespoons of the jelly mixture into each of six 150 ml (5 fl oz) stemmed wine glasses, and divide the lychees among the wine glasses. Refrigerate until the jelly has set. Spoon the remaining jelly over the fruit and refrigerate until set. Before serving, garnish with mint. Serves 6

645 ZABAGLIONE

6 egg yolks
3 tablespoons caster (superfine) sugar
125 ml (4 fl oz/1/2 cup) sweet Marsala
250 ml (9 fl oz/1 cup) thick (double/heavy) cream

Whisk the egg yolks and sugar in the top of a double boiler or in a heatproof bowl set over a saucepan of simmering water. Make sure that the water does not touch the base of the bowl or the egg may overcook and stick. It is important that you whisk constantly to move the cooked mixture from the outside of the bowl to the centre.

When the egg mixture is tepid, add the Marsala and whisk for another 5 minutes, or until it has thickened enough to hold its shape when drizzled off the whisk into the bowl. Whip the cream until soft peaks form. Gently fold in the egg and Marsala mixture. Divide among four glasses or bowls. Cover and refrigerate for 3–4 hours before serving. Serves 4

646 PASSIONFRUIT MOUSSE

5–6 passionfruit
6 eggs, separated
170 g (6 oz/3/4 cup) caster (superfine) sugar
1/2 teaspoon finely grated lemon zest
3 tablespoons lemon juice
1 tablespoon powdered gelatine
310 ml (10 3/4 fl oz/1 1/4 cups) cream, lightly whipped
40 g (1 1/2 oz) flaked or shredded coconut, toasted

Cut the passionfruit in half and scoop out the pulp. Strain, then measure out 3 tablespoons of juice and set aside. Add the seeds and pulp to the remaining juice and set aside. Put the egg yolks, 115 g (4 oz/1/2 cup) of the sugar, lemon zest and juice, and strained passionfruit juice in a heatproof bowl. Put the bowl over a pan of simmering water and, using electric beaters, beat for 10 minutes, or until thick and creamy. Remove from the heat and transfer to a glass bowl.

Sprinkle the gelatine over 125 ml (4 fl oz/1/2 cup) water in a small bowl and leave until spongy. Put the bowl in a pan of just-boiled water (the water should come halfway up the bowl) and stir until dissolved. Add the gelatine to the mousse mixture and mix well. Mix in the passionfruit pulp and leave until cold, then fold in the whipped cream.

Using electric beaters, whisk the egg whites until soft peaks form. Gradually whisk in the remaining sugar, beating until the sugar has dissolved. Fold the egg whites into the mousse mixture quickly and lightly. Spoon into eight 250 ml (9 fl oz/1 cup) ramekins. Refrigerate for 2 hours, or until set. Sprinkle with the coconut before serving. Serves 10–12

647 BERRIES IN CHAMPAGNE JELLY

1 litre (35 fl oz/4 cups) Champagne or sparkling white wine
1 1/2 tablespoons powdered gelatine
220 g (7 3/4 oz/1 cup) sugar
4 strips lemon zest
4 strips orange zest
250 g (9 oz) small hulled and halved strawberries
250 g (9 oz) blueberries

Pour 500 ml (17 fl oz/2 cups) Champagne into a bowl and let the bubbles subside. Sprinkle the gelatine over the Champagne in an even layer. Leave until the gelatine is spongy — do not stir. Place the remaining Champagne in a large saucepan with the sugar, lemon and orange zest, and heat gently, stirring constantly for 3–4 minutes, or until all of the sugar has dissolved.

Remove the pan from the heat, add the gelatine mixture and stir until thoroughly dissolved. Leave the jelly to cool completely, then remove the lemon and orange zest.

Divide the berries among eight 125 ml (4 fl oz/1/2 cup) stemmed wine glasses and gently pour the jelly over the top. Refrigerate for 6 hours or overnight, or until the jelly has fully set. Remove from the refrigerator 15 minutes before serving. Serves 8

648

649

650

648 BAKED RICE PUDDING

20 g (³/₄ oz) unsalted butter, melted
3 tablespoons short-grain rice
3 eggs
3 tablespoons caster (superfine) sugar
435 ml (15¹/₄ fl oz/1³/₄ cups) milk
125 ml (4 fl oz/¹/₂ cup) cream
1 teaspoon natural vanilla extract
¹/₄ teaspoon ground nutmeg

Preheat the oven to 160°C (315°F/Gas 2–3) and brush a 1.5 litre (52 fl oz/6 cup) ovenproof dish with the melted butter. Cook the rice in a saucepan of boiling water for 12 minutes, or until tender, then drain well.

Place the eggs in a bowl and beat lightly. Add the sugar, milk, cream and vanilla extract, and whisk until well combined. Stir in the cooked rice, pour into the prepared dish and sprinkle with nutmeg.

Place the dish in a deep roasting tin and pour enough hot water into the tin to come halfway up the side of the pudding dish. Bake for 45 minutes, or until the custard is lightly set and a knife inserted into the centre comes out clean. Remove the pudding dish from the roasting tin and leave for 5 minutes before serving. Serve the pudding with poached or stewed fruit. Serves 4–6

Note: For variation, add 2 tablespoons of sultanas or chopped, dried apricots to the custard mixture before baking.

650 APPLE SAGO PUDDING

80 g (2³/₄ oz/¹/₃ cup) caster (superfine) sugar
100 g (3¹/₂ oz/¹/₂ cup) sago
625 ml (21¹/₂ fl oz/2¹/₂ cups) milk
60 g (2¹/₄ oz/¹/₂ cup) sultanas
1 teaspoon natural vanilla extract
pinch ground nutmeg
¹/₄ teaspoon ground cinnamon
2 eggs, lightly beaten
3 small ripe apples (about 250 g/9 oz), peeled, cored
   and very thinly sliced
1 tablespoon soft brown sugar

Preheat the oven to 180°C (350°F/Gas 4). Grease a 1.5 litre (52 fl oz/6 cup) ceramic soufflé dish. Place the sugar, sago, milk, sultanas and ¹/₄ teaspoon salt in a saucepan and heat, stirring often. Bring to the boil, then reduce the heat and simmer for 5 minutes.

Stir in the vanilla extract, nutmeg, cinnamon, egg and the apple slices, then pour into the prepared dish. Sprinkle with the brown sugar and bake for 45 minutes, or until set and golden brown. Serves 4

649 LEMON MERINGUE PIE

MERINGUE
6 egg whites
pinch of cream of tartar
345 g (12 oz/1¹/₂ cups) caster (superfine) sugar

375 g (13 oz) sweet shortcrust pastry
3 tablespoons plain (all-purpose) flour
3 tablespoons cornflour (cornstarch)
230 g (8¹/₄ oz/1 cup) caster (superfine) sugar
185 ml (6 fl oz/³/₄ cup) lemon juice
1 tablespoon grated lemon zest
50 g (1³/₄ oz) unsalted butter, chopped
6 egg yolks

To make the meringue, beat the egg whites with the cream of tartar in a clean, dry bowl with electric beaters until soft peaks form. Gradually pour in the caster sugar, beating until the meringue is thick and glossy. Set aside until needed.

Grease a 25 cm (10 inch) top, 18 cm (7 inch) base, 3 cm (1¹/₄ inch) deep pie plate. Roll the pastry out between two sheets of baking paper into a 30 cm (12 inch) circle. Invert the pastry into the plate. Trim the edges. Re-roll the pastry trimmings and cut into three 10 x 2 cm (4 x ³/₄ inch) strips. Brush the pie rim with water, place the pastry strips around the top and use your fingers to make a decorative edge. Prick over the base with a fork. Cover and refrigerate for 20 minutes. Preheat the oven to 180°C (350°F/Gas 4).

Blind bake the pastry for 15 minutes. Remove the beads and bake for 15–20 minutes. Cool. Increase the oven to 200°C (400°F/Gas 6). Put the flours, sugar, lemon juice and zest in a pan. Gradually add 310 ml (10³/₄ fl oz/1¹/₄ cups) water and whisk over medium heat until smooth. Cook, stirring, for 2 minutes, or until thick. Remove from the heat and vigorously whisk in the butter and egg yolks. Return to low heat and stir constantly, for 2 minutes, or until very thick.

Spread the lemon filling into the pastry base, then cover with the meringue, piling high in the centre and making peaks with a knife. Bake for 8–10 minutes, or until lightly browned. Serves 4–6

651

652

653

654

651 MANGO SORBET

345 g (12 oz/1¹/₂ cups) caster (superfine) sugar
125 ml (4 fl oz/¹/₂ cup) lime juice
5 fresh mangoes (1.5 kg/3 lb 5 oz)

Place the sugar in a saucepan with 625 ml (21¹/₂ fl oz/2¹/₂ cups) water. Stir over low heat until the sugar dissolves, then bring to the boil. Reduce to a simmer for 15 minutes, then stir in the juice.

Peel the mangoes and remove the flesh from the stone. Chop and place in a heatproof bowl. Add the syrup and leave to cool. Place the mango mixture in a blender, blend until smooth, then pour into a shallow metal dish and freeze for 1 hour, or until it starts to freeze around the edges. Return to the blender and blend until smooth. Pour back into the tray and return to the freezer. Repeat three times. For the final freezing, place in an airtight container and cover the sorbet with a piece of baking paper and lid. Allow the sorbet to soften slightly before serving with tropical fruit. Serves 4

Note: You can use frozen mango if fresh is unavailable. Use 1 kg (2 lb 4 oz) frozen mango cheeks, softened, 170 g (6 oz/³/₄ cup) caster (superfine) sugar and 3 tablespoons lime juice, and follow the method as above.

652 WHITE CHOCOLATE MOUSSE

100 g (3¹/₂ oz) white chocolate melts (buttons)
125 ml (4 fl oz/¹/₂ cup) skim milk
2 teaspoons powdered gelatine
400 g (14 oz) low-fat French vanilla fromage frais
    or whipped yoghurt
3 egg whites
3 tablespoons passionfruit pulp
icing (confectioners') sugar, to dust

Place the chocolate and milk in a small saucepan and stir over low heat until the chocolate has melted. Allow to cool. Place 3 tablespoons boiling water in a heatproof bowl, sprinkle evenly with the gelatine, and stir until dissolved. Using a wooden spoon, stir the gelatine into the chocolate mixture.

Place the fromage frais in a large bowl and gradually stir in the chocolate mixture, a little at a time, stirring until smooth after each addition.

Beat the egg whites in a clean, dry bowl with electric beaters until soft peaks form. Gently fold the egg whites and the passionfruit pulp into the chocolate mixture. Divide the mixture equally among eight 125 ml (4 fl oz/¹/₂ cup) serving dishes or a 1 litre (35 fl oz/4 cups) glass bowl. Refrigerate for 3 hours, or until set. Serve with a light dusting of icing sugar. Serves 8

Note: It is important to have the ingredients at room temperature to ensure the texture is smooth.

653 LEMON GELATO

5 egg yolks
125 g (4¹/₂ oz/¹/₂ cup) sugar
500 ml (17 fl oz/2 cups) milk
2 tablespoons grated lemon zest
185 ml (6 fl oz/³/₄ cup) lemon juice
3 tablespoons thick (double/heavy) cream

Whisk the egg yolks and half the sugar together until pale and creamy. Put the milk, lemon zest and remaining sugar in a saucepan and bring to the boil. Pour over the egg mixture and whisk to combine.

Pour the custard back into the saucepan and cook over low heat, stirring continuously until the mixture is thick enough to coat the back of a wooden spoon — do not allow the custard to boil. Strain the custard into a bowl, add the lemon juice and cream and then cool over ice.

Churn in an ice-cream maker following the manufacturer's instructions. Or, pour into a plastic freezer box, cover and freeze. Stir every 30 minutes with a whisk during freezing to break up the ice crystals and give a better texture. Keep in the freezer until ready to serve. Serves 6

654 PETITS POTS DE CRÈME

420 ml (14¹/₂ fl oz/1²/₃ cups) milk
1 vanilla bean
3 egg yolks
1 egg
80 g (2³/₄ oz/¹/₃ cup) caster (superfine) sugar

Preheat the oven to 140°C (275°F/Gas 1). Put the milk in a saucepan. Split the vanilla bean in two, scrape out the seeds and add the whole lot to the milk. Bring the milk just to the boil.

Meanwhile, mix together the egg yolks, egg and sugar. Strain the boiling milk over the egg mixture and stir well. Skim off the surface to remove any foam.

Ladle into four 125 ml (4 fl oz/¹/₂ cup) ramekins and place in a roasting tin. Pour enough hot water into the tin to come halfway up the sides of the ramekins. Bake for 30 minutes, or until the custards are firm to the touch. Leave the ramekins on a wire rack to cool, then refrigerate until ready to serve. Serves 4

655

656

657

655 CHOCOLATE & PEANUT BUTTER PIE

200 g (7 oz) chocolate biscuits with cream centres, crushed
50 g (1^3/$_4$ oz) unsalted butter, melted
200 g (7 oz/^{3}/$_4$ cup) cream cheese
85 g (3 oz/^{2}/$_3$ cup) icing (confectioners') sugar, sifted
100 g (3^1/$_2$ oz/^{2}/$_3$ cup) smooth peanut butter
1 teaspoon natural vanilla extract
250 ml (9 fl oz/1 cup) cream, whipped to firm peaks
3 tablespoons cream, extra
3 teaspoons unsalted butter, extra
50 g (1^3/$_4$ oz) dark chocolate, grated
honey-roasted peanuts, chopped, to garnish

Combine the biscuit crumbs with the melted butter and press into the base and side of a 23 cm (9 inch) top, 18 cm (7 inch) base, 3 cm (1^1/$_4$ inch) deep pie dish and refrigerate for 15 minutes, or until firm.

Put the cream cheese and icing sugar in a bowl and beat with electric beaters until smooth. Add the peanut butter and vanilla and beat together. Stir in a third of the whipped cream until smooth, then gently fold in the remaining whipped cream. Pour the mixture into the pie shell. Refrigerate for 2 hours, or until firm.

Place the extra cream and butter in a pan and stir over medium heat until the butter is melted and the cream just comes to a simmer. Remove from the heat, add the grated chocolate, and stir until melted. Cool a little, then dribble the chocolate over the top of the pie to create a lattice pattern. Refrigerate for 2 hours, or until the topping and chocolate are firm. Remove the pie from the fridge, scatter over the chopped peanuts and serve. Serves 10–12

657 APPLE GALETTE

1 sheet frozen puff pastry, thawed
3 tablespoons apricot jam
1 granny smith apple
2 teaspoons raw (demerara) sugar

Preheat the oven to 210°C (415°F/Gas 6–7). Place a baking tray in the oven to heat. Trim the corners from the pastry to make a neat circle (use a large plate as a guide if you like).

Place the jam in a small saucepan and stir over low heat to warm through and thin. Strain through a sieve to remove any chunks of fruit and brush over the puff pastry, leaving a 1.5 cm (^{5}/$_8$ inch) border.

Peel, halve and core the apple, and cut into 2 mm (^{1}/$_{16}$ inch) thick slices. Arrange over the pastry in an overlapping circular pattern, leaving a 1.5 cm (^{5}/$_8$ inch) border around the edge. Sprinkle evenly with the sugar. Carefully place the galette on a lightly greased tray and bake for 35 minutes, or until the edge of the pastry is well browned and puffed. Serves 6

656 FREEFORM BLUEBERRY PIE

PASTRY
185 g (6^1/$_2$ oz/1^1/$_2$ cups) plain (all-purpose) flour
100 g (3^1/$_2$ oz) unsalted butter, chilled and cubed
2 teaspoons grated orange zest
1 tablespoon caster (superfine) sugar
2–3 tablespoons iced water

40 g (1^1/$_2$ oz/^{1}/$_3$ cup) crushed amaretti biscuits or almond bread
60 g (2^1/$_4$ oz/^{1}/$_2$ cup) plain (all-purpose) flour
1 teaspoon ground cinnamon
80 g (2^3/$_4$ oz/^{1}/$_3$ cup) caster (superfine) sugar
500 g (1 lb 2 oz/3^1/$_4$ cups) fresh blueberries
milk, for brushing
2 tablespoons blueberry jam
icing (confectioners') sugar, to dust

Sift the flour into a large bowl and rub in the butter with your fingertips until the mixture resembles breadcrumbs. Stir in the orange zest and sugar. Make a well, add almost all the water and mix with a flat-bladed knife, using a cutting action, until the mixture comes together in beads. Add a little more water if necessary to bring the dough together. Gather together and lift out onto a lightly floured surface. Press together into a ball and flatten it slightly into a disc. Cover in plastic wrap and refrigerate for 20 minutes.

Preheat the oven to 200°C (400°F/Gas 6). Combine the crushed biscuits, flour, cinnamon and 1^1/$_2$ tablespoons of the sugar. Roll the pastry out to a 36 cm (14^1/$_4$ inch) circle and sprinkle with the biscuit mixture, leaving a 4 cm (1^1/$_2$ inch) border. Arrange the blueberries over the crushed biscuits, then bring up the edges to form a freeform crust.

Brush the sides of the pie with the milk. Sprinkle with the remaining sugar and bake for 30 minutes, or until the sides are crisp and brown.

Warm the jam in a saucepan over low heat and brush over the berries. Cool to room temperature, then dust the pastry crust with sifted icing sugar. Serves 6–8

658

659

660

661

658 PANNA COTTA

435 ml (15¼ fl oz/1¾ cups) thick (double/heavy) cream
4 tablespoons caster (superfine) sugar
vanilla extract
3 sheets gelatine or 1¼ teaspoons powdered gelatine
250 g (9 oz) fresh berries

Put the cream and sugar in a saucepan and stir over gentle heat until the sugar has dissolved. Bring to the boil, then simmer for 3 minutes, adding a few drops of vanilla extract to taste.

If you are using the gelatine sheets, soak in cold water until they are floppy, then squeeze out any excess water. Stir the sheets into the hot cream until they are completely dissolved. If you are using powdered gelatine, sprinkle it onto the hot cream in an even layer and leave it to sponge for a minute, then stir it into the cream until dissolved.

Pour the cream mixture into four 125 ml (4 fl oz/½ cup) metal dariole moulds, cover each with plastic wrap and refrigerate until set. Unmould the panna cotta by wrapping the moulds in a cloth dipped in hot water and tipping them gently onto individual plates. Serve with the fresh berries. Serves 4

659 LEMON DELICIOUS

70 g (2½ oz) unsalted butter, at room temperature
185 g (6½ oz/¾ cup) sugar
2 teaspoons finely grated lemon zest
3 eggs, separated
3 tablespoons self-raising flour
185 ml (6 fl oz/¾ cup) milk
80 ml (2½ fl oz/⅓ cup) lemon juice
icing (confectioners') sugar, to dust
thick (double/heavy) cream, to serve

Preheat the oven to 180°C (350°F/Gas 4). Melt 10 g (¼ oz) of the butter and use to lightly grease a 1.25 litre (44 fl oz/5 cup) ovenproof dish. Using an electric beater, beat the remaining butter, the sugar and grated zest together in a bowl until the mixture is light and creamy. Gradually add the egg yolks, beating well after each addition. Fold in the flour and milk alternately to make a smooth but runny batter. Stir in the lemon juice. Don't worry if the batter looks like it has separated.

Whisk the egg whites in a clean, dry bowl until firm peaks form and, with a large metal spoon, fold a third of the whites into the batter. Gently fold in the remaining egg whites, being careful not to overmix.

Pour the batter into the prepared dish and place in a large roasting tin. Pour enough hot water into the tin to come one-third of the way up the side of the dish and bake for 55 minutes, or until the top of the pudding is golden, risen and firm to the touch. Leave for 5 minutes before serving. Dust with icing sugar and serve with cream. Serves 4–6

660 PLUM COBBLER

825 g (1 lb 13 oz) tin pitted dark plums, drained, syrup reserved
1 tablespoon honey
2 ripe pears, peeled, cored and cut into eighths

TOPPING
125 g (4½ oz/1 cup) self-raising flour
1 tablespoon caster (superfine) sugar
¼ teaspoon ground cardamom or ground cinnamon
40 g (1½ oz) unsalted butter, chilled and chopped
3 tablespoons milk, plus extra, for brushing
1 tablespoon caster (superfine) sugar, extra
¼ teaspoon ground cardamom or ground cinnamon, extra

Preheat the oven to 200°C (400°F/Gas 6). Grease a deep 18 cm (7 inch) round ovenproof dish. Put 185 ml (6 fl oz/¾ cup) of the plum syrup, honey and pear in a saucepan and bring to the boil. Reduce the heat and simmer for 8 minutes, or until the pear is tender. Add the plums.

For the topping, sift the flour, sugar, cardamom and a pinch of salt into a bowl. Rub in the butter with your fingers until it resembles fine breadcrumbs. Stir in the milk using a flat-bladed knife, mixing lightly to form a soft dough — add a little more milk if necessary. Turn onto a lightly floured surface and form into a smooth ball. Roll out to a 1 cm (½ inch) thickness and cut into rounds with a 4 cm (1½ inch) cutter. Spoon the fruit into the dish, then arrange the circles of dough in an overlapping pattern over the top — leaving the fruit in the centre exposed. Brush the dough with the extra milk. Mix the extra sugar and cardamom and sprinkle over the dough. Place on a baking tray and bake for 30 minutes, or until the topping is golden. Serves 4

661 STICKY BLACK RICE PUDDING

400 g (14 oz/2 cups) black rice
3 fresh pandan leaves
500 ml (17 fl oz/2 cups) coconut milk
80 g (2¾ oz) palm sugar (jaggery), grated
3 tablespoons caster (superfine) sugar
coconut cream, to serve
mango or pawpaw cubes, to serve

Place the rice in a large glass or ceramic bowl and cover with water. Leave to soak for at least 8 hours, or preferably overnight. Drain, then place in a saucepan with 1 litre (35 fl oz/4 cups) water and slowly bring to the boil. Cook at a low boil, stirring frequently, for 20 minutes, or until tender. Drain.

Pull your fingers through the pandan leaves to shred them and then tie them in a knot. Pour the coconut milk into a large saucepan and heat until almost boiling. Add the palm sugar, caster sugar and pandan leaves and stir until the sugars have dissolved.

Add the rice to the pan and cook, stirring, for 8 minutes without boiling. Turn off the heat, cover and leave for 15 minutes to absorb the flavours. Remove the pandan leaves. Spoon into bowls and serve warm with coconut cream and fresh mango. Serves 6–8

INDEX

A

B

C